AF126686

Europe

Europe

A New History

RODERICK BEATON

ALLEN LANE
an imprint of
PENGUIN BOOKS

ALLEN LANE

UK | USA | Canada | Ireland | Australia
India | New Zealand | South Africa

Allen Lane is part of the Penguin Random House group of companies
whose addresses can be found at global.penguinrandomhouse.com

Penguin Random House UK
One Embassy Gardens, 8 Viaduct Gardens, London SW11 7BW

penguin.co.uk

Penguin
Random House
UK

First published 2026

001

Copyright © Roderick Beaton, 2026

The moral right of the author has been asserted

Penguin Random House values and supports copyright.
Copyright fuels creativity, encourages diverse voices, promotes freedom
of expression and supports a vibrant culture. Thank you for purchasing
an authorized edition of this book and for respecting intellectual property
laws by not reproducing, scanning or distributing any part of it by any
means without permission. You are supporting authors and enabling
Penguin Random House to continue to publish books for everyone.
No part of this book may be used or reproduced in any manner for the
purpose of training artificial intelligence technologies or systems. In accordance
with Article 4(3) of the DSM Directive 2019/790, Penguin Random House
expressly reserves this work from the text and data mining exception.

Set in 12/14.75pt Dante MT Std
Typeset by Six Red Marbles UK, Thetford, Norfolk
Printed and bound in Great Britain by Clays Ltd, Elcograf S.p.A.

The authorized representative in the EEA is Penguin Random House Ireland,
Morrison Chambers, 32 Nassau Street, Dublin D02 YH68

A CIP catalogue record for this book is available from the British Library

ISBN: 978-0-241-62450-0

Penguin Random House is committed to a sustainable future
for our business, our readers and our planet. This book is made from
Forest Stewardship Council® certified paper.

MIX
Paper | Supporting
responsible forestry
FSC® C018179

For Fran

We must start with Europe, because of its physical variety and its natural genius towards excellence among men and governments; compared to the other continents it is also the most conducive to home comforts . . . The Romans, after subduing many untamed peoples . . . have socialized the antisocial and taught savages how to live an urban, constitutional life.

Strabo, *Geography* (first century CE)

No man is an *Iland*, intire of it selfe; every man is a peece of the *Continent*, a part of the *maine*; if a *Clod* bee washed away by the *Sea*, *Europe* is the lesse . . .

John Donne (1623)

Il n'y a plus aujourd'hui de Français, d'Allemands, d'Espagnols, d'Anglois même, quoi qu'on en dise; il n'y a que des Européens. (Today nobody is French, German, Spanish, even English any more, no matter what people say; there are only Europeans.)

Jean-Jacques Rousseau (1771)

Weder der Westen noch der Osten will Europa retten: Rußland will es erobern – Amerika will es kaufen. (Neither the West nor the East will rescue Europe: Russia wants to conquer it, America wants to buy it.)

Count Richard Coudenhove-Kalergi (1923)

Contents

List of Illustrations

Every effort has been made to contact all copyright holders. The publishers will be happy to correct any errors or omissions brought to their attention in future editions of this book.

1 Attic black-figure *lekythos*, *c.* 490 BCE, showing soldiers at the battle of Marathon. Hellenic National Archaeological Museum, Athens (EAM 14691), Photographic Archive, photograph Eleftherios Galanopoulos. Copyright © Hellenic Ministry of Culture / Hellenic Organization of Cultural Resources Development (HOCRED).

2 Marble bust of Herodotus (*c.* 484 BCE–*c.* 431 BCE), Roman copy, second century CE. Metropolitan Museum of Art, New York. Gift of George F. Baker, 1891 (Obj. No. 91.8). Photo: Metropolitan Museum of Art, NY.

3 The bay and battle site of Marathon (author photograph).

4 Detail of funerary *stele* of Panchares, son of Leochares, possibly one of the fallen at Chaeronea (338 BCE). Hellenic Ministry of Culture / HOCRED, Ephorate of Antiquities of Piraeus and Islands – Archaeological Museum of Piraeus, object no. MΠ 5280.

5 Alexander the Great (r. 336 BCE–323 BCE). Detail from Roman mosaic, Pompeii, *c.* 120–100 BCE. Museo Archeologico Nazionale, Naples. Photo: Giannis Papanikos / Alamy.

6 Wreathed head of Julius Caesar, obverse of a silver denarius coin, 44 BCE. The British Museum, London (R.6314). Photo: © Trustees of the British Museum.

7 The Pantheon, Rome, built on the orders of the emperor Hadrian, in the 120s CE (author photograph).

8 Marble bust of the emperor Caracalla (r. 211–217 CE), Roman, third century CE. Museo Archeologico Nazionale, Naples. Photo: NPL / DeA Picture Library / Bridgeman Images.

List of Illustrations

List of Illustrations

List of Maps

The states of Europe and western Eurasia in 2024, showing 'the shortest line' and 'grey area' in which 'Europe shades into Asia' (p.4)

The Roman Empire during the reign of Hadrian (117–138 CE)

PANNONIA

DACIA

DALMATIA

MOESIA

THRACIA

MACEDONIA

EPIRUS

ACHAEA

Athens

ASIA

Black Sea

Antioch

SYRIA

CYPRUS

CRETE

Mediterranean Sea

JUDAEA
Jerusalem

Alexandria

ARABIA

EGYPT

Red Sea

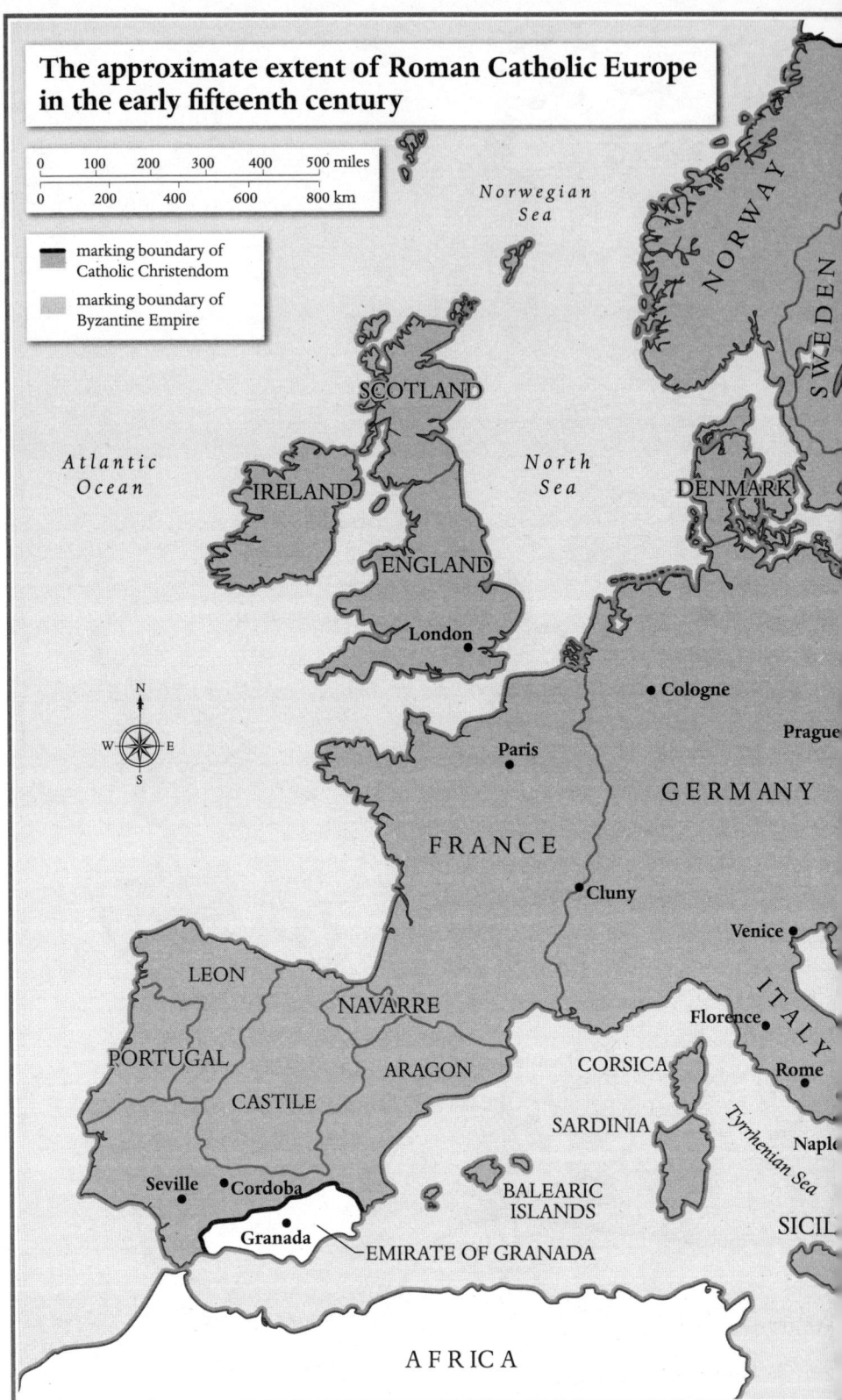

The approximate extent of Roman Catholic Europe in the early fifteenth century

| 0 | 100 | 200 | 300 | 400 | 500 miles |

| 0 | 200 | 400 | 600 | 800 km |

marking boundary of
Catholic Christendom

marking boundary of
Byzantine Empire

*Norwegian
Sea*

NORWAY

SWEDEN

SCOTLAND

*Atlantic
Ocean*

IRELAND

*North
Sea*

DENMARK

ENGLAND

London

• Cologne

Prague

Paris

GERMANY

FRANCE

•Cluny

Venice •

LEON

NAVARRE

Florence•

ITALY

PORTUGAL

ARAGON

CORSICA

Rome
•

CASTILE

SARDINIA

Tyrrhenian Sea

Naple

Seville   •Cordoba

BALEARIC
ISLANDS

SICIL

•
Granada

EMIRATE OF GRANADA

AFRICA

RUSSIA

POLAND

Kraków •

Vienna

HUNGARY

Baltic Sea

SERBIA

Adriatic Sea

BYZANTINE
EMPIRE

KINGDOM
OF THE
TWO SICILIES

IONIAN
ISLANDS

VENETIAN
MARITIME EMPIRE

BULGARIA

Constantinople •

Black Sea

CHIOS
(GENOA)

RHODES
(KNIGHTS HOSPITALLER)

CYPRUS

CRETE

Mediterranean Sea

Europe after the Treaty of Lausanne, 1923–1939

0 100 200 300 400 500 600 miles
0 200 400 600 800 1000 km

Greenland Sea

Barents Sea

ICELAND

Norwegian Sea

White Sea

NORWAY

SWEDEN

FINLAND

USSR (RUSSIA)

ESTONIA

LATVIA

LITHUANIA

North Sea

DENMARK

Baltic Sea

IRELAND

GREAT BRITAIN

NETHERLANDS

EAST PRUSSIA (GERMANY)

GERMANY

POLAND

BELGIUM

CZECHOSLOVAKIA

Atlantic Ocean

FRANCE

AUSTRIA

HUNGARY

ROMANIA

SWITZERLAND

YUGOSLAVIA

Black Sea

BULGARIA

ITALY

PORTUGAL

CORSICA (FRANCE)

ALBANIA

TURKEY

SPAIN

SARDINIA (ITALY)

GREECE

DODECANESE (ITALY)

Mediterranean Sea

MOROCCO

ALGERIA

TUNISIA

LIBYA

EGYPT

Europe's eastern frontiers, 1947–1989

| | 0 | 100 | 200 | 300 | 400 | 500 miles |
| 0 | 200 | 400 | 600 | 800 km |

the 'Iron Curtain'

frontier of the
Soviet Union before 1939

frontier of the
Soviet Union after 1947

*Norwegian
Sea*

NORWAY

SWEDEN

FINLAND

White Sea

USSR
(RUSSIA)

ESTONIA

LATVIA

LITHUANIA

*North
Sea*

DENMARK

Baltic Sea

• Kaliningrad

NETHERLANDS

• Berlin

EAST
GERMANY

POLAND

BELGIUM

WEST
GERMANY

CZECHOSLOVAKIA

BESSARABIA

FRANCE

SWITZERLAND

AUSTRIA

HUNGARY

ROMANIA

*Black
Sea*

ITALY

YUGOSLAVIA

BULGARIA

CORSICA
(FRANCE)

ALBANIA

TURKEY

SARDINIA
(ITALY)

GREECE

About This Book

Why a 'new' history? Why might we need one? And what makes this one new? The first answer concerns the very stuff of history: *events*. Even the existence, and certainly the nature, of Europe have been challenged in new ways since the spring of 2022. Russia's invasion of an independent state on Europe's borders was a timely reminder of the continent's age-old vulnerability on its eastern flank. Then the middle of the decade has seen an unprecedented (though not unforeseen) shift in the relationship between a US administration and the continent of America's birth. Eight decades ago, it was self-evident in Washington that the status of the United States as a global superpower depended on holding back the expansion of its rival, Russia, into Europe after the devastation of the Second World War; that calculation no longer holds good today.

Those simple facts, by themselves, have forced all of us who are, in the broadest sense, European to look at ourselves again, to take stock of where we came from and how we got here; even, perhaps, to re-examine the values and attitudes that bring us together and – more than ever today – also those that divide us.

To study history, I believe, is to look for patterns, to make sense of the things that happen and the actions of our fellow humans that affect all our lives. As they accumulate, these are the things that make us who we are; and so the patterns we find are also the ones that make sense of our own lives as individuals. When things change, when new and unexpected events suddenly reshape the world that we thought we knew around us, the effect is like the turning of a kaleidoscope – the whole pattern changes. We look at both the present and the past, and what we see lines up differently from before. History can't tell us what will come next, though none of us can resist trying to read it as though it could; but our perception of the present and our understanding of the past are both essential to how we *prepare* for the future. The story told in this book has been shaped by the changed and changing perspective of the mid-2020s; it could not have been told in this way before.

This history is new in another sense, too. A great many excellent histories of Europe, in English, have appeared over the last thirty years or so, from the very short to the very long (not least the nine-volume, multi-author *Penguin History of Europe*, to which I owe a great many debts, acknowledged in the endnotes to this book). But I couldn't help noticing that almost all of these, to varying extents, end up parcelling out the subject into the separate stories of regions or nations. There are good reasons for this: if you're trying to report everything that happened in granular detail you can't avoid focusing on the local and the specific. And the best sources on which every historian relies are usually the ones that have done precisely that. As a result, it's next to impossible in writing about Europe to avoid locutions such as 'Meanwhile, south of the Alps . . .', or 'In France, the Bourbon dynasty . . .'. I plead guilty too; but in every one of the chapters that follow I have tried my hardest to adjust the focus so that Europe *as a whole* appears in the sharpest outline and fills the screen.

In this I have been greatly helped by a different approach to the subject that goes back to the 1950s and has also seen an upsurge in recent years. This one derives from the branch of history known as History of Ideas. The Europe that is the subject of this book is as much an idea as a place; the story of its people is as much about shared, and changing, *identities* as about great or wicked deeds, pitched battles, invasions or revolutions.

Finally, writing this book completes a personal odyssey that began in 1973 – the year the United Kingdom joined the forerunner of today's European Union. That was also the year when I left the home where I had been born and brought up in one corner of Europe, in Scotland, to live and study in another small country at its opposite end, Greece. Greek culture and history would then become my specialist subject, from a doctorate right through to a thirty-year stint as a professor at a university in one of Europe's (and the world's) great metropolitan centres, London. But I have never stopped thinking about the questions that I first began to ask in the very different world of all those years ago: questions about the nature of nations, particularly small ones, and how they relate to the larger whole that is Europe. This book, begun not long after the United Kingdom had *left* the European Union (in January 2020), is my best attempt at an answer to those questions.

All this, I like to think, has equipped me to combine the dispassionate eye of a historian with a personal stake in trying to understand the multilayered identities that come with belonging to the changing Europe of today – in my own case, as simultaneously Scottish, British, an honorary citizen of another European nation, Greece . . . *and* European.

Introduction

What Do We (Think We) Mean by 'Europe'?

Everything changed on the morning of Thursday, 24 February 2022, when Russia invaded Ukraine. News media ever since have spoken of a new 'war in Europe', such as had not been seen since the end of the Second World War just over three-quarters of a century ago, in 1945. Even that phrase, bandied about everywhere, raises important questions: who, far away from the conflict zone, before that fateful morning, could even be sure that the contested lands were *in* Europe? Once it became clear that the government and people of Ukraine were determined to resist, in a matter of days the world had woken up to the reality that this was not just a war *in* Europe; it was a war *for* Europe.

Politically, on the face of it, the issues were plain enough. An independent state of some 40 million people found itself caught between the world's two most heavily armed military powers (US-led NATO and post-Soviet Russia) and between two ever more divergent economic and political systems (the European Union on its western flank, and authoritarian Russia with its client Belarus to the east and north). The Russian autocrat, Vladimir Putin, claimed Ukraine as Russian territory; a democratically elected government in Ukraine preferred alignment with its western neighbours. Suddenly, in the spring of 2022, everyone was talking about 'Europe' in a new way.

It wasn't just that the NATO alliance and the territorial integrity of its European members were potentially under threat (an argument persuasively, and understandably, amplified at every opportunity by the Ukrainian leadership); so was a whole set of moral, legal, political and cultural values that are deeply embedded in the political culture of most, if not all, European states as well as the institutions of the EU. As a perceptive columnist writing in the British daily newspaper, *The Guardian*, expressed it, as early as 2 March of that year: 'When the targets of Kremlin atrocity call out to "Europe" for help, they are appealing not to a geographical space but an idea. They are talking about security in the rule of law and democracy – the antithesis of Putinism.'[1]

That antithesis and that idea are not new creations of the twenty-first century. The moment we get beyond the relatively simple politics of the present moment, we realize that it isn't enough to invoke alleged glories or grudges going back to the end of the Cold War in 1989 or the Second World War in 1945; not even to the Great War of 1914–1918 that preceded it, nor, still farther back, to the adventures of Napoleon Bonaparte and the 'Concert of Europe' devised at Vienna in 1815 to prevent anything of the sort ever happening again. No, the idea that once again is at stake in the 2020s is as old as Europe itself. It was born a little over 2,500 years ago, among the city states of ancient Greece. So if we are to understand how we got where we are now, we have to start thinking all over again about the whole history of a continent, and above all, the history of the *idea* embodied, embedded, invested in that geographical space. And that is not simple at all.

This book reconfigures the history of Europe, from its distant beginnings to today, as the story of that idea. But first, in the rest of this Introduction, let's tease out some of the strands (sometimes overlapping, sometimes competing against each other) that go to make up that idea as it has evolved and continues to evolve in our own times.

Geography

Objectively, Europe doesn't even exist. Its presence could never be detected by any telescope trained on the Earth from Mars. But there it is in every modern atlas: the name 'Europe', or variations of it in different languages, written in more or less the same place, across the western end of the land mass that stretches all the way from the Atlantic in the west to the Pacific in the east. This land mass is conventionally known to geographers as Eurasia, a modern label that runs together the traditional names of Europe and Asia. Of its two parts, Asia is so much the larger that Europe is often called a peninsula on the western end of Asia (or Eurasia).[2] But that isn't quite accurate. A peninsula is, according to the word's Latin origin, 'almost an island'. To say that of Europe, when you look at a map of Eurasia, is quite a stretch. I prefer to think of Europe as a gigantic promontory, a piece of the total continent that stretches out, long and relatively thin, far to the west of the main land mass, into the surrounding seas.

This means that on three sides the boundaries of Europe are unambiguously defined by physical barriers. The land is bounded by the sea: in clockwise direction, by the Black Sea, the straits of the Bosphorus and Dardanelles, with the Sea of Marmara in between, then the Mediterranean, the Strait of Gibraltar, the Atlantic, the North Sea, and the Arctic Ocean with its inlet, the White Sea, to the east of Finland. Arguments about islands are arguments about politics, not geography: in geographical terms the continent includes, by definition, the islands of its continental shelf, some of which only became separated from the mainland in (geologically speaking) very recent times.[3] Europe's large islands include the British Isles and the islands of the Mediterranean, the latter all lying, conveniently for our purposes, much closer to the northern than the southern mainland.

That leaves the eastern flank. And here geography is of very little help at all. The eastern boundary of Europe has never been a matter of physical geography, for the simple reason that there isn't one. Except in its south-eastern corner, which is where the idea of dividing the world into separate continents first came into being in ancient times, there has never been any natural barrier to mark off Europe from Asia. In the eighteenth century, when Russia was in the process of becoming a European power, it became fashionable in some circles to see such a boundary in the Ural mountain range and the river of the same name that runs southwards into the Caspian Sea. Two hundred years later, during the Cold War, and as recently as the early 1990s, the phrase 'from the Atlantic to the Urals' could regularly be heard in the world of high politics. But despite the reported existence, 'High up in the Urals', of 'a cross marking the place where Europe stops and Asia starts', in practice those mountains and that river, far into Asia, have never served as the boundary of anything.[4]

In strictly geographical terms, the shortest line between the seas on either side, that could be said to mark off Europe as a promontory jutting out from Asia, runs from north-west to south-east, between Gdańsk on the Baltic and Odessa on the Black Sea – and even that leaves out most of Scandinavia, which has certainly formed part of Europe for most of the last thousand years. But it would be hard to make out any kind of real dividing line on that largely undifferentiated ground. We might do better, instead, to think of a grey area lying between the White Sea in the north and the Black Sea in the south. Somewhere in that broad, flat zone of steppeland, I would dare to suggest, with some linguistic sleight of hand, Europe shades into Asia.

All of which is a way of admitting that it's not the physical facts of geography that divide this single land mass into two named continents. This is where the behaviour, the attitudes and the perceptions of human beings take over.

History

If you lived at the southern end of the Balkan mainland or the nearby islands of the Aegean around 2,500 years ago, it would have made perfectly good sense to divide up the world you knew along the line of the straits that link the Black Sea to the Mediterranean: the Dardanelles (or Hellespont) and the Bosphorus. The Greeks of that time were great seafarers; they had settled all round the coast of the Black Sea, as well as the Mediterranean – 'like frogs around a pond', in the often quoted words of their most famous philosopher, Plato. And so they came up with another natural boundary: the river that they called the Tanais and we know today as the Don, which flows through south-western Russia into the Sea of Azov.

As to what happened if you travelled inland further north or west (beyond the immediate hinterland of the Mediterranean coastline), nobody knew for sure and most didn't much care. To the Greeks of the sixth century BCE, Europe was whatever lay to the west of the River Don and the Dardanelles. At the time, almost as many Greeks lived in Asia, around the coasts of what is now Turkey, as in Europe. The name 'Europe' began life as purely a geographical expression – though that would soon change dramatically, as we will discover in Chapter 1.

Half a millennium later, the Romans, starting out from their city state in central Italy, had conquered almost everywhere between the Atlantic and the Rhine (including most of Britain), and between the Mediterranean and the Danube. Their empire reached farther still, beyond Europe altogether, to encompass parts of today's Middle East, Egypt and the entire coastline of North Africa. This was a Europe that included only a small slice of today's Germany, no Scandinavia, and nothing of central or eastern Europe to the north of the Danube. It was not quite Europe as we think of it today – but it was still much the largest chunk of western Eurasia that has ever been united under a single jurisdiction. And it lasted for the best part of five hundred years.

By the time the Roman Empire began to fall apart in the fifth century CE, a new religion had taken root among its citizens; its emperors had turned away from the gods and goddesses and the religious practices of the ancient world and now looked to the One God of the Christians as the source of their earthly power. During the centuries that followed, the new local rulers who emerged to replace them invariably made the same choice. And in those days, where rulers led, their people followed. Christianity became all but universal throughout Europe. Politically, the continent was a patchwork; its shape on the map was constantly shifting. But regardless of where its boundaries lay at any particular time, Christian Europe came to be known as the *respublica christiana* (usually translated as 'Christian Commonwealth'), or Christendom, as historians call it today. Eventually Christendom would expand far beyond the bounds of the old Roman Empire. By the twelfth century, its reach included Scandinavia, today's Baltic states, what we now call central and eastern Europe, and the kingdom of a people called Rus in today's Ukraine.

During the eighteenth century, a new idea entered the European vocabulary. It was called 'civilization'. This was an idea based on the qualities associated with citizenship; it belonged to a tradition of political thinking that can be traced all the way back to ancient Greece and Rome. Nurtured by the intellectual movement that we call the Enlightenment, the idea grew to embrace all forms of rational inquiry, especially in scientific discovery and technological invention, medicine, law and politics, philosophy and the arts, and not least in the theory and practice of generating wealth through production and exchange (economics and trade, as we call them today).

As European intellectual elites began to think outside the box of revealed religion, 'civilization' began to replace or go hand in hand with Christianity as a defining characteristic of Europe itself. At the same time, civilization as an idea joined forces with religion to explain and justify the continent's imperial adventures abroad. Alongside the activities of Christian missionaries, which continued well into the twentieth century, European colonial administrators on other continents and politicians at home really believed that they were 'civilizing' people whom, at the time, it was perfectly accept-able to call 'savages', and worse.

Much has been written about the contradictions at the heart of this idea. On the one hand, Europeans from the sixteenth to the twentieth century were uniquely successful in exporting their ideas and their values throughout the rest of the world – as often as not, down the barrel of a gun. But as we'll see in more detail in the chapters that follow, time and again hard power would go hand in hand with soft power. It was thanks to European science, technology, medicine, and systems of trade and finance rooted in the Enlightenment that the population of the entire world has increased exponentially since then; almost everywhere, people live longer; diseases once fatal can be cured or prevented with medicines and vaccination. The global economy has boomed to an extent that previously would have been unimaginable. As a result, Europe today punches far above its weight, both economically and geopolitically, in relation to its share of our planet's inhabited surface.

But all this came at a terrible cost. In North America it is estimated that as many as 95 per cent of the indigenous population may have died as a result of the arrival of settlers from Europe; in Australia during the early period of colonization the equivalent figure may have been around 80 per cent.[5] Between the seventeenth century and the first half of the nineteenth, more than 11 million men, women and children were uprooted from Africa, to be transported by 'civilized' Europeans from one foreign continent to be sold as slaves to European settlers on another. As a track record, that hardly lives up to the blueprint for a bright, rational, ethical future, which was indeed, *as an idea*, one of the achievements of the eighteenth-century European Enlightenment. Calls for atonement, or even financial reparations, were increasingly being heard in the early 2020s.

Whether they like it or not – and some most emphatically do not – Europeans are the inheritors of that divided, and in some quarters divisive, legacy. For some historians today, the 'triumph of the West' is still something to be celebrated, not least because its end may be in sight; others choose to focus only on the dark side.[6] And that division is now being amplified and carried to far more extreme lengths in public discourse, especially on the internet. Wherever we stand on those issues, I would argue that triumphalism and hand-wringing are equally misplaced; whether we regard ourselves as Europeans or not, had these things not happened, most of us would never have been born, and certainly not into the world as we know it today. Perhaps it's the contradictions, every bit as much as the achievements and the atrocities, that define this particular civilization (among many others in the world, past and present) as European.

People on the Move

It may be timely to remind ourselves that every human being who has ever lived in Europe has been an immigrant, or a descendant of immigrants. Throughout much of the prehistory of our species, all but the southernmost shores of the continent were too cold to support human life. Geography tells us that until the technology existed to build boats capable of crossing open water, there was only one route in or out: by land from Asia. Our most distant direct ancestors are thought to have evolved somewhere in Africa around 60,000 years ago. But to establish themselves in Europe, their descendants would have had to trek the long way round, by way of the Middle East and skirting the Black Sea or the Caspian. By 10,000 years ago, boat-building had developed to the point that some of them could take shortcuts across the narrow straits that link the Black Sea to the Mediterranean, or go island hopping around the coasts, all the way to Britain and Ireland (though at the time these could still be reached by land). Some might also have crossed directly from Africa by way of the strait of Gibraltar – but except for a limited period, from the eighth to about the twelfth century CE, when most of today's Spain and Portugal came under the rule of Muslims from North Africa, that seems to have happened quite rarely.

By whichever route they came, the overwhelming direction of immigration was always the same: from east to west. The largest movements of new people into Europe seem to have coincided very roughly with the invention and then the spread of drastically new technologies: in the first case farming, around 8,000 years ago, and then, about three millennia later, the ability to extract the first metals from ores, and so to make durable tools and weapons out of bronze.

One or other of these mass movements most probably brought with it the precursor of the languages most widely spoken in Europe in historical times and today. The Germanic group of languages including English, the Romance group including French and Spanish, the Slavic including Russian, the Celtic languages of the north-western periphery, and the distinct branches represented by Greek and Albanian, all derive from this common origin, known as 'Indo-European' – so called because its descendants can be found right across an arc from northern India to Iceland. Traces of older languages that were once spoken in Europe, recognizable because they function in quite a different way from languages of the Indo-European group, can be found in Basque today, and in the ancient written records of the Minoans of Crete and the Etruscans of Tuscany. Hungarian, Finnish and Estonian may be distantly related to each other but not to the Indo-European family; their linguistic ancestors may have arrived, along with their speakers, either earlier or later.[7]

The details, timing and nature of these great movements of population in prehistoric times are still hotly debated by specialists working in several different disciplines; estimates of the proportion of the existing population displaced each time involve a large amount of guesswork. But it does appear that of the human populations that had reached Europe some 40,000 years ago, none was completely wiped out; even the Neanderthals, a species genetically distinct from *Homo sapiens*, we now know interbred with our direct ancestors and have left traces of their DNA in the human population of today. By comparison with those movements far back in prehistory, the most recent mass migrations into Europe, which happened between the fifth and the tenth centuries of our era, and are documented by written sources as well as by archaeology, were on a much smaller scale. And compared to any of these events in the distant past, it's worth noting that the flow of migrants or refugees in our own century, which arouses such intense political passions today, is still negligible as a percentage of the existing population.[8]

A consequence of all this was that once people got to Europe, there was nowhere else for them to go. For millennia, all migration routes ended in Europe. Out of the mix of populations that resulted grew the kingdoms, empires and republics of the Middle Ages and, eventually, the nations of today. There was a lot of moving around within Europe too. But with very few exceptions the long-term direction of travel remained the same: from east to west. And when the time eventually came for Europeans to burst out of their promontory and make their mark on the rest of the world, it was once again by setting out westwards that they did it, taking to the oceans. That had to wait until they had developed the skills and the navigational know-how to make such long voyages possible – which may be why the effect on every other continent, when finally it happened, was so dramatic. Once Europeans had circumnavigated the globe, conquering and in some cases permanently colonizing large parts of it, in the fullness of time the rest of the world would come to Europe too.

Today the European population is vastly more diverse even than it was before the colonial era. So how can we define Europeans? Who is European and who is not? No serious scholar nowadays believes that there was ever a single, original European race called 'Aryans'. That was a notion that became widespread during the nineteenth century and was taken to its destructive extreme by Germany's National Socialists, or Nazis, in the 1930s and 1940s. We now know that genetic differences among populations alive on the planet today (those that affect skin pigmentation, shape or colouring of eyes, for instance) are biologically insignificant. We are all one species.[9] Europeans, now as in the past, at the most basic level, must surely be defined as all those people who have made their home in Europe, wherever they may have come from, or however long ago their ancestors arrived.

Politics

There has never been a political state called Europe. For all the many things that Europeans have shared throughout their recorded history, they have not lived under a single jurisdiction since the collapse of the western Roman Empire in the fifth century; and much of the map of modern Europe wasn't even part of that.

Today, there are those who argue that Europe was so successful in dominating the rest of the world precisely *because* it was never unified. The first of six 'killer apps' that according to the historian Niall Ferguson enabled 'the West' to outbid 'the Rest' is 'competition': states, rulers, merchants, social classes, tax gatherers, soldiers, sailors and artists, he argues, achieved all that they did because they were constantly vying to outdo each other. A study by a leading economic historian of the ancient world goes even further. According to Walter Scheidel, the innovations that made the modern world possible all came about thanks to Europe's 'escape from Rome'. The collapse of the Roman Empire, he argues, was not only a good thing in itself; it was actually *necessary*, in order to turn Europe into the engine for the entire globalized economy that we know today.[10]

It's hard to see how the economic argument from hindsight could be proved or disproved. But for hundreds of years after Rome was sacked for the first time in 410 CE, everyone who lived in former Roman lands would daily have encountered the ruins of buildings, roads, bridges and the abandoned parts of towns and cities that extended far beyond the defensive walls that enclosed their own, much humbler homes. There was no getting away from the fact that the people who had once built and maintained these things had enjoyed prosperity and comforts, and lived among splendours, unknown to all but the most rarefied elite in later times.

For centuries, nostalgia for Rome ran deep. And it wasn't until the 1700s that standards of living and size of population in many parts of Europe began to outstrip what they had been in Roman times. Along with nostalgia went the idea, however wistful or fanciful, of restoration. Attempts to unify the continent by violent conquest (as, let's not forget, the Romans had once done) were made by the German king of the Franks, known as Charlemagne, at the end of the eighth century, by Napoleon Bonaparte in the nineteenth and by Adolf Hitler in the twentieth. None of those empires lasted.

During the sixteenth century large parts of Europe came under a single ruler, the Holy Roman Emperor Charles V, thanks to dynastic marriages among its ruling families. That empire didn't last either.

If not by conquest, could Europe be united by *consent*? Why should not its warring kings, princes and occasional republics join forces and bring peace and prosperity to their peoples, such as had once been enjoyed by the Europeans of the Roman Empire? Since the seventeenth century, this question has been asked again and again.[11] Today's European Union, established out of the former European Community in 1992, is one answer to that question – indeed the only plausible answer currently available.

With the creation of the EU, for the first time in its history, Europe acquired a political existence, defined boundaries, and even a capital city, Brussels. But the EU is not a nation. Citizens enjoy common rights by virtue of citizenship of member states, enshrined in treaties. These treaties allow for states both to join and to leave the Union; the rights of their citizens are determined accordingly. In the 2020s it is still anybody's guess how far widening of the EU might go, or deepening of the process of integration among some or all of its member states. Nor, even in the incontrovertible heartland of Europe as defined by geography and history, is every state a member: Britain, Norway and Switzerland each stand in a different relationship to Brussels – and those relations, too, show every sign of being in flux.

The forerunner of the EU, the European Community, had been born out of the ruins left by the Second World War. The political vision of its architects was set out in a document issued on behalf of the Community's (then) nine member states in Copenhagen, in 1973. Their aim, they said, was 'to succeed in the construction of a united Europe', one that would also be 'open to other European nations who share the same ideals and objectives'.[12] But ever since that call for new members began to be heeded in the 1980s, and while the foundations of today's enlarged EU were being consolidated, those 'ideals and objectives' began to meet with vehement resistance. Their opposite, 'euroscepticism', gained momentum in the political parties, the press, and public opinion of many member states, while on the outside, governments queued up to join and the entire heated controversy must still seem incomprehensible to most people living anywhere else in the world.

Today, while some see their future prosperity, security and harmony in 'ever closer union' among the peoples and states of Europe, others shun the notion of a 'European superstate' as a threat to their very identity. In reality a whole spectrum lies between the position set out in that 1973 document and the extreme eurosceptic belief that any form of supranational organization is pernicious and the continent's nation states should be free to get on with their own affairs without reference to anyone else beyond their borders. Regardless of whether it tends towards greater unity, integration, or even political union on the one hand, or the unfettered primacy of nation states on the other, every single idea on that spectrum is an *idea of Europe*. Scepticism or rejection of today's European institutions can't do away with Europe itself – a subject that continues to occupy the attention of a great many politicians, journalists and members of the general public, in many countries both inside and outside the European Union.

Identity

Most Europeans today probably still think of themselves first and foremost as citizens of a nation state, rather than of the EU. The picture is complicated still further by regional identities and loyalties. It suits political campaigners to make out that these identities, when they emerge, are in competition with one another; but in fact most of us, when we stop to think about it, would define our identity in multiple, overlapping ways. On public buildings throughout the European Union, and indeed in some states on its periphery, the blue banner of the EU, with its circle of twelve gold stars on a dark blue background, is a customary sight, flying alongside the national flag. There's nothing contradictory, still less controversial, about that double act. The same individual might be Catalan in Barcelona, Spanish in Brussels, and European in Cape Town or Beijing. A national passport or identity document is one form of identity, objectively established (though it can in certain circumstances be changed); how we each define ourselves subjectively is an altogether subtler, more complicated, business.

Much is made in political debates today about *national* identity and *national* allegiances. But it's worth remembering that, for all their profound impact since the early nineteenth century, these are newcomers in the way that human populations or their rulers have thought about themselves and their place in the world. Until the American Declaration of Independence in 1776 the idea that the collective self-determination of a nation's people might be a defined and achievable political goal, still less a yardstick of identity, was practically unknown.[13]

An attempt to define a *European* identity, essentially in political terms, formed part of that other Declaration, the one made two centuries later, in 1973, by the nine forerunners of the European Union:

> Sharing as they do the same attitudes to life, based on a determination to build a society which measures up to the needs of the individual, they are determined to defend the principles of representative democracy, of the rule of law, of social justice – which is the ultimate goal of economic progress – and of respect for human rights. All of these are fundamental elements of the European Identity.[14]

Few would disagree, probably, that these are the values or principles at stake in the confrontation with Russia over Ukraine in the 2020s; indeed they have been invoked in previous conflicts in which European nations have been involved, from the Cold War to America's 'War on Terror' of the early 2000s. Many governments outside the EU, as well as citizens worldwide, would no doubt subscribe to them too. But a set of principles, however praiseworthy or representative of majority public opinion at a given time, amounts to rather less than a rounded sense of identity.

In fact, all but one of the items on that list would probably have been unintelligible to an ancient Greek or Roman, would have seemed irrelevant if not even blasphemous in Christian Europe during the Middle Ages, and been viewed with deep suspicion, or worse, by the majority of European governments and many of their subjects before 1945. The immediate origin of most of these principles lies in the worldwide settlement at the end of the Second World War and the founding charter of the United Nations Organization, signed in June 1945. These in their turn drew heavily on ideas developed during the European Enlightenment of the eighteenth century. Of all the items on that list, only the rule of law stands out as a constant (even if it meant different things at different times and was all too infrequently enacted in practice) – and we will encounter it again in one form or another in the chapters that follow.

Perhaps more fundamental to a sense of European identity than any abstract principle was something else that was highlighted by that *Guardian* columnist back in 2022: Ukrainians, he wrote, were appealing to an 'idea' that was 'the *antithesis* of Putinism'. It was ever thus. The terms have varied over time: Greeks (or Romans) vs 'barbarians'; Christians vs 'heathens' or 'infidels'; 'civilization' vs 'savagery'; 'the West' vs 'the Rest'. It may not seem very edifying to identify the people of a continent, the makers of a civilization, and the political and intellectual architects of what is still sometimes called the 'free world' in terms of 'Us vs Them'. That certainly isn't the whole story. But it does, perhaps, help to explain why the idea of Europe has never gone away, in all the 2,500 years since it was first weaponized by the ancient Greeks in the service of their own existential battle for survival.

A history of Europe for our times, then, has to be far more than the story of a geographical space or of the peoples, nations, or states that occupy it. Identity lies at the heart of this story – and not just the competing identities that exist today, but the very different identities that have existed in the past and to which today's are the heirs. To understand the changing nature, content and significance of those identities we must now turn to the remote world of ancient Greece, where it all began.

The Beginning of History and the Invention of Europe

490 BCE–146 BCE

The last full moon of an Aegean summer was not long past. For a week now, down near the shore, the citizen-army of Athens had been encamped on rising ground, sheltering from the sun in a grove sacred to the demi-god Heracles. Below them, lined up along the beach, were the ships of the invaders – some six hundred of them. The empire of the Medes and Persians, the largest and most power-ful the world had yet seen, under its 'Great King', Daryaush, known to the Greeks as Darius, had taken to the sea in pursuit of new con-quests in the west. The city state of Athens, tiny by comparison, was one of a handful among the independent Greek states clustered on the European side of the Aegean Sea that had refused to submit; this punitive expedition was the result.

The year (by our system of counting) was 490 BCE; the place, the bay and plain of Marathon.

If the Persians were to break out of their beachhead, there would be nothing to stop them covering the 26-mile distance to Athens and entering the city unopposed. The Athenians knew what to expect if that were to happen. Their neighbours the Ere-trians, on the nearby island of Euboea, had also dared to defy the Great King. Eretria had held out for a week before the town was looted of everything valuable and burnt to the ground; by the time the killing was over, everyone left alive had been taken as a slave aboard the Persian ships. Fresh from the destruction, those ships had now crossed over the strait from Euboea as the shortest route to bring the expedition's fearsome cavalry within reach of Athens.

Even more deadly than the cavalry were the Persian archers. They were skilled at firing lethal showers of iron-tipped arrows high into the air, to fall among an enemy's tight-packed ranks, pierce the chinks of their body armour and cause havoc. The defenders were outnumbered too, perhaps by as many as two to one. Greek armies in those days were made up of citizens, mostly householders and farmers; they fought on foot, formed into squares called phalanxes. There may have been as many as 10,000 Athenians lined up that day to oppose the Persians. Even though all the city states of Greece faced the same threat, only one other, tiny Plataea, had sent a contingent to help, making perhaps another thousand men.

The story goes that the Greeks actually *ran* the distance of a mile that separated them from the enemy. That may have been an exaggeration. Each man would have been encased in a heavy bronze breastplate, with bronze greaves on his legs and carrying a heavy iron shield, adding some seventy pounds weight to his own. His helmet, also of solid bronze, covered his cheeks and nose, leaving only narrow slits for him to see what was directly ahead of him – and probably rather little to either side. In the heat of noon, his brains would have been close to boiling, even without the heat of battle. But on that day the men of the phalanxes had every reason to cover the distance quickly, to get past the range of the enemy's arrows.

The fighting lasted most of the day. By the time it was over, the invaders had been driven back to their ships; many were caught in a salt marsh behind the shore, and either drowned or were cut down by the Greeks as they struggled to free themselves from the water-logged ground. Fighting would have been hand to hand; spears, swords and axes thrusting, stabbing, slashing at armour and any exposed flesh. It would later be reported that precisely 192 Athenians had lost their lives that day, along with a smaller number of their Plataean allies, while Persian losses had been thirty times as many. No one knows how many were wounded, permanently maimed, or died later of their injuries, on both sides.

Even then, it was still too soon for the Athenians to be assured of their victory. There was nothing to stop the Persian fleet from sailing out of Marathon Bay, round the tip of Cape Sounion, and landing on the undefended shore right next to Athens itself. The only way to stop them would be to make a forced march, still in heavy armour, over the shoulder of Mount Penteli, to get to the city walls first. And that is what the Athenians did. The feat would be remembered for centuries afterwards, eventually to inspire a legend that would prove more lasting still. By the time the Persian fleet came within sight of Athens, their commanders could see the victors of Marathon once again drawn up and waiting for them. For some days the ships rode at anchor, then the order was given to set sail, back across the Aegean.[1]

The punitive expedition was over, but not the war. Ten years later, the Persians were back. Led by Darius's successor, Xerxes, in the summer of 480 BCE a huge amphibious expedition, launched from the eastern side of the Aegean, advanced right through the northern part of today's Greece, as far as the isthmus of Corinth. This time around, Athens was completely destroyed, the temples crowning its citadel, the Acropolis, set on fire. The battles of that campaign are scarcely less famous than Marathon: Thermopylae, where three hundred foot soldiers from the city of Sparta fought to the last man under their king Leonidas in a doomed attempt to hold the pass between the mountains and the sea; Salamis, the sea-battle in which the Athenians led by Themistocles destroyed the Persian fleet; and the final showdown at Plataea, the next year, where an alliance of Greek city states led by Sparta expelled the invaders for good. Only then were the Greek city states free to pursue their destinies in their own way.

'The Evidence of an Inquiry'

The Persian Wars, as these campaigns have been known ever since, would never afterwards be forgotten. Thirty years after Marathon, the battle would become the subject of a monumental painting in a public colonnade in the centre of Athens; seven centuries later, visitors still stood in front of it in awe, as we know from the description by one of them that we can still read today. Even after so long, the story of the battle was still being retold. There was evidently an appetite for new human touches to embellish it, too. In this way was born the legend that a messenger had run so fast to bring the news of the battle to Athens that he died on the spot after gasping out: 'We won.' Long after the independent Greek city states and the empire of the Medes and Persians had vanished for ever, when first the Romans and, later, medieval Christians faced enemies from the east, they still called them 'Persians', and claimed glory by association with Marathon and the Persian Wars that had begun as long ago as 490 BCE.[2]

In modern times, Europeans seeking the source of their own civilization have sooner or later found their way back to the same starting point. During the French Revolution, in the 1790s, for instance, the new revolutionary army was deliberately modelled on the citizen army of the Athenians; a small town in France even changed its name to Marathon. Famously, in 1846, the British philosopher and Member of Parliament John Stuart Mill addressed a British audience:

> The true ancestors of the European nations . . . are not those from whose blood they are sprung, but those from whom they derive the richest portion of their inheritance. The battle of Marathon, even as an event in English history, is more important than the battle of Hastings. If the issue of that day had been different, the Britons and the Saxons might still have been wandering in the woods.

By the end of the nineteenth century, German historians were celebrating 'the triumph of the free Hellenic [that is, Greek] circle of ideas . . . which gave us those cultural values from which we still draw our sustenance'.[3] In lighter vein at about the same time, one of the accomplishments expected of a 'very modern major-general' in the comic opera by W. S. Gilbert and Arthur Sullivan, *The Pirates of Penzance*, was to 'quote the fights historical / From Marathon to Waterloo, in order, categorical'. Out of the legend of the runner would be born the modern athletic contest that we know as the 'Marathon', run for the first time when the ancient Olympic Games were revived, appropriately enough in Athens, in 1896, and a fixture at every Olympiad since.[4] Today, the historical battle may have been eclipsed by its spin-off into sport; but the name of Marathon must surely have reached into just about every household on the planet.

Why?

What was it about that one battle, fought more than 2,500 years ago, that could generate such extraordinary name recognition so long afterwards? What did it take to turn the events of that August day in 490 BCE into the first 'great battle' of world history? Among countless other conflicts of the ancient world, what made the Persian Wars different? The answer must surely lie, not in anything that happened on the field, but in the *telling of the story* afterwards. And out of that telling would be born both history itself and the *idea of Europe*.

Once the fighting was over, the Greeks could just have heaved an immense sigh of relief, got on with their lives, and put it all behind them. For many people alive at the time, that probably was the top priority – not least because so many of the Greek states had chosen not to resist the invaders at all (some had even collaborated overtly). Instead, and often irrespective of what individuals or states had 'done in the war', the Greeks embarked on a communal celebration that lasted for fifty years, some would say for a hundred and fifty. Its echoes have never died down since, and are still with us today. It is only a slight simplification to call that celebration 'Greek civilization' or 'Classical Greece'.

The foundations for much of the arts, sciences, politics and law as we know them throughout the developed world had already begun to be laid among the self-governing citizen bodies of the Greek city states during the century before the wars. If the Persians had won at Marathon and beyond, all these new ways of thinking and doing things could so easily have been snuffed out. Instead, in the afterglow of the Greeks' unexpected victory, they took wing and reached new heights. In Athens, Aeschylus, Sophocles and Euripides perfected the art of tragic drama in the oldest stage plays that still survive; Athenians learned how to laugh at themselves too, as we know from the slightly later comedies of Aristophanes that lampooned public figures and fashionable notions, with no holds barred. This was the heyday of the marble temples designed and built by the Greeks to honour their gods. The work of painters doesn't survive, but sculptors such as Phidias created out of marble and bronze the figures in human likeness that today are among the world's most admired art objects.

Athens also led the way in establishing an early form of democracy. It seems the word (*demokratia*) was coined around 460 BCE; it means literally 'people power'. This was very different from the representative democracy that we know today: all male citizens participated in decision-making, and many offices of state were decided by drawing lots. Women had a very restricted role in public life, and the very large population of slaves none at all. Every Greek state had its own constitution; intense debates among citizens about how best to govern themselves gave rise to another newly coined word: 'politics' (*politika*), meaning originally 'the affairs of the city state', or *polis* in Greek.

By no means were all these states democratic, like Athens. But whatever the system chosen by the citizens – and it frequently changed – all were based firmly on a principle that was already deeply embedded in the self-government of the Greek city state: the 'rule of law' or 'equality before the law'. The Greeks made up a word for that too; they called it *isonomia*.[5] And that, as things turned out, would prove a more enduring and consistent legacy to later Europe even than the idea of democracy. As the Greek city states showed us long ago, you can have the rule of law without democracy; but you cannot have true democracy without the rule of law.

The decades after the Persian Wars were a time of extraordinary renewal, of rebuilding, new thinking and new creativity. Part of that involved a stock-taking of the recent past. What had happened, exactly, during those years of trial, while everything had hung in the balance? How had it been done? Among so many other inventions whose effects would echo down the ages, the time was ripe for an enterprising individual to 'demonstrate the evidence of an inquiry', as he modestly put it, into everything that had happened and, crucially, the reasons behind it.[6]

His name was Herodotus of Halicarnassus.

So far as we know, no one had ever attempted anything quite like this before. The epic poems, the *Iliad* and the *Odyssey*, attributed to a poet called Homer, may first have been written down as early as the eighth century BCE; they were already widely known and much loved long before the Persian Wars. But these epic stories, woven around a great war between a combined force of Greeks and the city of Troy, in today's north-west Turkey, are the stuff of legend. To this day no one knows whether there ever was such a war; and in any case the epics are mostly about the actions of larger-than-life heroes living in an imaginary bygone age. Herodotus was trying something completely different. For one thing he wrote in the relatively new and more down-to-earth medium of prose. Homer's poems were always sung, to the accompaniment of a musical instrument, before a rapt audience; originally they had been passed down by word of mouth from generation to generation. The new kind of writing could be read on the page (actually a scroll of Egyptian papyrus) and presented in public readings, for evermore, *exactly as its author had set it down.*

A permanent record of events, based on comparison of available sources and judicious weighing up of the evidence, and an investigation into their *causes*: these, together, are the essence of what, ever since Herodotus first put stylus to papyrus in or about the year 447 BCE, we have called 'history', after the Greek word meaning 'inquiry', that appears in the very first sentence of his book: *historie*.

Herodotus had been born in or about the year 484 BCE. His birthplace, the tiny Greek city state of Halicarnassus (today's upmarket and relatively unspoiled resort of Bodrum on the Aegean coast of Turkey), lay outside Europe; he himself had begun life as a subject of the Great King of Persia. The future historian would have been a child of five when the Persian Wars ended. By the time he began to write up the results of his 'inquiry', in his late thirties, to create what we call the *Histories*, the positive backlash from the war was already in full swing. Indeed, Herodotus must have been writing during the very same years when, on the Acropolis of Athens, the sacred buildings whose columns still dominate the city's skyline rose into the sunlight, in the grandiose project overseen by the statesman Pericles to replace the ruins left by the Persian sack of the city.

Herodotus's 'inquiry' wasn't only into *what* had happened. Writing a generation after the events he narrated, with access to many of those who had fought or had grown up in the aftermath, and in the climate of that time of reckoning, he offered his readers an attempt to explain *why*. What could have inspired his countrymen to fight in the way that they did – against such overwhelming odds? Part of the answer that he gives comes in the form of an imaginary speech – one of many that enliven Herodotus's narrative. Here, a pair of Greeks from Sparta confront a Persian dignitary and give him this explanation:

> What it is to be a slave you well know from experience, but you have never experienced liberty, to find out whether it tastes sweet or not. If you *were* to experience it, you would be urging us to fight for it not just with spears, but with axes too.[7]

Herodotus must have grown up literally alongside the new concept of liberty, or political freedom (*eleutheria*). The word seems to have become current among the Greeks very shortly after the final battle of Plataea in 479 BCE.[8] But liberty, as Herodotus's contemporaries understood it, was not absolute or unbounded. Another of those imaginary speeches, this time addressed to King Xerxes himself, explains why: 'Enjoying liberty, the Greeks are not in every respect free: they are subject to law, which they hold in far greater awe than your subjects do you.'[9] In this way the political freedom that the Greeks had fought to defend in the Persian Wars became inseparably entwined with that older concept that was already built into the very fabric of the Greek city state: *isonomia*, or the rule of law – thanks to Herodotus and the power of the written word, for all time.

Continents in Collision

Herodotus tells the story of the Persian Wars in a way that again and again talks up the shared identity of the Hellenes (the Greeks' name for themselves) and their potential for concerted action in a common cause – even if, in practice, as his narrative also shows unflinchingly, this was constantly undermined by the willingness of so many of the Greek city states to roll over before the invaders. Pitted against them are the *barbaroi*. In the aftermath of the wars, and as part of the cultural spoils of victory, the distinction between 'us' and 'them', between 'Hellenes' and 'barbarians', was becoming marked in a way it never seems to have been before – and not just in the pages of Herodotus.[10] Originally the word *barbaroi* had meant nothing more than 'foreigners', people who spoke a different language. But in the climate of the time its meaning was moving closer to the sense it has today.

Right from the start, the historian promises to preserve the memory of the 'great and wonderful deeds in evidence on the part of the Hellenes on the one hand and, on the other, of the barbarians'. Some scholars today make much of this even-handedness.[11] And it's true that Herodotus did very greatly extend the scope of his 'inquiry' to encompass an inexhaustible curiosity about non-Greek peoples and their ways. But that doesn't make him impartial. It would be anachronistic to say that the *Histories* present the Persian Wars as a 'clash of civilizations', because that phrase has acquired much additional baggage in modern times. Instead, in order to make sense of events for readers in the very different world of the fifth century BCE, Herodotus came up with a clash of *continents*. And this idea, so far as we can tell, was his own original invention.

Every Greek, for at least a century before Herodotus's time, had known that the world was divided into three continents: Europe, Asia and 'Libya', the Greek name for Africa. All three, as Herodotus himself pointed out, were known by the names of women. The origins of these names were lost in a mythology that was already ancient and partly forgotten in his day. The original *Europe* (usually called today by the Latin form of her name, 'Europa') had been a Phoenician princess abducted from her home in today's Lebanon and taken to Crete – either by Zeus, the king of the Greek gods in disguise as a bull, or (Herodotus's preferred version) by a crew of Greek pirates. Either way, as the historian also pointed out, the princess Europa never got to set foot on the mainland that would later bear her name.[12]

Herodotus evidently no more believed this story than we do. But he did find an imaginative way to mould it into an explanation of what the Persian Wars had been all about. According to the prologue to the *Histories*, the abduction of Europa had been just one among a series of intercontinental raids targeting royal ladies that had been going on for thousands of years. Neither side had taken these particularly seriously, Herodotus explains – surely tongue in cheek – until Paris, prince of Troy (on the Asian side of the Dardanelles), had stolen the most beautiful woman in the world, Helen of Sparta, from her husband Menelaus. This was supposed to have been the cause of the Trojan War, immortalized by Homer's monumental epic poem the *Iliad*. Greeks of Herodotus's time believed that that war had taken place some seven centuries earlier – and if it ever did, that date is probably not far wrong. It would be like blaming the battle of Agincourt for the state of Anglo-French relations today.

By this ingenious piece of revisionist myth-making, Herodotus manages to mobilize the myth of Europa, even to weaponize it. And his purpose, in the end, is serious: to persuade his readers that, from time immemorial, as he puts it, the Persians 'had regarded the

Greek world as permanently in a state of war against them'. There was a real division between 'barbarian' Asia and Greek Europe: 'the Persians claim Asia and the barbarian peoples living there for their own, while Europe and the Greek world they treat as having nothing to do with them'.[13] From that small beginning, 'Europe' in Herodotus's opening pages ceases to be a neutral geographical expression or a character in mythology and becomes geopolitical.

One of the great set pieces, later in the *Histories*, describes at length the crossing of the Hellespont (the ancient name for the Dardanelles) by Xerxes's army. Herodotus was not alone among Greek writers in presenting the unprecedented size of these forces as an enormity – a violation of the natural order and the limits set down for mortal humans by the gods. He describes in wondering detail how a double bridge of boats spanned the straits, strong enough to resist the current and the frequent gales that blow through the passage between continents; he relishes the anecdote that when the first attempt had been wrecked by a storm, Xerxes ordered his underlings to lash the sea with whips and throw iron fetters into it as a punishment. The Greeks loved stories in which pride goes before a fall; and Xerxes had further to fall than most. But Herodotus has a geopolitical point to make as well.

More than once he tells us that the Persians' goal in making this crossing was to conquer not just Greece but Europe itself: a land that was 'excellent to an extreme degree, and worthy to be ruled by the Great King alone among mortals'. 'Europe,' Herodotus has Xerxes promise his generals and courtiers, 'is a land no less in extent than our own, not inferior to ours and even more super-abundant'. Before the expedition had even set out, the way Herodotus tells it, Xerxes was boasting:

> . . . we will make the whole earth beneath God's heaven into Persian territory. The sun will not look down upon any land that shares a border with ours, but along with you I will make of all these lands a single country, once I have passed through the length and breadth of Europe. For I believe this to be true: there is not a city or a tribe

of humankind that will be left to give us battle, once those I speak of [that is, the Greeks] are eliminated.[14]

As Xerxes reaches the Hellespont and the momentous crossing from one continent to another is about to begin – it would take a whole week, day and night, for more than a million and a half men in arms to cross the bridge of boats – the Great King twice more repeats his determination to 'subdue the whole of Europe'.[15] Were he to have succeeded, it would have been nothing less than blasphemy, an offence against the gods, 'for one man to hold sway over both Asia and Europe' – this time according to a speech that Herodotus puts into the mouth of the Athenian general and victor in the battle of Salamis, Themistocles. And so, at the end of the story, the routed Persians are forced to abandon Europe and retreat back to Asia where they have come from – and where, as Herodotus has the satisfaction of reminding his readers in his concluding pages, they had always properly, and by their own account, belonged.[16]

It's hard to believe that any ruler of the Medes and Persians, surveying the world from his capital at Susa, today in western Iran, could really have set his sights on conquering the entire continent that lay beyond the Dardanelles. Herodotus himself admitted that he didn't in fact know how far Europe extended, or whether it was bounded by the sea to the north and east; but his contemporaries were well aware that the continent reached westwards as far as Cadiz on the Atlantic coast of the Iberian peninsula.[17] It would have been quite some conquest. And in Herodotus's telling, it was only the Greeks who had stood in the way and prevented it. A Europe united under Xerxes would have been a violation of nature, an abomination to the gods. This was the fundamental cause, according to Herodotus, both of the Persian invasions and of their eventual defeat by the Greeks. Ironically, perhaps, the inventor of history, the discoverer of historical causation, and the first to give a geopolitical identity to the continent of Europe was also the first eurosceptic – at least if the price of unity was to be autocracy imposed from Asia.

The First European Superstate

Philip II, King of the Macedonians, bore a terrible scar across the socket of his right eye, which he had lost in battle; another wound from another battle had left him with a pronounced limp. Philip was notorious for his hard drinking and for the drunken antics of his court; he had seven wives, not serially like the six married by Henry VIII of England, but several at a time. Citizens of Greek city states like Athens and Sparta could rarely find a good word to say about Philip or his people. The royal house of Macedonia was supposed to be descended from the Greek demi-god Heracles: that meant they counted as Hellenes. But when it came to the Macedonians themselves, their homeland lay far to the north, amid the mountains and lakes of the southern Balkans. Somewhere in this wild inland region, the Greek language and Greek customs shaded into others that in Greek eyes were irredeemably 'barbarian'. In the words of one prominent Athenian of the time, Macedonia was 'a place that used not to be able to provide even a slave worth buying'.[18]

Philip inherited his throne in 360 BCE (the consequence of yet another battle, in which his brother had been killed). More than a hundred years had passed since the end of the Persian Wars; about half that time since Herodotus had ended his *Histories*. In the meantime, the Greek city states had been plunged into a bewildering series of wars against each other. Of these, the Peloponnesian War that began in 431 BCE is much the best remembered – thanks to its historian, Thucydides. That one dragged on for twenty-seven years and brought both main players, Athens and Sparta, to their knees. But in truth the wars continued, off and on, for almost a full century – and still with no winner.

The Greek world of that time was like a microcosm of Europe in the eighteenth century. Athens, Sparta, Thebes and dozens of still smaller rivals jockeyed for position and formed temporary alliances – even with the old common enemy, Persia – so as to prevent any one of them from coming out on top. A favourite word of the time, another Greek invention, was *autonomia*, meaning literally that the city state was 'a law unto itself'.[19] Today we call it sovereignty. Ever jealous of their sovereignty and proudly refusing to give up an inch of it to a neighbour, the Greek city states could neither live together in peace nor prevail for long in war. That, too, is a situation eerily familiar, when you scale it up for the nation states of Europe in more recent times. Later European statesmen would invoke the 'balance of power' and the 'liberties of Europe'; in the smaller theatre of ancient Greece, they called it 'the liberty of Hellas'. The underlying principle was the same.

Stalemate among the city states gave the cue for Philip to bring his Macedonians onto the scene. Twenty years into his reign, he had expanded his kingdom to include, in today's terms, large parts of Bulgaria and Albania, most of the Republic of North Macedonia, all the European part of Turkey, and the northern regions of Greece that are still known by the ancient names of Macedonia and Thrace. Centralized, heavily militarized, and enriched by the exploitation of new discoveries of gold and silver, Macedonia was far stronger than any Greek city state, and more than a match for an alliance even of the strongest.

The test came in the summer of 338 BCE. Philip led his army south and was met by a rare tactical alliance between Athens and Thebes, two of the most powerful of the city states that had been at loggerheads for centuries. At the battle of Chaeronea, not far from Thebes, Philip's forces killed or took prisoner more than half of the Athenians and Thebans ranged against them. In the aftermath, nearly all the city states found themselves swept up into a nominal confederacy, with Philip as its Supreme Leader (*hegemon* in Greek). To many among the highly educated, articulate elite of Athens, in particular, this was tantamount to the end of Greek civilization; a judgement that would be repeated by historians writing about the ancient world in the eighteenth and nineteenth centuries and can still be heard among classicists today.

By taking control of the Greek city states and adding them to his dominions farther north in the Balkans, Philip had created something without precedent in this part of the world. One modern historian has called it 'the first nation state in Europe'.[20] But that is to look at it the wrong way round. Philip's Greek contemporaries can have had little idea of what *we* mean by a nation state; but they did have very definite ideas about what a Greek city state ought to be and how it should be run. And this was nothing like it. Not only were Philip's domains vast by comparison; they were ruled by a hereditary autocrat who governed through a warrior elite. Where were the citizen assemblies and the art of public speaking that were the pride of so many Greeks? Philip's subjects included not only the Macedonians, used to speaking Greek, but also Thracians, Illyrians, Paeonians and others who spoke different languages and worshipped different gods.

The Greeks loved to give names to things; but here they had a problem. The most you could say of Philip's motley subjects was that they all lived on the same continent. You couldn't quite call them 'Europeans', because the word barely existed yet. But one Athenian opinion-former, who was a rare fan, went out of his way to flatter Philip by telling him he possessed 'greater power than any of those who dwell in Europe'. The king's first biographer, who had known Philip personally, would concede, not without ambiguity: 'Europe had never produced a man like Philip son of Amyntas'. Had he wished, the same biographer also noted, Philip 'could by his efforts have ruled over the whole of Europe'.[21]

Far from being a forerunner of today's nation states, what Philip had created was a superstate that forced peoples and ethnicities unwillingly together under a single ruler. And it was this superstate – minuscule by modern standards, but in this part of the world unprecedented for its time – that would go on to make Europe's first indelible mark on the rest of the planet.

Milking his new position for all it was worth, Philip was now poised to exploit the never-quite-forgotten existential clash with Asia. Within a year of his victory over the Greek city states, he announced to the assembled delegates of the Greek city states in spring 337 BCE that he was going to launch a new war against the Persians.[22] No effort was spared to present the expedition as a revenge match against the invader of a century and a half before. The recently subjected city states might grumble, but they could hardly refuse when they were ordered to send their best fighting troops for the campaign: *theirs* were, after all, the wrongs that were now to be avenged. What better way could there be, from Philip's point of view, to bind them into his new superstate? No doubt with an eye to a propaganda opportunity, while preparations for the expedition were in full swing, and an advance guard of Macedonians was already pushing into Anatolia, Philip chose to name his newborn daughter Europa.[23] No one was to be in any doubt that Europe and Asia would soon, once again, be ranged in battle against one another.

In the event, before the main part of the expedition could set out, Philip was assassinated in broad daylight before thousands of spectators gathered in the theatre of his capital city, Aegae – ironically enough as he followed a procession of images of the twelve deities of Mount Olympus, with his own making a thirteenth. It now fell to his son and heir Alexander (known ever afterwards as 'the Great') to follow through on his father's promise. The combined forces of Macedonia and the Greek city states set out in the spring of 334 BCE. We have no direct evidence for Alexander's motives; the histories of these events that have come down to us were written with the benefit of several centuries of hindsight. But from what later historians tell us, Alexander, no less than his father, had an eye for a propaganda opportunity.

The army that Alexander ferried across the strait of the Dardanelles was a mere fraction of the size of the amphibious force that Xerxes had mobilized in the opposite direction a century and a half before. But it was still the largest that had ever been mustered under Greek command.[24] According to one account, the twenty-one-year-old Alexander, Supreme Leader of the Greek confederacy and commander-in-chief of the expedition, stood in the prow of the leading ship; as it came to shore, 'he, first among the Macedonians, hurled a spear from the deck then going ashore himself plunged it into the earth, in this way showing that he was ready to receive the land of Asia from the gods as conquered by his spear'. According to another, 'halfway over he slaughtered a bull as an offering to Poseidon and poured wine from a golden cup into the sea to propitiate the [sea-spirits, the] Nereids'. A newly built altar marked the spot 'where he left the shore of Europe and another where he landed on the other side of the strait'.[25] The impieties of Xerxes were not going to be repeated this time around.

Once ashore, Alexander visited the site of Troy and laid a wreath on the supposed tomb of Achilles, the greatest of the Greek heroes who had fought in the Trojan War of legend, according to Homer in the *Iliad*. In reality, the epic poet had never so much as mentioned Europe or a conflict between continents; it was Herodotus and his tongue-in-cheek explanation for the age-old and immutable enmity between Europe and Asia that Alexander was channelling by these actions. A few days after that, Alexander won his first battle against an army sent by Darius III, the latest Great King of the Medes and Persians.

Europe was on the front foot. But no one now could pretend that what was at stake was the rule of law, still less the political liberty that the Greek city states had discovered through their resistance to the Persian invasions and had since squandered. Alexander and his father Philip before him were simply doing what Darius and Xerxes had each tried to do in their turn. The difference was that Alexander (in the short term) succeeded. And this time there was no Herodotus to tell his readers that it would be an abomination and an affront to the gods for one mortal human being to rule over two continents.

By the time Alexander died, in Babylon in 323 BCE at the age of thirty-two (most probably from natural causes), he had conquered all of south-western Asia as far as the southern shore of the Caspian Sea and the eastern frontiers of today's Afghanistan. His army had even crossed Pakistan and the River Indus, to reach into India as far as Amritsar. All the former Persian Empire was now his, from the Hindu Kush to Egypt as far south as today's Aswan and as far west as the oasis of Siwa – and all this on top of the extended superstate in Europe that he had inherited from his father.

Some three centuries later, rumours had become established that at the time of his death Alexander had been working on plans to transfer whole populations from Asia to Europe and vice versa. His aim, according to the historian Diodorus of Sicily, had been 'by means of intermarriage and acquired affinity, to bring the largest continents together in a state of shared concord and familial harmony'.[26] Modern historians mostly treat these claims with a pinch of salt, and probably rightly. But if not Alexander himself, then somebody during the intervening centuries had at least thought up such a drastic way to overcome the geopolitical fissure between continents that had been conjured into existence by Herodotus. A grand vision indeed, but it was not to be.

Instead, after Alexander's death his Macedonian generals fought among themselves, much as the Greek states had done of old, but now on a much larger scale, to determine who would succeed him. After a generation of conflict, not one but three kingdoms emerged, under self-proclaimed kings known as the 'Successors'. One successor kingdom was based in each of the three known continents: Asia, Africa and Europe. Whatever Alexander's intentions might have been, the *effect* of his campaigns was to prove very different from just one more land grab by a greedy imperial power. The military force that made it possible had been raised by a newly consolidated kingdom on European soil, the first of its kind. But in hindsight the Macedonian military machine would turn out to be the tail wagging a dog of a different breed altogether. Because wherever Alexander's armies went, they took with them the Greek language, which within a very few years would become the common currency of everyday business and education across a broad swathe of three continents.

Embedded in the language were the philosophy, the arts and architecture, science, and much else that had been so finely honed by the Greeks in the aftermath of the Persian Wars – including even those political ideas about freedom, the sovereignty of independent states, and the rule of law that had all, in practice, been put into abeyance, first by Philip and then by Alexander. Europe was already beginning to export something akin to its stock-in-trade in centuries to come – and by means that would become all too familiar, too, the world over. As soft power spread out on the back of hard power, its effects would prove much longer lasting.

Federal Solutions

Back in Macedonia, a little over a century after Alexander's death, an obsequious courtier addressed these words to the king who had inherited the superstate created by Philip II: 'Master of Europe, by land and sea supreme ruler over mortals, no less than Zeus over the immortal gods . . .'[27] The reality was rather different. The European portion of Alexander's short-lived empire was the least favoured of the three; by 200 BCE the centre of action had moved eastwards into Asia and south across the Mediterranean to the newly founded Greek mega-city of Alexandria on the Egyptian coast. And already a new power was on the rise, in Italy to the west, that threatened to eclipse the Greek world altogether. That power was Rome.

Even in their own backyard the Macedonians had never managed to stamp their authority permanently on the Greek city states that Philip II had brought to heel after the battle of Chaeronea in 338 BCE. The confederacy he had imposed on them had already been a dead letter by the time Alexander died, fifteen years later. But Philip's high-handed treatment had given a new twist to the kaleidoscope that was the Greek world of the fourth century BCE. The perfect sovereignty that the cities had prized for so long, and had fought so bitterly among themselves to maintain, was no longer a viable option. Might there be something in the federal idea after all? With the relatively big players, Athens, Sparta and Thebes, all cut down to size, it was the minor city states – some four hundred of them by this time – that led the way in a striking political innovation.

The concept had been around for some time; but it had only been seriously tried at a very local level, often in out-of-the-way places that the Greeks of the city states looked down on as backward. In the chaos that followed the death of Alexander, many of the city states of southern Greece banded together into genuinely federal unions. It has been reckoned that by about 300 BCE between 40 and 50 per cent of the Greek city states then in existence belonged to such a confederacy.[28]

Political leaders and strategists now began to devise ways to pool sovereignty and ensure the equitable rule of law across a number of previously sovereign member states, while still allowing each to maintain its own identity, constitution and laws. One of the largest and best organized of these federal unions was known as the Achaean League, which brought together most of the cities and regions of the southern Greek region known as the Peloponnese. By the middle of the second century BCE the prospects for the Achaean League could not have been brighter – or so it would appear from an insider's account written at about that time. Polybius was simultaneously a citizen of Megalopolis, in the wilds of Arcadia, and of the federal League. His father had held several political and military offices in the League; Polybius in his youth had been expected to follow the same path – until a dramatic change in his fortunes, when he was in his mid-thirties, set him on the way to becoming a historian instead. He (and we) would have the Romans to thank for that, as we will discover shortly.

Federal efforts had failed in the past – 'since', as Polybius put it, all too truly, 'none could set aside the interests of their own supremacy for the sake of shared liberty'. But now, he went on:

> . . . almost all of the Peloponnese resembles a single city state, with the difference only that its inhabitants do not live within a single circuit wall, while in other respects everything is identical or nearly so, both for the whole and for each individual city . . . Nowhere else will you find a truly, thoroughly democratic system based on political equality and free speech or a purer policy than exists among the members of the Achaean League.

These principles, Polybius believed, were the best bulwark against what he called the 'enslavement of fatherlands', whether by home-grown 'tyrants' or external enemies.[29] The trouble was, some 'fatherlands' (that is, city states) had been less willing than others to be roped in. Sparta, once the strongest military state in the Peloponnese and fiercer than most in standing up for its own sovereignty, had only been incorporated a generation before the time when Polybius most probably wrote his glowing account. Never a cooperative member, it would be Sparta's bid to break loose (Spexit?) in 148 BCE that would trigger disaster for the Achaean League.[30]

Because of what happened next, the Greek experiments in federal pooling of sovereignty during the third and second centuries BCE had no sequel in the ancient world. But they would never be forgotten either. Polybius's *Histories* would be rediscovered during the Renaissance; the model of the federal republic would be revived in the mid-eighteenth century by the French political philosopher Montesquieu, later to influence the drafting of the Constitution of the United States of America, as well as the constitutions of some of its individual states. In Europe, from the Swiss Confederation in 1848 to the post-Second World War German Federal Republic, the model as described by Polybius has proved both an inspiration and a challenge. And of course the dilemma faced by those federal unions more than two thousand years ago seems uncannily to prefigure, today, the one faced by the European Union in its dealings with current, former and potential future member states.[31]

Back in the second century BCE, these developments were rapidly being overtaken by that rising power in the west, in Italy, that was already beginning to change the shape and the meaning of Europe yet again. This was the city state and republic of Rome.

The Romans we will get to know through their own words and their own idea of themselves in the next chapter. But those words and that idea would not be crafted until surprisingly late in the day, by which time the Roman state would already have reached the height of its power, and its greatest minds would often draw on hindsight to account for how they had got there. For now, we can best trace the rise of Rome through the impact it made on the Greeks, who were still the only people in Europe writing history, at least that has survived for us to read today.[32]

The first serious confrontation between the Greek world and its future rival and conqueror came in 280 BCE. In that year, Pyrrhus, king of Epirus in north-west Greece and a neighbour of Macedonia, chose to invade Italy. Pyrrhus was a younger cousin of Alexander, and had inherited a taste for conquest, as well as a contingent of captured Persian war elephants that had been sent back as trophies from the east. If his cousin could conquer Asia, Pyrrhus would try his luck in the opposite direction. The elephants caused mayhem in Italy. But Pyrrhus's victories over the Romans were costly, giving rise to the phrase 'pyrrhic victory' that we still use today. Never to be forgotten, either, was the Greek king's first sight of a Roman army making camp and preparing for battle. Turning to one of his generals, Pyrrhus is said to have remarked, 'The way these barbarians keep discipline has nothing barbarian about it.'[33] After campaigning for five years, he gave up and went home.

As they got to know them better, most Greeks quickly came to the same conclusion about the Romans as Pyrrhus had done. After all, Greeks living in cities all round the southern coasts of Italy had been doing business with their northern neighbours for several centuries before Pyrrhus made his brief foray. Both the Romans and the Etruscans, further north in Italy, used versions of the alphabet that had first been devised, around 800 BCE, to write Greek. The Etruscan city states bore at least a passing resemblance to Greek ones; little noticed until the fourth century BCE, Rome itself appeared, to Greek eyes, to be just another of the same. Indeed, at least one Greek commentator at the time thought that Rome actually *was* a Greek city.

Romans worshipped gods and goddesses that looked and behaved just like their Greek counterparts; though the Latin names were different, the stories told about them were immediately recognizable.

Already by the fifth century BCE, Greeks knew that this Italian people claimed to be descended from Trojan exiles who had supposedly migrated across the Mediterranean after the legendary sack of Troy by the Greeks. That in itself says a lot about how the two peoples saw one another. The emerging Romans had chosen to insert themselves into a quintessentially *Greek* story – but they also chose to identify with the opposite side.[34] From the Greek point of view, confronting the rise of Rome would not be like resisting the Persians. As Pyrrhus had observed, these foreigners were not so very foreign either.

The first time a Roman army entered the southern Balkans, by sea across the Adriatic, was in 229 BCE. Like Pyrrhus's intervention in the opposite direction, this was a brief affair.[35] But it was a harbinger. It is once again Polybius who takes up the story. Written between 167 and shortly after 146 BCE, the surviving parts of his *Histories* are our earliest source for the first stages of Roman expansion beyond Italy. Polybius's own life had been shaped by these events. The Achaean League had sat on the sidelines while the Roman legions battled it out against the Macedonian kingdom. But when that war ended with the crushing defeat of Macedonia's last-ever king, the mythologically named Perseus, in 168 BCE, the victorious Romans proceeded to round up a thousand of the most prominent citizens of the Greek states and carry them off to Rome as hostages to ensure the good behaviour of their relatives back home. Polybius was one of them.

The hostages' captivity seems not to have been too onerous – except that it lasted eighteen years and by the time they were allowed home fewer than a third of them were still alive. Polybius was lucky enough to form a lifelong friendship with the Scipio family, one of the most illustrious and best connected of the Roman aristocracy. In this way, he had access to the highest echelons of Roman society. And that is how one of the prospective leading lights of the Achaean League ended up, instead, becoming the first historian systematically to chronicle and try to explain, as he put it,

'how and by what kind of a political state almost the entire inhabited world came to be conquered and fell under the single rule of
the Romans in just under fifty-three years – an event like nothing
that had ever happened before'.[36]

How had the Romans done it? The historian's rationally trained
mind sought the answer in the ways the Romans organized their
society, their government and their armies. But with the benefit of
hindsight, we can see today that it was the failure of either Macedonia or the Greek city states to create a unified political system
on European soil that left the way open for the Romans to fill that
role instead. It may be, as some modern historians have suggested,
that given time the Greek federal experiment might have become
embedded and even have proved a match for the concentrated
power of Rome.[37] And Polybius himself, although he avoids making
the comparison directly, must surely have seen that 'to have brought
about that supreme achievement, the unity of the peoples of the
Peloponnese', which is what his fellow countrymen had done, fell
a long way short of the Romans 'subduing almost the entire inhabited world and achieving a mastery unrivalled in the present and
impossible to surpass in the future'.[38] The Greek world, despite the
spectacular exploits of Alexander the Great in the east, was just too
small to fill the European stage.

The *coup de grâce* came in the year 146 BCE. Two years after
Sparta's attempted exit from the Achaean League, the Romans'
ruling body, the Senate, had been called upon to arbitrate. But to
the horror of Polybius, the Achaean leaders decided to risk everything in a spectacular and ill-judged act of defiance. The Roman
response was swift and brutal. During the summer of that year, an
army fielded by the League was defeated outside the city of Corinth
by the Roman consul Lucius Mummius. In the immediate aftermath, the Achaean League was disbanded; Corinth was razed to
the ground, its treasures looted, and most of its people either killed
or enslaved. According to a decree of the Roman Senate, no one
was ever to live there again; a whole century would pass before that
decree would be rescinded.[39]

No one could doubt, now, that Europe had a new master, and that was Rome. The nearest thing to a European union that the ancient world ever knew would be achieved not by consent, through federal solutions like the Achaean League, but by force of arms. Which is why it is still better known to history as the 'Roman Empire'.

2.

'Power without End'

146 BCE–337 CE

Rome was always about power – how to gain it, how to wield it and how to keep it. In 146 BCE the Greek city of Corinth was not the only one to experience the annihilating edge of that power. The same year saw the final act in an existential struggle between the city state of Rome and its rival Carthage, on the North African coast of what is now Tunisia. At stake was supremacy in the western Mediterranean and its European hinterland. And just like the earlier wars between Greeks and Persians, this one would determine whether it would be Europe or another continent that would shape the history of this part of the world from that time on.

It had been a close-run thing. Over a period of more than a century, the Romans had been engaged in no fewer than three all-out wars against Carthage. These have been known ever since as the 'Punic Wars', from a Latin adjective meaning Carthaginian. During the Second Punic War, which began in 218 BCE, the Carthaginian general, Hannibal, brought a huge army equipped with elephants the long way round from North Africa, via Spain's Mediterranean coast and across the Alpine passes in midwinter, to attack the Romans in the rear in their own Italian homeland. Two years later, after losing two battles in Italy with the loss of tens of thousands killed, it really did look as though Rome would be wiped off the map. The historian Titus Livius (known in English as Livy), writing some two centuries later, imagined the scenes in Rome like this:

Never while the city itself was still safe had there been such great terror and uproar within the walls of Rome . . . No other people, afflicted with such a great weight of catastrophe, could have avoided being wiped out . . . In the midst of such ills and without definite news they could think of no plan and were distracted by the loud lamentations of the women indiscriminately wailing over the fate of the living and the dead in almost every house . . .[1]

In the distress of the time, bizarre things had happened that clearly horrified the later historian. Two Vestal Virgins, priestesses dedicated to chastity, were found to have broken their vows; one was buried alive, the other killed herself, while a male culprit was clubbed to death by the high priest of the city himself. On the advice of an oracle, 'unusual rites were performed: one of them consisted in burying alive in the cattle market a pair of Gauls, male and female, and a pair of Greeks' – all highly 'un-Roman' behaviour, in Livy's opinion.[2]

And yet, Rome had been saved – more because Hannibal failed to follow up his victories than from any other cause, as Livy would also concede. Dogged persistence had enabled the Romans to regroup and carry the fight back to North Africa. In 201 BCE a Roman army defeated Hannibal decisively on his home ground, at the battle of Zama, fought close to Carthage. That left Rome holding the upper hand, and able to dictate the terms of peace. But peaceful co-existence with a defeated rival was not to the taste of the Roman Senate. On flimsy pretexts, the senators provoked a Third Punic War in 149 BCE. This one ended in the total destruction of Carthage three years later, which brings us back to 146 BCE when the same fate befell Corinth.

The oft-repeated story that salt was ploughed into the Carthaginians' fields to prevent them from ever again bearing crops is a modern embellishment. But it's true that Carthage, like Corinth, was systematically looted, buildings were stripped of their roofs, and the surviving population sold into slavery. Here, too, the edict went out that the city was never to be inhabited again – though here, too, eventually it would be rescinded.[3] In charge of the destruction was Scipio Aemilianus, the Roman aristocrat who had befriended Polybius, the Greek historian, during his captivity in Rome, and had taken him along to watch. According to Polybius, 'Turning round to me at once and grasping my hand Scipio said, "A glorious moment, Polybius; but I have a dread foreboding that someday the same doom will be pronounced on my own country." '[4]

Whether Scipio ever said anything of the sort is open to question. But the victors can never for a moment have doubted that if the fortunes of war had gone the other way, the fate of Carthage would have been their own. The rise of Rome to dominate Europe and beyond was rooted in that zero-sum struggle for survival. No longer just another of southern Europe's hundreds of city states, Rome had begun to lay the foundations of its future empire.

'The Public Thing'

Built on seven low hills overlooking a bend in the River Tiber, some 25 miles inland from its mouth, the city of Rome could trace its origin back to the year 753 BCE. Twin brothers named Romulus and Remus had allegedly been fathered by Mars, the god of war. Cast out as infants, they had been rescued and suckled by a she-wolf until a kind-hearted shepherd took them in. As young adults, between them they came up with a plan to build a new city on the hills overlooking the place where the she-wolf had found them. But they couldn't agree which hill to start with. So they quarrelled, and Romulus killed Remus. The survivor got to name the city after himself. Violence was in there from the very beginning.[5]

This was the story that, seven hundred years later, when Livy wrote it up in the definitive version, Romans were still telling themselves about their most distant past. Almost as much shrouded in myth is the tale of Rome's seven kings; their reigns seem improbably long if it's true that the last of them was driven out in 509 BCE. That became the moment, as it would long afterwards be reconstructed by Livy, for the Romans to discover their own version of political liberty – and it sounds very like its Greek equivalent, as it emerged at much the same time in the aftermath of the Persian Wars.

The second book of Livy's history begins at this point: 'Of the free Roman people, their acts in peace and war . . . and the rule of laws overruling that of men I now shall write – a liberty made all the sweeter by the overbearing behaviour of the previous king.'[6] Whatever exactly had happened back then, one consequence of those early upheavals would remain deeply embedded in the Roman psyche for the next thousand years: the Latin for 'king' – *rex* – would remain a dirty word, never again to be used for a Roman ruler, even long after one-man rule had returned to what would by that time have become an empire.

Polybius, writing in the second century BCE, had admired the perfect, self-correcting balance, as he saw it, of the unwritten Roman constitution. The Senate, an aristocratic body, made the laws and the most important decisions; executive authority was exercised by elected officials, the two consuls, who held office for a year at a time; through these and other elected offices, the common people had a say, though this was much less than in a Greek democracy. Modern historians are sceptical that the Roman system can ever have worked quite so neatly, and there is some suspicion that, when it did, that may have been because later Romans had been reading Polybius.[7]

Be that as it may, the essence of the system was summed up in the phrase *Senatus PopulusQue Romanus*: the Roman Senate and People. The initials SPQR would also have a very long afterlife – and are still stamped by the municipality of Rome on drain covers throughout the city today. The Romans called their state 'the public thing', or *res publica* in Latin, the origin of the modern word 'republic'. That term, too, would continue in daily use for centuries after the last republican institutions had become mere adjuncts of imperial rule. Even after their empire had reached its fullest extent, elite Romans would never entirely lose the mentality of the ancient city state that had shaped their institutions in the early centuries.

By the first century BCE, the *res publica* had developed a highly sophisticated concept of the interlocking relationships linking political liberty, the rule of law, and the rights and duties of citizens. The philosopher, politician and practising lawyer Marcus Tullius Cicero, during the middle years of that century, recognized that 'if liberty was the precondition of citizenship, citizenship was its guarantee'; 'the defining trait of a free people was the enjoyment of equal rights under the law'.[8]

For ancient Romans, the making and observance of laws were practical matters; while the Greeks had established the underlying principles, the beginning of the legal profession and of codified rules for regulating the behaviour of citizens is to be found in Rome. That is why, in the words of one legal historian, writing at the end of the twentieth century, Roman law 'over the centuries . . . has played an important role in the creation of a common European culture . . . [L]awyers of different periods have found what they needed at the time. It has indelibly impressed its character on European legal and political thought.'[9] In this way, ideas that had originated in the Greek city states in the aftermath of the Persian Wars would become a blueprint for the legal systems of an entire continent.

In its dealings with its neighbours, Rome started out little different from many another city state of Europe's Mediterranean hinterland. A citizen army was expected to defend the city against all comers; in practice, as often as not, that meant pre-emptively taking the fight to the enemy. Traditionally, Roman men were expected to be disciplined soldiers, while women kept out of public view as dutiful wives and mothers. Indeed the Latin word *virtus*, which meant both moral uprightness and valour in battle, is derived from *vir*, meaning a fighting man (which also gives us 'virile').

Autonomy, or absolute sovereignty, was taken every bit as seriously in Rome as anywhere in the Greek world. The Greeks had fought each other to a standstill in the name of this principle. But in Italy the Romans' competitors were less evenly matched. To their north were the city states of the Etruscans; a number of different Italian peoples inhabited the centre and south of the peninsula; perched all round its southern coastline was a plethora of cities that had been settled by Greek immigrants, centuries before. Each time the Romans won a local feud or, later, a regional war, they would co-opt the losers to fight on their own side and call them 'allies'. The resources and armed forces of these new-found friends could then be called upon to swell Roman coffers and Roman armies for the next campaign. Athens and Sparta had tried this too, in their day – but sooner or later a sufficient number of their rivals would always band together to level the playing field again. Nothing like that happened in Italy. In a zero-sum game, the Romans took more and more autonomy for themselves, and left less and less for anybody else. By the time the wars against Carthage were over, Rome controlled the entire peninsula.

And so the *res publica* grew into something that looked less and less like a city state. By about 100 BCE the 'Roman Senate and People' ruled over most of Spain, a wide strip of southern France bordering the Mediterranean, the whole of Italy including the islands of Corsica, Sardinia and Sicily, most of today's Croatia, Albania and Greece, as well as small overseas enclaves in Tunisia and Anatolia. Modern historians often describe this dramatic expansion as an incipient 'Mediterranean empire', or even take later Roman claims at face value and speak of a 'world empire'. No one today has any idea what the senators and army commanders may have planned – if, indeed, there was ever any conscious, coherent plan at all.[10] But the reality of Roman rule at the beginning of the first century BCE is plain to see on a map: this was a *European* empire, with forward outposts on the facing coasts of Africa and Asia.

It would not be long before so much success abroad triggered crisis at home. The political balance that Polybius had described through an outsider's rose-tinted spectacles was proving impossible to sustain. During a period of just over a century, from 133 BCE to 27 BCE, the *res publica* came close to imploding – at the same time as it exploded outwards across western Europe and the eastern Mediterranean. Paradoxically, it was struggles for power at home that drove the new phase of conquest.

It began with the assassination of an elected official, Tiberius Gracchus. In 133 BCE a mob of his political opponents stormed the Capitoline Hill, where votes were being counted, and clubbed him to death. (This was the original Capitol, after which the seat of the US legislature would be named some two thousand years later.) Twelve years after that, Tiberius's brother Gaius would be killed in similar circumstances. In the words of the most recent historian of ancient Rome, murder had become a 'political tool'.[11] The brothers' offence had been to try to push through reforms that in modern times have sometimes been interpreted, anachronistically, as an early form of socialism. The issues were more complicated than that; but behind these political murders lay a new and vicious polarization of Roman society, which would soon be tearing at the fabric of the state. Modern parallels are not hard to seek.

During the century that followed, the Republic was rocked by a series of civil wars. One, which began in 91 BCE, was about who had the right to benefit from Roman citizenship – a direct symptom of the mismatch between city state and growing empire. Two decades after that came a revolt by the slaves that Romans relied on for their workforce. In 73 BCE a runaway slave by the name of Spartacus gathered together tens of thousands of his fellows and threatened to march against Rome. It took two years of vicious fighting all over southern Italy before the slaves and their supporters were defeated and Spartacus was killed. In the aftermath, six thousand of the survivors were crucified and left to die slowly, hanging from crosses, along the length of the Appian Way leading towards Rome. Intended, no doubt, as a deterrent and a demonstration of how brutal the Roman state could be when threatened, this act also perhaps betrays how deeply insecure it was at this time.[12]

But the greatest threat of all to the stability of the Roman system came not from slaves or foreigners but from the generals in command of the Senate's own armies. Already during the 80s BCE, victorious generals had led their troops into Rome and occupied the city. One, Lucius Cornelius Sulla, had gone farther, in 81 BCE, to proclaim himself *Dictator* (a Latin word for a role designed to last no more than six months in order to deal with a civic emergency); but Sulla held on to it. In the first of several purges of fellow citizens, thousands of Romans were put to death, some on Sulla's orders, some on those of his opponents. But then, at the end of two years, his self-appointed tasks completed, Sulla bowed to Roman convention, surrendered his authority and retired to his country estate. The next generation of military strongmen would not be so accommodating.[13]

The rivals this time were Gaius Julius Caesar and Gnaeus Pompeius Magnus, better known as Pompey; 'the Great' (Magnus) was his own addition to his family name. During the 60s BCE, Pompey led a massive naval expedition into the eastern Mediterranean to wrest back control of the seas from pirates. Having dealt with them, Pompey went on to roll up some of the remnants of the kingdoms that had succeeded the 'Successors' of Alexander in the Levant. A decade later, between 58 and 51 BCE, Caesar no less famously subdued the whole of Gaul, made up of today's France, Belgium, a strip of western Germany and much of Switzerland. He also more briefly led forays across the Rhine and the English Channel (respectively in 56 and 55 BCE). Caesar's campaigns created the most rapid expansion that the empire ever saw – and probably also the most destructive of human life. Totting up the casualty figures claimed by Caesar himself in his sparely written *Commentaries on the Gallic War*, the naturalist Pliny the Elder, a hundred years later, calculated that 1,192,000 of the enemy had been killed by Caesar's legions in this conquest – a figure broadly accepted by historians today.[14]

When Caesar returned to Rome from Gaul in 49 BCE, he brought his army with him. This action set off a new civil war against Pompey. Caesar won, and Pompey fled to Alexandria, where he was murdered on arrival. Egypt was still (just) independent under the last of the 'Successors' to Alexander: a woman, for once, and a feisty one at that. Cleopatra VII made a tactical alliance with Caesar and also bore him a son, named Caesarion, or 'little Caesar'. Back in Rome once more, in January 44 BCE, Caesar went one better than either Sulla or Pompey had done before him and persuaded the Senate to grant him the title and the powers of *Dictator* for life. To emphasize the point, Caesar at the same time became the first Roman ruler to have his own face imprinted on coins, just like a king.[15]

Caesar was due to leave Rome again on 18 March, to lead a new military campaign in the Middle East. Three days before that, on the Ides of the month according to the Roman calendar, he was assassinated by a group of fellow senators on his way to a meeting of the Senate. Caesar had lived for just two months after being declared *Dictator*, supposedly for life. And it was the *Senatus*, the old oligarchy based on wealth, not the *Populus*, that had done the deed. Just so deep, among the Roman elite, ran the age-old horror of monarchy.

But one-man rule did not die with Caesar. Systems of government that had worked well for a city state had been close to breaking point for the better part of a century. Now they snapped. Two more civil wars followed. In the first, it took two years before the armies of Brutus and Cassius, the leaders among Caesar's assassins, were defeated outside Philippi, the city in Macedonia that owed its name to Philip II. The victorious legions on that occasion were led by Mark Antony – a former supporter of Caesar who had whipped up the Roman crowd to a frenzy at his funeral – together with Caesar's adopted son and heir, Octavian, who had been only nineteen years old at the time of the murder. A decade later, Antony split from Octavian and formed his own alliance with Cleopatra of Egypt – incidentally creating one of the great romantic stories of all time. Antony and Cleopatra lost. Both committed suicide, and Caesar's son by Cleopatra, Caesarion, now an adolescent, was put to death by the victorious Octavian, on the grounds that another Caesar would be one too many.[16]

Rome once again had a sole, absolute ruler – who by this stroke was able to add Egypt to the growing list of Roman territories. Octavian knew better than to risk any association in the public mind with the hated idea of kingship. Instead, in 27 BCE he devised for himself a new title which means more or less 'Revered One': *Augustus* – and this is the name by which Rome's first emperor has ever since been known. *Imperator*, another of his titles, had for centuries meant nothing more than the commander of an army, and the final victor in the Roman civil wars was certainly that. Only later would *imperator* become the Latin word for 'emperor' and the origin of its equivalents in many modern languages. At the same time, *imperium* (literally, 'power'), which up to that time had usually been applied to a military command or, in civil life, a term of office, quietly morphed to mean an empire. Within a few years, everyone would accept, whether they liked it or not, that this was what the Roman *res publica* had become. The power that had subdued a continent and reached across the Mediterranean was now concentrated in one man.[17]

Pax Romana

The forty-year reign of Augustus marks a turning point in the history of Europe. For a full two centuries after the end of the civil wars, Roman society and Roman government brought peace, stability and prosperity on a scale never before seen and not matched again until modern times. This period has been known ever since as *Pax Romana* (Roman peace) or *Pax Augusta* (the peace of Augustus). As the latter name suggests, it was peace imposed from the top; it was peace imposed by power.

Modern judgements of the Roman Empire at its heyday run the full gamut. At one extreme, it has been called a 'kleptocracy' built upon 'institutionalized terror'. At the other, according to the British historian Edward Gibbon, writing in the 1770s at the height of the European Enlightenment:

> If a man were called to fix the period in the history of the world, during which the condition of the human race was most happy and prosperous, he would, without hesitation, name that which elapsed from the death of Domitian [96 CE] to the accession of Commodus [sole emperor from 180 CE].

Gibbon concluded that even the 'absolute power' wielded by emperors had been tempered during the second century CE by 'the guidance of virtue and wisdom'. A more nuanced view, for the 2020s, comes from the historian Mary Beard, who reminds us that a Roman emperor 'did not rule alone, or in a vacuum'. In a study of how imperial rule actually worked, Beard has thoughtfully examined the varied ways in which 'collaboration and cooperation – well-meaning or not' enabled the empire of Augustus and his successors to function.[18]

In the first euphoria of the Augustan peace, Romans themselves, at least those who belonged to the educated elite, pulled out all the stops to celebrate what had been achieved. The greatest poets of the age vied with one another to please the emperor and their own wealthy, highly placed patrons; but at the same time they were putting into elegant verse what many ordinary Romans were most probably thinking about themselves at the time.

Written between 29 BCE and the poet's death ten years later, the *Aeneid* by Publius Vergilius Maro, better known as Virgil, tells the epic story of Aeneas, the ultimate ancestor of the Romans according to legend. Fleeing the sack of Troy along with his father Anchises, his son Iulus and the surviving Trojans, 'dutiful Aeneas' endures shipwreck and multiple hazards, including a love affair with the queen of Carthage, Dido, whom he jilts in order to fulfil his destiny and prepare the way for the foundation of Rome. Having made it to Italy, Aeneas has then to fight a series of battles to secure a permanent home and intermarriage for himself and his people with the local Italians. In the telling of this story, Virgil subtly builds on the two much older Greek epics, the *Iliad* and the *Odyssey*, to create what is often called, albeit with some anachronism, the 'national epic' of ancient Rome.

The poet makes full use of hindsight to pepper his tale with prophecies for a glorious future. In the most famous of these, Jupiter, the father of the gods, for the first time names the Romans as a people, and goes on:

For them I set neither boundary nor season,
power without end or limit shall be theirs.

Later in the poem, when the hero visits the world of the dead, he is treated to a pageant of future Roman history. It includes this injunction to Aeneas's descendants:

Be mindful, Roman, by your power to rule over peoples.
Let these be your arts: to impose the habits of peace,
to spare the defeated and vanquish the proud.[19]

This was very much a blueprint for the age of Augustus, when the poem was written; and it has been invoked in self-justification by many later European empires too.

Virgil's contemporary, Horace (Quintus Horatius Flaccus), was a courtier as well as a poet. In an ode written in about 11 BCE, Horace praised the emperor for restoring peace at home and abroad. The 'age of Caesar' (at once the family name and a future imperial title):

. . . has revived the antique arts
by which the Latin name and Italian
strength and fame have grown so great
that the prestige of their power
now reaches from the rising of the sun
to its setting in the west.[20]

The Roman obsession with power (*imperium*) was as much in evidence as ever under the *Pax Romana*. But perhaps paradoxically, from the time of Augustus onwards, what had been won by violence began to be consolidated and maintained by consent, as much as by coercion. Both together were needed to keep the peace – and to lay down its enduring legacy to Europe for later times.

*

The world of the 'Roman peace' has been described as a 'world of cities' – just like modern Europe (and that is no accident). In the eastern provinces, cities were nothing new: great numbers of them had been founded under Alexander the Great and his 'Successors' – no longer politically independent as they had been in ancient Greece, of course, but otherwise very much on the Greek model. In western Europe outside Italy, on the other hand, urban life, civic architecture or town planning on any scale had been unknown before the Roman conquests; now these began to appear everywhere.[21] Roman cities had paved streets, public buildings such as temples, law courts, markets and bath-houses, piped water (often brought from great distances by stone-built aqueducts whose arches still span river gorges today), drainage systems and sewers. Well-to-do houses faced inward from the street, with accommodation arranged round a central *atrium*, and for those who could afford it an enclosed, colonnaded garden; walls were painted in vibrant colours with abstract patterns or scenes from mythology. A form of under-floor heating was provided, known as a hypocaust, by the circulation of hot air from a wood- or charcoal-fired furnace.

Along with these comforts and conveniences, people who lived in cities were able (and expected) to acquire the quality of *civilitas*. By this term was meant not only what it sounds like, but also, more fundamentally, 'civic virtue'. Closely related, in the minds of educated Romans, was the broader concept of *humanitas*, roughly equivalent to 'civilization', as that term has been understood since the eighteenth century. As well as meaning 'humanity' or 'humaneness', this word came to carry additional, subtler meanings: in the now dated language of the classic nineteenth-century Latin–English dictionary, *humanitas* was glossed as 'Mental cultivation befitting a man, liberal education, good breeding, elegance of manners or language, refinement'.[22]

But not all the trappings of Roman civic life would strike us, today, as in any way civilized. First of all there was the ubiquitous presence of slaves and slave-markets; the entire economy (in modern terms) of both town and country in the Roman Empire was based on the labour of a category of human beings who could be bought and sold, routinely tortured to provide evidence in a court of law, beaten or in extreme cases even killed by their masters. And then there were the blood sports that attracted huge crowds to venues specially designed for the purpose. An amphitheatre consisted of two traditional Greek semicircular theatres put together to make an oval arena, entirely surrounded by tiers of seats. Gladiators, the stars of the shows, were slaves trained to fight with a sword against other slaves, who might be variously armed. For all contestants the only hope of surviving lay in hacking their opponents to death for the amusement of the spectators. In other spectacles, gladiators took on exotic wild animals; criminals who lacked the privileges of citizenship could be 'thrown to the lions', to be savaged and devoured – again for the delectation of a huge and appreciative crowd.

From the time of Augustus onwards, in most of the European provinces of the empire, every self-respecting Roman city, and many a smaller town or army camp, would have its amphitheatre. In the Balkans, Anatolia and the parts of the Middle East that Rome now controlled, cities instead retained their Greek-style theatres that had been designed for the performance of drama, music and dance. In all those places where Greek continued to be the language of culture and education, amphitheatres never caught on – though there are stories of theatres being repurposed for these gory entertainments. The vicious streak at the heart of Roman civilization, acknowledged in the myth of Romulus, the first Roman, murdering his brother Remus, would remain part of its legacy to later Europe – as can be seen in the institution of bullfighting that continued into modern times in Spain and the south of France. Spanish bullrings almost exactly reproduce the design of the ancient amphitheatre. At Arles in Provence, the ancient Roman amphitheatre was actually used for a form of bullfighting in the nineteenth and twentieth centuries.

For an empire to function, cities had to be connected with one another. Previous generations of Roman engineers had pioneered the building of paved roads across the landscape of Italy and some of the nearer provinces. Road-building really took off under Augustus. The result was a network of 372 named roads of a total length somewhere between 50,000 and 60,000 miles, with twice as many miles of regional roads constructed to a lower standard.[23] Bridges spanned rivers far and wide – some of them still standing today. A courier system connected every province with the capital, so that the emperor could always be informed of what was going on. At the centre of the entire system, Augustus set up a huge pillar in the Roman Forum, called the Golden Milestone (*miliarium aureum*); all distances were measured from this spot – the origin of the proverbial expression, 'All roads lead to Rome'.[24]

Along those roads the legions marched to expand or defend the frontiers; horse-drawn wheeled vehicles carried people and goods in every direction. Recent studies of human remains have revealed how mobile was the population of the empire; soldiers would routinely be recruited in one province, spend their years of service in several others and end their days somewhere else again. But civilians, probably traders, could also cover great distances in the course of a career. A tombstone found near Hadrian's Wall in Britain had been put up by a man from Palmyra in Syria to commemorate his British wife, who had come from just outside London.[25] For four and a half centuries after Augustus became emperor in 27 BCE, freedom of movement for citizens and the relatively free flow of trade (though not without local tariffs) were daily facts of life throughout the Roman Empire.

Europe, the way educated Romans saw it, was 'the foster-mother of the [Roman] People (*populus*) which has vanquished all other peoples (*gentes*)', in the words of one geographer writing in the first century CE; for good measure he added that it is also 'by a long way the most beautiful land on earth'. Another, almost a century earlier, had praised the natural advantages of the European climate and terrain; combined with Roman force of arms, these had been sufficient to make this continent more conducive than any other to the development of 'urban, constitutional life' – or, as a later age would call it, civilization.[26] But why stop at just one continent? Baked into the idea of Roman power was also the idea of Roman *universality*. That had been the point of Jupiter's promise to Aeneas in Virgil's poem. It would be no accident that in times to come, the name 'Roman' would become inextricably entwined with the Greek word *catholic*, which means 'universal'.

That was in theory. But despite the generous disposition of the father of the gods as reported by Virgil, by the time Augustus died in 14 CE, the Roman Empire did have limits. A devastating fightback by German tribes beyond the Rhine, five years earlier, had done wonders to concentrate Roman minds. According to the historian Tacitus, writing a century later, it had been Augustus's own wish, expressed at the end of his life, that the empire in future 'should be concentrated within the limits' formed by 'the sea of Ocean or distant rivers' (apparently meaning the Rhine, the Danube and the still more distant Euphrates).[27]

Even so, the age of conquest was not quite over. During the century after Augustus, the legions would cross the sea into Britain in 43 CE, and the Danube into modern Romania between 101 and 106. Briefly, a decade later, Roman power would push across the Middle East to reach the shores of the Persian Gulf. But that was a conquest too far – as the emperor Hadrian immediately recognized when he took up the reins in 117 CE. It was time to return to the wise words of Augustus and set bounds after all. Hadrian took Augustus's idea further; for the first time, so far as we know, during the reign of Hadrian physical markers began to be imposed upon the landscape to define the limits of Roman power. The most famous, and lasting, of these is the wall across northern Britain that still bears the emperor's name. But at the same time work started on building a wooden palisade in Germany between the Rhine and the Danube. Beyond the Mediterranean, a line of frontier posts faced the Sahara desert and – for once in Rome's history, by peaceful means – Hadrian negotiated an agreed line of demarcation along the Euphrates river.[28]

The empire that Hadrian began to enclose within these boundaries was at least double the size that it had been two hundred years earlier. In essence, it was as much as ever a *European* empire – as Augustus's dying wish and Tacitus's words had clearly implied that it should be, even if neither thought to name it as such. This was a Europe protected, beyond its Mediterranean edge, by forward bulwarks in Anatolia, the Middle East and North Africa (as would happen again between the 1830s and 1950s), and most vulnerable, as always, from the flat lands that open out across today's central Europe towards Asia. From the time of Hadrian onwards, the empire would be on the defensive. And for the first but not the last time, Europe was putting up border fences to keep the rest of the world out.

Roads to Freedom

The idea of political liberty, which had been born out of the victory of the Greeks over the Persians and the expulsion of the early kings of Rome, had never been forgotten. But if you lived in the Roman Empire at any time after Augustus had become emperor, there was no getting away from the fact that that, too, had been placed under strict limits. The locutions of the old republican city state – the *res publica* and the 'Roman Senate and People' – were still sacrosanct. But everybody knew that the reality was a monarchy in all but name.

Tacitus, who was probably finishing his historical account of the early emperors during the first years of Hadrian's reign, was frank about what had been lost: 'The condition of the state had been turned upside down . . . Everyone, deprived of equality, hung on the commands of the ruler.' Where election to public office still existed, it was blatantly manipulated, making the 'encroaching condition of slavery the more detestable'.[29] Born into the senatorial class, Tacitus, if he had lived in an earlier century, would have been expected to play a prominent part in political life. As it was, horrified by the fate of fellow senators who had been put to death on the orders of several recent emperors, and the public burning of tracts that had been written in their defence, he concluded that the best thing he could do would be to tell the true story as a historian: 'Now that Rome has virtually been transformed into an autocracy, the investigation and record of these details concerning the auto- crat may prove useful.' There was, Tacitus believed, a *moral* lesson to be learnt from writing and reading history. But even with all the privileges of his class, background and education, he knew there was nothing he could do to change it.[30]

At the heart of Roman absolutism lay a curious paradox. Emper- ors were frequently honoured while alive in ways that traditionally had been reserved for the gods; once they were dead, every emperor from Augustus onwards became *divus* (deified, or made into a god). Temples would be built, prayers addressed and public sacrifices carried out, all in the name of a deceased emperor. But if it was dangerous to say the wrong thing about the current occupant of the imperial throne, dead ones who had gone to join the immortal gods were fair game. Despite Tacitus's anxieties, no one intervened to prevent him setting the record straight, either during his lifetime or afterwards; many of the home truths he set down, just over two thousand years ago, we still can read today.

And Tacitus was not the only one. His younger contemporary, Suetonius, got away with narrating the often scurrilous personal lives and violent deaths of the Caesars, from Julius, the precursor of them all, to the tyrannical Domitian (safely assassinated and gone to join the immortals in 96 CE in time for Suetonius to publish his work a couple of decades later). The poet Juvenal, who like Sueto- nius wrote during the first decades of the second century, invented the genre we still call satire. Driven by what he himself called *saeva indignatio* (savage indignation), Juvenal directed his barbs against all the human weaknesses and abuses he observed around him in daily life in Rome. These voices from the imperial period bear wit- ness to a self-awareness, to the possibility of critique, indeed to a moral consciousness, that would become vital parts of Rome's later legacy to Europe. The essence of *humanitas* may lie less in what the Romans *did* than in what they *wrote* – and in the freedom they still enjoyed that enabled them to write it at all.

That was one kind of freedom. Philosophers and educators talked about another. Many of the Roman elite subscribed to the philosophical system of thought known as Stoicism. According to the Stoics, the goals of each individual life were to be 'free, self-sufficient, untroubled by suffering'. The way to attain these was 'to draw back into the little allotment that is the self . . . to be free and to view things as a man, as a human being, and as an animal subject to death . . . to preserve your own self at all times in freedom, living generously, simply, decently'.[31]

These words belong to no less a person than the philosopher-emperor Marcus Aurelius, who reigned from 161 to 180 CE and left a kind of private diary, written in Greek, and now commonly known as the *Meditations*. Even the most powerful man in the world of his day was perplexed by perennial questions about the meaning of his own life; even the emperor himself had his work cut out to achieve the *inner* freedom that came from overcoming hopes, fears and the cares that went with his office. Marcus was a rarity, perhaps unique among world rulers, in thinking these things and writing them down. But if Marcus Aurelius had enjoyed the benefit of a more refined education than was available to most of his subjects, the anxieties that troubled him seem to have been very widely shared at the time. You didn't have to be an emperor to have an inner self, a soul even, and to long to set it free.

Philosophy was one route to that destination; and the Stoics, like all the Greek and Roman philosophers before them, relied on human reason as the means to get there. But rational philosophy could never be for everyone; religion, on the other hand, and more or less by definition, was. By the time of Augustus, alongside the traditional worship of the gods and goddesses who had always been the protectors of the city of Rome, new cults, with their beliefs and practices, were spreading far and wide, more often than not through the ranks of the legions. The cults of the Egyptian goddess Isis, the Greek healing god Asclepius and the Persian sun-god Mithras all seem to have promised their devotees some form of personal salvation; often this would be embodied in rituals called 'Mysteries', whose content would prove to be among the ancient world's best-kept secrets.

One of these new sects would ultimately stand out from all the rest. From an obscure corner of the eastern empire, from the province of Judaea, during the 30s and 40s CE, the first followers of Jesus of Nazareth began to disseminate his teaching beyond their own immediate Jewish community. These followers believed that Jesus had been the Messiah, or in Greek 'the Christ', meaning 'the anointed one', who according to Jewish prophecies would succeed to the mantle of the ancient kings of Israel and liberate its people. Jesus himself had been crucified by the Roman authorities in Jerusalem in or about the year 30 CE. But for the Apostle Paul, who first began to preach the 'Good News', or Gospel, to an empire-wide audience, Jesus had been the Christ in quite a different sense.

Writing to members of the embryonic sect in Galatia in central Anatolia, probably in the year 49 CE, Paul introduced himself as 'an apostle, not by human appointment or human commission, but by commission from Jesus Christ and from God the Father who raised him from the dead'. Jesus as the Christ, Paul continues, had 'sacrificed himself for our sins, to rescue us out of this present age of wickedness'. The tiny groups addressed by Paul in this and subsequent letters that would later be collected and preserved in the New Testament were already by this time becoming known by the name of *Christianoi*, or 'Christians'.

To be baptized as a Christian meant not only to follow the moral precepts taught by Jesus ('love, joy, peace, patience, kindness, goodness, fidelity, gentleness, and self-control', as summed up by Paul in that first letter); it also offered *freedom* of a kind that could never be available to the rational Stoics or the followers of any other Greek or Roman philosophy. 'Christ,' writes Paul to the Galatians, 'set us free, to be free men.' What he meant by that he would spell out a few years later, when writing to the Christian community that had already become established in the empire's capital: 'in Christ Jesus the life-giving law of the Spirit has set you free from the law of sin and death'.[32]

The four Gospels that preserve the record of Jesus's life and teaching would not be written until the last decades of the first century and the beginning of the next. But already, from these letters addressed by Paul to the first generation of Christian converts, it's clear to see how the new religion must have appealed powerfully to the mixed population of an empire that was ruled from the top down; Christianity, by contrast, in its early years, was destined to make converts from the bottom up.

It has been argued that in 'bring[ing] together basic features of Jewish and Greek thought to create something new', Paul introduced a new 'universal' concept of freedom, an *individual* freedom which is also 'freedom of conscience'.[33] In fact, the discovery of the individual belonged more broadly to the Greco-Roman world of the time; but the letters of Paul, and early Christian teaching more generally, at once addressed that individual in quite a new way and offered a prospect of freedom that could not be touched by the power of emperors, no matter how coercive: 'Render . . . unto Caesar the things which are Caesar's, and unto God the things that are God's,' says Jesus, according to St Matthew's Gospel. The ancient world had never seen anything quite like this before: 'So you are no longer a bondservant, but a son; and if a son, then an heir of God through Christ.' Or, as the Christian writer Tertullian would put it in the early third century: 'One mighty deed alone was sufficient for our God – to bring freedom to the human person.'[34]

These ideas had originated outside Europe. They were still marginal within the Roman Empire at the time when Tertullian was writing, some decades after the death of Marcus Aurelius in 180 CE. But the time would come when their legacy would define what it meant to be European.

A final gift of freedom during the Roman Empire brings us back, albeit in a limited way, towards the ancient liberties that had been enjoyed by citizens of the Greek city states and of Rome itself in its early days. It came from an unlikely quarter, but also the only one with the power to confer it; that is to say, from an emperor himself.

The emperor in question has become known to history by the nick-name Caracalla, which refers to the soldier's cloak he apparently wore. Caracalla's posthumous reputation was given a new lease of life by his lurid role as one of the villains of the 2024 Hollywood blockbuster film *Gladiator II*. The villainy was real enough, but far more enduring in its effect was a decree that he issued in the year 212. With the stroke of a pen (or stylus in those days), Caracalla transformed every subject of the Roman Empire, who was not a slave, into a full Roman citizen.

This was a grant of rights and freedoms that would last as long as the empire; nothing like it would ever be attempted again until the Maastricht Treaty of 1992. For centuries, Roman citizenship had been a sought-after and jealously guarded privilege. At the time of the edict, fewer than a third of the free men and women living in the empire would have been full citizens. Suddenly *everybody* was (except of course for the invisible multitude of slaves). Quite why the emperor did it was a bit of a mystery to contemporaries, and historians today are still guessing.[35] But Caracalla was a military man; he would have known that an emperor's job was above all to hold the frontiers. It would make sense to ensure that everybody on the inside had an equal stake in defending them.

The effects reached into every corner of the empire and many aspects of the new citizens' lives. From Hadrian's Wall in the north of Britain to today's Gibraltar and Tangier, from the banks of the Rhine to the banks of the Euphrates and the first cataract on the Nile, the entire population (other than slaves) now enjoyed the same rights and shared the same obligations. Within the next few years, new legal texts would be drawn up to spell out, more fully than ever before, exactly what these were.[36] Regardless of where people came from, what language they spoke, which gods they worshipped, still less the colour of their skin (which seems to have been little noticed in the Roman Empire), all were now subject to the same rule of law; all enjoyed the same freedoms and shared the same obligations that set them apart from slaves at home and the rest of the world abroad. Caracalla's edict turned out to be far more than a bureaucratic measure: its long-term consequence would be to redefine identity for everyone. From now on, all the empire's subjects would *think of themselves* as Romans. The *idea* of Europe could never afterwards be separated from the idea of Rome.

An Empire Transformed

But what 'Rome' itself meant was changing. Caracalla lasted only five years after issuing his edict. He was assassinated in Mesopotamia in the spring of 217, literally stabbed in the back on the instigation of one of his own generals, while he was preparing to lead a campaign against Rome's perennial Middle Eastern foe, the Parthians. This was to prove the pattern for the next seven decades. It was the army, now, that made emperors, and unmade them too. Most of the twenty-three *augusti* who reigned during that time would end up the same way as Caracalla, after even shorter reigns.

Roman armies were no longer led by larger-than-life figures, such as Pompey and Caesar, who would compete to send back home the spoils of foreign conquests. Ever since the late 160s and 170s CE, when Marcus Aurelius had to set aside his philosophical speculations to lead a series of campaigns against Germanic tribesmen on the Danube frontier, the legions needed to be organized for defence, not conquest. The empire employed more soldiers than ever. And they had to be paid. Once upon a time, if they lived long enough to retire on a pension, the legionaries could expect to be settled on land that they and their descendants could farm in perpetuity. But land was running out. And so was ready cash. By the late third century, the silver coins being minted contained so little silver that they were almost worthless. Attempts to reform the currency and introduce price controls only made things worse. The empire was in an economic crisis; the only available solutions seemed to be to tax its citizens more heavily and to centralize the machinery of government.

The evidence of archaeology suggests that the empire's European heartland was already showing signs of decline during this century. City populations shrank in size; even Rome, by the year 300, may have been home to no more than a third of the population that had lived there a hundred years before. Plagues in the 160s CE and again during the next century may have been among the causes. When cities and towns shrank, defensive walls sprang up around them; according to one modern account, Roman Europe in the third century was already beginning to 'look more and more medieval'; Rome itself acquired new city walls in the 270s – and even today, what remains of the Aurelian Walls is truly massive.[37]

Externally, the most obvious new threat came from the empire's south-eastern borders, far away from Europe in the Middle East. Romans and Parthians had been eyeballing one another for hundreds of years along a fluctuating frontier zone that stretched from Armenia in the north to the Persian Gulf in the south. In 226 an Iranian dynasty, known as the Sasanids, set about vigorously reviving the power and glories of the long-vanished Persian Empire of Darius and Xerxes.[38] The struggle between Rome and Sasanian Persia for mastery of the Middle East would last for a full four hundred years and draw the remaining centres of Roman power to the very edge of the European continent and into Asia. Compared to that, the Germanic tribesmen with their periodic raids across the Danube or the Rhine must have seemed like no more than an irritant.

In the meantime, the empire was quietly but drastically reinventing itself to deal with changing circumstances. Diocletian, who came to power in 284, is remembered today for an ambitious programme of reforms; among these was the division of the empire into an eastern and a western half, each ruled by one senior co-emperor and two juniors (called 'Caesars'), together adding up to a 'gang of four' known collectively as the 'tetrarchy'. Paradoxically, though, along with the division of authority at the very top, and seemingly in contradiction to it, from the last years of the third century onwards, the administration of the empire became more centralized and top-down than ever. For the first time a professional bureaucracy sprang up and grew exponentially. The state became more 'extensive and coercive' than it had ever been before; it exercised 'greater control and oversight' not only over the workings of the bureaucracy but over the behaviour of its citizens.

One modern historian has called this a 'total system'; perhaps it was not far off from what we might call, today, totalitarian. The flip side of Caracalla's gift of common rights and freedoms, in the changed circumstances of half a century later, turned out to be a growing expectation that all Roman citizens should behave and think in the same way.[39] What the empire's subjects thought or believed in private had never much mattered to the state authorities. Now, increasingly, it did. And this is how religion first became the political issue in Europe that it would continue to be until at least the seventeenth century.

The state religion of ancient Rome had always been a matter of public performance; so long as you fulfilled your obligations in public, it was nobody else's business what you thought or believed. The minority sect known as Christianity had been spreading throughout the empire (and indeed well beyond its borders) since the middle of the first century. When it earned official mention at all during the first two hundred years of its existence, Christianity would be contemptuously dismissed as a *superstitio*. It was only when Christians came into conflict with the secular demands of the state that they made it into the historical record. If their actions in public were deemed to be seditious they could be executed, as Jesus had been for the same reason. But apart from the notorious pogrom instituted by the emperor Nero in 64 CE, when the Christians of Rome had been scapegoated after a devastating fire, adherents of the new religion had generally been left alone.

It was in the middle of the third century that this began to change. First the emperor Decius in 249, and then another short-lived successor, Valerian, a decade later, ordered every citizen to make public sacrifices to the traditional gods of the state. Christians who refused would be killed, often with horrible brutality by gladiators or wild beasts in the amphitheatre. As it happened, both persecuting emperors came to bad ends within a short time. Decius became the first-ever emperor to die in battle – against an incursion across the Danube by Germanic tribesmen known as Goths. The humiliation of Valerian was even worse: captured on the battlefield by the Persians, along with most of his army, the emperor of the Romans was reputedly used as a footstool by the Great King; when he died in captivity not long afterwards, 'his skin was plucked off him, and when it had been stripped from his flesh, it was dyed red so that it could be placed in the temple of the gods of the barbarians as a memorial of their brilliant victory'. So, at least, our Christian source informs us, with unmistakable relish.[40]

Quite why Diocletian chose, along with his junior emperor Galerius, to start a new persecution in the year 303 is hard to tell. According to most modern estimates, Christians in the empire at this time can have amounted to no more than 10 per cent of the population – in the western provinces probably well below that. But when Christian 'martyrs', as they became known, from the Greek word for 'bearing witness', showed themselves willing to die for their beliefs and endure extreme torments under the public gaze, the severity of the measures taken against them had the effect of catapulting a minority issue to the very top of the political agenda.[41]

Diocletian abdicated in 305, the only Roman emperor ever to do so voluntarily. His four successors who made up the 'tetrarchy', far from working together as intended, soon launched into a war of elimination for the top job. As civil war convulsed the empire, a defining issue for each of the contenders turned out to be whether to back this minority religious sect or try to eliminate it altogether. It was too late to go back to simply ignoring it. And so the stage was set for the greatest of all the transformations that would change the whole nature of the Roman Empire for as long as it lasted.

Flavius Valerius Constantinus was a capable (and probably ruthless) army officer from the south of today's Serbia. The little that we know about his origins and early life hardly looks like preparation to become the emperor Constantine I, Constantine the

Great, even Saint Constantine, as he still is commemorated by the Orthodox Church. It is difficult to form a sense of what Constantine might have been like as an individual, because everything that has ever been recorded about him was written in the light of what happened afterwards. On the other side of the coin from the praises of Christian contemporaries stand the executions of his eldest son (by a previous marriage) and his current wife for reasons of state that have never been sufficiently explained.[42] And then there's the colossal seated statue of himself that he commissioned in Rome. Only the head and a few fragments survive; but they still have the power to intimidate. The eyes, now lacking the coloured inset stones that would have intensified the effect, look far above the viewer – not upwards towards the heavens, but coldly, towards something of more interest elsewhere. And there is a cruel set to the mouth.

Be that as it may, when Constantine defeated his last surviving co-emperor, Licinius, in battles fought at Adrianople in Thrace and on the Asian shore of the Bosphorus at Chrysopolis in July and September 324, it was the climax of a campaign that had been fought on a ticket of liberating the persecuted Christian population of the eastern empire. Constantine had committed himself to the Christian cause twelve years previously, after winning a battle against another rival on the outskirts of Rome. On that occasion a weather phenomenon in the sky had convinced him that he would conquer under the sign of the Cross on which Jesus had been crucified. Ever since, Constantine's motives have been the subject of speculation. Had he perhaps always been a secret sympathizer? Or was he simply a pragmatist who found himself thrust by circumstances into collaboration with a religious minority whose ideas he barely understood, until it was too late to extricate himself? Might Christianity have appealed to such an authoritarian figure as a tool to restore civil order after decades of turmoil? We will never know.[43]

The upshot was that within a year of his final victory over Licinius, Constantine had placed himself as the official patron of the

Christian Church and promptly summoned the first-ever council of its leaders from all over the empire to decide exactly what should be the 'correct belief' (*orthodoxy* in Greek) of Christians from that time on. The Nicene Creed, the statement of belief still recited in Christian churches all over the world, was first formulated at that council, held at Nicaea (today's Isnik in north-west Turkey) in the summer of 325. Twelve years later, Constantine would complete his long-drawn-out personal conversion when he received Christian baptism on his deathbed in 337.

By the time of his death, whether or not he ever realized this, Constantine had changed the nature both of Christianity and of his own office. From its humble beginnings as a bottom-up movement spreading out from Judaea in the decades after the execution of Jesus, Christianity had become a top-down religion, backed – and soon to be imposed – by the full might of Roman power, concentrated in the person of the emperor. And the nature of that power, too, had subtly, and as it turned out, irrevocably changed. '*Imperium* without end or limit' was now subject to a power that was higher still. In the words of Constantine's confessor: 'the image of the higher kingdom is reflected in the emperor who, beloved of God and in imitation of the Superior Being, by his governance steers the helm of all the world's affairs'.[44] From that time on, every earthly monarch in Europe would be expected to act as viceroy for the Christian God on earth. This was the beginning of what would later be called the 'divine right of kings'.

To commemorate his victory Constantine did something else that was almost as momentous in its consequences. On the European shore of the Bosphorus, opposite the site of his final battle, he ordered the building of a new city on top of a crumbling old Greek one called Byzantium. Following a long-established custom, he named it after himself: Constantinople, or City of Constantine. The empire by this time was full of cities named after emperors who had once passed that way – there were dozens of Hadrianoples for instance (Adrianople in Thrace would prove the longest-lasting of them, its name still preserved in the Turkish form, Edirne). But this one would prove to be much more than just another Roman vanity project. Soon to vie in importance with Rome itself, and eventually to overtake it, Constantine's city, perched on the very edge of Europe, would remain for a thousand years the capital of an empire that would proudly proclaim itself at once Roman and Christian.

3.

'Waiting for the Barbarians'

337–800

In the summer of 376, only a couple of generations after the death of Constantine, an event took place on the Roman frontier the like of which had never been seen before:

> Once the emperor's permission to cross the Danube and settle in parts of Thrace had been granted, the work of transportation went on night and day. The Goths embarked by troops on boats and rafts and canoes made from hollowed tree trunks. The crowd was such that, though the river is the most dangerous in the world and was then swollen by frequent rains, a large number tried to swim and were drowned in their struggle against the force of the stream.

We owe this account to a Roman army officer and amateur historian by the name of Ammianus Marcellinus, who was writing not long afterwards. Replace the Danube with the Mediterranean or the English Channel, and the picture of desperate migrants drowning in an attempt to reach safety and make new lives for themselves in Europe seems chillingly familiar. So too, perhaps, does the acquiescence of the emperor, who had agreed to accept them.

The story soon darkens further. The Roman authorities found themselves unable even to count the new arrivals, let alone to provide the basic necessities for them to find accommodation and food. Taking advantage of the chaos, a second group of Goths, as large as the first, crossed the river without authorization. Ammianus goes on to tell us how he was reminded of Xerxes leading his

Persians across the Hellespont into Europe, more than eight centuries before. In language that sounds all too like the daily currency of Europe and North America in the 2020s, the Roman historian talks of 'a countless swarm of peoples pouring over the provinces', and laments 'the critical situation resulting from the opening of our frontier and the eruption of armed men from the barbarian lands like lava from Etna'. He himself would not live to see more than the beginning; but history would prove him right when he saw in these events 'the destruction of the Roman world'.[1]

Historical parallels, however, can be misleading; and this one risks distorting our understanding of what happened nearly two thousand years ago, as well as of the challenges we face today. Yes, there are troubling similarities between patterns of migration in the twenty-first century and the mass movements into Europe that began with German-speaking Goths crossing the Danube in the summer of 376. The parallels have often been talked up for blatantly political ends; and in order to counter them some serious historians, anxious to distance themselves from the anti-immigrant rhetoric of their own time, have even leant the other way, to question whether the Roman Empire ever really did fall. Maybe what happened wasn't so cataclysmic after all, but rather a series of transformations that certainly changed Europe, but less dramatically, and left much of the old edifice still functioning, if in new ways? Anticipating those revisionists, as long ago as in 1904, the Alexandrian Greek poet C.P. Cavafy had wondered, in the much-quoted poem whose title serves as the title for this chapter: what might have happened if the expected barbarians had failed to arrive? 'Those people were some sort of a solution,' the despairing speakers in the poem, left high and dry, are forced to conclude. How, indeed, can you tell the story of Europe without 'barbarians'?[2]

The 'barbarians' who are the subject of this chapter were real enough, even if we do put the old Greek and Roman word for them in inverted commas. If we are to understand how Europe was transformed during the four centuries after the death of Constantine in 337, there's no getting away from populations on the move, often in great numbers and over distances of thousands of miles, at what must have been great hardship to themselves as well as distress to those on the receiving end. But what happened *then* was actually a lot less like anything happening today than some would have us believe.

First of all, as we saw in the Introduction, the overwhelming movement of peoples into Europe over many millennia has been from Asia, across steppes, rivers and narrow passages of sea. Twenty-first-century migration across the Mediterranean (and also in the Americas) has been from south to north. This is an entirely new pattern of population movement, driven by civil collapse in the world's hottest regions, which in turn may be at least partially explained by the effects of global heating. (Changes in climate, far from Europe, most probably lay behind the population movements that Ammianus witnessed too.) But the biggest difference between the 'barbarians' who began to arrive at the end of the fourth century and the migrants, refugees or asylum seekers of today is that the latter arrive as individuals or in small family groups, usually thrown together while in transit from many different starting points. Crucially, they do not come armed and in force, prepared to fight their way in.

According to the best modern estimate, the total number of Goths massed on the far bank of the Danube in the summer of 376 may have been around 200,000 men, women and children. Approximately one-tenth of those would have been warriors in arms.[3] It was as a *warrior* force that Ammianus feared them. And he had good reason to. Almost immediately after they arrived, fighting broke out between the Gothic warriors and the local armed forces, which were probably already outnumbered. Two years later, in August 378, the Roman legions faced an assembled force of disaffected Goths outside the city of Adrianople (Edirne). The emperor Valens himself took part in the battle and was killed, along with somewhere between 10,000 and 20,000 legionaries. No wonder Ammianus claimed to hear, in the sound and fury of the battle of Adrianople, 'the death-knell of the Roman cause'.[4]

There is no parallel for *that* in the annals of recent immigration into Europe (or America, for that matter). On the other hand, Ammianus several times paints a vivid picture of the Goths' wagon-trains, drawn up in a defensive circle, while the warriors roamed to forage and plunder.[5] That sounds very like familiar images from films set in the American West during the nineteenth century. The truth is that the newcomers to the Roman Empire a millennium and a half ago had a great deal more in common with those 'pioneers', descended from Europeans, on another continent in a later era, than with the unarmed and dispersed refugees and asylum seekers of today.

This chapter tells a story of the meeting and melding of peoples, of extreme and widespread violence, political fragmentation, economic collapse – descent, if you will, into 'barbarism'. But there's a barb at the end of it: just as the barbarians of yesteryear had become Romans, granted full citizenship since the time of Caracalla, so the barbarians who came after would turn into . . . *us*. Out of their multiple encounters with the existing Roman population, with each other, and with whatever still remained of the civilization they had overturned, would be born the Europeans whose descendants would shape every aspect of the life of the continent as we know it today.

Who Were the Barbarians?

Romans had always been aware that beyond the reach of their rule lived people whose way of life was very different from their own. The word to describe such people had been collecting baggage ever since the aftermath of the Persian Wars, when it had become the label of choice among Greeks to mark out the common enemy. Now taken over into Latin, by the third century CE a 'barbarian' was anyone who lived outside the Roman *imperium*. The elite Romans whose words we can still read were deeply contemptuous of these barbarians; they thought nothing of killing large numbers of them if it would ensure the safety of the empire – or amuse their fellow citizens during a sultry afternoon in the amphitheatre. On the other hand, the Roman sense of superiority over the barbarian wasn't (or wasn't usually) racist, in today's terms. To be a barbarian was considered a regrettable condition, a state of deprivation, one that very obviously fell short of *humanitas*. But that could always be fixed; after all, most Roman citizens had been barbarians once – or their parents or grandparents had.[6]

Seen through Roman eyes, not all barbarians were the same. The closer they lived to the frontier, the more they would have become adapted to cross-border trade; their system of agriculture might not be so very different from the Roman, just more primitive; some (like the Gauls subdued by Julius Caesar in the first century BCE) might even live in towns. Roman influence clearly permeated the frontiers. The farther you went beyond them, the more barbarous became the barbarians. In Caesar's day, more primitive, fiercer and more deadly on the battlefield than the Gauls were the *Germani*, who lived on the other side of the Rhine. The most primitive of all, according to Caesar's account, were the ones even farther away who lived by hunting and fighting, refused to grow crops or ever settle in one place, and made do with a diet of milk, cheese and meat.[7]

A century and a half after Caesar's time, Tacitus devoted a whole treatise to 'Germania', the lands beyond the Rhine, in which he named dozens of different tribes or peoples. Here, too, the most physically distant are those at the farthest remove from anything that could be called *humanitas*. The Fenni (possibly ancestors of later Finns or Lapps) 'are astonishingly wild and disgustingly poor. They have no weapons, no horses, no homes. They eat wild plants, dress in skins and sleep on the ground.' On the plus side, at least, since they took no notice of either god or man, Tacitus reckoned that the Fenni had 'gained the ultimate release: they have no needs, not even for prayer'. Of the legendary half-men half-beasts that were supposed to inhabit places even more distant, the patrician historian decides to 'express no opinion'.[8]

These and other ancient accounts of barbarians are often dismissed today as stereotyped and shaped by the tastes and conventions of the Roman elite. But modern archaeology doesn't really contradict this picture (though traces of the yeti-like creatures have still to be found). Archaeological evidence reveals a 'three-speed' Europe at this time. The areas under Roman rule, unsurprisingly, were home to the most intensive agriculture and the densest populations. Beyond those, an inner zone several hundreds of miles deep corresponded to most of Germany and today's central Europe. There, farming communities had to move frequently as the soils quickly became unproductive and people lived at a considerable distance from each other. Farther east still, in a third zone, farming gave way to the nomadic pastoralism of the steppe-land where Europe shades into Asia. The peoples of those remote regions lived by hunting and from the flocks that they would move in seasonal cycles to ensure the best grazing – much as described by Tacitus.[9]

Given these disparities, there must have been a constant incentive for those less prosperous to be drawn westwards. While the Roman Empire was at the height of its prosperity, to cross over the Rhine or the Danube and seek Roman citizenship would have been the equivalent of the sought-after 'green card' that since the Second World War has conferred the right of foreigners to live and work in the United States. And so the legions were stationed along the frontiers, to man the walls, palisades and forts that since the time of the emperor Hadrian had divided the Roman world from the rest. When barbarians did come over, it was invariably on terms and conditions set by the Romans. Over the centuries, the empire had developed hard-headed policies towards those whom today we might call economic migrants, refugees or asylum seekers. Men of fighting age were made welcome as the pre-gunpowder equivalent of cannon fodder for the army. Their dependants, on the other hand, would be dispersed and settled in different regions. As one modern historian puts it, 'All immigrants became soldiers or peasants' – unless they were unfortunate enough to end up as slaves.[10]

This was broadly still the situation when Constantine was succeeded by his sons in 337. Quite why it changed has been hotly debated ever since. Beginning with Edward Gibbon's six-volume

Decline and Fall of the Roman Empire, published between 1776 and 1788, over two hundred different answers have competed for the attention of specialists and the general public alike.[11] And in modern times, every generation has seen its own predicaments mirrored in those centuries of turmoil. But change it did. And there is no better place to take up the story than with that crossing of the Danube in the summer of 376. The Goths didn't arrive out of nowhere. It was desperation that drove them to cross into Roman territory. Ammianus tells us as much as a well-informed Roman could have hoped to learn about the causes of that desperation.

Early in 376, news had begun to filter into the empire: far away, somewhere to the north of the Black Sea, a previously unknown barbarian people was on the move. They were called Huns, and according to Ammianus they were 'the seed-bed and origin of all the destruction' that was to follow. The historian must have been relying on hearsay; no Roman had probably yet seen any of these people up close. But this is what he had been told:

> . . . they are so prodigiously ugly and bent that they might be two-legged animals . . . Still, their shape, however disagreeable, is human; but their way of life is so rough that they have no use for fire or seasoned food, but live on the roots of wild plants and the half-raw flesh of any sort of animal . . . They have no buildings to shelter them . . .

The Huns, Ammianus goes on, fight with bows and arrows from horseback; rarely can they be separated from their animals; they even sleep clinging to 'their beasts' narrow necks'. 'None of them ploughs or ever touches a plough-handle. They have no fixed abode, no home or law or settled manner of life, but wander like refugees with the wagons in which they live.'[12]

It was these Huns who had displaced the Goths from where they had been living, in today's Ukraine, Moldova or Romania, to congregate on the banks of the Danube and seek refuge on the Roman side. Some, at least, of those Goths had already been in contact with

the newly Christian empire. We know this because the first translation of the Christian Gospels into a Germanic language seems to
have been made by one of them during the reign of Constantine's
successor in the 340s. On the Roman scale, the Goths belonged to
the relatively less barbarous category of barbarians – unlike the
Huns who were pushing them towards Europe.[13]

That may have been one of the reasons why, when the Gothic
leaders petitioned Valens to be allowed to cross, the emperor was
initially sympathetic. At the time he had been leading an expedition
against the Persians – it was always this more organized enemy in
the Middle East that concentrated Roman efforts during these centuries, until it was too late. The Gothic petitioners had to go all the
way to Antioch (today's Antakya, on the Mediterranean coast of
Turkey) before they could catch up with Valens. Whatever he may
privately have thought of the request, the emperor allowed himself
to be persuaded that here was just the source of extra manpower
for the legions that he needed for the war in the Middle East; more
settlers farming the land would yield even more taxes to pay for it. It
sounded like win-win. So he gave permission and it all began.[14]

Their bloody victory over Valens and the legions did the Goths
little good. Their numbers were formidable, but their warriors were
no match for city walls that had been built to withstand a siege.
First they directed their efforts towards nearby Adrianople, but they
were beaten back. Then they marched on Constantinople, already
by 378 one of the largest cities of the empire and its eastern capital.
Here, too, they were thwarted by the city's fortifications. Four years
later, in 382, a treaty confined the Goths to the rural areas that they
had already effectively occupied in Thrace and the southern Balkans.[15] It was an uneasy peace. The Goths had a great deal farther to
travel yet. And two decades later their wagon-trains would become
entangled with others more recently arrived, as the European frontier of the empire collapsed altogether.

As if all this were not enough, tensions between the empire's two
imperial capitals, Rome and Constantinople, reached the point of

open civil war in 394. When the emperor Theodosius unexpectedly died in January the next year, the only pragmatic solution seemed to be to split the empire, with one of his two sons ruling over the western half, the other in the east. This time the division would prove permanent.

A decade later, in the autumn or early winter of 405, a new force from beyond the Danube crossed the eastern Alps and entered Italy. Where they had come from and quite who they were nobody seemed to know. Probably they were German-speakers, like the Goths, but had started out from further north in the Balkans. Then on New Year's Eve, on another part of the frontier, a Roman army was attacked and defeated near its outpost on the eastern side of the Rhine, near today's Mainz. A mixed force, apparently made up of several distinct peoples, crossed the Rhine into the Roman province of Gaul. Of these, the Vandals and Suevi apparently spoke Germanic dialects, but they had started out from different points in eastern Europe; the Alans, who came with them, had originally been nomads of the Eurasian steppes, and spoke a language related to Persian.

What had brought all these people together, where exactly they had come from, and what drove them to move in such numbers and in armed force, was as much a puzzle to contemporaries as it is to us today. At the same time another Germanic group, the Burgundians, moved in to occupy the lands left behind by this incursion, to straddle the old Roman frontier of the Rhine. The Burgundians are the first of all these groups on the move whose descendants would remain recognizable in the later medieval history of Europe, and whose name is still attached to a region (though not the same one) today.[16]

With such a bewildering array of armed groups on the move, it's not surprising that identities – and no doubt loyalties too – became more fluid than ever. After all, Roman citizenship had already, for more than two centuries, been for *everyone* who lived inside the empire. And all sorts of new people were now not only on the inside but often in a position to call the shots. To try to quell these latest upheavals, the empire found itself having to negotiate with the 'barbarian' groups that had arrived earlier; whole legions were raised from Gothic immigrants. By far the most competent of the generals available at the time was one Stilicho, who happened to be of part-Vandal, part-Roman parentage. Stilicho seems to have been a loyal servant of the empire. But he soon found himself embroiled in an ongoing 'cold war' between Rome and Constantinople, and was eventually accused of treason and executed in a palace coup – which only made the empire's plight even more desperate.[17]

Such resistance as could be organized against the Vandals, Suevi and Alans in Gaul, far from driving them back across the Rhine where they had come from, had the unintended consequence of diverting them, instead, across the Pyrenees into Spain. Five years later, by 411, these groups had taken over the entire Iberian peninsula, with no one to stop them. And that meant that both Gaul and Spain, with all their revenues, were lost to the administrative centre of the western empire in Italy. Not only were identities in flux; so were the whole shape and nature of Europe.

The Earthly City and the City of God

In the midst of all this turmoil, the remnants and descendants of those Goths who had been settled in the Balkans after the battle of Adrianople in 378 once again take centre stage. The story of this group is one of the best documented, and extraordinary, of all the upheavals of this time. Consistently, ever since they had first petitioned the emperor Valens to be allowed into the empire, the leaders of these Goths had sought two things: land where they could live and grow crops to feed their dependants, and employment for their men in the Roman army. In today's language, their goal was integration into the empire, not conquest.

The treaty signed in 382 had lasted only a few years. Since then, the wagon trains of the Goths had set out through the Balkans, down to the southern tip of Greece, then back up along the entire length of the Adriatic coast. For a time they had briefly threatened northern Italy, before being shunted by Stilicho back to the western Balkans, more or less to where they had first been settled twenty years before.[18] The Goths now had a new leader. His name was Alaric; he had probably been a young child at the time of the crossing of the Danube in 376. Sometimes fighting alongside the Romans, sometimes against them, and latterly in a fragile alliance with Stilicho, Alaric had been for some time a thorn in the side of the Roman administrations in both east and west. Stilicho had gone to his death leaving unpaid a debt of four thousand pounds in gold owed by the Roman state to the Goths for services already rendered. When the Senate showed no inclination to pay up, Alaric led an army, perhaps 30,000 strong, into Italy.[19]

No fewer than three times, between 408 and 410, Alaric's Goths laid siege to Rome. The city was no longer the effective capital of the empire in the west; that role had passed to Ravenna, further north and (at that time) a port city on the Adriatic coast. This was where the hapless emperor Honorius was holed up. But Rome was still the seat of the Senate, and the senators were some of the wealthiest people in the empire. Alaric shuttled back and forth, with a contingent of his troops, between Rome and Ravenna. Up to the last minute, the senators could have bought off the besiegers. Honorius could have granted the military rank and honours that Alaric claimed as his due; it would have been neither the first nor the last time that such a thing happened. Obstinately, emperor and Senate refused, contemptuous, to the last, of these 'barbarians' at the gates. Alaric finally gave the order to sack the city. For three days, beginning on 24 August 410, the city founded by Romulus almost twelve hundred years before was systematically looted. The Senate House was set on fire; the treasures that Alaric had been unable to lay his hands on by negotiation were now seized by force and carried off.

Ancient and modern accounts often highlight the fact that the Goths, in the course of their wanderings, had been fully converted to Christianity; supposedly they treated sacred buildings and holy relics with respect. The assault by Alaric's Goths has even been called 'one of the most civilized sacks of a city ever witnessed'. But only a few decades had passed since Ammianus Marcellinus had described Rome, in his history of his own times, as 'a city destined to endure as long as the human race survives'. Ammianus had been a Roman of the old school, sceptical of the Christianity that he saw burgeoning all around him, a believer in 'the divine providence which has attended the growth of Rome from its cradle and guaranteed' that destiny. For people like Ammianus (who was almost certainly no longer living by 410), what had happened was literally unthinkable.[20]

Christians, too, recognized that with the fall of the 'eternal city' an era had ended. The monk St Jerome, living far away in the much greater safety of Jerusalem, wrote when the news reached him: 'The brightest light of the whole world is extinguished; indeed the head has been cut from the Roman empire. To put it more truthfully, the whole world has died with one City.'[21] But the response that would come to dominate Christian thinking throughout western Europe for the next thousand years came from the African bishop of the Roman city of Hippo, in today's Algeria. Later canonized as a saint in the Roman Catholic Church, Augustine was deeply versed in classical Latin literature as well as the still evolving theology of the early Christian Church. Shortly after the fall of Rome, Augustine began work on his *magnum opus*, known in English as *City of God*. Running to over a thousand pages in the standard English translation, its subject is not the physical fabric of an urban space (*urbs* in Latin), but rather the city as a community (*civitas*), the origin of the concept of *civilitas* which for Romans came close to the meaning of 'civilization' today.

The *civitas* that had been Rome had been destroyed; however, Augustine set out to persuade his readers, 'The Heavenly City outshines Rome, beyond comparison. There, instead of victory, is truth; instead of high rank, holiness; instead of peace, felicity; instead of life, eternity.' With some chutzpah Augustine even appropriated the lines from Virgil's *Aeneid* in which Jupiter had promised to the Romans 'power without end or limit', and he turned them, instead, into a promise made by 'the one true God' to the Christian faithful.[22] Rome was on the path to fulfilling its destiny in a way quite different from anything that anyone, from Virgil in the first century BCE to Ammianus Marcellinus four hundred years later, could ever have imagined.

Forces had been unleashed across Europe that nobody could control. The sack of Rome was only the latest horror among many. As the Christian bishop of today's Auch, in south-west France (a long way from the Rhine frontier), wrote shortly after the incursions of 406: 'All Gaul was filled with the smoke of a single funeral pyre.'[23] In Italy, the Goths led by Alaric still had nowhere to go, once they had finished with Rome. Alaric himself died shortly afterwards, while trying to embark his people and their wagon trains on ships to take them to the still-prospering Roman provinces in North Africa. When that failed, the wagons were hitched to the horses once again, and a travel-weary people began the long trek that would take them right round the Mediterranean coastline from southern Italy until they reached the south of Spain.

Finally, eight years after the sack of Rome, a new Roman administration was once again strong enough to impose its will. The successor to the ill-fated Stilicho, Flavius Constantius, had wrested back control of much of Gaul in the name of his emperor, who was still Honorius at Ravenna. The upturn in fortunes would prove only temporary; but on the strength of it a new treaty brought the Goths back from Spain and settled them in the south-west corner of Gaul – the very part of the country where the bishop of Auch had been smoked out by the destruction of a few years before.

Even that would not be the end of the odyssey of the Goths. In the course of half a century two or three generations had followed their wagons from north of the Black Sea, backwards and forwards across southern Europe, to wind up some 2,000 miles from where they had started. From the time of this settlement, these descendants of the first groups to cross the Danube came to be known by the name of Visigoths, or western Goths, to distinguish them from their kin who would shortly follow them for part of the route and end up farther east, in Italy.

Meanwhile the mixed groups of Vandals, Suevi and Alans who had moved into Spain had been fighting among themselves. In 428 a new king of the Vandals, Geiseric, set his sights on the rich pickings of the empire's African provinces, as Alaric had done not so long before him. Ferrying an army across the Strait of Gibraltar, Geiseric proceeded to sweep along the African coast. St Augustine, in Hippo, died with his life's work recently completed, just as Geiseric's troops began to lay siege to the city in August 430. Carthage, the greatest city of Roman North Africa, fell in 439; the rump empire in Italy had now been deprived of grain and tax revenues from its most lucrative remaining provinces.

Back in Europe, those who could afford to were abandoning the collapsing or sacked towns and retreating to their country estates. Under the new dispensation, instead of paying taxes to a central authority, they employed their own militias to protect them. They made what deals they could with the new warlords who now held the power of life and death in their region. The Roman state had failed these landholders. What else could they do? One of their number, who owned an estate near today's Lyon, complained bitterly about being 'placed . . . among long-haired hordes, having to endure Germanic speech, praising often with a wry face the song of the gluttonous Burgundian who spreads rancid butter on his hair'.[24]

But the worst was yet to come.

'Europe's Despoiler'

By 440 those fearsome nomadic horsemen whose westward movement had set the whole line of dominoes falling in the first place, the Huns, had occupied the Hungarian Plain and reached the Danube. Whether they still lived as nomads isn't clear, but they had lost nothing of their reputation for ferocity. Wherever they went they absorbed the populations that were unable to flee before them and recruited them into an embryonic 'Hunnic empire'. By threatening raids across the river into Roman territory their leaders succeeded in extracting substantial amounts of gold from the emperor in Constantinople as protection money. In 441, united under a new leader, Attila, they upped the stakes and attacked the eastern empire in Thrace. Unlike the Goths who had come this way seventy years before them, these Huns had learned how to build siege engines and capture towns. A second campaign in 447 brought them close to Constantinople itself and left a trail of destruction all the way from the Danube to southern Greece. Precisely what persuaded Attila to turn his attention westwards, two years later, isn't known; but the eastern empire was enjoying an economic boom at this time and had gold to spare. Protection money undoubtedly came into it once more.

In any case, in the spring of 451 Attila led a huge force into Gaul. Unlike the Goths, these new invaders were pagans (we know no more about their religion than we do about their language). Christians on the receiving end, whether Roman or German, thought this latest visitation had to be a punishment for their sins. The label 'scourge of God' traditionally applied to Attila may be a later invention; but according to one of the Roman ambassadors who had met him: 'He was a man born into the world to shake the nations, the scourge of all lands, who in some way terrified all mankind by the dreadful rumours noised abroad concerning him.' For another Christian, who wrote an account of these events a few decades afterwards, Attila was simply 'Europe's despoiler'; he had 'swept like a broom through almost the entire continent, sacking and destroying towns and citadels' wherever he went.[25]

At the far end of this trail of destruction, Attila was defeated in the summer of 451 in a closely fought battle in northern France. Thanks to reinforcements from the recently settled Burgundians and Visigoths, the Roman generalissimo in the west at this time, Aetius, carried the day. A similar scenario was played out again, a year later. This time the Huns' warpath led them across the north Italian plain. The city of Aquileia at the head of the Adriatic was the first to be sacked (according to legend, prompting the survivors among its inhabitants to move out to the nearby lagoon and lay the foundations for Venice). Next came Milan further west, one of several imperial capitals in the fourth and fifth centuries. But despite all the sound and fury, this second campaign by Attila in Europe fizzled out. A planned attack on Rome never happened. Instead, the Huns retired back across the Danube, where Attila died not long afterwards, around 453, allegedly bursting a blood vessel after heavy drinking on the night of his latest wedding. The 'Hunnic empire' that had briefly coalesced during the previous decades broke up within a few years; the Huns themselves as a distinct people or an organized force disappear from history shortly afterwards.[26]

But if Rome had been spared the attentions of 'Europe's despoiler', the city would still be sacked for a second time just two years after Attila had departed from Italy. In 455 Geiseric's Vandals crossed the sea from Carthage and landed near the mouth of the Tiber. Aetius was no longer there to mastermind the defence; the year before, he had gone the way of several previous generalissimi, in this case murdered by the emperor himself in front of his astonished counsellors. And so at the end of May 455, Geiseric was easily able to accomplish what, almost seven centuries earlier, the Carthaginian general Hannibal had failed to do in seventeen years of war. It was this second sack of Rome that earned for the Vandals the proverbial name that would long outlive them. The destruction was apparently even greater this time; loot and prisoners were loaded onto ships and taken back in triumph to North Africa.

After two more decades of efforts to put the Roman Empire in the west back together again, its 'noiseless fall' came about in 476. For long enough by this time, real power had lain not with the reigning emperor but with his senior commanders. In that year, one of those commanders dared to do what several of his predecessors, including the ill-fated Stilicho and Aetius, had not: Odoacer led a revolt, deposed the newly crowned, underage emperor (ironically named

Romulus, after the mythical founder of Rome), and in Ravenna declared himself *king*.

Of all these things, the most shocking to traditional Roman sensibilities must surely have been the last. Almost a millennium had gone by since the last king had been run out of Rome. But Odoacer, himself seemingly of mixed parentage from beyond the Danube, counted these days as a Goth; most of the troops who had put him on his throne spoke a dialect of German among themselves; their form of Christianity, known as Arianism, differed in points of belief from the official Roman Nicene Creed. But Latin was still the only common language that everybody understood, and to all intents and purposes the language of writing and administration. So Odoacer styled himself, in Latin, as *rex*. In Ravenna and throughout Italy the Roman system of administration limped on; only now, for the first time, under explicitly 'barbarian' management. The first foundations for a new kind of Europe were beginning to be laid.[27]

Further west the Visigoths, with no one to stop them, began to spread out southwards from the lands they had been granted in south-west France. Soon they too would establish a kingdom, this time in the Iberian peninsula; this was to prove the last of the migrations of this group, which had begun a full century before. And in the other direction, as the short-lived 'empire' of the Huns in today's Hungary collapsed, a new mass migration of Goths crossed over the Danube into Roman territory. Once again vast wagon trains set out across the Balkans, carrying women and children, farmers and their implements and livestock, and escorted by formidably armed warriors. Once again, the walls of Constantinople and the astute diplomacy of the eastern empire deflected them westwards towards softer targets.

Between 489 and 493 these Ostrogoths (or 'eastern Goths'), as they would soon become known, fought their way into Italy. Ravenna surrendered after a three-year siege; at a banquet meant to celebrate the new-found peace, Odoacer was murdered by the Ostrogoth leader himself. Theoderic the Ostrogoth now became king not only of Italy but of large parts of the western Balkans and south-eastern France as well. During the reign of Theoderic, from 493 to 526, Ravenna experienced an astonishing revival: most of the churches with their stunning gold-leaf mosaic decoration that draw the admiration of visitors today were built during this time.[28]

Meanwhile, in northern Europe a new Germanic force had begun to coalesce to the east of the Rhine. During the fifth century, separate warbands were subdued and rival leaders eliminated until by the end of the century a single ruler emerged to command a larger group that now began to be known collectively as the Franks. Much of the early history of the Franks is cloaked in legend. It would be retold a century later by the Christian bishop Gregory of Tours. The Franks had been pagans when they first began to cross the Rhine and enter Gaul. At first they had attacked and destroyed churches; the Christian population had been fair game. But in 496, after a seemingly miraculous escape during a battle against another pagan tribe, their king, Clovis, had himself baptized as a Catholic Christian. According to Gregory, his entire people spontaneously, thanks to divine prompting, elected to follow him.[29] However it was managed, this was a pattern that would be repeated very often during the coming centuries.

Then in 507, at a place now called Vouillé, near Poitiers in western France, a decisive battle was fought between the Franks, led by Clovis, and the Visigoths. With the Visigoths defeated, the Frankish kingdom extended throughout most of the old Roman province of Gaul. Of all the peoples on the move during these turbulent centuries, the Franks had covered the shortest distance. They were also the first to establish a political state, called Francia, which would eventually give its name to one of the nations of modern Europe.

By the early sixth century the map had been drastically redrawn. And it would continue to be redrawn for some centuries yet. But what exactly had changed? Some historians place emphasis on the remarkable continuity of institutions from the late Roman Empire to the emerging kingdoms of the west. In Italy under Theoderic, in Visigothic Spain and in newly minted Francia, the new rulers worked with the existing population to perpetuate a form of civil order that was often based quite closely on what had gone before. They had no other models to follow, after all; and the ancestors of the new ruling class had been in contact with the Roman Empire for generations before them: they knew how the system worked. Christianity clearly played a large part here: every incoming group (except the Huns, who had promptly gone away again) sooner or later adopted Christianity. So St Augustine's City of God could remain an ideal for all to aspire to, even as the earthly city fell into relative obscurity. While the urban fabric of the Roman city had all but disappeared from western Europe, the concept of *civilitas* still lived on, not least in the Latin language.

Central to that concept, and no less important for the future development of Europe, was the weight that the new rulers placed on the Roman legal system. During the sixth century the Franks and Visigoths promulgated their own law codes – complete with their own variations and different priorities, to be sure. But even in lands that in practice were often lawless, the principle of the rule of law and the value of written laws applicable to all continued to be upheld.[30]

Only on the far fringe of the continent was the picture different. In Britain, always an outlier in the western empire, seaborne invaders from the Low Countries and northern Germany obliterated all trace of Roman institutions. Christianity had to be reintroduced (by a different St Augustine, no relation to St Augustine of Hippo) at the very end of the sixth century; it would take centuries for the rival Anglo-Saxon kingdoms to come together into medieval England; the British Isles would not be politically united again until 1707.

A question that has greatly vexed historians since the late twentieth century has been the scale and nature of the movements of people that accompanied the collapse. Rulers and elites were replaced throughout the continent – no doubt about that. But what about the ordinary people? The population of Roman Europe had already been thoroughly intermixed, long before the first 'barbarians' had begun to arrive. No serious historian now believes that specific homogeneous groups, the direct ancestors of modern nations, moved in to displace the existing people of any region. Proof enough is evident in the languages of the continent today: the national languages of Portugal, Spain, France, Italy and three of the four official languages of Switzerland, along with a multitude of local dialects, are all direct descendants from the Latin spoken for centuries by the Roman citizens of those same regions. During the period of migrations, and for centuries afterwards, populations continued to mix – a process still going on to this day.

We simply don't have the evidence to estimate with any accuracy the number of 'barbarians' that must have moved westwards into Europe during the fourth, fifth and sixth centuries. The numbers were certainly large; but even if standing Roman armies sometimes found themselves outnumbered, and allowing for the mass movement of whole family groups, not just armed warriors, it has been estimated that incoming 'barbarians' can have amounted to no more than between 2 and 10 per cent of the existing population.[31]

On the other hand, we also know that the overall population declined during the upheavals of these centuries, probably quite sharply. In these circumstances, the descendants of incomers, who had grabbed the best lands and the best positions at court, were more likely to be among the survivors than the peasants or the sons and daughters of city-dwellers, former Roman officials or landowners who had been displaced. The evidence of archaeology certainly suggests that most parts of western Europe experienced a huge drop in material comforts and standards of living – in some areas to a level lower even than had existed before the Romans arrived. What had happened to the west is sometimes called by theorists 'systems collapse'.[32] Next would come the turn of the eastern empire – but not yet.

'The Empire That Would Not Die' – But Very Nearly Did

After Odoacer's coup in Ravenna in 476, the only Roman emperor left standing was the one who ruled from Constantinople. The upheavals that had put an end to the empire in the west had left their mark throughout the southern Balkans too. But the eastern capital itself, strategically placed to control the waterways that separate Europe from Asia, had been able to block the movement of armed warriors and their wagon trains across the straits into the richest of the empire's remaining possessions, which by this time lay to the east and south, outside Europe altogether. Ruled from its new capital overlooking the Bosphorus, the eastern Roman Empire was beginning to look very much like a European state in exile.

During the very time of the collapse in the west, Constantinople was still approaching its heyday. The city's Theodosian Walls, named after the reigning emperor, Theodosius II, were completed in 413, just three years after Rome had been sacked by Alaric's Goths. Still a formidable part of the cityscape of Istanbul today, these massive fortifications would remain unbreached for close on eight centuries. By the beginning of the sixth century the population of Constantinople would reach its all-time peak before modern times, estimated at almost half a million inhabitants.[33]

This was the Roman Empire inherited by Justinian I, who came to the imperial throne in 527. Justinian is probably best remembered today for the monumental codification of the entire corpus of Roman law that he commissioned within a year of taking office, and still bears his name. The 'Roman law' that today underpins the legal systems of many European states is essentially based on the work of Justinian's legal teams. Justinian was also the first Roman emperor to link the rule of law and citizenship in the empire explicitly to the Christian religion: 'We command that those who follow this law shall embrace the name of Catholic Christians', declares the preamble to the compilation.[34]

At a time when in the west cities and public buildings were being abandoned and very little new was being built at all, Justinian's reign of thirty-eight years saw an ambitious programme of new and restored fortifications, bridges, aqueducts and above all churches in the east, some of which are still standing today. Dwarfing all others is the great church of the Holy Wisdom, known by its Greek name of Hagia Sophia, in the centre of Constantinople. For a thousand years the largest building in the world, Hagia Sophia was completed in astonishingly quick time: begun in 532, after a riot burnt down the old church on the site, it was finished in 537. The design was new, based on a rectangular plan and capped by a central dome – a plan that would be followed by eastern Orthodox churches to this day, as well as in the west from the Renaissance onwards, and throughout the Muslim world in the traditional design adopted for the mosque.

To cap it all, while Justinian's new church was beginning to rise towards the skyline of his capital city, in 533 he sent his trusted general, Belisarius, at the head of a fleet into the Mediterranean. Belisarius's orders were to take back control of the empire lost to the Romans in the west. The 'reconquest', as it is usually called, took twenty years to complete – and inevitably, even then, it still left most of Europe under 'barbarian' rule. But the Vandal state in North Africa was abruptly extinguished; Carthage and St Augustine's Hippo became Roman cities once more, and would remain so for more than a hundred years.

In Europe, Rome was taken by Belisarius at the end of 536; Ravenna, the Ostrogothic capital, in 540. By 553, all of Italy, the western Balkans, a strip of coastland in southern Spain, and all the large islands of the Mediterranean were back within the Roman Empire. In Ravenna, the new churches that had been built on the orders of Theoderic the Ostrogoth were given their finishing touches, especially to their interior decoration. This was how the recently completed church of San Vitale came to be adorned with the magnificent mosaic portraits of Justinian, his empress Theodora and their imperial retinues that visitors still admire today. The message was clear: the Roman Empire was coming back to Europe.[35]

But the forces that had already changed the face of a continent would prove too much for either Justinian or his successors to resist for long. Bubonic plague, arriving from Asia in 542, took its greatest toll on the crowded and still-thriving cities of the eastern empire. During four months that summer, in Constantinople, as many as 100,000 people may have died of the plague – equivalent to one in four of the population.[36] Ever-simmering war with Persia boiled up again in the 540s; not for the first time or the last, the price for shoring up defences in the Middle East would be to leave frontiers undefended in Europe. We first hear of the people who would later become known as Slavs beginning to cross the Danube in or about 518. The early Slavs moved and settled in small groups, apparently without leaders who could command or organize large forces. A more immediate threat seemed to be posed by the Avars, a Turkic-speaking people who appeared at the same time. Former nomads like the Huns before them, the Avars brought a very similar style of warfare; in their turn, they too would create a short-lived but powerful 'empire' on the Hungarian plain.[37]

In the late 570s and 580s, groups of Avars and Slavs banded together to launch a sustained assault on the southern Balkans. One contemporary source claimed that around the year 580 'Slavonians' had taken over all of Greece and most of Thrace (including today's south-eastern Bulgaria and European Turkey). Two years later came the first of a series of sieges of Thessalonica; the city was only saved, according to an account written shortly afterwards, by the personal intervention of its patron saint, Demetrius. The massive city walls, most of which still stand today, had the effect of leaving the city as an island of Roman urban life in a countryside dominated by Slav settlers and Avar warriors.[38]

And then in the first years of the seventh century, the war on the eastern front entered its endgame. The Roman emperor Hera-clius, who ruled in Constantinople from 610 to 641, very nearly lost everything when the Persians advanced through Anatolia and approached the Asian shore of the Bosphorus in 615. The Balkans were once again left fatally exposed; Avars and Slavs took full advantage. Thessalonica was besieged for a second time – saved again, it would be reported, thanks to St Demetrius. A decade later, the Persians were back, and this time made it all the way to the Bosphorus. Not to be left behind, the Avars and the Slavs laid siege to the capital on the landward side.

For ten days, beginning on 29 July 626, the eastern Roman

Empire was reduced to just Constantinople itself, plus the islands of the Aegean and the lands in the west that had been reconquered by Justinian. But the Romans still had command of the sea; there was no way for the two enemies, dug in on each side of the Bosphorus, to join up. The siege collapsed. Heraclius had already left the city in a daring attempt to lead an army the long way round, into Persia across the foothills of the Caucasus in today's Azerbaijan. Two years later, the emperor's gamble paid off and he won his war after all. After such a close call, it really did look as though the Roman Empire in the east was about to be restored.

But the cost had yet to be reckoned. The tide of war had brought destruction all the way to the walls of Constantinople and then back again to the Persian capital on the eastern bank of the Tigris, in today's Iraq. Before either empire could begin to get back on its feet, a new force, bursting almost literally out of nowhere, would put an end to both Roman and Persian rule throughout the Middle East.

The Arab tribesmen of the south-eastern frontier zone and their relatives living beyond it, in the region the Romans called 'Arabia Deserta', had sometimes served the Roman legions as mercenaries, at other times had launched raids into Roman territory. This was a familiar pattern. Seen through Roman eyes, the Arabs must have looked like just another local variation of the Goths, Huns, Avars and others who had appeared on the European frontiers at intervals over the last two and a half centuries. But there was one enormous difference. The commanders of the first armies to enter Roman territory from Arabia, Abu Bakr and Umar I, also known as Caliph Omar, were acting in the name of the leader who had first brought the tribes together during the previous decade and had died in 632. This was the Prophet Mohammed, the founder of a new religion, Islam, based upon the ancient Jewish principle of monotheism and on the personal revelation granted to Mohammed and preserved ever afterwards in the Muslim holy book, the Koran.

The holy war, or *jihad*, launched simultaneously against both the Roman and the Persian empires in the 630s was more than a war of conquest; it aimed to win converts to the new religious faith. And it proved spectacularly successful. While in Europe the newcomers had either shared the religion of the Roman Empire before they arrived or would sooner or later adopt it, in the Middle East the Arabs created a whole new civilization based on the religion they had brought with them. With conversion came a new language: to this day Arabic remains the language of almost every state and the vast majority of people living in the regions of the Middle East and North Africa that had once been Roman and Christian.

The Roman cities of the eastern empire, so recently recaptured from the Persians, went down like ninepins before Umar and his forces. In the battle of the Yarmuk, fought at the point where the gorge of the river of that name emerges into the plain of Galilee beneath the Golan Heights – today at the meeting point, and closed borders, of Jordan, Israel and Syria – an army sent out from Constantinople was roundly defeated in August 636. In the aftermath, some cities surrendered; others were besieged and sacked. The entire Middle East became the Muslim Caliphate, ruled from its new capital in Damascus.

Within ten years of reaching the Mediterranean coast, Umar's forces had begun to commandeer the ships they found in the ports they captured, and then went on to build their own. A Muslim fleet appeared for the first time off Constantinople in 654. At the same time an Arab army marched all the way through Anatolia to the opposite shore of the Bosphorus. Only a storm that providentially scattered the enemy fleet saved the city from assault that time. At the end of the next decade the Arabs were back; naval blockades in the Sea of Marmara lasted on and off until 678. By the turn of the new century the situation was desperate. Constantinople had lost all its provinces in North Africa, all the way to Morocco and the Atlantic coast; Muslim armies had returned to Anatolia.[39]

The third and last Arab siege of the city began in August 717. It lasted a full twelve months. At the end of that time, it was the besiegers who were starving. According to a later Greek account, the Arabs had been reduced to eating their own faeces and the corpses of their comrades. By August 718, a new caliph had come to power in Damascus, and the siege was called off.[40] Once again, Constantine's strategically sited city had prevented an enemy from crossing the straits that separate Europe from Asia. And the survival of the capital, almost alone among the cities of a once-mighty empire, ensured that something, at least, of the old Roman ways of thinking and doing things would continue.

Christian emperors would rule from Constantinople for seven more centuries; they and their subjects would insist until the end that they were Romans, and that their state was the direct continuation of the *res publica* that had once been founded on the banks of the Tiber by Romulus. There was one important difference, though. Because the city lay in the *east*, where the majority language had always been Greek, the language and culture of this empire were not Latin but Greek. This is one reason why modern historians almost always call this medieval civilization 'Byzantium' or 'the Byzantine Empire', after the original Greek name for Constantine's city, and its people 'Byzantines', although they themselves never did.[41]

The Byzantines, as we too must call them from now on, had come through their near-death experience – but only just.

How the West Was Won

In the east the advance of Islam had been halted at the Bosphorus. But only seven years earlier, at the opposite end of the Mediterranean, the strait that separates Europe from Africa had proved no barrier when an Arab expeditionary force landed on the south coast of Spain in the early months of 711. Their leader's name, Tariq, would ever afterwards be commemorated in the modern name of Gibraltar ('Tariq's Mountain' in Arabic). Much larger Muslim forces soon followed, chiefly made up of converted Berber tribesmen from North Africa. By the time the Byzantine capital celebrated its reprieve in 718, very nearly the whole of the Iberian peninsula was in Muslim hands. All that remained of Christian, Visigothic rule in Spain was the tiny kingdom of Asturias in the north-west. This was the only time, so far as we know, that the European land mass has been successfully invaded from the south, directly from Africa.

For a time it looked as though the impetus of *jihad* in the west might carry Islam even farther. In 732 a Muslim army advancing northwards into today's France reached almost as far as the River Loire, before it was turned back in a battle fought near Poitiers. Edward Gibbon, writing at the time of the European Enlightenment, opined that, had the outcome gone the other way, 'the interpretation of the Koran would now be taught in the schools of Oxford, and her pulpits might demonstrate to a circumcised people the sanctity and truth of the revelation of Mahomet'. In reality, the battle of Poitiers may have been a more modest clash with an advance raiding party, rather than a decisive turning of the tide. Whatever the truth, the line of demarcation remained where it had been before, at the Pyrenees and the Cantabrian mountains that separate the north coast of Spain from the hinterland to the south.[42]

In command of the Christian forces at Poitiers had been the strongman of the Frankish kingdom. Since all records at the time were kept in Latin, we know him and his descendants by the name Karolus; to his own people he would have been Karl. The Frankish aristocracy spoke a form of German among themselves, but to converse with the majority of their subjects they had to get used to several local variants of Latin. One of these would eventually crystallize into modern French – which is why the victor at Poitiers is universally known today as Charles, with the addition of the nickname Martel, which means 'Hammer'. No wonder the chronicler of the battle, writing in Latin shortly afterwards, was at a loss for what to call the troops under Charles's (or Karl's) command. Descended from pre-Roman Celts, from Romans, from Visigoths, Franks and other transient inhabitants of Gaul during recent centuries, the men must have spoken as many languages and dialects among them. And so the chronicler came up with a new word for them. He called them *europeenses*.[43] At a time when the old Roman identity must have been no more than a distant memory to most people, and stable kingdoms had yet to coalesce, what else could you call them but 'Europeans'?

Stability depends on the legitimacy of the ruler and the system of government. Both of these were in short supply in Europe's west during the decades after the battle of Poitiers; there was no equivalent to the legitimacy that Byzantine emperors could claim through direct continuity from imperial Rome. And so the Franks became the first to find a way to invent one. Charles Martel had been content to serve the descendants of King Clovis as the power behind the throne. But ten years after his death in 741, his son Pippin deposed the last of the old dynasty (known as Merovingians) and had himself crowned king of the Franks in his stead. Faced with a strong backlash among the Frankish nobility, in the summer of 751 Pippin and his supporters turned to the highest authority they could find in the Christian Church in the west. And in this way a new shaping force began to emerge in the political life of the continent. This was the institution that we now know as the papacy.[44]

Bishops of Rome had for several centuries considered themselves to be something more than ordinary bishops. Partly this was the inheritance of Christ's disciple, St Peter, who according to tradition had been martyred in the city; there was also the lingering legacy of Rome as the imperial capital. Around this time the bishops of Rome began to distinguish themselves by the title 'pope' (from the Greek word for 'father'). In Rome and central Italy, popes were more than spiritual leaders; they were also secular rulers, with considerable power and wealth behind them. And in 751, the same year that Pippin set out his claim to the Frankish throne, that position had just come under a new and acute threat. Most of northern Italy had been ruled for some time by the Lombards, another Germanic people who had arrived two centuries earlier. When Pippin's envoys reached Rome in 751 the Lombards had just ousted the Byzantines from Ravenna. Would Rome be next? In this emergency, an alliance between the spiritual authority of the pope and the hard power that had been visibly demonstrated north of the Alps by Pippin's father, Charles 'the Hammer', was, you might say, made in heaven.

One pope gave his written blessing to Pippin's coronation as king of the Franks in 751. Two years later the pope's successor took the unprecedented step of crossing the Alps in person. During several months spent as Pippin's guest in northern France, this pope anointed his host for a second time as the legitimate monarch of the Franks. That finally put paid to muttering among the Frankish nobility. Pippin and his successors were secure. In return for this favour, the pope begged Pippin to send an army of Franks against the Lombards. That would happen, but not immediately.

In the meantime, we don't know which pope it was during the second half of the eighth century, but one of them commissioned a brilliant forgery, which would not be exposed for what it was until seven centuries later. If the papacy now had the power to make (and perhaps also unmake) kings, that role, too, would require legitimacy. A document that first began to circulate at this time, known as the Donation of Constantine, purports to be a decree drawn up by the first Christian emperor shortly after his conversion, more than four hundred years earlier. According to this decree, Constantine had delegated supreme spiritual authority over the empire to the bishop of Rome in his day, and to his successors in perpetuity. It was a bold claim, and it was set out in uncompromising terms: 'Where God has established the head of the Christian religion, it is not right that an earthly ruler should have jurisdiction . . . Anyone who violates this shall be bound over to eternal damnation.'[45]

In the bargain between the Frankish kings and the popes in Rome during the years after the death of Charles Martel, the foundations for medieval Christendom in the west were being laid. Events would soon prove that the popes had chosen well – as would be demonstrated during the reign of Pippin's son and successor, another Karl, later to be known to history as Charles the Great, or Charlemagne, whose dynasty would be called 'Carolingian'.[46]

Charlemagne came to the throne as king of the Franks in 768. Almost immediately he embarked on the first of a total of fifty-three campaigns that during his long reign would extend the boundaries of the Frankish kingdom in every direction. One of the first of these would be against the Lombards, whom he roundly defeated in 774 – to the great satisfaction of successive popes thereafter. During the rest of the century his armies would march south-west into Muslim Spain, north-west into Brittany, north-eastwards up to the Baltic coast of Germany, and eastwards to take in today's Bavaria, Switzerland, Austria and much of Hungary. In a war of mutual attrition lasting more than three decades, the leaders of the pagan Saxons of today's Germany were forced to accept Christianity; before long, their people would follow.[47]

By the turn of the next century, Charlemagne had not only brought much of the old western Roman Empire back under one rule, he had created a Christian kingdom that extended eastwards far beyond the old Roman boundaries of the Rhine and the Danube. As the year 800 drew to a close, the stage was set for the capstone to be set in the arch whose twin pillars, the hard power of the Frankish kings and the soft power of the papacy, had been carefully built up during the past half-century.

The shape of Europe had changed out of all recognition since Hadrian had begun setting boundaries to the Roman Empire, almost six centuries earlier. So had its identity – which was entirely, now, a matter of religion. Europe was wherever Christian rulers ruled. And it really was a matter of *rule*. Christians in huge numbers would continue to live and thrive for hundreds of years in the Islamic world. By the eighth century, Christian communities had spread right across Asia as far as China.[48] But in none of those places were Christians in charge. In Europe, they were. One after another, 'barbarian' warlords, kings and princes would continue to follow the examples of Constantine I of the Romans, and Clovis of the Franks, to bring the new religion to their people from the top down.

The result was that in the still-forming kingdoms of the west, just as in the Byzantine Empire in the east, *Christendom*, or Christian Europe, would be defined by systems of government and ways of organizing society that drew their authority and claimed their legitimacy from the same ultimate, higher power: the One God of the Christians.

4.

A Tale of Two Empires

800–1204

Charlemagne must have cut a commanding figure, standing six feet three inches tall among the crowd of worshippers and dignitaries attending Mass on Christmas Day in the year 800. This was no ordinary celebration: the place was St Peter's Basilica in Rome; the celebrant was Pope Leo III. The crowd had evidently been primed for something special that was about to occur. Charles 'the Great' has been described by his most recent biographer as 'a practical, down-to-earth man with a down-to-earth sense of humour (his jokes show that): someone [who] "felt good in his own skin"'. So far as we know there was no joking that Christmas Day; but the king had every reason to feel good. As he rose from prayer, according to the oldest surviving account, written not long afterwards, 'Pope Leo placed a crown on his head and he was acclaimed by the whole people of the Romans: "To Charles *augustus*, the God-crowned great and pacific emperor of the Romans, life and victory!"'[1]

To be a king was one thing; and Charles, as king of the Franks and Lombards, was already a king twice over. But no new emperor had been acclaimed in Rome for more than three hundred years. And no Roman ruler, ever, had held the Latin titles of both 'emperor' (*imperator*) and 'king' (*rex*), as Charlemagne did from this time on. 'By the mercy of God', as his official designation expressed it, Charles was having it both ways – at once looking back to the defunct dispensation of ancient Rome and forward towards something as yet to be determined.[2]

An anonymous courtier shortly afterwards gushed in elegant

Latin verse: 'Rex Carolus [is] the world's head, the love and ornament of his people, Europe's worshipful apex, best father, hero, Augustus' – and for good measure, the builder of a 'second Rome'. This form of words, too, looks simultaneously backwards and forwards. Since the 1950s, it has been customary to extract from it the phrase 'Father of Europe' and apply it to Charlemagne – as though its author could have foreseen either the later Holy Roman Empire or the initiatives that would lead to today's European Union. In reality, both the language and the terms of praise are drawn from the ancient world. *Pater patriae* (father of the fatherland) had been an honorific title awarded by the Senate to the most distinguished citizens of the Republic and later to many reigning emperors. But there *was* something new after all: the *patria* had always been Rome, whether understood as a small city state or a world empire. Now, for the first time, the fatherland was called 'Europe'.[3]

New Romes

The idea of Charlemagne as the heir to imperial Rome evidently went back well before the time of his coronation as emperor. Building work for his new capital city at Aachen, in today's German *Land* of North Rhine-Westphalia, had begun in the 780s. During the following decades, his palace and church would be adorned by materials and artwork arduously transported all the way from Rome and Ravenna. Among these were columns made of the rare purple-coloured stone known as porphyry and the equestrian statue of Theoderic, the Ostrogoth king of Italy who had ruled from Ravenna – evidently co-opted by Charles as a role model. It has been argued that the immediate inspiration for Charles's new European empire may have been not so much ancient Rome as Christian Ravenna, which for two hundred years had been the outpost of Constantinople in the west.[4]

In other ways, too, Charlemagne reached back towards traditions that had come close to being lost during the chaos of several centuries. He himself never properly learned to write (itself a revealing reflection of his times), but he did make serious efforts to encourage those who did. Latin learning flourished once more at Aachen and in provincial centres, as well as in monasteries throughout his realm. His first biographer, Einhard, writing within twenty years of his subject's death, had been steeped in the literature and history of the Roman Republic and Empire. The preface to Einhard's biography even refers to Charlemagne's empire as the '*res publica* of the Franks'; its author modestly introduces himself as a 'barbarian' in awe of the treasures of the Latin language and Latin learning which he hopes he has mastered sufficiently for his purpose.[5]

As a Christian ruler, Charlemagne seems to have modelled himself on the later Roman emperors, from Constantine onwards, who had attempted to resolve disputed matters of faith and where necessary to legislate to ensure uniformity of belief and practice. The inscription on his tomb describes him as the 'great and *orthodox* emperor', using the Greek word for 'correct belief' that had first been coined in the time of Constantine. Charles was the heir of Rome also in the importance he attached to the rule of law. Ever since the time of their conversion to Christianity, the Franks had followed the example of the Romans in producing law codes. But Charles, rather as Justinian had done in Constantinople almost three centuries earlier, set about revising and harmonizing these, at the same time updating them for the needs of his new empire. In this way the Roman legal tradition, and the older Greek concept of equality before the law, also took on a new lease of life in his revived empire.[6]

Last but by no means least, Charles knew perfectly well that he wasn't the *only* Roman emperor around. That title still belonged to the emperors in Constantinople – and Constantine's city had routinely been called the 'second Rome' for at least a couple of centuries before Charles's anonymous courtier claimed that title for *his* new capital at Aachen. Both before and after Charles's coronation as emperor, there are tantalizing hints that officials on both sides had an eye on reuniting the two halves of the empire that had been forced ever further apart by the events of recent centuries.

In the early 780s an engagement between the Byzantine co-emperor, Constantine VI, and Charles's daughter Rotrud had been arranged. As both were aged about eleven at the time, the marriage would have to wait. It may have been Charlemagne who called it off, perhaps worried that an eastern emperor might in future lay a claim to his own lands in the west; or it may have been the young emperor's mother, the formidable Irene, who ruled jointly with him after the death of her husband Leo IV in 780. Either way, nothing came of it. Then in 797 Constantine rebelled against Irene, who had her son blinded and took the imperial title for herself – the only time in Roman or Byzantine history when a woman ruled in her own name.[7]

At the moment when Charles received his crown as emperor in Rome in 800, there were those on both sides who believed that the eastern throne was in effect vacant – so shocking was the idea of a female ruler in those times. A marriage between a western *augustus* and an eastern *augusta* would resolve the supposed power vacuum in Constantinople at the same time as bringing the whole of the old Roman Empire back together. Did the often-married Charles ever seriously consider marrying Irene? Might she have been prepared to put her own lands within his power in order to hold on to her imperial title? There are hints at both possibilities in the diplomatic moves recorded at the time. But then Irene was toppled by a palace coup in 802, and the opportunity had gone for good.[8]

Einhard in his biography of Charlemagne laconically reports that after his coronation in Rome, 'the Roman emperors [in Constantinople] were angry about it'. But relations would soon be patched up. In 812 a deputation arrived at Aachen from Constantinople. A newly crowned emperor in the east, Michael I, solemnly conferred on Charles the titles of 'emperor and *basileus*' (the Greek title of all Roman and Byzantine emperors). And in a letter to his eastern counterpart dictated shortly before he died, two years later, Charlemagne tactfully assigned to Christ himself the credit for 'the long sought and always desired peace [achieved] in these times between the eastern and the western *imperium*'.[9]

After the upheavals of half a millennium, the Roman Empire in Europe was back in business. A Roman emperor once again held sway in both east and west; the bounds of the Christian continent had even been greatly extended. What, really, had changed?

The answer was, of course: just about *everything*. For one thing, there was now not *one* Roman Empire but two. When the original empire had been divided, first by Diocletian at the end of the third century and then for good at the end of the fourth, it had been an arrangement handed down from above. During the four hundred years covered by this chapter – a period also known conventionally as the 'High Middle Ages' – we're no longer talking about the two halves of a single empire, but about two separate successors to the Roman Empire of old. And on closer inspection, neither of those quite measured up to all that it claimed, in the first years of the ninth century.

In the east, for all their touchy insistence on their unique right to inherit the Roman imperial title, emperors ruled over a state that in terms of its size, wealth and military strength wasn't greatly different from the larger kingdoms of the west, either before or after Charlemagne.[10] By the time that Constantinople began to recover after the Arab siege in 717 and 718, most of its former territory, revenue and manpower had been lost to the Muslim caliphate. Even in the capital itself the population had been reduced to about a tenth of what it had been in its heyday – though the city was still, by some margin, the largest in Europe. Much of the urban space enclosed by the impregnable Theodosian Walls had been given over to kitchen gardens; untended houses had been left to fall down.

The public spaces of Constantinople were still peopled with hundreds of marble and bronze likenesses of long-discredited gods and goddesses, along with emperors and dignitaries who had once been famous. But no one seemed to know any more who most of them were, or why they had been put there. Stories circulated about evil demons that lurked inside them. The house still stood where wealthy aristocrats had once congregated in a Senate modelled on the venerable Senate of Rome; surely, one bystander asked himself, it must have been built by a man called Senatus? At least, in Constantinople in the century of Charlemagne, there were still people able to read and write, as was no longer the case in most of the west, outside monasteries and the courts of princes. But what they wrote, as those anecdotes show, betrays how far the links with the Greco-Roman past had frayed, even at the heart of the eastern capital.[11]

At the opposite end of Europe, the realm that Charlemagne had knocked together by force of arms and the strength of his own larger-than-life personality would soon fall apart. The Franks still clung to a traditional system of inheritance that went back long before there had ever been a Frankish kingdom, let alone a Europe-wide empire. When the 'Father of Europe' died in 814, the empire passed to his only surviving son, Louis the Pious. Had his other sons survived him, Charlemagne would himself have carved up his lands among them – indeed, there's no evidence that he had originally intended to pass on the imperial title at all. As things turned out, the carve-up was delayed by a generation. But after Louis died in 840, *his* three sons claimed more or less equal portions; in 843 the empire was formally split into three separate kingdoms. From then on it was downhill all the way.[12]

There was also a more fundamental flaw in Charlemagne's imperial project. Once upon a time, Rome had taxed its citizens, especially its farmers, to pay the wages of its soldiers. In the east, the Byzantine Empire still did. But many centuries would pass before any state in western Europe would again be able to redistribute resources so efficiently or on such a scale. Frankish kings, even when they were additionally crowned as Roman emperors, relied on the private armies maintained by local landowners. For these services, the ruler was expected to provide favours in return; more often than not, these would take the form of a share of the booty or land seized on campaign. As the favours mounted up, the landowners gained wealth and power at the expense of the centre, and had less and less incentive to heed the next call to arms. Instead, they would spend more of their time and energy jockeying for influence or even fighting local wars on their own account. And once the empire had reached its maximum extent, there were no more lands and precious little booty to hand out.[13]

Then to cap it all, beginning during the reign of Charlemagne and intensifying ferociously thereafter, the ninth and tenth centuries saw armed groups of men on the move again, intent on plunder, disruption and conquest. Neither of the 'two Romes' would be unaffected by the havoc they brought with them.

The Last of the Barbarians

The Vikings, also known as Northmen or Norsemen, came by sea, from Scandinavia. Even the existence of these lands had barely made it into the written record before this time; with the exception of the mainland portion of Denmark, you have to go a very long way round to reach any part of Scandinavia from the rest of Europe by land. What drove the Vikings to venture across the seas has been a mystery ever since their longships began to appear off the coasts of western Europe in the last years of the eighth century. Unlike the Goths, Huns or Avars before them, so far as we can tell, they weren't being pushed out of their own homes by people moving in from further east. On the other hand, their homelands were poor in most resources except the trees that, with the right technology and enough determination, could be felled and made into ocean-going ships. And once launched across the waves, whatever it was that drove them, the new arrivals did not come in peace.[14]

Within a century, the Vikings in their ships had encircled the entire continent – by sea in one direction, through the great rivers on the edge of Asia in the other. Heading west across the open seas they attacked the coasts of France and reached as far inland as Paris by way of the River Seine. Further afield they preyed on the Christian kingdom in northern Spain and the Muslim al-Andalus to the south. Entering the Mediterranean they raided the mouth of the Rhône and in 860 set their sights on the fabled riches of Rome – though if the later story of this expedition is true, their prey turned out to be not Rome at all but the far more modest town of Luni farther north on the borders of Tuscany and Liguria.[15]

Other Vikings set out in the opposite direction, across the Baltic and then by way of river systems as far as the Black Sea. From there they set up a lucrative trade in furs and slaves with the Muslim Abbasid caliphate to the south. In the same year as the abortive attempt on Rome, descendants of Viking traders crossed the Black Sea from today's Ukraine with two hundred ships, intent on sacking Constantinople. Unable to breach the Theodosian Walls, they devastated the suburbs instead, before heading back the way they had come.[16]

By the turn of the tenth century the descendants of these raiders had made new homes on European shores and were starting to change their ways. In England, King Alfred of Wessex sealed a deal to keep the Danish settlers of eastern Britain out of his own kingdom by persuading their leader to turn Christian. In 911, in northern France another descendant of Viking raiders took the same step and brought all his people with him – in return for a permanent grant of land in what would soon become Normandy (named after its 'Norsemen' founders). Over the next three centuries the Normans, as the descendants of those Vikings came to be known, would become a powerful force all round the periphery of Europe – conquering much of Britain in 1066 and ruling over an independent kingdom as far away as Sicily and southern Italy in the eleventh and twelfth centuries.

During the same period, the Scandinavian homelands of the original raiders would begin to form kingdoms of their own. In due course the rulers, there too, would convert to Christianity and impose their adopted religion on the rest of their people. In this way these northern lands would enter the European fold. Farther south, on the eastern margins of Europe, the descendants of Viking traders had by this time come to be known by the collective name of 'Rus'; soon they would adopt the dominant Slav language and culture of the region – and would bequeath their name to Russia and Russians of later times.

Finally, Viking settlement wasn't confined to Europe. Ocean-going longships reached Iceland, beyond the European continental shelf altogether, in the 870s – bringing, almost certainly, the first human inhabitants to that volcanic land. Later expeditions would create settlements on the coasts of Greenland and North America. Those would prove only temporary; but the descendants of the Viking settlers of Iceland are still there today. The age of European conquest and colonization by sea was still far in the future; but the Vikings of the ninth and tenth centuries pointed the way.

Back in Europe, as one threat diminished, another rose up in its wake – this time on land. During the decades after 900, it was the turn of Magyar nomads from the Asian steppes to sweep westwards. Very much like the Huns and Avars before them, or the Mongols who would come later, these were fierce warriors who fought on horseback. Their language, the ancestor of modern Hungarian, is unrelated to the major language groups of Europe. Like the Vikings, the Magyars when they first arrived were pagans. They plundered churches and monasteries all over central Europe.

It was an all-too-familiar story; and the outcome would fall into a pattern that was also familiar – though perhaps for the last time in European history. After losing a battle fought near the southern German city of Augsburg, in August 955, the Magyars would soon cease to be raiders, convert to Christianity, and begin to live more and more like the neighbours who had arrived before them, in a kingdom centred upon today's Hungary.

The Frankish army that defeated the Magyars was led by Duke Otto of Saxony, who also held the title of King of East Francia – that is to say, of one of the splinter kingdoms left over from Charlemagne's empire in today's Germany. As he left the battlefield, Otto was hailed by his troops as 'Father of the Fatherland, Master of the World and Emperor'.[17] This was very like the praise that had been lavished on Charlemagne a century and a half earlier; and a like reward would duly follow. On 2 February 962, in Rome, Otto was crowned by Pope John XII as Emperor of the Romans. In this way was born the Holy Roman Empire, as it would come to be known in later centuries. Founded on an ambiguous notion of equivalence between spiritual and temporal authority, or as we might prefer to say today, between soft and hard power, the Holy Roman Empire would last for almost a millennium, until 1806 to be precise.

'On How to Run an Empire . . .'

By the middle of the tenth century, that other Roman Empire that today we call 'Byzantine', perched on Europe's south-eastern edge, was once again on the up. Constantinople had survived attacks from all sides, with not only its defensive walls intact, but safely nestling inside them the basic institutions of the old Roman political system. The Senate might have been long forgotten by the man on the street, but the imperial bureaucracy, which went back to the time of Diocletian, flourished in the capital as never before. Indeed, as other sources of income dried up, serving the emperor became the most sought-after route to wealth and influence. Taxes continued to be raised and spent by the imperial treasury. Unlike in the west, power was still firmly rooted at the centre.

While in southern Germany Otto was still rallying his forces against the Magyars, in Constantinople an emperor was busy compiling handbooks on administration for the benefit of his successor. Constantine VII could not have been more different from the warlike Otto. Something of an invalid throughout his life, he was reputed to prefer books, learning and long hours of study to the battlefield. A contemporary described him as 'tall, broad-shouldered and erect in bearing, with a long face, an aquiline nose, a glint in his eye' – perhaps caused by his reputation for enjoying his wine – 'and a fair complexion'. A stickler for protocol, both religious and civil, Constantine was a born administrator; indeed, in today's terms, a compulsive micro-manager. He was evidently effective as a politician too: in 945, at the age of forty, he had finally reclaimed his throne from a usurper. For the rest of his life he would trumpet his legitimacy by adopting the title 'Porphyrogenitus'. Literally meaning 'born in the purple', this was an allusion to a bedchamber lined with the precious purple-coloured granite from Egypt known as porphyry, and traditionally the birthing-place for the offspring of the reigning emperor.[18]

One of Constantine's handbooks is known as the *Book of Ceremonies*. In it, according to its opening paragraph, 'is set forth the harmonious order of the imperial centre'. That was a pious throwback to the time of the first Constantine, when for the first time the Roman Empire had been imagined as the earthly reflection of the kingdom of heaven. The same 'harmonious order' was still expected to hold the centre of that empire together in the 950s.[19]

Of course, Constantine Porphyrogenitus and his formidable array of experienced civil servants knew very well that the actual state of affairs was very different. Another of the emperor's handbooks, compiled around the year 950, has become known by the Latin title: *De administrando imperio*, or *On How to Run an Empire*. This one is mostly about foreign policy. Beyond the empire's borders, in every direction, it is perfectly clear that *disorder* prevails. On every side the empire is threatened by actual or potential enemies – not excluding even the 'Franks', as the Byzantines generally called all their Christian neighbours in the west. And the handbook explains how to deal with them.

Top of the list of risks comes the westward movement of wild, heathen peoples across the steppes that lie to the north of the Black Sea. Much of the text is thought to be a digest of intelligence and diplomatic reports, but in a passage evidently written by the emperor himself, in a more personal style, he warns his son: 'All the tribes of the north have, as it were implanted in them by nature, a ravening greed of money, never satiated, and so they demand everything and hanker after everything . . .'[20] At first glance this might look like a rehash of the old Roman stereotype about 'barbarians' beyond the frontier. But no – and indeed, Constantine generally avoids that term. The art of running an empire, in the mid-tenth century, is based on a subtler understanding of what it is that makes your enemies tick. Why not flatter them and buy them off, rather than fight them?

Constantine's civil servants were well aware of the devastation brought by the Magyars to central Europe. But they knew, too, that these invaders were only one part of a wider problem. The Magyars might be invincible in the west (as they still were in 950), but they in their turn were on the run from another nomadic people who had originated in central Asia and now occupied the northern shores of the Black Sea. These were the Pechenegs. Intelligence reports indicated that the Magyars lived in terror of the Pechenegs. So did the Rus (the descendants of Vikings and their Slavic-speaking subjects, now ruling from their capital at Kiev). The same was true, even closer to Constantinople, of the Bulgars, whose kingdom occupied most of the central Balkans. The way to keep all these potential troublemakers at arm's length was therefore to reach out to your enemy's enemy: send gold to the Pechenegs. The opening chapters of Constantine's handbook explain in detail how this policy was supposed to work – as indeed it did for the best part of a century and a half. No wonder that *On How to Run an Empire* was kept under lock and key, as a 'secret and confidential document'.[21]

Constantine Porphyrogenitus and his contemporaries would not have seen it in quite this way, but with the benefit of hindsight *we* can see that the imperial capital, strategically guarding the straits between Europe and Asia, was still ideally placed to limit the armed movement of peoples from east to west.

Constantine's handbooks also reveal how vital to the eastern empire was the exercise of soft power through diplomacy. Byzantine officials had been honing the art for centuries. This was how the rulers of the Bulgar state in the Balkans had been persuaded to adopt Christianity back in the 860s; after Constantine's time, in 989, Vladimir, prince of the Rus, would follow. With little of the violence that Charlemagne had unleashed against the pagans of western Europe, the eastern empire was also pushing the bounds of Christendom outwards, indeed well beyond the reach of the imperial state. One diplomatic expedient (though Constantine himself thought this was rather bad form) was to send a royal bride to marry the prince of a newly converted people. Another, which was never tried in the west until the Reformation of the sixteenth century, was to offer them the sacred scriptures of the Christian religion in their own language.

Both the Bulgars and the Rus, by the time of their conversion, were largely, if not entirely, Slavic-speaking. Back in the 860s, two learned brothers from Thessalonica, known to history as Cyril and Methodius, had been commissioned to devise an alphabet, based on the Greek one, so that the Slavic language could for the first time be written down. This alphabet is still known as 'Cyrillic' after the younger of the brothers, and today is used to write Russian, Ukrainian and several languages of the Balkans. Using this alphabet, Methodius translated the Bible into the language that we know today as Old Church Slavonic, and which is still used for the liturgy in Orthodox churches wherever a Slavic language is spoken. It is thanks to this exercise of soft power in the ninth and tenth centuries that the eastern, Orthodox branch of Christianity has remained the predominant religion of south-eastern Europe, as well as of Russia, ever since.

But soft power was only ever going to be one part of the story. Beginning before the time of Constantine Porphyrogenitus, and continuing for a whole century afterwards, the eastern empire once again expanded by military force. In the Mediterranean, Crete and Cyprus were regained from the Muslims in the 960s; repeated attempts to oust them from Sicily would ultimately fail, but did bring the Byzantines back to rule parts of southern Italy – thereby creating a long-running bone of contention with their counterpart, the Holy Roman Empire in the west.

In the Balkans, Basil II, who reigned from 976 to 1025, has gone down in history with the nickname 'the Bulgar-Slayer' for his brutal conquest of the empire's Slav neighbours to the north. Once it was over, in 1018, according to a story that would begin to circulate half a century later, the emperor ordered some 15,000 Bulgar captives to be blinded and sent back to their king in batches of a hundred, each led by an officer who had been spared the sight of a single eye for the purpose. True or not, this anecdote, reported by historians on the winning side, gives a flavour of how the Byzantines could talk up their own hard power when they chose.[22]

By the time Basil died in 1025, the centralized state based on Constantinople had reached out in every direction. As well as reclaiming all of the Balkans, which had been lost to Roman power some five centuries before, the Byzantine state had pushed the political boundaries of medieval Europe far to the east, to take in much of today's Turkey, Armenia and Georgia. Constantinople was once again one of the largest and wealthiest cities in the entire world; certainly, it far outstripped any other in Europe. Its population seems to have reached a level not seen since the sixth century, before the onset of the plague during the time of Justinian – once again nudging up towards half a million.

The arts and learning flourished; new churches and public buildings arose in Constantinople and in other cities and towns. From its straitened condition of three centuries before, after the Arab siege, the Byzantine Empire had become truly an empire once more, taking control of new territories and ruling over a variety of different peoples.[23] Its rulers saw themselves as the successors of Constantine, the first Christian emperor, who had founded their city. The old Roman concept of the state as 'the public thing', translated into Greek as *politeia*, still retained its hold. Emperors were not above the law; and the principle of the rule of law remained as strong as ever. According to one of the most learned and influential churchmen of the eastern empire, Patriarch Photius, writing in the ninth century: 'The *politeia* is constituted of members and limbs, in a like manner to human beings, and the greatest and most necessary parts are the emperor and the patriarch.'[24] In practice, rival contenders would often fight hard and dirty to win the imperial throne; but once an emperor received his crown and the holy oil of his office, no one was ever in doubt as to who was boss in Constantinople.

. . . And How Not To

In western and northern Europe, by contrast, there was a vacuum of leadership at the very top. Instead of functioning as the two most vital organs of a single body, the Holy Roman Emperor and the western equivalent of the patriarch, the pope, were constantly circling one another – in the words of one modern historian, 'locked in a dance that each struggled to lead, yet neither was prepared to release his partner and go solo'.[25] At stake was that vacant top job.

The trouble was that, after Charlemagne, no ruler in western Europe would ever again concentrate so much political and military power around a single centre. While Charlemagne had been flattered in his lifetime as 'Father of Europe', the best that a contemporary chronicler could do for Otto I, after *his* coronation as emperor, was to call him 'lord of *almost* all Europe'.[26] Otto and his successors in the tenth and eleventh centuries ruled over a territory made up of today's Germany, the Low Countries, eastern France, Switzerland, Austria, the Czech Republic, Slovenia, and Italy as far south as Rome. This was a sizeable portion of the continent; indeed it was much the largest political unit anywhere west of Constantinople. But Christian Europe now stretched much farther still, from Ireland to Poland, and would soon be reaching into Scandinavia and the hinterland of the Baltic.

There seems to have been a general understanding that an emperor had a higher status than any other ruler. But in the west, however holy and Roman they might claim to be, very few of those emperors would ever successfully impose their will on other rulers or their subjects – and never for long. On the other hand, the administrative hierarchy of the Church, from archbishops and local bishops down to humble parish priests and deacons, and a whole parallel world of monasteries governed by their own rules, worked in much the same way everywhere. The entire system was generously endowed by donations and tithes (a form of taxation that went directly to the Church) paid by the faithful. As a result, popes sat at the top of a continent-wide hierarchy that controlled much of the available wealth and was not limited by the boundaries of states. Always in the background, and sometimes in the foreground, was St Augustine's vision of a 'city of God' that far transcended the long-dismantled but never-forgotten empire built by the ancient Romans. The stage was set for a struggle between hard and soft power that would prove long and bitter.

Time and again an emperor would depose a pope and appoint another more amenable to his wishes; but popes were more than able to fight back. Pope Gregory VII came to the papal throne in 1073 determined to push the claims to papal power farther than ever before. A brief and uncompromising document called *Dictatus Papae* ('What the Pope Said') was issued in 1075. It opens by defining the universal, or Catholic, Church as 'Roman' for the first time, with 'the Roman pontiff' as its head. The pope's rights include all ecclesiastical appointments; all princes are to kiss his feet. Other articles state 'that it may be permitted to him to depose emperors', while 'he himself may be judged by no one'. Two further articles hint at even more far-reaching powers: 'we ought not to remain in the same house with those excommunicated by him'; according to the final one, the pope 'may absolve subjects from their fealty to wicked men'.[27] This was going considerably further even than the forged Donation of Constantine, which dated from the time of Charlemagne; and it was dropped into a world in which the relationship between pope and emperor was far less cosy than it had been back then.

In January 1076 the young Henry IV, already a king in the German lands north of the Alps and emperor-designate, deposed Pope Gregory. The pope responded by excommunicating Henry. This was more than a religious sanction; it licensed all Henry's enemies at home to rebel; in theory, no devout Christian could even give him shelter. The following winter, word reached Henry that the pope he had deposed was on his way to southern Germany to rally Henry's own lords and bishops against him. In a panic the emperor fled across the snow-covered Alps, with his wife and young son, desperate to intercept Gregory before he could reach Germany. On 25 January 1077, Henry arrived at the hilltop fortress of Canossa in northern Italy. The winter was exceptionally cold that year, and the pope kept him waiting, 'clad in wool, barefoot, freezing, in the open air outside the castle for three days with his followers'. Humbly, the uncrowned emperor begged to be forgiven and received back into the Christian fold. Graciously,

Pope Gregory conceded. On the face of it, and for the time being, the rift was healed.[28]

The exact significance of this encounter has been debated ever since. Was it a draw? Or had the pope come out on top?[29] The sequel would muddy the waters further, as Henry and Gregory would each depose the other again three years later. In the end it would be a pope chosen and installed by himself who would crown Henry as emperor in Rome in 1084, more than twenty years after he had come of age and legally become emperor. As the eleventh century drew towards a close, the top job in what we may now call Roman Catholic Europe was still vacant. But not for much longer.

It was in any case further down the social scale that the most far-reaching changes of those times were afoot. Changes to the world's climate brought warmer than average temperatures between about 950 and the early 1300s. It's presumably no accident that the population of Europe more than doubled during the same period. Detailed cause and effect are harder to work out, but new and more productive methods of agriculture must have played a part.[30] Military technology was developing at the same time: from the humble stirrup that would allow a heavily armoured warrior to fight with a lance on horseback, to siege engines, ever more elaborate castles, and the crossbow. All over Catholic Europe the figure of the mounted knight in armour changed the profile of the fighting forces that kings or princes could field, and in centuries to come would also generate a whole mythology, known loosely as 'chivalry' (from the French word for a horse, *cheval*).

Just as widespread, from the middle of the tenth century, was the exponential growth of monasteries and other religious institutions. This wasn't exactly a grassroots movement, either; you had to be wealthy to set up a monastery or a convent, an abbey or a priory, though the monks and nuns who populated it might be drawn from all social classes. The gold standard was set by the Benedictine monastery at Cluny, in Burgundy, endowed by Duke William of Aquitaine in 910 and run from then on by abbots who were answerable only to the pope. Affiliated institutions sprang up all along the pilgrimage routes that by 1000 criss-crossed western Europe.

Cluniac monasteries attracted donations from kings and knights who had sins to atone for. During the decade after the debacle between Henry IV and Pope Gregory at Canossa, a great new abbey began to rise on the site of the original foundation at Cluny. Monks and the patrons of religious establishments during the next centuries would form a profoundly interconnected network from end to end of Catholic Europe, cutting across the often-shifting jurisdictions of kings and princes.

Beginning in 1088 they were joined by a new kind of institution that in time would come to be known as the 'university'. The first of these was established, at least so tradition has it, in the Italian city of Bologna that year. Within a century others had followed at Oxford and Cambridge in England, in Paris, and Salamanca in Spain; what we now call higher education had begun. The wandering scholar and the penniless student, along with the 'chivalrous' knight errant, were taking to the roads to generate another mythology that is still with us today. And then there were the merchants and townspeople who had largely disappeared from western Europe with the demise of the Roman Empire. Towns and cities were growing again, especially in Italy and along Europe's coasts, all the way from the North Sea to the Mediterranean.

None of these developments was in any way top-down; none was directed by a king, an emperor or a pope. And despite plenty of regional variety, all of them spread remarkably uniformly throughout 'Roman Catholic' Europe. Everywhere, kings and princes held court, built castles and waged war against each other in much the same way. The knight on horseback, with his 'fewtered' lance and the stirrups needed to get him aloft, was as familiar a sight in Kraków in Poland as in the Bayeux Tapestry that depicts the Norman conquest of England in 1066. The same can be said of the Spanish frontier lands between Christendom and Islam where the Castilian nobleman Rodrigo Díaz de Vivar, known as El Cid, was beginning to make a name for himself in the same year. Monastic orders reached into every corner of the continent; so did students and scholars, along with the lessons they learned and taught, and the Latin language in which they did so.

Roman Catholic Christendom was on the way to becoming a European union of sorts.[31] Though nobody seems to have noticed this at the time, it was also catching up with the eastern empire fast. And perhaps it was the very *decentred* nature of all these novelties that was beginning to give western Europe the edge?

Then in 1095, in the northern Italian city of Piacenza, an unprecedented plea for help was received and read aloud. It came from no less a person than Alexius Comnenus, the emperor of the Romans in the east.[32] From the viewpoint of Constantinople, if you needed something from western Europe, there was only one person to ask, and it wasn't the Holy Roman Emperor (who was still Henry IV). The call that came from the east was addressed to the current pope, Urban II – who suddenly became the most powerful person in all of Europe.

A Pan-European Adventure

A new movement of nomadic warriors westwards out of central Asia had been in full swing once again during the eleventh century. This time the newcomers were Seljuk Turks; their previous homeland had lain somewhere to the east of the Caspian Sea. Converted to Islam on their travels, they captured the Abbasid capital, Baghdad, in 1055 and took over what was left of the fragmenting Muslim caliphate. In 1071, at Manzikert, near Lake Van in today's Turkey, the Byzantine army was defeated by the Seljuk sultan and the emperor taken prisoner. During the next twenty-five years most of Anatolia was lost to Constantinople. By 1095 the Seljuks were in possession of the fortress city of Nicaea, less than a hundred miles from the capital, on the Asian side of the straits. The 'empire of the Romans' in the east was being forced back towards the bounds of the continent it had started out from, in the days of ancient Rome.

Exactly what the emperor Alexius wrote to Pope Urban II in the summer of 1095 has been lost to history; but the broad outlines can be inferred. Byzantine armies by this time relied very heavily on foreign mercenaries, and never more so than now, when they had been deprived of their largest recruiting grounds at home, in Anatolia. What Alexius most needed was manpower – and also the siege engines that would be necessary if Nicaea was to be retaken. In that kind of military technology western Europe was already ahead. Since he was appealing to the spiritual leader of Roman Catholic Christendom, Alexius evidently framed his appeal in the name of their shared religion. The Turks were not only threatening to extinguish Christianity in the east; they were desecrating the holy places in Jerusalem and the lands where Christ had lived and died. These places, of course, had been ruled by Muslims for centuries; but now, so the word went out, Christians were being killed and hideously tortured by their new masters. The future, even the survival, of Christendom as a whole was at stake. Could the pope coordinate a military effort from the west to support Alexius's beleaguered armies in Anatolia?[33]

And there was a subtext. For several centuries before this time, the more that popes in Rome had tried to assert their authority over all Christians everywhere, the greater the irritation they had aroused in Constantinople; the eastern empire had after all never experienced the kind of power vacuum that existed in the west. The church hierarchies and ritual practices of eastern and western Christendom had drifted apart over time. Differences in doctrine and details of ritual, small enough in themselves, had become entrenched. When representatives of the pope had visited Constantinople to try to resolve them with the patriarch of the day, the two parties had ended up excommunicating one another.

That had been in 1054. Sometimes called, in retrospect, the Great Schism, the event marked the formal separation between the Roman Catholic and the Eastern (or Greek) Orthodox Churches. And despite repeated attempts, and several near misses, the separation remains in place today. Technically, it meant that the two halves of Christendom were no longer in communion with one another. On both sides, during the years leading up to 1095, attempts had been made to heal the split. Now, in return for military assistance, Alexius was bound to offer concessions to the pope. For Urban II, the prospect must have seemed irresistible: not only was he struggling to shore up the authority of his office at home, against continuing opposition from Gregory's old adversary, Henry IV; but here was a god-sent opportunity to extend it farther and embrace the eastern empire too.[34]

The pope seized that opportunity with both hands. And so began the movement that we now know as the Crusades, although that name would not appear until much later.

Outside the cathedral in Clermont-Ferrand, in the centre of today's France, on 27 November 1095, the pope preached a sermon to the assembled crowd. Once again, the precise words of what he said have been lost; but from the rather different versions that were written down afterwards by two clergymen who had been present, several points are clear. First of all, the pope presented the threat to Christians far away in Jerusalem and Constantinople as a threat right here in the country of the Franks who were his audience; this was a threat to 'all the faithful' – a type of call to battle that would be heard again and again down the centuries, not least in the 2020s. Both accounts describe the Turks (incorrectly) as 'Persians', suggesting that Urban was echoing the terms of the appeal he had received from Alexius – in Greek, the legacy of Marathon and the ancient Persian Wars had never been forgotten.[35]

Then there was civil strife and disorder at home. Papal sermons at the time were full of denunciations of the misrule that prevailed among Catholic Christians; popes were after all promoting their own authority in a world where kings and local warlords were regularly fighting against each other. Now, according to both versions of Urban's speech, here was their chance to come together in a worthy cause, and fight against a common enemy abroad. One of the two versions goes farther:

> . . . this land which you inhabit, shut in on all sides by the seas and surrounded by the mountain peaks, is too narrow for your large population; nor does it abound in wealth; and it furnishes scarcely food enough for its cultivators. Hence it is that you murder one another, that you wage war, and that frequently you perish by mutual wounds.

The audience is enjoined, instead, to '[e]nter upon the road to the Holy Sepulchre; wrest that land from the wicked race, and subject it yourselves. That land which as the Scripture says "floweth with milk and honey", was given by God into the possession of the children of Israel.'[36] In these words, written down within a few years of 1095, whether or not they were truly spoken by Urban himself, we can see that the possibility of worldly benefit was there, right from the beginning of the crusading enterprise, in the minds of at least some of those who took part. The seeds of the whole movement that would later come to be known as European colonialism had been sown by the end of the eleventh century.[37] Whatever else they were, the Crusades would prove to be Europe's first colonial venture overseas; and the undefined homeland that is too narrow for the crusaders sounds very like Europe itself.

But by far the chief, and perhaps in reality the only, reward promised by Pope Urban on that day was a spiritual one: the 'remission of sins'. For once, the phrasing is identical between the two accounts, the best guarantee we could have that the words in question are authentic.[38] What form, precisely, this remission was to take in 1095 is still far from clear. Later appeals in the same spirit would spell it out further. So successful, for centuries before this, had been the Christian promise of eternal life that the natural human fear of death had long ago been overtaken by fear of everlasting punishment afterwards. The bravest, brashest knight in armour might tremble before the scenes of Hell painted in vivid colours on the walls of churches all over Christendom. Now the highest religious authority in the land was telling you that if you were prepared to risk everything in *this* life in the service of the holy cause, you would be spared punishment for your sins in the next.

The response was phenomenal. As many as 80,000 may have answered the call in the months after Urban's sermon. They came from just about every part of western Europe, from the Christian kingdoms of northern Spain to the eastern borders of today's Germany, from the English Channel to the toe of Italy. Some may even have volunteered from as far away as England and Denmark.[39] Entirely characteristically at this stage of the crusading movement, crowned heads were absent: Henry IV, still the Holy Roman Emperor, had been excommunicated yet again; so had the king of France (whose title is misleading, as Philip I controlled little of the country that now bears that name). The leaders, instead, were five powerful landholders from different parts of today's France and southern Italy. Making up the rank and file were 'sergeants, squires, engineers, archers, crossbowmen, infantry troops, steersmen and sailors', all backed up by an 'array of household servants, officials and hangers-on: priests, clerks, pages, valets, cooks, dog-handlers' and more than a dozen other callings, including 'minstrels and laundresses'.[40]

By the summer of 1097 the full force of the crusaders had crossed over the Bosphorus from Europe into Asia and laid siege to Nicaea. The city was taken. The shock effect of the arrival of reinforcements from so far away, and on such a scale, rolled back the Seljuk gains in Anatolia. The Byzantine Empire would not again find itself under such pressure on that front for almost a century; its restored presence in western Asia would last for even longer. Alexius had got what he wanted – but at a price that had yet to be reckoned.

Already, by the time that Nicaea was recaptured, it had become apparent that the crusaders and the Christian empire they had supposedly arrived to defend had diametrically different agendas. Alexius, his generals and his civil servants had no interest in pursuing a holy war in the Middle East; they were simply trying to reclaim their own territory from the Turks. The crusaders, for their part, had never seen themselves as mercenaries recruited to fight in someone else's war. For most of them, Anatolia was merely a stepping stone towards their real goal: the Holy Land and in particular Jerusalem.[41] The allied forces of east and west parted company not long after the end of the siege of Nicaea. They would never really cooperate again. The crusaders profoundly distrusted the 'Greeks', whom they came to regard as both treacherous and heretical, while the other side was contemptuous of these brutish, boorish 'barbarians' who, far from serving the emperor's wishes, it soon turned out had become a permanent, and far from welcome, presence on their own turf.

Jerusalem was sacked by the crusaders on 15 July 1099. In the words of a devout Christian eyewitness, who had travelled with the crusade all the way from Le Puy, near Clermont-Ferrand:

> Some of the pagans were mercifully beheaded, others pierced by arrows plunged from towers, and yet others, tortured for a long time, were burned to death in searing flames. Piles of heads, hands and feet lay in the houses and streets, and indeed there was a running to and fro of men and knights over the corpses.

The same witness saw nothing incongruous in the immediate sequel: 'A new day, new gladness, new and everlasting happiness, and the fulfilment of our toil and love brought forth new words and songs for all', as the victors gathered in the Church of the Holy Sepulchre, with 'clapping of hands, rejoicing and the singing of a new song to the Lord'.[42]

The capture of Jerusalem in 1099 marked the beginning of a western European presence in the Levant that would last for just short of two hundred years. At their height in the first half of the twelfth century, four newly established 'crusader states' stretched from the district of Urfa in today's southern Turkey, via a narrow strip of Mediterranean hinterland, all the way to the southern tip of today's Israel and Jordan on the Gulf of Aqaba. Known collectively by the French name *Outremer* (Overseas), they were ruled by an elite that was mostly French in origin. But we also hear of Scottish, English, German, Bohemian, Bulgarian and Hungarian immigrants.[43] Even so, there were never enough settlers to make these states viable in the long run. Over time the predominant pattern of population movement, from east to west, that the Crusades had seemed to reverse, would reassert itself. And the march of the Turks into Europe, which had been averted by the First Crusade, would resume in earnest in the fourteenth century.

Meanwhile, back at home, the call to risk everything in a do-or-die adventure in strange lands had entered deeply into the imagination of European Christians – including millions who never left their own hearthside. Coinciding with the emergence of regional spoken languages into writing, the first century of the Crusades generated a whole new type of storytelling. Folk memories and popular histories half-remembered from earlier centuries were dusted off, given a new literary polish, and repurposed as exemplary tales of heroism. In these, idealized Christian knights gave their all for the defence of Christendom: *La Chanson de Roland* ('The Song of Roland') in Old French, the *Nibelungenlied* in Old High German and *El Cantar de mio Cid* ('The Song of El Cid') in medieval Spanish are the most famous. The 'Arthurian cycle' of stories and poems in Middle English and Welsh belong to the same tradition.

Before long, and again very much a product of the crusading spirit, the 'medieval romance' would be born. Proliferating in most of the languages of Europe, and enormously popular over a period of almost five centuries, from the late twelfth until the early seventeenth century, romances would tell of outlandish adventures and 'romantic' love between the sexes, all governed by an overarching moral code, known by the French term *cortesie*, or courtliness. Stereotypes of modern storytelling, particularly in films and video games, such as the knight in shining armour, the damsel in distress waiting to be saved, and the notion of 'chivalry' or 'chivalrous behaviour' all derive from the first century of the Crusades. Perhaps the most enduring and the most novel of all was the idea of 'adventure' itself – a newly coined word in several European languages (*aventure* in French, *Abenteuer* in German, and so on) that has stayed with us ever since.

If these were among the imaginative responses to the Crusades, in their turn they helped to fuel the zeal of real crusaders on the ground. During a period of just over a century after the capture of Jerusalem, three more Europe-wide expeditions were mounted, each of them initiated by a religious call in the west, and all designed to reinforce the crusader states at a moment of crisis. The Second Crusade began with a naval expedition that set out from the south of England and took in the conquest of Lisbon from its Muslim rulers in 1147 – for the first time extending the scope of one of these expeditions outside Anatolia and the Middle East. This time, the expedition was joined in the Holy Land by two of the most powerful rulers in Europe: Louis VII of France and the German king, Conrad III, who styled himself 'Emperor of the Romans' despite not actually having been invested by the pope. But after a disastrous attempt to capture Damascus, one by one the leaders gave up and turned for home. As a result, in the words of the Jerusalem-born chronicler William of Tyre, writing in the 1170s, 'from that time onwards the condition of the Latins [that is, Catholic Christians] in the East became visibly worse'.[44]

When Jerusalem fell to the Kurdish leader Saladin in 1187, the response from Europe took the form of the Third Crusade. This was perhaps the most ambitious of them all. Richard I ('Lionheart') of England took part, along with his bitter rival Philip II of France and the formidable Frederick Barbarossa, the German king who this time really did bear the title of Emperor of the Romans and would lose his life on the way to the Holy Land in 1190. Knights from all over Europe were falling over one another to sign up: in the words of one witness, 'it was not a question of who had received the cross but of who had not yet done so'. But Jerusalem held out against all their efforts; in 1192 the retreat began. The casualty rate this time seems to have been the highest of any of these expeditions, estimated by contemporaries at somewhere between 50 and 75 per cent; some contingents were all but wiped out.[45]

The next attempt fared even worse. The Fourth Crusade set out by sea from Venice in 1202. The Venetian republic was generally more interested in trading than crusading and drove a hard bargain: its galleys would ferry the knights, along with their horses and equipment, to Egypt on their way to the Holy Land – but they would have to pay for the service. This time, however, the surge of recruits to the cause failed to materialize. The Venetians still expected to be paid in full; but the crusade could not muster enough cash to meet the bill. Thanks to a series of events that were entirely unforeseen and largely unplanned, the expedition wound up, not in Egypt, but moored in the Bosphorus, outside Constantinople, instead. The Byzantine Empire was in the midst of a succession crisis; one of the rival claimants to the imperial throne, a young man by the name of Alexius, had fled to the crusaders and promised them all the money they needed, if only they would help him gain his birthright. But the plan backfired. Once installed as emperor, Alexius was murdered by his own people. When no money was forthcoming, the Venetian ships forced their way into the narrow inlet of the Bosphorus, known as the Golden Horn, that led to the heart of Constantinople.

On Monday 12 April 1204 the Theodosian Walls of the Byzantine capital, which had resisted all attempts to breach them for eight centuries, were overtopped by wooden siege engines carried on the decks of Venetian galleys. Crusaders scrambled across the ramparts, fought their way to the nearest gates and opened them to their comrades. The greatest city of Christendom was savagely sacked and looted by Christian knights who had 'taken the cross' to defend their faith against the infidel.

Of all the Crusades, this was the one that would prove to have the most lasting impact on the later history of Europe. A movement that had begun with a plea from the eastern empire for help in the defence of Christendom had ended up turning against the very people it had been meant to support. In the months and years that followed, the remains of the Byzantine Empire would be dismembered, with most of its European provinces falling to princes from the west or the growing colonial power of Venice. The Byzantines would regain their capital city half a century later, in 1261; the Byzantine state would limp on for the best part of another two centuries, a shadow of its former self. But the long-term effect of the Fourth Crusade would be fatally to weaken the defence of Europe by eliminating the continent's strongest strategic bulwark in the south-east.[46]

After 1204, nobody could doubt that Christian Europe was defined, and in many ways ruled, by the Church that Pope Gregory VII had been the first to call 'Roman Catholic' back in 1075. The Fourth Crusade had put an end to the parallel lives of a western and an eastern empire, each a successor to ancient Rome. Augustine's 'city of God' had ousted both, with a single role model for all of Europe to follow – the blueprint for what might be termed the 'holy European union' of the later Middle Ages.

5.

Breaking Out – Breaking Up

1204–1556

Pope Innocent III took a poor view of human nature in general. 'Man has been formed of dust, clay, ashes,' he wrote in a treatise that would become something of a bestseller for its times, 'and, a thing far more vile, of the filthy sperm . . . His evil doings offend God, offend his neighbour, offend himself.' No wonder, then, that man's 'destiny is to be a putrid mass that eternally emits a most horrible stench'. Elected in 1198, this was the pope who four years later urged the crusaders on their ill-fated mission that would end in the sack of Constantinople. Afterwards, when the news reached Rome of the full horror of what had happened, even such a natural pessimist was appalled. But Innocent was also a pragmatist. What had been done was hardly Christian in spirit, but it could still find its place as an unintended part of a programme that Innocent had inherited from his predecessors and would bequeath to the popes who followed him during the next century.[1]

That programme would be fully spelt out, a decade later, during two weeks in November 1215. In the Great Hall of the Lateran Palace in Rome, one of the largest ever Councils of the 'universal' Church brought together some five hundred bishops and archbishops, with almost ten times that number of junior clergymen, from all over Europe and the crusader states. Representatives of several monarchs also attended (including two rival candidates for Holy Roman Emperor). Nothing on such a scale had been attempted since Constantine I had convened the Council of Nicaea in 325, a year after the victory that had established him as the first Christian emperor of Rome.

From Constantine until after the time of Charlemagne it had always been the emperor who would summon this kind of conclave. But no longer. Innocent III left nothing to chance; the Fourth Lateran Council (or Lateran IV, as it has generally been known ever since) had been two full years in the making. The initiative was entirely the pope's; so was the making of the agenda. And given the number of resolutions (seventy-one), and the short time actually allotted to discussion, it seems likely that many of these had been written in advance, to be merely voted through by the attending churchmen. This was the pope's Council.[2]

Essentially the upshot was to consolidate definitions of religious practice, belief and regulation that would remain the bedrock of the Roman Catholic religion ever afterwards. Among these was the doctrine of Purgatory. Churchmen had long recognized a gap in the traditional teaching about the afterlife. If after death you went to either eternal damnation in hell or eternal salvation in heaven, it was hard to see how those who took up arms in a crusade could be rewarded with the 'remission of sins' that had been promised; there had to be a mechanism available in the hereafter that would give effect to the popes' offer. Purgatory – the place of purging, or cleansing – had emerged as the answer. There, through graded suffering, souls might eventually redeem themselves until they were fit for heaven. Prayer, and particularly the benediction of popes and other clergy, could shorten the time spent in Purgatory.[3] By formally adopting this belief into official Catholic teaching, the Lateran Council also unwittingly created the fault line that would come close to destroying the Catholic Church three centuries later and would split Europe apart for almost as long again.

Another development that would cast a long shadow was a new strong line against 'heretics', meaning anyone whose religious beliefs or practices deviated from those officially approved. From this time on, the rooting out of heresy would increasingly be a duty laid on religious and secular leaders alike. A new set of legal practices, known by the Latin term *inquisitio*, would make it easier to denounce anyone suspected of heresy; torture and imprisonment were approved as means to extract confessions. The horrors of the Spanish Inquisition of the sixteenth and later centuries were still some way in the future; but already the extreme penalty for those convicted was to be burnt to death in a public spectacle. And such spectacles were becoming more frequent throughout Europe.[4]

Along with the crackdown on Christian deviation, the 'canons', or resolutions, issued at the conclusion of Lateran IV also included new and more systematic sanctions against Europe's long-established Jewish communities. This was when Jews were for the first time required to dress differently from Christians, forbidden to appear in public at Easter time, and liable for punishment for uttering the name of Christ. Expulsions of whole Jewish communities, from this time on, as a result would become much more frequent.[5] In the same spirit, the struggle against the 'infidel' abroad was to be resumed. Pope Innocent had already made up his mind to announce a new crusade to reclaim the Holy Land; this duly became the final resolution of the Council. (The Fifth Crusade would at least get as far as Egypt – after Innocent's death – but this one would prove no more successful than most of its predecessors.)

While the Council was in session, the pope also seized the opportunity to make more directly political interventions. One of these was over the perennially vexed question of who should rightfully be the next Holy Roman Emperor. Another, brought all the way from England, was the document known as Magna Carta, that King John had been obliged by his rebellious barons to sign only five months before. Often taken to be a first sign of Europe's political evolution towards representative democracy, Magna Carta placed legal limits on the powers of a reigning monarch. But Innocent was not impressed. The English rebels found themselves the latest victims of papal displeasure, and joined the growing list of the excommunicated, while 'Bad King John' became officially a vassal under the protection of the pope. England was not the only kingdom to be treated in this way. The list of papal vassals included Aragon, Sicily, Denmark, Bulgaria, as well as, in effect, the German lands ruled by Frederick II (who was also the pope's candidate for the now largely symbolic title of emperor).[6]

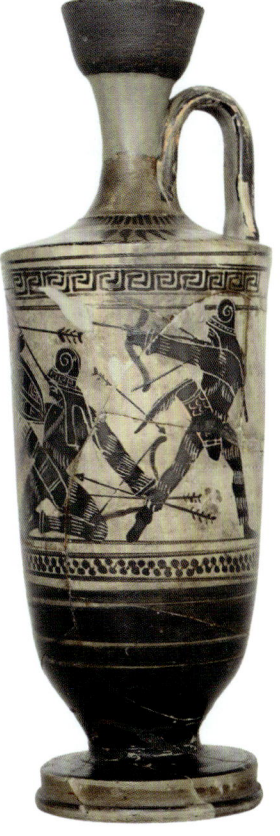

1. (*left*) Greek infantrymen
and Persian archers at the
battle of Marathon (490 BCE).
Two sides of an Attic black
figure *lekythos*, probably made
shortly afterwards.

2. (*above*) Herodotus of
Halicarnassus (*c.* 484–*c.* 431
BCE). Roman copy of a
fourth-century BCE bust.

The bay and battle site of Marathon today, from the slope of Mount Penteli.

4. *Stele* (gravestone) of Panchares, son of Leochares, believed to be one of the fallen at Chaeronea (338 BCE), showing a scene from the battle in which the city states of Athens and Thebes were defeated by King Philip II of the Macedonians (detail).

5. (*left*) Alexander the Great (ruled 336–323 BCE). Roman mosaic from Pompeii, *c*.120–100 BCE (detail).

6. (*above*) Julius Caesar, 'the first Roman ruler to have his own face imprinted on coin just like a king' (p. 50). Denarius of 44 BCE.

7. 'Rome was always about power' (p. 42) – as can still be experienced by the visitor to the city today, looking up at the Pantheon, built on the orders of the emperor Hadrian in the 120s CE.

8. Caracalla, sole ruler of Rome from 211 to 217 CE, 'transformed every subject of the Roman Empire who was not a slave into a full Roman citizen' (p. 63). Marble bust from the emperor's lifetime.

9. Colossal statue of Constantine (ruled 306–37 CE), the first Christian emperor of Rome, as reconstructed in 2022. Only the head and a few fragments of the original survive.

10. (above) 'Ammianus several times paints a vivid picture of the Goths wagon-trains, drawn up in a defensive circle, while the warriors roamed to forage and plunder' (p. 74). This image dates from the fifteenth century.

11. (left) Attila the Hun (c. 406–53 CE), as imagined by the French painter Eugène Delacroix in 1843.

12. The interior of Hagia Sophia, Constantinople, completed on the orders of the emperor Justinian in 537.

13. Charlemagne's church at his capital city, Aachen, late eighth to early ninth century.

14. Mosaic portrait of Justinian (ruled 527–65), S. Apollinare Nuovo, Ravenna, 6th century.

15. Charlemagne, King of the Franks (reigned 768–814), crowned as Emperor of the Romans on Christmas Day, 800, as imagined by Albrecht Dürer in 1514.

16–17. An emperor and a higher power: the Byzantine emperor Constantine Porphyrogenitu (ruled 913–59) crowned by Christ (*left*); the Holy Roman Emperor Henry IV waits at Canossa in 1077 to be admitted by Pope Gregory VII (*right*).

18. The sack of Constantinople by the Fourth Crusade in April 1204. Detail of a fifteenth-century miniature.

9. The Fourth Lateran Council, November 1215 (Matthew Paris, *Chronica Maiora*, 1259).

10. Mongols, also known as Tatars, in action *c*. 1330: the martyrdom of John the New Moldavian fresco, Voronet, Romania, 1547).

21. 'In paintings such as the *Arnolfini Portrait*, of 1434, by Jan van Eyck, Europeans literally begin to confront their own selves reflected in a mirror' (p. 152). Detail.

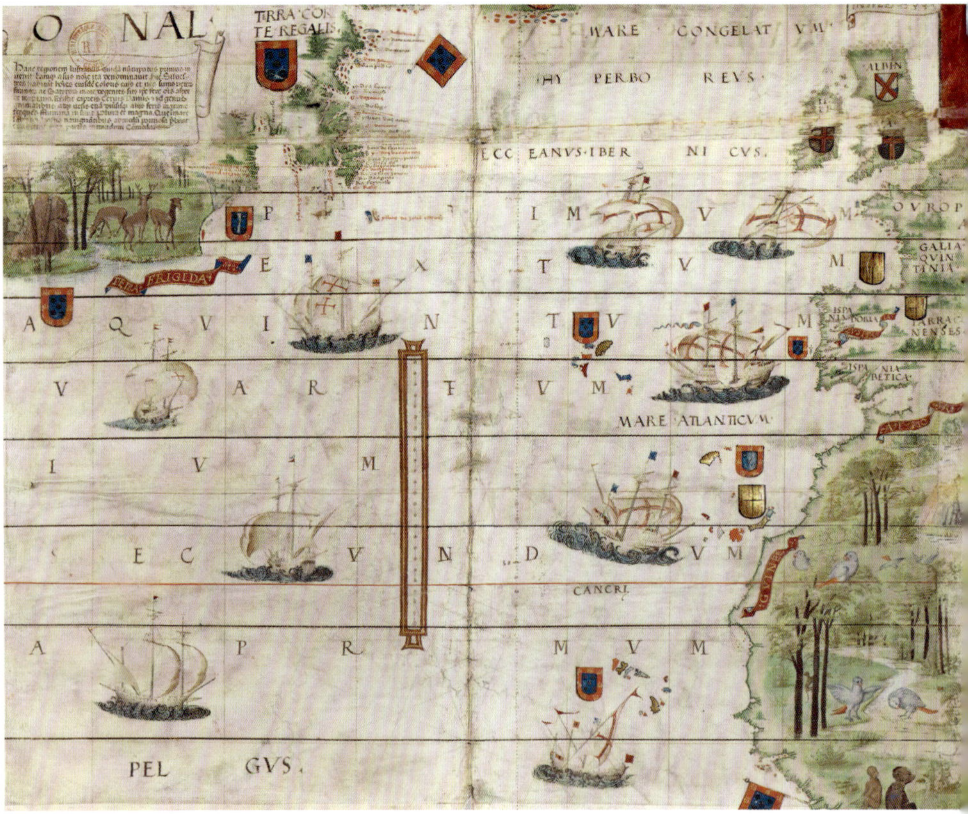

22. European ships crossing the Atlantic Ocean, from the Miller Atlas, 1519. Europa ('ovropa') is labelled over northwest France.

The canons that were promulgated at the end of the Fourth Lateran Council on 30 November 1215, together with a burgeoning body of ecclesiastical legislation known as 'canon law', were not the laws of any one kingdom or political state. They might be variably enforced in practice, but in theory they added up to a legal system and a concept of the Christian subject before the law that applied throughout Catholic Europe. Pope Innocent's programme has been called 'an attempt to create a legitimate pan-European order'. Even if it never entirely succeeded, it has been argued that Innocent III and his immediate successors 'laid the foundation for modern Europe'.[7]

On the map, Roman Catholic Europe in 1215 looked not very different from the continent that we know today. But as an *idea*, the Europe of Innocent III and the Fourth Lateran Council was as different from anything modern as it also was from the Roman Empire that it finally and irrevocably replaced. This chapter tells the story of how that idea came to be tested to destruction, while Europe burst like a seed-pod across the world's oceans.

Dante's World

A century after the time of Innocent III, the Florentine poet and philosopher Dante Alighieri gave eloquent and articulate expression to the political and theological vision that had gradually come to define Christian Europe ever since the time of Charlemagne. Dante (as he has been generally known since his lifetime) was writing at the very time when in reality that vision was beginning to recede for good – during the first two decades of the fourteenth century. He had himself fallen victim to the poisonous internal politics of his native city and was living as a political exile in one Italian city state after another – under pain of death by fire or decapitation should he ever return to Florence.

The old rivalry between popes and emperors was back, and with a vengeance. Dante had been of the pope's party. But then, disillusioned, he had come to pin his hopes, instead, on the next Holy Roman Emperor, who was expected to be Henry VII, after his election to the title of King of Rome in 1308. It was probably during the next five years, while Henry tried to stamp his imperial authority on the Italian city states on his way to be crowned as emperor in Rome, that Dante drafted an erudite treatise called *On Monarchy*. In it, he argued that the Roman Empire had been ordained by God for the fulfilment of the 'end and purpose of all human civil society' (or as a later age would have put it, of 'civilization'). Drawing on some quaint arguments culled from Virgil's *Aeneid*, Dante further argued that Rome's founders had combined the virtues of all three known continents. Of these he gave pride of place to Europe – and to his native Italy, as 'Europe's noblest part'. 'Nobility' counted for a lot in Dante's scheme of things. And he was in no doubt that Catholic Christendom – Europe, in other words – was the direct, divinely appointed successor to the empire of ancient Rome.[8]

The authority of the emperor, Dante went on to argue, derives not from the Church or the pope but directly from God himself. This had been pretty much the position in the time of the Christian Roman emperors Constantine and Justinian – both of them among Dante's heroes. The solution to the world's many ills, Dante believed, would be a clear separation between the powers of Church and State, of pope and emperor. Each had been divinely ordained for his role by God; therefore neither had the right to usurp the authority of the other.[9] It was a neat philosophical solution to an age-old problem that politically had proved insoluble. If it could ever have been put into practice it might have turned the whole of Europe into something rather resembling the Byzantine Empire as it had been before the Fourth Crusade – though if that had happened, it's anybody's guess what its legacy might have been to the Europe of today.

When Henry VII died of fever in August 1313, having had to fight his way to Rome and then been crowned as Holy Roman Emperor not by the pope but by the cardinals among his own supporters, Dante's grand political scheme died with him. But Dante Alighieri was a poet as well as a political philosopher, and he was not done yet. In all probability, he was already well advanced on his poetic masterwork and one of the greatest literary achievements of the European Middle Ages. The dry treatise, *On Monarchy*, had been written in Latin prose; but when it came to poetry Dante joined the growing number of writers, all over Europe, who were beginning to forge an expressive and subtle literary idiom out of the spoken language of their time and place – in Dante's case, the Tuscan dialect of Italian.

Usually known today as the *Divine Comedy*, Dante's *Commedia* (its original title) takes its reader through the three realms of the Catholic Christian afterlife: Hell, Purgatory and Paradise. Dante was a polymath, fully conversant with all the branches of knowledge available in his day. He drew on this knowledge to depict the earth as a sphere with every other heavenly body revolving round it. Below the earth's surface, in circles of fire and other torments, until the frozen core is reached, lies the place of eternal damnation. High above, in spheres radiating out from the moon and sun to the fixed stars and the fiery zone beyond, known as the 'empyrean', the spirits of the blessed are assigned places in a hierarchical order with God himself in the outermost layer. In between, again consisting of a hierarchy of concentric circles, lies the intermediate zone of Purgatory, which had only become an official part of Catholic doctrine a century before.

The poem imagines a totally ordered universe; but in place of the impersonal physical force that since the time of Isaac Newton in the seventeenth century we have learnt to call gravity, Dante imagines something far more human that holds it all together, governing every aspect of our lives and the world around us. Many readers have found the moral judgements of Dante's God harsh, even cruel, the rewards of his milky realms of Paradise pale by comparison with the vivid torments of Hell. But the universe of Newton, Einstein, or today's quantum physics is not much kinder. And there is something rather wonderful about the affirmation that closes the whole poem – an idea that would have been incomprehensible to an ancient Greek or Roman, and may perhaps represent the other side of the coin from Pope Innocent's visceral disgust at the human condition. In the last of the poem's approximately 15,000 lines, the celestial voyager is granted a glimpse of 'the *love* that directs the motion of the sun and of the other stars'.[10]

In the *Commedia* Dante conjures up a theological equivalent of geopolitics for the early fourteenth century: the inhabited world stretches from Cadiz in the west to the River Ganges in the east. Jerusalem, the site of Christ's crucifixion, is placed, with some geographical licence, at the centre of this northern hemisphere. Opposite Jerusalem, in the equivalent position south of the equator – where no one could yet have reached from Europe at this time – in a daring and original leap of the imagination, Dante creates a physical space for Purgatory, on a mountain that rises out of the ocean to reach all the way up to Heaven.[11]

In the twenty-sixth canto of *Inferno* (*Hell*), the poet has the fabled Greek voyager-hero Ulysses, also known as Odysseus, tell of his last, doomed voyage far beyond the Strait of Gibraltar, which traditionally had always marked the limit of the known or knowable world. The lines in which Ulysses inspires his men to follow him into the unknown would strike many an admiring echo in later times; uncannily they seem to prefigure the spirit of the actual voyages on which Europeans would soon begin to set out:

> O shipmates, you who through a hundred thousand
>> perils have forced a passage to the West,
>> to this small vigil that remains to us,
> to this last portion of our sensual life,
>> do not deny the experience of a world
>> beyond the sunset, where no people live.
> Give thought to those who were your ancestors:
>> you were not granted life to live like beasts,
>> but through the path of virtue to seek knowledge.

After months at sea, the mariners spot an impossibly high mountain on the horizon, little knowing that this is Purgatory. In Dante's universe, this is the farthest that even the bravest, most determined human being can reach independently of the divine will. As the shade of Ulysses in Hell laconically explains to the poet, a sudden storm sank the ship, 'as pleased another' (meaning the Christian God, whom the hero could never have known).[12]

Soon, it would be Dante's perfectly ordered cosmos that was in headlong retreat.

From Silk Roads . . .

During Dante's lifetime, Europe's place on the map of the world and in the minds of those who lived there was already being transformed. The impetus came from outside. And since there was still only the one way in, that meant: from the east. The agents of this change are variously known to history as Mongols or Tatars. After devastating the lands of the Rus and the kingdoms of Poland and Hungary between 1238 and 1241, the Mongols would be remembered for centuries in the folklore of those regions as subhuman 'dogmen' – dog-headed creatures unleashed from hell. The name 'Tatars' sounded like 'Tartarus', the ancient Latin name for the nether world; and so these 'Tatars' quickly came to be known as 'Tartars', a word that has since entered many, if not all, European languages with the proverbial sense it has today. To an English chronicler of the time, writing at a safe distance, the 'Tartars' were 'an immense horde of that detestable race of Satan'.[13]

Even by comparison with the Huns, Avars or Magyars of earlier times, the Mongols excelled in the exemplary cruelty they showed to their victims, in their sheer numbers and in their effectiveness on the battlefield. As their warrior bands penetrated all the way to the Adriatic, in vengeful pursuit of the defeated King Bela of Hungary at the end of 1241, it seemed that nothing could stop their advance. Then at the beginning of the next year the story took an unexpected turn. The Mongols abandoned the hunt for Bela; within a few months all their troops had vanished from Europe. It would be some time before Europeans could work out what had happened. Thousands of miles to the east, at Karakorum in today's Mongolia, the Great Khan, Ogodei, had died in December. It would take the Mongols five years of infighting before they found a successor; their warriors on the European front had more pressing concerns far away, at home.[14]

But there was more to it than that: there was something about the Mongols that made them different from every previous invader from the east. Recently united into a formidable continent-wide force by Ogodei's more famous father, the warlord Genghis Khan, the Mongols had become the first people to control the entire land mass that lies between Europe and China; soon, indeed, they would conquer China itself. Theirs was the largest single political entity that had existed anywhere in the world up to that time, perhaps of any time; it was larger, even, than the Russian Empire that in later centuries would be in many ways its heir.[15] With the whole of Asia to rule over, the Mongols had richer pickings to pick from than Europe. And so, from being a terrible threat, they became for Europeans quite literally a golden opportunity.

When Dante mentions 'Tartars' at all, it is as the craftsmen of the most exotic, luxurious, highly coloured fabrics imaginable – clearly already a legend in Italy in his day.[16] The famed 'silk roads', which for centuries had tenuously connected China, via central Asia, with the ports of the Black Sea and the Levant, and ultimately with Europe, had suddenly opened up as never before – thanks to the Mongols. Travel and trade by land across Asia for the first time became a real possibility for Europeans. And those who made the journey came back with scarcely believable tales of the wonders and riches they had seen.

The accounts that began to circulate under the name of the Venetian trader and explorer Marco Polo, at the end of the thirteenth century, may have been exaggerated. But the evidence of archaeology in central Asia confirms the Mongols' 'particular love of gold', their penchant for amassing it and then for using it as a means of long-distance exchange. Decades of plunder had made these nomads into the wealthiest people on the planet. As a matter of principle, it seems, their leaders still lived in tents, as their ancestors had done – but these could be elaborate affairs, 'constructed using golden nails and with interiors decked out in gold'. Whole cities could be constructed in this way. Aptly, the Mongols at the height of their power and wealth have been described as 'imperial nomads'.[17] No wonder the Europeans who reached their domains were dazzled.

And so it began to dawn on some, at least, in Europe that when it came to material benefits, God's perfectly ordained world of Christendom lagged far behind a semi-mythical east. China and 'the Indies', it now emerged, were home to riches far beyond anything available to Christians in the west. Enterprising Europeans wanted a share for themselves. And the way was now open. According to the Florentine merchant Francesco Pegolotti, writing at the end of the 1330s, the entire land route from the Black Sea to China was 'perfectly safe, whether by day or by night'.[18]

Why, then, did so *few* set out from Europe to make the journey? We know the names, and something of the experiences, of those who left a record of their travels. Before Pegolotti, in the thirteenth century there had been the Flemish friar William of Rubruck, who had been sent on an embassy to the Great Khan by the king of France; there was the pope's emissary Giovanni da Pian del Carpine, charged with the unlikely prospect of converting the Mongols to Christianity (eventually they would opt for Islam instead). And of course there was Marco Polo, who had been taken along by his uncles on a trading expedition that began in 1271 and lasted more than twenty years. But despite the incentives and the undoubted 'lure of the east', when Europeans did venture beyond their homeland in a big way it would not be overland.

Apart from the Mongols themselves, it was not *people* that moved along those newly opened roads. Once again, the direction of travel remained the same as it always had been: from east to west. The gap in technological know-how between China and Europe began to be filled, with all the inevitability of a lock gate opening. Often it was no more than the straightforward transfer of a labour-saving device – such as the humble wheelbarrow; the technique of forging cast iron to make stronger, more durable tools; or the magnetic compass as an aid to navigation. More far-reaching was the ability to make paper out of wood pulp. Writing materials had been prohibitively expensive in Europe ever since the Arab conquest of Egypt in the seventh century had put papyrus, the staple of the ancient world, out of reach. Paper had been made in China since the first century BCE; the first manufacture in Europe dates from 1276. It would take longer (until the second half of the fifteenth century) for another Chinese invention, the technology of printing, to become the most transformative of all.[19]

More dramatic and more immediate in its effects was the arrival of gunpowder. Fireworks had been known in China for centuries; it was probably under the Yuan Dynasty which began in 1279 (that is, the period of Mongol rule) that the explosive potential of gunpowder was first harnessed in China to make a weapon. The first cannon in Europe seems to have been fired in the year 1326 – five years after the death of Dante. Europeans may not have been the inventors of firearms; but they certainly exploited to the full the technological know-how that had come to them from the east.[20]

Far deadlier even than the new killing power of artillery was a different sort of arrival by the same route. Where people and goods were on the move, animals, parasites, and the bacteria and the viruses they carried moved with them. The plague known to history by the later name of the Black Death may have started out in the Tien Shan mountain range of central Asia; it probably reached Europe aboard ships transporting grain from ports on the northern shore of the Black Sea.[21] Between 1347 and 1351 the first wave of the pandemic swept all the way to the British Isles in one direction and the Iberian peninsula in the other. Over the next century successive waves would bring more deaths to every part of the continent; smaller, more local outbreaks would continue until almost the end of the eighteenth century.

In Florence, where the plague raged from March until July 1348, an unexpected consequence was the invention of the literary genre we now know as the short story. The *Decameron*, by Giovanni Boccaccio, purports to be a record of the yarns that seven young Florentine noble ladies and three young men told to each other to while away the time during a period of shared isolation in a country retreat. In his introduction to the work, written very shortly afterwards, Boccaccio vividly describes what it had been like to live in the city while the plague had been at its height.

Its symptoms included 'certain swellings in the groin or the armpit, some of which were egg-shaped whilst others were roughly the size of a common apple'. Then as the pandemic progressed, 'many people began to find dark blotches and bruises on their arms, thighs and other parts of the body'. Nobody knew the cause, and of course there was no remedy. 'At all events,' Boccaccio concluded, 'few of those who caught it ever recovered, and in most cases death occurred within a few days' after the appearance of the first symptoms. Even more shocking was the contagiousness of the disease, which Boccaccio compared to 'a fire racing through dry or oily substances'. Even to touch an article of clothing that had been worn by someone infected would bring death to people and animals alike. When the city's graveyards were full, 'huge trenches were excavated in the churchyards, into which new arrivals were placed in their hundreds, stowed tier upon tier like ships' cargo'.[22]

Up to half the entire population of Europe may have died of bubonic plague during the fourteenth century, in some communities perhaps even more. According to one estimate, out of a possible 80 million Europeans alive in 1346, 25 million may have died in the four years of the first wave. Looking back from the perspective of today, the arrival of the Black Death has often been taken to mark the end of the Middle Ages in Europe. If it is true that in the years after 1300 there had been 'too many people for the technology of the time to handle', then nature's deadly remedy had raced along the silk roads far faster than the technological changes that would eventually support many more.[23]

All the more surprising, therefore, that it was in the hundred and fifty years after the first visitation of the Black Death that a depleted European population began to break the bounds of its own continent in a manner and on a scale that had never been imaginable before.

. . . *To Sea Lanes*

In 1352 the Black Death was at last receding from Europe. In Constantinople, rivals for the little that was left of the former Byzantine Empire were at each other's throats. It was an empire in name only; ever since the city had been recaptured from the successors to the crusaders, almost a hundred years before, Constantinople had been little more than the capital of a city state, not much bigger and a good deal less powerful than several in Italy. Its emperor, John VI Cantacuzene, was locked in a deadly civil war against his predecessor – and, as things would turn out, his successor too – John V Palaeologus.

Both sides had routinely, for some time, been recruiting Muslim Turks as mercenaries from the Asian side of the straits to fight against each other in Europe. Orhan, the son of Osman, emir of Bithynia on the southern shore of the Sea of Marmara, enjoyed particularly good relations with Cantacuzene; following a long-established Byzantine custom, these had been sealed by marriage to the emperor's daughter – though with the telling difference that, now, there was no expectation that the bridegroom would abandon his religion and become Christian. No one alive at the time could have been expected to foresee this, of course – but Osman, who had died back in 1326, would later give his name to the dynasty and empire known as the Ottomans, or Osmanli, that would last until 1923.

So far, each time a Turkish force had fought on European soil, the mercenaries had taken their pay at the end of the campaign and gone back home. But in 1352, Orhan's son, Suleiman, instead dug in with his troops on the Gallipoli peninsula, on the European side of the Dardanelles, and refused to leave. When an earthquake devastated the region two years later, Suleiman took advantage of the situation to bring over 'a great crowd of Osmanlis with their wives and children to take possession of the deserted towns and villages'. Ottoman Turkish colonization of south-eastern Europe had begun.[24]

During the next decades Ottoman armies, no longer mercenary forces in the pay of Christians but fighting under the banner of Islam, conquered most of the southern Balkans up to the Danube. By the end of the fourteenth century the Ottoman capital had been moved across the straits to Adrianople (today's Edirne in the European province of Turkey); their latest ruler, Bayezid, had promoted himself to the rank of sultan. Constantinople, cut off from the rest of Christian Europe, was placed under siege in 1394; it would be accidentally reprieved eight years later only thanks to a new intervention by the Mongols in Anatolia.[25] Just over a century had passed since the last of the crusader outposts in the east, the port of Acre (today the Israeli town of Akka), had fallen in 1291. Now the momentum of the Crusades was being put into reverse. It was Europe's turn to be on the receiving end of a holy war. The prevailing momentum, millennia old, from east to west was making itself felt once again.

And despite last-ditch attempts to ride to the rescue of Constantinople during the first half of the fifteenth century, it was westward that Europeans, too, found themselves increasingly looking. The slow process of reconquering the Iberian peninsula was almost complete: only the Muslim kingdom of Granada, in the south, still held out against the Christian kingdoms of Castile and Aragon that were already beginning to lay the foundations for modern Spain. As the century wore on, the Muslims of Granada would find themselves under exactly the same pressures as the Christians of the Balkans had experienced a few decades earlier. But while an Ottoman sultan might relish the prospect of a whole continent before him, ripe for conquest (much as Xerxes is alleged to have done some two thousand years before), you couldn't go far beyond Granada without ending up in the sea. Hard-pressed from the east, where else did Europeans have to go?

Up to this time, the Atlantic Ocean had proved an impassable barrier. Only the Vikings, with their short-lived settlements in Greenland and Nova Scotia, had crossed it and returned to tell the tale. They had also populated Iceland, but their descendants were still there and making it a going concern; for anyone else, a land of volcanoes and tundra on the edge of the Arctic Circle offered limited prospects anyway. Since the days of the Vikings, increased trade throughout the continent had brought advances in shipbuilding and techniques of navigation; long-distance trading routes were now flourishing along the whole length of the Atlantic seaboard, from the British Isles and the North Sea all the way round to the Mediterranean. It was becoming possible to cover longer distances by sea than ever before.

The first Europeans to reach the Canary Islands, off the northwest coast of Africa, had landed in 1341. (It may have been reports of an early, distant sighting of the volcanic peak of Teide on Tenerife, 15,000 feet high, that had inspired Dante to his imaginative construction of Purgatory, some three decades earlier.) But Atlantic voyages really took off in a big way in the next century, during the very years when the Ottomans were pushing forward into the other end of southern Europe and consolidating their hold. Under the direction and personal sponsorship of the younger son of the king of Portugal, known to history as Henry the Navigator, the uninhabited islands of Madeira and the Azores were claimed and colonized between the 1420s and the 1440s; the Cape Verde islands, off the African coast, in 1456. Before long, Portuguese ships would be sailing all the way down the Atlantic coast of Africa and round the Cape of Good Hope to enter the Indian Ocean from the south.[26]

Constantinople finally fell to the forces of the twenty-one-year-old Ottoman sultan, Mehmed II, on Tuesday, 29 May 1453. This once-great imperial city of Christendom had been a mere outpost of Christian Europe for some time. But the news of its loss sent shockwaves reverberating around the continent. 'The Catholic faith is wretchedly wounded, our religion shamefully confounded, and the name of Christ damned and greatly oppressed,' declared the diplomat, man of letters and future pope Enea Silvio Bartolomeo Piccolomini, in an address to an assembly of notables and churchmen in Frankfurt-am-Main a few months later. It was one thing for Christians to be vanquished in Asia and in Africa, the speaker went on – an allusion to the failure of the Crusades in the Levant and Egypt; but 'now truly we have been stricken and felled in Europe, that is to say in our own fatherland, in our own house, in our seat'.[27]

The loss of Constantinople had jolted into existence a whole new way of thinking about Europe: once again as a 'fatherland' (*patria*), as in the time of Charlemagne – but this time one in retreat, under pressure, in desperate need to rally and defend itself. Shortly before he became Pope Pius II in 1458, Piccolomini developed his theme to the length of a whole book. *De Europa (On Europe)* was followed by *De Asia (On Asia)* three years later. The clash of continents, which had first been dreamt up by Herodotus, sprang back into life in these learned disquisitions on geography and recent history. And for the first time, in the opening chapter of *De Europa*, the Latin word *europaei*, soon to become standard, and adapted into many other languages, appears as the name for its people.

As pope, Piccolomini did his best to rouse his fellow Europeans for a new crusade to recapture Constantinople. But the impetus for further adventures in the east was long gone. By this time Europeans were already launched upon the oceans of the world. The tide of history was flowing westwards. In its path lay the last Muslim kingdom in the Iberian peninsula. Barely four decades after the fall of Constantinople, Mohammed XII, the last sultan of Granada, surrendered the city's palace-fortress, the Alhambra, to King Ferdinand of Aragon on 2 January 1492.

Four months after that, the Catholic Monarchs, as Ferdinand and his queen, Isabella of Castile, were now known, agreed the terms of a contract with an Italian sea captain from Genoa who had been pestering them for years with a pet project. This was to sail westwards across the Atlantic and reach 'the Indies' by a route that had never before been tried. Described by contemporaries as 'an imposing, charismatic figure, tall and ruddy', Christopher Columbus left mainland Spain with three small ships on 3 August 1492, to make the first ever European landfall, so far as is known, in the Caribbean two months later.[28]

This rapid sequence of events was more than a coincidence. Columbus himself spelt out the connections in the account of his first voyage that he addressed to his patrons shortly afterwards. It begins with the glad sight of 'your Highnesses' banners victoriously raised on the towers of the Alhambra', when Columbus claims to have been present at the siege of Granada some months before. It continues, 'Therefore having expelled all the Jews from your dominions in that same month of January [Columbus's memory was faulty here: it was actually March], your Highnesses commanded me to go with an adequate fleet to . . . India.' The purpose of the voyage, according to Columbus, was to convert the inhabitants of east Asia to Christianity, on behalf of 'your Highnesses as Catholic princes and devoted propagators of the holy Christian faith [who] have always been enemies of the sect of Mahomet and of all idolatries and heresies'.[29]

The obsession with 'idolatries and heresies' had been growing in Catholic Europe since at least the time of Pope Innocent III. It was fuelled by fear of Islam. And fear of Islam, in turn, had never been greater, now that the Ottomans had advanced so far into Europe. Before long, the remaining Muslims in the Iberian peninsula would be subjected to the same treatment as the Jews: forced either to convert or to abandon their homes for ever. For more than a century to come, the activities of the Spanish Inquisition would be directed mainly towards the descendants of converts from Islam or Judaism. Thousands who were suspected of lapsing back into their old or their ancestral faith would be arrested, interrogated under torture, and in extreme cases burnt to death in the publicly staged execution known in medieval Portuguese as *auto da fé*, or 'act of faith'.

Columbus seems additionally to have proposed to the monarchs, in all seriousness, that the riches he would bring back from the Indies would enable them to complete the long-abandoned work of the Crusades and reconquer Jerusalem after all. Alternatively, if he was successful in circumnavigating the globe, he might even be able to stop off in the Holy Land on his way back; by taking the Muslims by surprise, in the rear, the goal of the Crusades might yet be achieved.[30] It so happened that King Ferdinand, along with his other titles, was nominally heir to the defunct crusader Kingdom of Jerusalem. Ancient prophecies about the end of the world, and the 'last world emperor' laying down his crown at the Holy Sepulchre there, were once again in vogue. In some circles, at least, the atmosphere was more highly charged still, because the year 1492 was reckoned to mark the end of the seventh millennium since the Creation: perhaps it was the destined role of King Ferdinand of Aragon to fulfil these prophecies and usher in the Second Coming of Christ?[31]

All this goes to show that the thinking and the intentions that led to the first – and in the event permanent – presence of Europeans in the Americas were very much a product of the age. They were also thoroughly muddled. Columbus himself, by the time he had completed his fourth voyage to the Caribbean in 1504, was at once convinced that he had discovered the 'earthly Paradise' and that its inhabitants, as non-Christians, could most usefully be sent back to Spain as slaves. His contract in 1492 had given him permission to take possession of the lands he would discover in the name of his sovereigns; and indeed whenever he reported back, after each of his voyages, he would proudly enumerate the conquests he had made.

But Columbus also believed, and had persuaded his patrons, that he was heading for the lands of the 'Great Khan' of the east; surely this ruler would not take kindly to having his territory annexed by Christian monarchs he had never heard of? To be on the safe side, the expedition had been furnished with diplomatic letters from Ferdinand and Isabella addressed to the 'princes' of those parts, to be delivered as its leader saw fit. And then there was the quest for gold, which had piqued the ambitions of Henry the Navigator and many others. Columbus found rather little of it (that would be left to others, after him), but he still did all he could to talk up the riches of the lands he had reached.[32]

Trade, plunder, conquest, religious conversion, the triumph of Christianity over Islam, or even the final dissolution of the world – any or all of these were in prospect as Columbus set out. Had it not been for Columbus, presumably someone else would sooner or later have crossed the Atlantic – now that the technology and navigational know-how had made such voyages possible. It would not be long before another Italian, known in English as John Cabot, set out from Bristol in 1497, to land in either Maine or Newfoundland, and from Portugal Pedro Álvares Cabral reached Brazil in 1500.

But Columbus was the first. And something of his own individuality would therefore be stamped, ever afterwards, on Europe's relationship with the new world that he had brought within the horizons of Europeans. To his dying day, Columbus refused to accept that the islands he had reached lay close to a previously unknown continent. His conviction that the people he encountered there were Indians led to the island group being known ever afterwards as the West Indies; long after he had been proved wrong, the native inhabitants of the Americas would more often than not be known as 'Indians' in all the languages of Europe. Columbus's entire project was based on a false premise: going against the best scientific opinion of the time (which was close to being correct), he had seriously underestimated the circumference of the earth. Had Columbus known the truth, would he have set out? Would his backers have backed him?

In any event, within thirty years after 1492, the Atlantic was being criss-crossed by ships setting out from almost every part of Europe's western seaboard. Rivalry between the united Spanish kingdoms of Castile and Aragon on the one hand and the kingdom of Portugal on the other resulted in a remarkably precocious ruling by Pope Alexander VI. Only a few months after Columbus had returned to Spain to give an account of his first voyage, the pope responded to appeals from both sides by drawing an imaginary line from pole to pole that ran more or less down the middle of the Atlantic. That was in June 1493. To the west of that line, any newly discovered lands could be claimed by the Catholic Monarchs; to the east, by the Portuguese.

A year later a formal treaty was drawn up between the competing parties in the Spanish town of Tordesillas, overlooking the River Duero that had once marked the frontier between Christendom and Islam. This time the line down the Atlantic was moved further west – paving the way, although nobody could know this then, for the Portuguese claim to Brazil in the sixteenth century (which is why Brazil is the only state in South America today that has Portuguese rather than Spanish as its majority language). Once again Pope Alexander gave his blessing to the agreement – in this way seemingly claiming papal supremacy over the entire world.[33]

But if the pope thought new voyages and new conquests were simply a matter for the kingdoms of the Iberian peninsula, he would soon be proved wrong. 'I should be very happy,' Francis I of France is said to have exclaimed shortly afterwards, 'to see the clause in Adam's will that excluded *me* from my share when the world was being divided.'[34] And it wasn't just the French. Semi-licensed pirates, known as privateers, from England as well as France began to prey on Spanish ships on the high seas. It would not be long, either, before the Dutch would join in, eventually to claim possessions in the Caribbean, while English, French, Dutch and Spanish colonists would all fight for their share of the North American continent until the late eighteenth century.

In the half-century after Columbus's first voyage, driven by similarly mixed and often muddled motives, the *conquistadores* Hernán Cortés and Francisco Pizarro overwhelmed the great empires of Central and South America: respectively of the Mexica, or Aztecs, in the 1520s and the Inca in the 1530s. Quite how they did it has been much discussed ever since. Technology certainly helped – including the ships and navigational instruments that could get them there, the steel armour, guns and horses that had all been unknown until that time in the Americas. Astutely exploiting these advantages, as well as internal divisions among the native populations, tiny

Spanish forces succeeded in subduing swathes of territory that by 1580 would be almost as large as the whole of Europe itself. Sheer luck played a part too. By that year, a world empire ruled by a European dynasty reached from California and Chile in the west, via a string of Portuguese coastal possessions in Africa and India, to the East Indies and the Philippines so as, in the words of William Shakespeare, writing in the next decade, 'to put a girdle round about the earth'.[35] For better or for worse, and certainly irreversibly, Europe had 'gone global'.

And it was *Europe* that had done this – not Spain, or Portugal, or France, or England, or the Netherlands; not Italian, Spanish or Portuguese sailors and navigators; not German or Italian bankers. All these, and more, played their parts; none had a monopoly. No people from another continent has ever attempted anything comparable in historical times (the Chinese, famously, had the technology and might have done so, but chose not to).[36] Not since our species, *Homo sapiens*, first began to spread out across every other continent from Africa, some 60,000 years ago, has any single movement of peoples had such far-reaching consequences for the entire world – consequences that the entire world is still coming to terms with today, more than half a millennium after Columbus sailed westward to reach the Indies.

Discovery at Home

Even before these explosive encounters with previously unknown peoples on other continents, Europeans had been embarking on a different kind of voyage of discovery closer to home: the discovery of *themselves*. The intellectual and artistic movement known as the Renaissance (literally: 'rebirth') is usually traced back to the Italian poet, scholar and papal courtier Francesco Petrarca, better known in English as Petrarch. Born during the lifetime of Dante, Petrarch had lived through the first wave of the Black Death. He is credited with having been one of the first Europeans of his age to begin systematically to seek the roots of their own civilization in the pre-Christian, classical past.

The word that we use today, 'civilization', had not yet been coined, so Petrarch and his successors fell back on the term that the ancient Romans had used to sum up their way of life: *humanitas*. This is why Petrarch and those who followed in his footsteps came to be known as 'humanists'. What is often called the 'humanism' of the Renaissance had nothing to do with the secularism of a later age. Indeed, most of the artistic achievements that we still most readily associate with it were religious in purpose (think of the domed cathedral of Florence, Michelangelo painting the walls and ceiling of the Sistine Chapel in Rome, the sixteenth-century epic poems of Ludovico Ariosto and Torquato Tasso celebrating historic battles between Christianity and Islam). Being a 'humanist' was no bar to the highest religious offices. Even popes could count as humanists – among them Pius II with his learned treatises on Europe and Asia.[37]

Petrarch and those who came after him sought out manuscripts that had lain forgotten for centuries in monastery libraries. They could make their discoveries without travelling great distances or facing physical dangers. Especially in Italy, where the visible remains of Roman civilization lay all around them, they had only to see what was in front of their eyes. Humanists could afford to be armchair explorers, or at least to limit their exertions to touring from one monastic library to another. And sometimes what they were looking for came to *them*. During the last years of the tottering Byzantine Empire, while Constantinople was surrounded by the Turks, and then in the aftermath of its fall, scholars fleeing westwards brought with them manuscripts written in ancient Greek and, no less valuable, their intimate knowledge of that language.

As the cultures of the eastern and western halves of Christendom had drifted apart during the Middle Ages, knowledge of Greek had disappeared from the west. Petrarch, late in his life, was proud to possess a manuscript of Homer's *Iliad*, but when he died in 1374 he had not been able to learn enough Greek to read it. A century later, courses in ancient Greek were being taught in universities all over Italy; a century after that, in all of Europe. As elite Europeans rediscovered the ancient Greek maxim, *know thyself*, they also learned to trace the roots of their *humanitas* all the way back to its distant origin in the world of the classical Greek city states.

Questions about good government, and especially how to regulate the affairs of small states frequently warring among themselves, were as relevant in fifteenth-century Italy as they had been among the city states of Greece two thousand years before. And it wasn't just philosophers who addressed these issues: two of the most influential books of political theory written in the early sixteenth century, *The Prince* by Niccolò Machiavelli and *Utopia* by Thomas More, were the work of political actors capable of operating at the highest level in their respective realms, the Florentine republic and the kingdom of England. Their learning and their *humanitas* might not have been enough to save their careers (the one lost his job, the other his head); but the questions they were asking had not been aired in public for a thousand years. And they have continued to be debated ever since.

This turn towards the classical past left its mark on just about every aspect of activity among Europe's elites – beginning in Italy, and from about 1500 fanning out across the continent. Architects began to design churches and other grand buildings using mathematical proportions and styles learned from the handbook of architecture by Vitruvius that had been prepared for the first Roman emperor, Augustus. Lifelike representations of human figures carved out of stone or cast in bronze once again began to people urban spaces. Carried over into painting, the same principle led to the beginning of individual portraiture. The mathematical exploration of perspective led to a whole new realism in two-dimensional representation. In paintings such as the *Arnolfini Portrait*, of 1434, by Jan van Eyck, Europeans literally begin to confront their own selves reflected in a mirror.[38] In literature, alongside the romances of the Middle Ages, ancient literary genres leapt back into life – none more spectacularly than drama, whose rediscovery, along with the revival of the theatre as a form of entertainment, would give us the works of Marlowe and Shakespeare in England, Racine, Corneille and Molière in France, Lope de Vega and Calderón de la Barca in Spain, Goldoni in Venice, Georgios Chortatsis in Venetian-ruled Crete, and many others.

Humanitas in the fifteenth and sixteenth centuries went far beyond the fields that we nowadays designate as Humanities. Modern medical science began with the rediscovery of the works of Galen, the physician and philosopher who had written in Greek in the second century CE. In the physical sciences and astronomy, the more advanced technology of the age enabled pioneers such as Galileo in Italy and Copernicus in Poland to propose new answers to questions that had first been articulated by the ancient Greeks.

All of this, we now know, was made possible by one thing that the Middle Ages had largely had to do without. That was money. The flow of raw materials and manufactured goods around Europe had been increasing at an ever faster rate for several centuries. As the continent recovered from the effects of the Black Death, and as the population once again began to increase during the sixteenth century, trade in precious commodities brought opportunities for profit, plunder, or both together, on a scale that had never been conceivable before. Modern systems of commerce and banking effectively began at this time. From the 1520s onwards, silver from South America would become the basis for a booming cash economy throughout Europe.[39]

And it wasn't just goods and people that were on the move. Fastest moving of all in the new Europe that was emerging around 1500 were *ideas*. What made this possible was a new invention that revolutionized the way books were produced and circulated – and in the process fuelled the rapid growth of literacy among the European population.

The technology of printing had evolved centuries before in China. The Chinese technique had been to carve a whole page from a single block of wood, that could then be impressed upon paper any number of times; it seems to have been a goldsmith by the name of Johannes Gutenberg, in the German city of Mainz, around the year 1450, who hit upon the idea of using metal to cast the reverse shape of each individual letter of the Roman alphabet. Known as movable type, this innovation crucially built upon the much older technology represented by the Greek and Roman alphabets; the result would be to create the most efficient means of preserving and reproducing human language ever devised before the digital age. And once the first presses had been set up, this invention, too, in digital terms, 'went viral' throughout Europe. By 1520 more than 250 printing houses were operating, almost all of them in cities, from Oxford to Rome, from Lisbon to Kraków. Before long, the spread of what social historians call 'print culture' would become a defining characteristic of Europe itself.[40]

But above all, to be European, by the turn of the sixteenth century, still meant to be a Catholic Christian. Even as it continued to succumb to Ottoman advances in the Balkans and the Mediterranean, Catholic Europe had by this time reached its largest extent. Back in 1386, the last of the large-scale, top-down conversions of a pagan people had brought the dukedom of Lithuania into the orbit of western Christendom, in a union with the kingdom of Poland, later to become known as the Polish-Lithuanian Commonwealth. From the Arctic Ocean to the Mediterranean, from the Atlantic coasts of Ireland and Portugal to (more or less) the Dnipro river in today's Belarus and Ukraine, the Christian sacraments were celebrated in the same way; the same words of the Nicene Creed were spoken; with the exception of precariously tolerated groups, notably Jews, everyone professed the same beliefs in public and in private. Canon law, as amplified and reinforced by the Fourth Lateran Council back in 1215, was at least in theory applicable everywhere.

Politically, on the other hand, Catholic Europe has been described as a 'kaleidoscope', rather as the ancient Greek city states had once been, only on a much larger scale. Some 500 separate jurisdictions existed, of every conceivable size from the sprawling Holy Roman Empire to the most modest principality or self-governing city. Systems of government varied in their details; some of the smaller states were even republics. But most were ruled by monarchs. And thanks to a gradual innovation that had been taking place over the centuries, kings and princes (occasionally, these days, even queens) were almost always supported by representative assemblies drawn from the wealthy and powerful among their subjects; to a greater or lesser extent, the sovereign would, in turn, be answerable to them. In most parts of Europe, some sort of rudimentary parliamentary system existed below the monarch; royal power was therefore not quite absolute. Armies were no longer levied from the local warlords who had once formed the medieval aristocracy; in the new cash economy they were more often made up of mercenaries, who could be hired from anywhere.[41]

This was the Europe in which the heir to the ramified titles and fortunes of the Habsburg dynasty was elected as Holy Roman Emperor on 28 June 1519, with the title of Charles V – and set himself the task of pulling it all together.

The Last of the Caesars

Charles had been born in 1500 in the Flemish city of Ghent, at that time part of the Burgundian Netherlands. By the age of nine he was already heir to four separate kingdoms and dozens of smaller fiefdoms (including the title to his native Burgundy, much of which had recently been absorbed by France). In 1516, when Ferdinand of Aragon died, Charles had become in effect the first king of a united Spain. His grandfather, Maximilian, was already Holy Roman Emperor. Since Charles's father had died young, it was Charles whose election to the top post Maximilian exerted himself to promote during his last years. When that finally happened, it was thanks to blatant bribery and in the face of determined competition from the two most powerful rival dynasties in Europe: the Valois king of France and the Tudor Henry VIII of England. Once elected, Charles ruled over a motley collection of states reaching from the Iberian peninsula to the Balkans, from the Mediterranean to the North Sea and the Baltic. It has been estimated that approximately 40 per cent of the population of Catholic Europe were his subjects.[42]

The accident of birth that brought all these territories under the control of one man was not entirely accidental: Charles's Habsburg forebears had been playing the dynastic game of thrones with skill and determination for several generations; they had ended up also lucky in the outcome. Charles's first language was French; of necessity he would learn to function in Dutch, Spanish, Italian and German; towards the end of his life he would even master Latin, which was still, as he himself acknowledged, the 'universal' language.[43] Lacking a true mother tongue (his mother Juana of Castile was Spanish, but played no part in his upbringing after the age of four) and without a local patrimony of his own (since the Duchy of Burgundy no longer existed), Charles seems always to have thought on a European scale. His goals throughout his adult life, so far as we can tell, were to unite Christian Europe and to defend it against the newest threat from Islam in the form of the Ottoman Turks. To achieve those goals he determined to stamp out heresy at home, and to embody and uphold an ideal of honour embedded in centuries of chivalric romances, going back to the time of the Crusades.

His prospects and his achievements were magnified in words, paint and print throughout his reign. Courtiers compared him to Alexander the Great, to the Roman emperor Augustus and to his namesake Charlemagne. His Grand Chancellor and right-hand man for many years, Mercurino Arborio di Gattinara, even saw him as the embodiment of Dante's ideal of universal monarchy. Routinely, Charles would be addressed by the ancient Roman imperial title, *Caesar*. Among many famous paintings, one by Titian shows him in full armour, mounted, and carrying a lance longer than his horse, in the aftermath of a victory in 1547; another, probably commissioned by his banker, shows him seated, in the dark velvet robes of a civilian and respected capitalist. Charles V, with his jutting, drooping lower jaw (the result of inbreeding) and craggy expression of wary bellicosity, would dominate Europe in word and image throughout his thirty-seven-year reign as emperor.[44]

And thanks to the new medium of print, and a related craze for map-making in the sixteenth century, Europe itself acquired a new image to match. In 1537 an Austrian draughtsman devised a map in which Europe was personified 'in the shape of a virgin'. By turning the page so that west is at the top, Johannes Putsch (Latinized as Johannes Bucius Aenicola) ingeniously represented the Iberian peninsula ('Hispania') as the face and head that wears Charles's own imperial crown. Italy forms the strong right arm, clasping in its hand the 'orb and cross', the traditional insignia of the papacy; central and eastern Europe make up the body and skirts. The British Isles are tacked on as a pennant tied to the sceptre held in Europe's left hand, and much reduced in scale. Versions of this image were included in one of the most widely read geography books of the century in its later editions. Now retitled *Europa Regina* (Queen Europe), this anthropomorphized continent was, it seemed, made for its emperor, Charles V, and vice versa.[45]

But despite all the hype and the enthusiasm in many quarters, imperial monarchy would turn out to be an anachronism in the sixteenth century. Nobody knows quite why it happened, but Europe simply would no longer consent to be governed in this way.

At one end of the social scale, resistance came from rival monarchs. Their own dynasties had long been engaged in exactly the same game of one-upmanship as the Habsburgs and feared they were now about to lose out. Charles V fought more battles against Christian kings and princes than he ever did against the Turks. In the course of more than twenty years of on-and-off war between the emperor and King Francis I of France, a mercenary army loyal to Charles set its sights on Rome in May 1527. When the leader was killed in the first assault, there was no one to restrain the troops; once they had broken into the city, they ran amok for ten days. Somewhere between 8,000 and 10,000 Romans were slaughtered – far more than during the sack by Alaric the Goth or by the Vandals, a little over a thousand years before. According to one eyewitness, 'the extent of the destruction means that Rome will not be Rome again in our lifetimes, or in 200 years'.[46]

Although it had no more been intended than the sack of that other former capital of the Roman Empire, Constantinople, back in 1204, this one would represent another nail in the coffin of any idea of building a new Europe on the foundations of the empire of old. Nostalgia for an always elusive 'universal monarchy' in Europe was giving way to a new obsession that would dominate the politics and the wars of the continent for at least the next two hundred years, perhaps even until today: the idea of a 'balance of power' among competing states.[47]

Further down the social scale, the nature of those states was beginning to change too. For centuries, monarchs had ruled over territories whose boundaries were determined by gains and losses on the battlefield and by marriage alliances among power-ful families – precisely those things that had concentrated so much power in the hands of Charles, even before his election as emperor. In these 'dynastic states', as historians often call them today, any sense of shared identity among the people who happened to live there was incidental, if it existed at all.[48]

But now a consciousness was beginning to develop, among elites in several different parts of Europe, that the inhabitants of a par-ticular region, or the speakers of a common set of local dialects (such as German, Italian, French or Spanish), possessed character-istics, and therefore also rights, that belonged to them alone. In an indicative sign of the change that was coming, at the end of the fifteenth century, the Electors and the Diet (an assembly of high-ranking nobles and churchmen) had begun referring to the 'Holy Roman Empire *of the German Nation*'.[49] This was rather less than a formal title; and 'nation' in those days was a much vaguer and less resonant term than it would later become. But it did mean that all three candidates for election in 1519 had been expected to demon-strate how *German* they were.

Charles's male ancestors had come originally from a German-speaking area of what is now Switzerland; Habsburgs had been ruling German-speaking Austria for some time before this. But when his backers wrote that their candidate was 'German by blood and disposition, by birth and tongue' and 'a German born and educated, who is also able and adept at speaking and writing in the German language', they revealed nothing true about Charles, but a great deal about how the new criterion for election had come to be understood. To ram home the point, when the seven Electors had taken their bribes and swallowed their misgivings, they presented Charles's representatives with a document to be signed before he could take up office. The 'Election Capitulation', as the document became known, committed the emperor-elect to employ only Germans in the imperial service, to make his settled home in (an undefined) Germany, and not to bring with him any 'foreign' troops from his other dominions.[50]

This new way of thinking wasn't confined to German-speaking Europe. Already before this, as king of Castile and Aragon, Charles had been subjected to very similar pressures from the *Spanish* aristocracy. While he had been away making his peace with the German Electors, violent revolts broke out in several parts of Spain. The movement of the *comuneros* was quickly put down without his intervention. But the idea that a monarch ought to be answerable to his subjects, visible in the places where they lived, and able to speak to them in their own language, was gaining ground.

Of all the challenges to Charles's authority the most consequential came not from kings or princes, nor from rich and influential subjects, but from a thirty-four-year-old monk with a troubled conscience and a part-time teaching role at the local university in the Saxon town of Wittenberg. Martin Luther's target was not the emperor or the empire. The subject of the intemperate letter that Luther sent to his archbishop in 1517 was the rather abstruse one of the sale of indulgences. It all stemmed, originally, from the 'remission of sins', which had once been promised to those who went on Crusade, and had been formalized into the doctrine of Purgatory by the Fourth Lateran Council. What had begun as an appeal to the 'knightly' values of noble self-sacrifice had degenerated over time into a simple financial transaction – not unlike the insurance business of more recent times.

An indulgence was a piece of paper that granted the bearer, or a departed loved one who might be assumed to be already in Purgatory, some remission in the afterlife from punishment for the sins they had committed while alive. By the second decade of the sixteenth century, as printing expanded all over Europe, indulgences were rolling off the presses and selling on an industrial scale; indeed this was one of the means by which successive popes aimed to recoup the cost of rebuilding the Basilica of St Peter's in Rome, which was then being planned.

Luther's objections were theological as well as the obvious ethical ones. The 'Ninety-five theses', written in Latin, in which he laid them out were probably not actually nailed to a church door in Wittenberg, as later legend would have it.[51] But the backlash in ecclesiastical circles lit the fuse of Luther's famously fiery temper; escalation followed. Three years later, in 1520, under threat of excommunication, which duly came in June that year, Luther took to the sixteenth-century equivalent of the airwaves. The same printing presses that were running off certificates of indulgence by the thousand were now mobilized to disseminate a devastating series of critiques, not just of the papal money-spinner but of the very institution of the papacy itself. Luther would prove a prolific polemicist; unlike his 'Ninety-five theses', his books and pamphlets were written in German for everyone to read – or to be read aloud for the benefit of those who could not. And suddenly everybody *was* reading them and talking about them.

In April 1521 escalation went all the way to the top; Luther was called to give an account of himself before the emperor at that year's meeting of the Diet in the German city of Worms. Unsurprisingly, Charles insisted on the integrity of his role as 'Defender of the Faith'; to permit heresy 'or a diminution of the Christian religion to rest in the hearts of men through our own negligence would bring permanent dishonour on us and our successors', he is recorded as saying. To which Luther did not, in fact, reply, 'Here I stand; I can do no other.' But the gauntlet had been thrown down; there was no going back.[52]

Here the story might have ended. A century earlier, the Bohemian preacher Jan Hus had been burnt at the stake in the southern German city of Konstanz for less offence than Luther had caused. In England, another critic of papal authority, John Wycliffe, had died in his bed before anyone could convict him, but his remains had been dug up, posthumously excommunicated and incinerated. Luther can have been under no illusions about the risks he ran. What was different this time? Almost certainly without intending to, Luther had tapped into an overlapping series of discontents. Several of those were specifically German ones: there were issues about taxation; there was resentment at Charles's reliance on advisers and officials from southern Europe, who spoke a different language and perhaps *thought* differently too; there was distrust of an emperor who, now that they had met him, the nobles could see for themselves was a lot less German than they had been led to expect.

One of the Electors had been Frederick, Duke of Saxony; and Martin Luther was his subject. After the Diet was over, Frederick arranged for Luther to be whisked away to the safety of his castle known as the Wartburg until the dust had settled. Frederick seems to have been unmoved by Luther's theology; what was at stake for the Elector was rather his own *political* authority on his home ground.[53] And so Frederick became a staunch defender of a declared heretic – something that would have been scarcely imaginable a century earlier. Other princes and nobles were sympathetic, too, from a variety of motives. Once Luther had survived his condemnation at Worms, and was soon free again to preach and to publish, it was too late to put the genie back in its bottle.

What we now call the Reformation had begun.

And the forces unleashed soon proved impossible to control – least of all by Luther himself. In 1524, again spread far and wide by the medium of print, a raft of demands by the German peasantry included the right for communities to elect their own priests – in effect to break with Rome and the empire, as Luther had demanded.

The 'Peasants' War' lasted for a year and spread beyond the borders of the empire to convulse Poland, Hungary and the newly independent Swiss cantons. It has been called 'Europe's greatest rebellion' before the French Revolution of 1789. Of some 300,000 who took up arms, at least a quarter lost their lives. The revolt was suppressed in the end, and disowned by Luther. But it would prove a harbinger of things to come.[54]

After a staged protest at another Diet, this time in 1529, the reformers came to be known as 'Protestants'. On the face of it, what was at stake was the salvation of immortal souls. But the Reformation, as well as the Catholic fight-back that would become known as the Counter-Reformation, was just as much about where people felt that they belonged in *this* world, and who had the right to tell them how to live their lives. As European Christendom began to break apart, between the 1520s and the 1550s, Europeans were starting to define themselves more precisely in terms of where they lived, the language they spoke, the taxes they paid and to whom, and how they managed their affairs at a local or regional level.

Charles V won very many of his battles, some spectacularly: over the French at Pavia in 1525, against the Ottomans in North Africa ten years later, against an alliance of German Lutheran princes in 1547. But in the long run he lost each of his wars. By the mid-1550s, the Ottoman advance into eastern Europe and the Mediterranean had been slowed but not halted. Regional monarchies, following the example of Francis I, had seized the initiative and were showing the way: when Henry VIII repudiated the authority of the pope and declared himself head of the English Church, he was not so much breaking with Europe as jumping on a bandwagon that was already rolling across the continent. The Peace of Augsburg, an uneasy compromise brokered in 1555, in effect conceded that the Reformation could neither be reversed nor completed: its terms allowed rulers to impose their own preferred version of the Christian faith within their borders.

It may have been in recognition of all this that Charles announced his decision to abdicate. He surrendered the last of his offices in July 1556, in Brussels, before leaving for retirement in Spain; he died there two years later. The last of the Caesars, it has been said, had ruled over an 'impossible empire'. No one could seriously be expected to keep it going in future; and so, among the settlements that ended his reign, was the formal division of his realms. Charles's brother Ferdinand inherited central and eastern Europe and would in due course be elected Holy Roman Emperor; his son would succeed him in Spain and the Netherlands as King Philip II.[55]

Seen in retrospect, the reign of Charles V represented the last chance for Europe to build on the remarkable religious and cultural unity of Catholic Christendom and create a unified political system to match. As late as the 1530s, it has been argued, something of the sort might still have been possible.[56] Instead, the 'holy European union' of the later Middle Ages, which had been cemented in place by Pope Innocent III three centuries before, peeled apart during those years. But could *anyone* have succeeded where Charles failed? Each of the formidable forces ranged against him was perhaps a symptom of a larger cause. Could it be that the sudden opening up of new worlds, both abroad and (thanks to the Renaissance) within, had irrevocably destabilized the ordered universe that had been so memorably evoked by Dante? Ideas of an earthly kingdom that perfectly mirrored the heavenly one above, or an imagined 'City of God', which went back to the earliest years of the Christian Roman Empire, began to falter before the vastness of the world's oceans and the astonishing variety of its previously unknown inhabitants. Perhaps 'breaking out' was itself the root cause of 'breaking up'?

6.

Becoming European – Inventing Civilization

1556–1789

Writing home from Vilnius, the capital of today's Lithuania, in the 1580s, a German merchant by the name of Samuel Kiechel reported:

> In addition to the Lutherans, the city has all sorts of religions and sects, all of which have their churches and public observances, such as Catholics, Calvinists, Orthodox or Muscovites, Anabaptists, followers of Zwingli, and Jews, who have their own synagogue and place of worship. Then there are also the heathens or Tatars, and all of the religions, congregations, and sects have freedom of conscience, in which no one is troubled.[1]

In today's more secular, pluralist Europe, this seems unremarkable – how else could it be? But in an age when almost everyone's identity was still determined by their religious beliefs and practices, the variety of forms of worship reported in Vilnius was very much the exception. And even there, it would not last for long.

The Protestant Reformation split Europe more or less horizontally from end to end. Only Italy and Spain were relatively untouched by the reforming movement. In Spain, Charles V, his son Philip II and the already powerful Spanish Inquisition were better placed than most to nip it in the bud – and since Spanish rule extended across most of northern and southern Italy, the same applied there too. Central Italy was directly ruled by the pope; the power of patronage, backed up by a Roman Inquisition instituted as late as 1542, ensured that cries of 'Antichrist' were unlikely to gain much traction there. Elsewhere, Protestant communities thrived, often in uneasy competition with Catholic neighbours or fellow subjects, in just about every region of Europe – from Scotland and Scandinavia in the north to the southern foothills of the Alps, and from the Atlantic coast of France to the Polish-Lithuanian Commonwealth and Transylvania in the east.

Luther had unleashed a tide of what today we would call religious fundamentalism: in place of the institutional structures of the Catholic Church, the only authority was now to be the word of God as written down in the Bible; the only route to salvation lay through faith alone, with no other intermediary than scripture. But as fundamentalists have discovered time and again, the same words on a page can be interpreted in different ways by different readers; faith can mean belief in different things in the eyes of different believers – hence the variety of previously unheard-of sects that Samuel Kiechel found rubbing along together in Vilnius.

Calvinists were followers of Jean Calvin, who in French-speaking Geneva had preached that not only can sins not be remitted in the afterlife, but each one of us is preordained to be either saved or damned; this is the doctrine known as predestination. In German-speaking Zurich, Huldrych Zwingli had taught *his* followers to deny that Christ is really present in the Eucharist, or Holy Communion. In Strasbourg, on the dividing line between French- and German-speaking Europe, some even questioned whether Jesus had ever been divine. Most radical of all were the Anabaptists, who insisted that only adults, already educated in the faith, could be baptized. In a world where most infants never made it into adulthood, and traditional belief held that the unbaptized went straight to Hell, this horrified not only Catholics but also most other Protestants.[2]

Among these bewildering varieties, the Peace of Augsburg recognized only a 'Lutheran' Church; rival 'Reformed' Churches in different parts of Europe would have to make their way as best they could. The Anglican Church of England was (and is) only one of many such, as is the Presbyterian Church of Scotland. Soon Protestant authorities would be at least as demanding and intrusive as the Catholic Inquisition had ever been in regulating the details of how people worshipped, what they were supposed to believe, and even their personal behaviour. The overturning of centuries-old traditions often involved wholesale destruction; churches and monasteries were looted and destroyed – some never to be rebuilt. People fared even worse. The burning of those condemned as heretics was no longer a monopoly of the Catholic Church; no sanction was too extreme for those convinced that they, and they alone, possessed the transcendent truth of the Christian faith.

Even in those parts of Europe where Protestantism never gained a foothold, lives were radically changed by the Reformation. The Catholic fight-back went far beyond the military campaigns of 'defenders of the faith' such as Charles V and Philip II or the political jockeying of the German-speaking states. A Council of the whole Church had been summoned in 1545 in the city of Trento at the foot of the Italian Alps. Historians writing in English call it the Council of Trent; its proceedings were published in Latin and refer to the city by its ancient name, Tridentum, which is why the reforms it introduced are generally known as 'Tridentine'. In the course of a decade and a half of on-and-off deliberations, it became clear that if Christendom was to be brought back together again, it wasn't going to be by reaching out to those who had broken away; the split had already gone too far for that.

The Council's thorough overhaul of the organization and governance of the Church did go some way towards meeting the initial demands that had triggered the Protestant revolt: in what has been termed 'a major case of shutting the stable door after the Lutheran horse had bolted', the sale of indulgences was banned.[3] But essentially the Tridentine reforms were defensive. Also known as the 'Counter-Reformation', their effect was to double down and reinforce the authority of the papal office and the hierarchy of the Church – the very things that Luther and his successors had most vehemently and most consistently challenged.

The final session of the Council, in 1563, devised a new title, which was first used by Pope Pius IV a year later: 'Bishop of the Universal Church'. An institution that did not even command the allegiance of Christians in roughly half of Europe was reasserting its claim to supremacy over the entire world. All new entrants to the priesthood had to swear an oath of obedience to the pope. 'Uniformity', 'unity' and 'centralization' became the watchwords of the Counter-Reformation. But it remained to be seen how far that uniformity could be rolled out across a continent so deeply divided.[4]

Taken together, the Peace of Augsburg in 1555 and the conclusion of the Council of Trento in 1563 had the effect of fixing the pieces of the European kaleidoscope in mid-turn. The pattern that resulted was as random as it looked; sooner or later the pieces must surely move again. Before long, it would be clear to most parties that nothing had been resolved at all; when the kaleidoscope next began to turn, the violence unleashed would convulse the whole of Europe for more than a century. And that happy harbinger of a diversity of faiths living side by side, which the German merchant had observed in Vilnius, would go the way of all the rest.

Wars of Religion

The compromise that had been thrashed out at Augsburg boiled down to the neat Latin phrase that would be coined some decades afterwards: *cuius regio eius religio*. The neatness becomes lost in translation (roughly: 'whoever rules the state decides on the religion'); the point was that it was the *rulers* who got to decide. Individuals who disagreed could decamp and go somewhere else – and many thousands did just that; but wherever they settled, they would still be expected to conform. The terms of the Peace of Augsburg were only ever intended to apply to the Holy Roman Empire. And within that sprawling and increasingly devolved territory they did more or less keep the peace for a little over half a century.[5] But elsewhere in Europe, most rulers soon found themselves struggling to impose unity at home and as often as not would also be dragged into destructive wars against other states on the opposite side of the religious divide. Religion was politics; and most politics were about differences of religion.

First up was Scotland. In 1559 a revolt by some of the Scottish nobility, backed by 'mob violence' and fanned by the 'fiery preaching' of a convert to the Calvinist sect of Protestantism, John Knox, set up a new, radically reformed Church and led to several years of civil war.[6] It was in the course of these events that Mary 'Queen of Scots', one of the most romanticized of all the characters in this turbulent period of history, lost her throne in 1567 – and her head twenty years later. Mary's cousin, Elizabeth I of England, was more successful in imposing the unique 'Anglican' form of Protestantism on her subjects, but at the price of excommunication by the pope in 1570. And in 1588, it was only their weather that saved the English from conquest by the seaborne 'Armada' sent by Philip II to reclaim their country for Catholicism.[7]

By that time the Spanish-ruled Netherlands had been in revolt for more than two decades. Religion and what we would nowadays call 'national' identity had been intertwined since the very beginning of the Reformation, when Luther had addressed one of his polemical tracts to the 'princes of the German nation'. The long-running Dutch revolt against Catholic, Spanish rule, no less than the defiant stand by Protestant England, would later be reframed as *national* struggles. But the horrific violence that began in the Netherlands in 1566, and three centuries later would inspire dramas by Goethe and Schiller, was at least as much driven by religious fervour and mutual hatred between Catholics and Protestants.

France, the largest state in Europe by this time, was probably the worst affected of all during the second half of the sixteenth century. Reformers desecrated churches and destroyed images in 1562; in retaliation later that year, hundreds of Protestants (known in France as Huguenots) were murdered in many different parts of the country. From then until 1598 the French monarchy imploded under the impact of no fewer than eight civil wars, all of them fundamentally fought over religion. The worst of the violence was triggered on 24 July 1572, St Bartholomew's Day, when the Huguenot leaders, who had gathered in Paris for a royal wedding, were murdered in a pre-emptive strike ordered by the king's council. The rank-and-file populace then rushed in to complete what panicky politicians had started: in Paris during the next three days, Catholics went on the rampage and cut down Huguenots wherever they could find them. In other parts of the country the killing continued for even longer. It has been estimated that as many as 3,000 French Protestants lost their lives in Paris alone – and perhaps double that number across the rest of France.[8]

This round of strife came to an end when Henry IV granted rights and some degree of protection to the Huguenots in the Edict of Nantes, in 1598. Henry was a pragmatist who had been by turns a Catholic and a Protestant before converting back to Catholicism in order to receive the French crown in 1594. But his efforts at reconciliation were cut short by a Catholic assassin's dagger in 1610, and would begin to unravel shortly afterwards.

The passions unleashed across Europe by these conflicts had broken free of any attempt by rulers or elites to control them. These were murderous times: following the killing of Henry III in 1589, Henry IV was the second king of France to be assassinated by a religious zealot within a few years; he had already survived a dozen or so attempts when the last succeeded. By the end of the sixteenth century, Europeans could no longer define themselves simply as Christians, as they had been doing for centuries. Fragmented identities had sprung up instead, along with the labels to match: Protestant, Lutheran, Catholic, Reformed, Calvinist, Anabaptist, and many others.

The differences that set these sects apart had moved on from the theological 'theses' of a Martin Luther or the dynastic ambitions of princes. *Everybody* was now involved, down to the humblest Transylvanian or German peasant, or the Edinburgh street-seller Jenny Geddes, who in 1637 is alleged to have thrown a stool at the minister in St Giles' Cathedral and shouted, 'Dost thou say Mass at my lug?' ('in my ear') – sparking yet another civil war.[9] Europeans everywhere were turning on one another, ready to kill and be killed in the struggle to define their new, competing identities.

All this reached its frenzied and protracted climax during the first half of the seventeenth century. In 1618 the terms of the Peace of Augsburg finally broke down: within the Holy Roman Empire, the emperor and his Catholic allies determined to eradicate Protestantism from their domains. Protestant resistance made a dramatic beginning in the 'defenestration of Prague': imperial delegates were thrown out of a high window of the royal palace, to land ignominiously, if unharmed, in a dungheap. But despite some initial successes, a Protestant alliance within the empire never quite came together. Protestant states outside it soon became involved: the fledgling Dutch Republic, still locked in its century-long struggle against Spanish rule; a newly assertive, Lutheran Denmark; and the ambitious King Gustav Adolf of Sweden, who would lose his life in a battle fought hundreds of miles from his homeland, near Leipzig. England and Scotland, their crowns recently united in the person of King James I and VI, sat on the sidelines – but that fact in itself would prove to be one of the causes of the religious civil wars that in turn would rage across the British Isles between 1638 and 1660.

What became known as the Thirty Years War was largely fought on the lands of the Holy Roman Empire (by this time roughly equivalent to German-speaking Europe). By the time the war came to an end in 1648, most German states had been plundered numerous times by each other, by Catholic troops from France or Spain, by Protestant troops from the Netherlands, Denmark or Sweden, or by some lethal combination of all of these – horrors most vividly brought to life in the first German-language novel, *The Adventures of Simplicius Simplicissimus* by Johann Grimmelshausen, first published in 1668. Modern historians estimate that the German population was reduced by between six and eight million, equivalent to something between 20 and 45 per cent – a far higher proportion than in either of the two world wars of the twentieth century.[10]

When peace negotiations finally began, in 1643, they had to be held in two separate cities, 30 miles apart. By this time the conflict had spilled far beyond even the widest imaginable boundaries of the German-speaking empire. A total of 196 different states, from one end of Europe to the other, took part. Among significant players that had originally been part of Catholic Christendom, only England and Poland stood aloof, both of them distracted by continuing internal conflicts of their own.[11]

The treaties that were eventually signed at Münster (for the Catholics) and Osnabrück (for the Protestants) on 24 October 1648 would ever afterwards be known as the Peace of Westphalia. Their terms, once again, essentially froze into place a stalemate between the two Europe-wide parties. In much of central and eastern Europe, Protestants were forced into exile or obliged to convert; but elsewhere their rights were confirmed or even strengthened. There would never again be any question of a single form of Christianity defining the entire continent. Rulers – and increasingly their populations too – were going to have to learn to live with irreconcilable differences in religious belief and behaviour.

Wars among States

If the Peace of Westphalia had few outright winners or losers, it did at least bring peace to the ravaged German states for almost a century. In the rest of Europe, the wars continued, eventually to engulf the entire continent once again. But the Thirty Years War and the compromises that ended it marked a sea-change. What had begun as a confrontation between religious blocs ended up entrenching a newly emerging concept of European identity. Modern historians often call this the 'European state system'; a Swedish architect of the Peace set out its purpose as 'to conserve the equilibrium of all Europe'.[12]

Even while the warring parties had been tearing apart the German-speaking centre of the continent, kings and their counsellors were coming up with new grounds to justify their actions; these became known as 'reasons of state'. The chief minister to Louis XIII of France, Cardinal Richelieu, despite the religious affiliation of his office, had declared as early as 1616 that 'the interests of a state and the interests of religion are two entirely different things';

by the time the Peace of Westphalia was sealed in 1648, in the words of one modern historian, 'Europe was beginning to follow Richelieu's principle: religion and politics need not be identical.'[13]

A hundred years after Charles V had tried, and failed, to unite Europe under a single monarchy, European rulers had become fixated on the alternative idea that had begun to gain currency during his reign: the new 'state system' was all about the 'balance of power'. Beginning with the Westphalia treaties, and continuing through the wars and the terms of peace during the next century and a half, the common goal running through European geopolitics was to *limit* the power of any one state or ruler. Modern historians have described these conflicts as a 'struggle for supremacy' or 'pursuit of glory';[14] but the wars that came after 1648 were generally seen by those who waged them as *defensive*. It was fear of each other, often expressed as the fear of 'encirclement', that motivated rulers and their counsellors during those centuries. In a nutshell, European states were behaving very much as the Greek city states had done in ancient times.

The catalogue of wars tells its own dismal story. The Franco-Spanish war that began in 1635 overlapped with the Thirty Years War and fed into it; but since both belligerents were on the same (Catholic) side, you couldn't call this one a war of religion. By the time it was over in 1659, the balance of power between these two states had shifted decisively: Spain was no longer the great power it had been in the time of Charles V and Philip II; France, the loser back then, was now on the way up.

In northern Europe, between 1652 and 1674 England fought no fewer than three wars against its suddenly prosperous seafaring rival, the Dutch Republic. During the same period Sweden tussled with Poland for control of the shores of the Baltic; at the beginning of the eighteenth century both would lose out permanently when a new power, Russia, emerged on the eastern borders of Europe in the Great Northern War. The long reign of Louis XIV of France (as sole ruler from 1661 to 1715) provoked a string of wars: while Louis invoked 'reasons of state' to protect France from being dominated by encircling neighbours, the said neighbours ganged up in a shifting set of alliances to avoid being dominated in their turn.

The last of Louis's wars, known as the War of the Spanish Succession, began in 1701 and ended with the Peace of Utrecht, made up of a series of treaties signed in the Dutch city between 1713 and 1715. Wars named after other 'successions' followed. The War of the Polish Succession was fought in the 1730s, of the Austrian in the next decade. The most far-reaching of all, with perhaps the greatest number of competing states, and fought across several continents as well as the world's oceans, is known as the Seven Years' War and lasted from 1756 to 1763. The war's lasting impact was greatest in North America and the Indian subcontinent; in both spheres Britain gained decisive advantages over its colonial rival, France. Finally, when Britain's American colonists went to war in 1775 in support of their claim to independence from the mother country, that conflict, too, quickly evolved into a European war, as France, Spain and the Netherlands all jumped upon the opportunity to curtail the influence of Britain nearer home.

The only lasting winners out of any of those conflicts were the Americans, who won their independence in 1783. In Europe, one war after another ended in the same kind of stalemate as the Peace of Westphalia. Fortunes rose and fell, but only on a relative scale. New states came to prominence, notably the Dutch Republic in the seventeenth century and the Kingdom of Prussia, most of it part of Poland today, during the eighteenth. Britain, formed out of the union of the parliaments of England and Scotland in 1707, had begun to outstrip its European rivals overseas and build up a fighting navy that by the early 1800s could plausibly aspire to 'rule the waves'. Losers to varying degrees and at different times were Spain at one end of the continent and Poland at the other. But there was no knock-out blow. And no end to the wars.

The driving force behind all these conflicts was essentially the same – and it was no longer religion (although religious passions were frequently still whipped up when they could be mobilized to generate popular enthusiasm). In the courts and cabinets of Europe, the rules of the game were fully understood and equally taken for granted by all. When the Dutch leader William of Orange rallied his people against invasion of their lands by the troops of Louis XIV in 1672, he did so in the name of the 'liberties of Europe'. An official in the French foreign ministry in 1729 expressed the fear that the current Holy Roman Emperor, Charles VI, was trying 'to elevate himself to the absolute ruler of Germany, which would indeed overturn the balance of power in Europe'.[15] On that occasion for once there was no war – but the assumption was baked in: if your neighbour looked like becoming too strong on his own ground, that was reason enough to send in the army – for the sake of something called 'Europe'.

Europe as a concept was quietly taking the place of Christendom – indeed the text of the treaties that made up the Peace of Utrecht (the last of them in February 1715) may mark the last official appearance of the Latin phrase, *respublica Christiana*, with the meaning of 'Christendom' or 'Christian commonwealth'.[16] Far from being a commonwealth, Europe was now more like a playing field on which a varying number of teams all played at once; battles were fought both on and off the pitch, as states that were not yet nations struggled to secure a place for themselves in the European league table. Just like modern sporting competitions, it was all about winning, but there was no real prize to be won. And of course it was far more deadly. In the eyes of all, it was a zero-sum game. Even the peaceful pursuit of wealth through trade – which was hugely expanding throughout this time – was understood and practised in the very same way. In commerce, no less than on the battlefield, 'beggar my neighbour' was the watchword.[17]

As the eighteenth century drew towards a close it was becoming evident that the 'state system' was failing. Europe ought to have collapsed – but instead was steadily exporting its ways and its battlegrounds across more and more of the planet. Why? Much has been written about the spirit of competition and a 'Protestant work ethic' that drove the success of 'the West' – but these terms sound more like descriptions of behaviour than explanations of the causes.[18] To understand what happened next, we have to take account of two huge changes that had been going on during the same centuries. One of these was on the ground, where Europe was learning to live with new, powerful neighbours on its eastern borders; the other was in the minds of some, at least, of its inhabitants.

Eastern Approaches

The Ottoman Turks, back in the fifteenth century, had been only the latest in a long line of newcomers who had entered Europe from Asia by force of arms. Beginning with the Goths who had crossed the Danube in 376, and continuing intermittently for almost a millennium until Mongol horsemen fought their way to the shores of the Adriatic in 1240, the mayhem caused by these outsiders had always ended in one of two ways: either they would sooner or later adopt the religion and much of the way of life of those they had conquered – in other words become Europeans – or they would go away again, as the Huns had done in the fifth century, and the Mongols in the thirteenth. But the Turks (as Europeans nearly always called them then), Osmanli (as they called themselves) or Ottomans (as most historians prefer to call them today), would prove to be different.

After the fall of Constantinople, Pope Pius II had done his level best to muster a new crusade to try to retake it, as we saw in the last chapter; when that failed, he had one last shot left in the Christian locker. In 1461 the pope addressed a long, florid letter to Sultan Mehmed II. In it he acknowledged the sultan's power over huge swathes of Asia, Africa and Europe; to match, the pope offered the prospect of *legitimacy* as a universal emperor, if only Mehmed would convert to Christianity and bring his people with him. What a great 'abundance of peace' would be the result, Pius wrote. Waxing lyrical, and blending Virgil's praise for the first Roman emperor, Augustus, with the prophetic Book of Isaiah in the Old Testament, the pope expanded on his theme:

The age of Augustus would return, what the poets call the 'Golden Age' would be renewed. The leopard would lie down with the lamb, the calf with the lion; swords would be transformed into plough-shares . . . the land would prosper, towns and cities would be rebuilt . . . How great would be your glory for having restored peace to the world! . . . How much everyone would love you, respect you, praise you, as the author of general peace and salvation for all! . . . No one among mortals will exceed you in power or glory.[19]

In hindsight, this episode seems simply bizarre, so much so that most histories of the period don't even mention it. But it may hold an important clue to how *being European* was still understood in the century before Europe began to break out across the oceans – and to break apart at home. It had been the very same Pius II, in his pre-papal days as the diplomat and humanist Enea Silvio Bartolomeo Piccolomini, who had lamented the Ottomans' devastation of the European 'fatherland' and had published an account of the geography and history of its people. For Piccolomini, to be European wasn't a matter of race or origin, but of religious faith and all the rest of the cultural traits that went along with it. In the mind of a fifteenth-century humanist pope, there was no reason why Turks should *not* become Europeans – by becoming Christians. This was the way it had always been done. And the sultan's reward (not that this was in the gift of even a pope) would be to become the acknowledged and legitimate master of all of Europe.

But times had changed. Sultan Mehmed never answered this letter, and may not even have received it. It would not be through the age-old route of religious conversion that Turkey would become a European power, to the extent that it ever has – and that may well be the principal reason why the process has never been completed, to this day. The conqueror of Constantinople had no need of the blessing of any pope to style himself, in Greek, 'emperor of the Romans' and 'heir to Alexander the Great'. Mehmed even had his portrait painted, in the latest style of the Italian Renaissance, by the Venetian painter Gentile Bellini; he invited men of learning and culture from the west to visit his capital. Some historians even suggest that Mehmed in his later years turned himself into something of a 'Renaissance prince' on the European model.[20] That must surely be an exaggeration; but Mehmed's career does suggest that other ways of becoming European, besides the traditional one, were becoming imaginable in the fifteenth century. And the ruler of an empire spanning three continents was in a position to pick and choose.

In the next century, Süleyman I, remembered ever afterwards as 'the Lawgiver' among his co-religionists, but as 'the Magnificent' by awestruck European contemporaries, made it clear that in his book there was only ever going to be one emperor in Europe, one inheritor of the imperial legacy that went all the way back to ancient Rome, and that was the Ottoman sultan. What Pope Pius had offered his predecessor on conditions, Süleyman was determined to take for himself, by right of conquest.[21]

Süleyman came to the throne in 1520. The start of his reign coincides almost exactly with that of Charles V as Holy Roman Emperor; he would rule for even longer, until 1566. During the 1520s Süleyman's armies punched through the western Balkans and took possession of much of Hungary. In 1529 they laid siege to Vienna for three weeks; but Ottoman forces had reached the end of their supply lines and became literally bogged down in the flooded plains of central Europe. For more than a century and a half after that, a fortified frontier, almost a thousand miles long, ran from the northern Adriatic to the foothills of the Carpathian mountains in today's Slovakia, and from there along the southern edge of the Polish-Lithuanian Commonwealth to end up at the Dnipro river to the east of Kyiv.[22] South of that line, the ambiguously named 'Turkey in Europe' or 'European Turkey' would become an acknowledged reality in the languages of Europe.

At sea, in 1565, an Ottoman fleet tried, and failed, to seize the strategic island of Malta. And six years later, during the short reign of Süleyman's successor Selim II, off the western coast of today's Greece, defeat at the battle of Lepanto decisively put an end to the Ottoman advance into Europe through the Mediterranean. Even so, by the middle of the seventeenth century, 'Turkey in Europe' included not just the entire coastline and hinterland east of the Adriatic, but almost all the islands too.

In 1683, Vienna once again came under siege. For two months, the defenders were cut off; all the cats in the city (euphemistically renamed 'roof rabbits') were killed for food; there were even reports of rats being trapped and eaten.[23] The decisive battle was fought outside the city on Sunday 12 September. In its aftermath, the besiegers were driven not only from the city gates but hundreds of miles back through the Balkans.

In 1699, for the first time, the sultan's representatives signed a formal treaty of peace with an alliance of European powers. Up to that time, when Ottoman officials had negotiated with other states, they had done so from a position of superiority; the sultan was 'king of kings' and no Christian ruler was his equal. But after the retreat from Vienna through Hungary, the age of Ottoman conquest was over. Diplomacy, more often than not, would take the place of war from that time on.[24] 'Turkey in Europe' had not only become a recognized player on the European stage; it was beginning to play by the same rules. And to the great convenience of every other European state, the Ottomans would now direct their firepower not towards Europe but against their new rival on Europe's eastern borders. That rival was Russia.

At the time of the Ottoman conquest of Constantinople, the only surviving state that still professed the eastern Orthodox branch of Christianity had been the Grand Duchy of Muscovy, with its capital in Moscow. A century later, the Grand Dukes had fought free of the last remnant of the Mongol Empire in western Asia, and taken for themselves the title 'Tsar', or 'Czar', derived from the ancient Roman imperial title, 'Caesar'. The Grand Duchy was well on the way to transforming itself into the Russian Empire. Some Orthodox churchmen even began to promote the notion that Moscow was the true successor to Constantinople (traditionally the 'new' or 'second Rome'), and should therefore be known as the 'third Rome'.

But Moscow was still a long way from Europe. As late as 1657, Louis XIV of France could address a letter to a ruler of Muscovy who it turned out had been dead for twelve years. The game of states, or balance of power in Europe, could safely leave nascent Russia out of account: according to an Austrian ambassador writing at the very end of the seventeenth century, 'none but the Tatars fear the armies of the Tsar'.[25]

All that changed when Peter I ('the Great'), of the Romanov dynasty, became sole ruler in 1696. Peter was the first Russian leader to set his sights squarely on the west, on Europe; and he came at first not as a leader of armies but as a tourist. For eighteen months, in 1697 and 1698, the tsar travelled, semi-incognito, through Lithuania and Prussia to Hanover, then to Amsterdam and London, returning by way of Dresden, Leipzig, Prague, Vienna and Kraków in Poland. In the Netherlands and in London's docklands, Peter set himself to learn about shipbuilding, naval strategy and forms of government quite unlike anything he had ever experienced at home. 'English freedom is not appropriate' for Russia, he is reported as saying; but he did carry back with him many new ideas, not least about men's fashion (he made Russian aristocrats shave off their beards) and how to build a modern navy.[26]

It was this last ambition that brought Russia territorially into Europe. Between 1700 and 1721, in the Great Northern War, Peter pitted his forces against the regional European powers Sweden and Poland. The tug of war went all three ways, but Peter would win out in the end. An early victory on the River Neva, which flows into the Gulf of Finland, gave him the opportunity he had been seeking. In May 1703 his engineers began to lay the foundations for a new city on marshy land at the mouth of the river, to be known, after his own patron saint, as St Petersburg. It was built in record time: in 1712 the capital was officially moved there from Moscow. Soon, St Petersburg would become the headquarters of a newly created Russian navy. Aptly, the new Russian capital has been called 'not a new Rome but a new Amsterdam'.

Built very largely upon a semicircular network of canals, the town planning and the architecture of today's St Petersburg indeed very much resemble a Dutch city. Even its name, in Russian, actually reproduces the *Dutch* form: *Sankt Peterburg*. The city that arose upon this unpromising terrain was Russia's opening towards Europe, designed largely by Italian, German and French architects, and very visibly intended to *look* European. But the method of its building relied entirely on the autocratic traditions of the Russian state that Peter had inherited. St Petersburg was built by slave labour; according to the estimate of one foreign observer at the time, as many as 100,000 serfs and conscripted labourers may have died during the construction.[27]

As Peter continued to win victories in the Great Northern War, European ideas about Russia had to change to keep up. In 1709 the Prussian diplomat and mathematician Gottfried Wilhelm Leibniz observed:

> The Tsar henceforth will attract the consideration of Europe and will play a big part in general affairs . . . It is commonly being said that the Tsar will be formidable to the whole of Europe, that he will be as though a Turk of the North.

When the war was over, in 1721, Peter took for himself the ancient Roman title of 'Imperator'. For the first time since 1453 there was a Christian emperor in both east and west. From that time until the last of the Romanovs was deposed in 1917, the ruler of Russia would be known not only as 'Caesar' (Tsar), but throughout the courts of Europe as 'Emperor'.[28]

During the next decade even the notional physical borders of Europe moved far to the east. It was a captured Swedish geographer in the service of Peter the Great who first conjured up the idea that the European continent extended all the way to the Ural mountain range.[29] That would place Moscow, and the traditional territory of Muscovy, also within the limits of Europe. But what really turned Russia into a European power during the eighteenth century wasn't lines on a map or even natural barriers; it came down to plain geopolitics. Just like its great rival the Ottoman Empire to the south, the Russian Empire, from the time of Peter the Great until the end of the First World War, would be ruled from a capital city unquestionably situated in Europe.

Of all Russia's rulers (of any period) the one who did most to bring that country closer to Europe was neither a tsar nor a Romanov. Catherine 'the Great', as she would become known, was German by birth; she had been married at an early age to the last of the male bloodline of Peter I. After her Romanov husband was deposed and murdered in 1762, Catherine ruled in her own right as tsarina and empress for the next thirty-four years.

One of Catherine's first acts in power, in 1766, was to summon representatives from all over Russia to ratify a new code of laws. Known as the *Nakaz* ('Instruction'), and promulgated the next year, the resulting document declares uncompromisingly in one of its opening articles (according to the contemporary official translation): 'Russia is an European State.' Together with other administrative reforms that came later, the *Nakaz* did go some way towards reforming aspects of Russian society and administration along European lines; Catherine's (highly selective) support for new ideas and technologies originating in Europe has been much discussed. But the *Nakaz* stopped well short of introducing the rule of law, as that concept was understood in Europe. Another article states (again in that official translation): 'The Sovereign is absolute; for there is no other Authority but that which centres in his [*sic*] single Person, that can act with a Vigour proportionate to the Extent of such a vast Dominion.'[30]

During the reign of Catherine the Great hostilities with the Ottoman Empire ratcheted up. After six years of war, a treaty signed in 1774 for the first time gave Russia control of a large part of the northern shores and hinterland of the Black Sea, mostly in today's Ukraine. Crimea was annexed in 1783. Four years later, Catherine launched a new war, apparently with the serious aim of reconquering the old Byzantine capital and renaming it Tsargrad, or Caesar City.[31] She won that war, too, though not decisively enough to make good the claim to the Ottoman capital. Ambitions for Tsargrad would have to be shelved – to be revived over a hundred years later, during the First World War.

The door was still open, as of necessity it had always been, to outsiders to *become European*. But the terms of engagement had changed. By the eighteenth century, nobody expected an Orthodox Russian emperor, any more than the Muslim 'Grand Turk', to change his religion (Catherine, indeed, had been brought up as a Lutheran before converting the other way in order to marry a Romanov and become *Russian*). With their capital cities respectively on the Gulf of Finland and the European shore of the Bosphorus, the two empires bordering Europe to the east were ambiguously at once on the inside and the outside, 'European' up to a point but only so far. They were never going to be Catholic Christian – but then, by this time, neither was half of Europe.

An equilibrium had been reached between Europe and each of these powerful neighbours: in 1718 the Treaty of Passarowitz, signed with the Ottoman Empire, agreed territorial limits that would hold, more or less, for the best part of a century. The Treaty of Nystad, three years later, brought stable relations with Russia that would last for about as long. During the eighteenth century, as Europeans fought among themselves in the name of the 'balance of power', and the empires on their borders were preoccupied with fighting each other, the continent had never been less threatened from the east. In the words of Edward Gibbon, writing towards the century's end and contrasting his own times with the decline and fall of the Roman Empire that was the subject of his monumental work:

> Cannon and fortifications now form an impregnable barrier against the Tartar horse; and Europe is secure from any future irruption of Barbarians; since, before they can conquer, they must cease to be barbarous. Their gradual advances in the science of war would always be accompanied, as we may learn from the example of Russia, with a proportionable improvement in the arts of peace and

civil policy; and they themselves must deserve a place among the polished nations whom they subdue.[32]

For the first time, perhaps ever, there were no more barbarians on the frontiers. If, as Cavafy's poem 'Waiting for the Barbarians' had it, 'those people' had once been 'some sort of a solution', it must surely be time to find a new one. We now call that solution the 'Enlightenment'.

Beyond Religion, beyond States

The roots of the Enlightenment go all the way back to the earliest years of the Reformation. With the removal of the Churches' monopoly on what people could believe – by definition, they couldn't *all* be right – the process of self-discovery that had begun with the Renaissance gathered momentum. By the seventeenth century, a 'scientific revolution' was well advanced. New revelations about the universe went hand in hand with discoveries and speculations about *how* human beings are able to perceive that universe and know what they know about it. Philosophers and mathematicians such as René Descartes in France and Isaac Newton in England came up with mathematical explanations for how the natural world works, based on experiment, observation and the rigorous application of reason – which is why they would earn for themselves the name of 'rationalists'.

During the same century, a few pacifically minded individuals began to ask, in the same spirit: could there be a *rational* alternative to the religious divisions and 'reasons of state' that did nothing but perpetuate warfare in Europe?

In France, the former chief minister to Henry IV devoted the long years of his retirement, after his royal master's assassination in 1610, to elaborating what he called a 'Grand Design'. Maximilien de Béthune, ennobled by his royal master as the Duc de Sully, outlived Henry by just over thirty years – more than half of which were also the years of the Thirty Years War. In 1638, while more and more continental states were being drawn into the carnage of that war, Sully went public with 'an elaborate scheme to redraw the frontiers of Europe and create supranational institutions'. The fiction that the Grand Design had actually been the brainchild of the late king has been exposed as just that – but Sully was nothing if not loyal, and the royal name attached to it ensured that people took notice.[33]

To replace the huge imbalances among the existing states of Europe, the entire map of the continent was to be redrawn. According to Sully's 'design', some fifteen new states would co-exist in a kind of federation. This was explicitly to be modelled on the abortive experiments in the same direction that had been tried by the ancient Greek city states, almost two thousand years before. Ultimate authority was to rest not with kings, emperors or popes, but with a great representative council, or senate. This sounds in today's terms more like the European Commission, whose members are appointed by national governments, than the elected European Parliament. Instead of the much-vaunted and elusive balance of power that actual sovereigns claimed to be fighting to maintain, the 'tidy mind' of this former Chief Minister and Superintendent of Finances envisaged an 'equilibrium' among evenly matched forces. This has been compared to Newton's later demonstration of the gravitational forces that keep the planets in their orbits: a bold attempt, perhaps, to impose a *mathematical* solution on a geopolitical problem.[34]

After Sully's death in 1641, the Grand Design was left to gather dust, while 'reasons of state' and the even grander designs of Louis XIV fuelled the next round of European wars during the rest of the century and beyond. It was as a reaction to those wars, around the turn of the next century, that Sully's ideas were dusted off and adapted to the changed circumstances of the time.

William Penn is best remembered as the founder of the British colony of Pennsylvania in North America and its capital city, Philadelphia. In 1693, back in England, Penn published an essay whose title says it all: *An Essay towards the Present and Future Peace of Europe, by the Establishment of an European Dyet, Parliament, or Estates.* Penn was a leading figure in the Protestant sect known as Quakers; one of the Quakers' basic tenets is pacifism. And just as the architects of European unity in the aftermath of the Second World War would later do, Penn made it clear that his main object was peace.

Instead of trying to redraw the map, as Sully had done, Penn proposed a parliament made up of representatives of the European states that existed in his day. Of the powers that bordered Europe to the east, Sully had excluded both Orthodox Muscovy and Muslim Turkey from his scheme. Penn was prepared to be more inclusive: 'If the Turks and Muscovites are taken in, as seems but fit and just,' he wrote, the total number of delegates would reach ninety.[35] In the event, Penn's ideas would prove more influential in his adopted continent of America, where they would play an important part in the formulation of the Constitution of the United States, almost a full century later, than they ever would in the Old World of Europe.

A few years after Penn, a minor French aristocrat in holy orders, Charles-Irénée Castel de Saint-Pierre, returned to the theme of the Grand Design and worried away at it, to the extent of three wordy volumes and several revisions, over a period of twenty-six years, beginning in 1712. As it happened, shortly after the first of these volumes appeared, Saint-Pierre had the opportunity to experience peacemaking in practice, when he served as a secretary to the French delegation negotiating the Peace of Utrecht. But it seems his thinking was influenced less by this brush with *Realpolitik* in action than by Sully's Grand Design and by his own pacific instincts. Saint-Pierre's *Project to Render Peace Perpetual throughout Europe* was based, like Penn's much shorter essay, on the real states that could be found on a map. This time, Muscovy was in – updated to become 'Russia' in the final edition and promoted to fourth in importance among them all; but Muslim Turkey was once again out. All were to send their representatives to sit in the 'senate', the supreme body of what was now, for the first time, in the edition of 1713, called a 'European Union'.[36]

Like many of those whose ideas run ahead of their time, none of these men came up with a convincing plan for how to get from here to there. None had access to councils of state, or the ear of any among the kings or princes who would have had to give up some of their own power in order to bring it about. Another two hundred years would pass before anyone in a position to do so would take these proposals seriously; still, they were a start.

A Civilization for all the World

In the meantime the ideas that would spark the Enlightenment and do more than anything else to define Europe from the eighteenth century onwards began with a deceptively simple premise: 'I lay it for a certain ground, that every intelligent being really seeks happiness,' wrote the English philosopher John Locke in his *Essay Concerning Human Understanding*, first published in 1690.[37] This starting point was not exactly new. Aristotle had said much the same in the fourth century BCE. But for centuries Christianity had taught that earthly existence is a preparation for judgement in an eternal afterlife, a set of travails to be endured in the hope of heavenly reward. And not even the ancient Greeks had imagined that general happiness could be achieved by a steady and systematic improvement of the material conditions in which people lived.

During the eighteenth century, the idea took hold all over Europe that it was possible to make things better in the here and now. No doubt this was a response to actual improvements in living conditions, which were going on at the same time – perhaps in a sort of feedback loop? As one modern historian of the Enlightenment puts it, 'This was betterment conceived in a historical perspective, the perspective of the "progress of society".'[38]

The new way of thinking was not in itself – or was not *necessarily* – opposed to the Christian religion. A few voices would be overtly anti-religious, and many more would be raised against aspects of institutional Christianity, especially as represented by the Catholic Church. But the mainstream was content to rub along with inherited, and deeply ingrained, practices and beliefs. The Enlightenment, it has been argued, could only have happened in Europe, because of the shared inheritance of Christendom: 'It was, in a sense, a form of secularized Christianity.'[39]

The Enlightenment is often associated with particular centres: France (usually meaning Paris), Scotland (Edinburgh) and several of the German states, giving it a northern European focus. But thanks to printing, newspapers and new forms of sociability, such as coffee houses and 'salons' where men (usually) would gather to discuss the issues of the day, the ideas of a relatively small number of highly educated thinkers would be disseminated very widely throughout the continent and its islands. And despite the hazards of travel in those days, leading figures of the Enlightenment often covered great distances, regularly crossing and recrossing the frontiers of states, even those at war with one another: from Paris to St Petersburg, from Edinburgh to Rome, in one case even from Corfu, via Constantinople and the German cities of Leipzig and Halle, to today's Ukraine.[40]

One of the most far-reaching achievements of the Enlightenment was the *Encyclopédie, ou Dictionnaire raisonné des sciences, des arts et des métiers* (*Encyclopaedia, or Systematic Dictionary of the Sciences, Arts and Crafts*). Its seventeen massive volumes, published in Paris between 1751 and 1772, contain some 72,000 articles, illustrated by eleven supplementary volumes of engraved plates; almost all the self-styled *philosophes* who make up the French Enlightenment contributed. The word 'encyclopaedia', the editor-in-chief, Denis Diderot, explained, was modern but based on ancient Greek roots; it was intended to mean 'joined-up knowledge'. The avowed aim of the project, he went on, was nothing less than to 'change the common way of thinking'. And evidently it did. Despite repeated difficulties with censorship, the volumes rolled off the presses. The first edition was hugely expensive, but still made a modest fortune for its printer; later editions were made accessible to a wider public. It has been estimated that by 1789 between 14,000 and 16,000 copies of the *Encyclopédie* may have been in existence in France.[41] The age that gave birth to the *Encyclopédie* was called, in its own time, the 'age of reason' – a label that has stuck. By the exercise of reason, human beings could find their way towards the betterment that was now to be the object of their existence.

A preoccupation for almost all the major figures of the Enlightenment was how to overcome the bitter divisions between rival forms of the Christian faith, which still existed in the eighteenth century, across Europe and within individual states. This was the time when the French term *tolérance* became current, along with its English equivalent, 'toleration'. Exactly what this might mean, and how to establish reasonable limits to it, were much debated. The long article on the subject in the *Encyclopédie*, which appeared in 1765, is at its most eloquent in highlighting the horrors that the opposite of toleration had brought upon Europe and might again, given the chance:

> Calvinists, Roman Catholics, Lutherans, Jews and Greeks [of the Orthodox Church], all will devour one another like wild beasts; the places where the Gospels reign will be distinguished by carnage and desolation; Inquisitors will be our masters; the Cross of Jesus will become the badge of crime; and his disciples will become drunk on the blood of their brothers . . .

Instead, the writer proposes a 'general rule': 'Give inviolable respect to rights of conscience in everything that in no way disrupts society.' Bland, perhaps – but the appeal to individual conscience was beginning to be heard in many quarters, as Europe began slowly to put the devastation of its religious wars behind it.

The writer of this particular article, Jean-Edme Romilly of Geneva, extends his list of Christian sects to include Judaism. The emergence of Europe's Jewish communities from the enforced segregation of the ghetto begins with the Enlightenment. Others among the *philosophes* would extend the principle of *tolérance* still farther, to bring about what one modern commentator has called a radical 'rethinking' of European attitudes to Islam.[42]

No less important were ideas about law and liberty. At a time when most European states were governed by more or less absolutist monarchies, enlighteners looked back to ancient Greece and Rome to seek solutions to issues of their own day. This was the thrust of one of the most influential works of the period, *The Spirit of the Laws*, published by Charles Louis de Secondat, Baron de Montesquieu, in Geneva in 1748. Later in the century, it would become routine to 'define Europe as a space of "fundamental laws" '; just as in ancient Greece, it was the principle of the rule of law (however imperfectly applied) that distinguished the people of Europe from those of other continents.[43]

Some of those ideas caught the attention of Europe's most powerful rulers – and not for the negative reasons that might have been expected. From Sweden to Portugal, from Tuscany to St Petersburg, emperors, kings, princes, even a powerful minister acting in the name of his sovereign, would embrace some, at least, of the new ideas. Among the 'enlightened despots' of the eighteenth century, as a later age would dub them, Frederick II of Prussia, Catherine II of Russia and Joseph II of Austria stand out. These, and others less grand, read the works of the *philosophes*, corresponded with some of them, on occasion made them welcome at court. After all, if the race was on to improve the condition of their subjects, should not the rulers be there in the vanguard?

Frederick 'the Great' was something of a philosopher himself (he wrote in French, the language of the *philosophes*, not his native German) and liked to present himself as the 'first servant of the state'. A prince, he wrote, has duties to his people, and 'should often recall to mind that he is a man just like the least' of them. Frederick imagined a relationship with his subjects in which they came to him and said: 'We need you to maintain the laws which we wish to obey, to govern us wisely, to defend us; for the rest, we require that you respect our liberty.'[44] The 'enlightened despots' of the eighteenth century may have been more despotic than enlightened, by the standards of later times. But at least they showed a lively intelligence, and an intellectual curiosity, not found among authoritarian leaders today. As a result, in many parts of Europe, rulers were scarcely less eager than philosophers to pursue the project of betterment. Almost everywhere, methods of agriculture were improved, advances made in medicine and public education, roads and canals built. Trade and commerce were booming; taxes were raised more efficiently than at any time since the last years of the Roman Empire.

Along with new ways of thinking went new ways of doing and making things. This time the impetus came from neither philosophers nor kings. It came from inventors and entrepreneurs, and for once was concentrated in one small corner of Europe, one that until relatively recently had not been a big player on the European stage. In 1769, in Britain, the Scottish engineer James Watt obtained a patent for a novel type of engine that worked by the power of steam, heated in a cast-iron chamber by burning coal; in partnership with the factory-owner Matthew Boulton, Watt went on to design machines that would drive pumps for canals and mines – in this way generating huge savings in the production and transport of the very raw material that fuelled them, and so creating a virtuous circle. Other inventions at the same time made it possible for workers to produce cloth and fabrics on a scale that we now call 'industrial', generating paid employment for the many and eye-watering profits for the few who owned and operated the new factories.

The Industrial Revolution had begun. Before long its effects would begin to transform Europe, and then the world, in ways that could hardly have been foreseen in the second half of the eighteenth century. For the time being, it was enough that the productive power of human labour was being magnified exponentially by new machines and new ways of working; energy was being harnessed that dwarfed the muscle-power of humans or horses. Who, now, could deny that human lives could be made better by human efforts?

All this called for a new word to describe it. That word was *civilization*. It was coined in French, from a Latin word meaning 'civic' or 'civil', which in turn derives from the Latin for 'citizen'. It seems to have made its debut in print in a book of economic theory published in 1756.[45] 'Civilization' combined the ancient Roman concept of *humanitas* with Christian virtues inherited from the intervening centuries. Overlaid upon both were attitudes to urban (or urbane) sociability, politeness (itself derived from the ancient Greek word for a city, *polis*) and 'progress', which were very much products of the time. Civilization had *begun* with the philosophers of ancient Greece – the *Encyclopaedia* was very clear about that.[46] But Europe in the eighteenth century had visibly progressed even farther than the ancients had been able to do. To explain this, historians devised models of the 'stages' through which human society had developed: from the primitive or 'savage', through intermediate forms of social organization all the way to the present, and still improving, 'civilized' condition enjoyed in Europe.[47]

There was plenty of scope, here, for crude claims that Europeans were superior to other peoples of the world; some of the overtly racist theories that would emerge during the nineteenth century can be traced back to ideas formed during the Enlightenment. (Indeed, a passing remark made in 1753 by the Scottish pioneer of the human sciences, David Hume, would lead to his name being stripped from a landmark building of the University of Edinburgh in 2020.) But by and large the historians and philosophers of the Enlightenment were willing to learn from what they knew of distant peoples. The second half of the century saw new systematic voyages of exploration, notably by Captain James Cook from England and Antoine de Bougainville from France, that combed the islands and mainland coasts of the southern hemisphere as far away as Australia and New Zealand. Several prominent figures of the Enlightenment took a great interest in what they could discover about China. Did the Chinese Empire add up to an alternative kind of civilization? they wondered.[48]

Encounters with non-Europeans (even if they mostly happened in the imagination and on the page) brought with them a healthy opportunity for self-criticism. Montesquieu, as early as 1721, had held up a mirror to contemporary Europe by imagining how it might appear to outsiders. In his *Persian Letters*, first published in that year, a pair of cultured Persian gentlemen arrive on an extended visit to Paris, engagingly described by one of them as 'the seat of government of the empire of Europe'. The book was enormously popular, went into several editions, and started a vogue that would last throughout the century.[49]

A particularly devastating critique of European smugness was launched in French in 1759, while the Seven Years' War was at its height. Its author was François-Marie Arouet, known by the pseudonym Voltaire. *Candide, ou L'Optimisme*, to give this short novel its full title, takes its motley cast of characters (who hail from different parts of Europe and the New World) through a series of grotesque adventures in search of a happiness that continues to elude them. At every turn, their misfortunes make a mockery of the oft-repeated mantra of Candide's former tutor Dr Pangloss, that 'all is for the best in the best of all possible worlds'.

At the end the group is reunited on a small farm on the shores of the Sea of Marmara, not far from the Ottoman capital, Constantinople. There, Candide encounters a simple Turk who seems to enjoy all the good things of life, without ever visiting the nearby city or taking any notice of what goes on there. Having 'meditated deeply', Candide concludes, in the novel's often-quoted final words: 'we must cultivate our garden'. The condition nearest to happiness that actually exists in the world is to be found on the very edge of Europe, among neighbours who it just happens are not European Christians at all, but Muslim Turks. It's not only 'optimism' that Voltaire's tale has debunked by the end, but also traditional assumptions about Christian Europe.[50]

A more serious critique of the Enlightenment project itself was launched, from within its ranks, in the 1750s and 1760s. Jean-Jacques Rousseau is best remembered today for his treatise *Du contrat social* (*On the Social Contract*), published in 1762; its first chapter opens with the oft-quoted words, 'L'homme est né libre, et partout il est dans les fers' ('Man is born free, and everywhere is in chains'). Rousseau's distinctively different take on the 'pursuit of happiness' dates from the previous decade, when he had entered a competition for a prize essay launched by a provincial French learned society. The subject was a question that could probably never even have been asked at any time before the Enlightenment: 'What is the origin of inequality among men?' Rousseau's answer can be summed up in one word, even though that word had yet to reach the public domain: *civilization*. According to Rousseau, we had all been much more equal – and therefore, he argued, happier – before ever we learned to speak and organize ourselves into the social groups that would eventually grow into cities and nations.

The idea of the 'noble savage' didn't begin with Rousseau, but he did make it very much his own. If civilization itself was the cause of the evident inequalities that divide mankind, Rousseau then set himself, in his essay *On the Social Contract*, to propose a system of government that would make the best of a bad job. And here he came up with a far-reaching idea, one that had not been aired since the time of the ancient Greek city states and the Roman Republic, and even then not in quite so radical a way.

According to Rousseau, every human society is founded on the principle that 'Each one of us, in common, places his person and all his power under the supreme direction of the general will; and as a corporate body we receive every individual member as an indivisible constituent of the whole.' Sovereignty, in other words, is derived not from the rulers but from those who are ruled. This was a very different kind of social contract from the one imagined by Frederick II of Prussia. The siren call of the 'general will' or collective 'will of the people' would be heard again and again in Europe in times to come, challenging that most consistent of all the European values reaffirmed by the Enlightenment: namely, the rule of law.[51]

Less shocking to the polite circles in which Enlightenment thinkers moved, but in their way almost as radical, were the researches of a Protestant pastor who had been born and educated in Prussia and spent much of his life in Riga, the capital of today's Latvia. His name was Johann Gottfried Herder. The *philosophes* loved to generalize, to find common denominators in their search for a happiness that they thought could be more or less identical in any human society, any-where in the world. Herder in many ways shared that outlook, but with a difference: indeed, he argued that it was the *differences* mark-ing off one individual and one society from every other that make us all human. Herder is often remembered today as the father of the discipline of anthropology, thanks to his exhaustive studies of many different societies, published during the 1780s. Nations, he argued, acquire their particular 'character' through interaction with their physical environment and through sharing a language, along with the stories, beliefs and memories embedded in it and handed down from one generation to the next.

These two counter-currents from the tail end of the Enlighten-ment would make a lasting impact on ideas of Europe during the next century and beyond. In the meantime, by the second half of the eighteenth century, despite the doubts and objections of some, and in defiance of the reality of near-constant warfare and a 'state system' perpetually on the verge of collapse, the Enlightenment had coalesced around its own idea of Europe. Montesquieu, who died in 1755, had already observed that 'Europe is one state made up of many provinces'. Voltaire, mindful of the inheritance from European Christendom, or *respublica christiana* (and himself rather succumbing to the lure of optimism), had put it like this, eight years before the publication of *Candide*:

> Already for a long time one could regard Christian Europe (except Russia) as a sort of great republic divided into several states . . . all in harmony with each other, all having the same substratum of reli-gion, although divided into various sects; all possessing the same principles of public and political law, unknown in other parts of the world.[52]

Even Rousseau, at the beginning of the 1770s, was prepared to concede that 'Today nobody is French, German, Spanish, even English any more, whatever people say; there are only Europe-ans. They all have the same tastes, the same passions, the same customs . . .' – though, this being Rousseau, it was their vices, not their virtues, that he was talking about.[53]

The idea of 'civilization' was the creation of all Europe, not of any one state or region, religion or sect. But it was also a process; for Europeans of the late eighteenth century that process knew no bounds. The 'pursuit of happiness' might have begun in Europe, but in principle it ought to be a goal for all mankind – and indeed achievable by all. It was in this spirit that the phrase crossed the Atlantic to find its way into the American Declaration of Independence in 1776 – and that Edward Gibbon, five years later, could argue, in the continuation of the passage quoted earlier:

> . . . the experience of four thousand years should enlarge our hopes, and diminish our apprehensions: we cannot determine to what height the human species may aspire in their advances towards perfection; but it may safely be presumed, that no people, unless the face of nature is changed, will relapse into their original barbarism.[54]

How wrong can you be?

7.

'The Lightning of the Nations'

1789–1871

On Sunday 12 July 1789, late in the afternoon, in the Garden of the Tuileries, outside the old city walls of Paris, the Greek medical doctor and self-taught classical scholar Adamantios Korais was out walking with a friend. Suddenly a commotion was heard in the street, and gunshots. Everybody ran to find out what was going on. A troop of dragoons entered the gardens, apparently on their way from the royal palace at Versailles to the centre of Paris. An elderly passer-by had his face slashed by a dragoon's sabre. The horrified strollers fled for their lives. During the next forty-eight hours tensions grew across the city. Writing to a friend back home, shortly afterwards, Korais described how groups of Parisians had begun raiding barracks and armouries, and helping themselves to weapons – including, he says, even cannon.

On Tuesday afternoon, 14 July, a mob laid siege to the fortress-cum-prison, the Bastille. After a three-hour stand-off the gates were forced, the commandant and his deputy beheaded on the spot. Korais continues his story:

> It was six o'clock in the evening, and I had gone out as was my habit, to read the English newspapers in the coffee house – don't imagine that with all this uproar and commotion I would keep indoors! . . . On my way I encountered the victors of the Bastille, accompanied by three or four hundred thousand of the common people, who were parading all about the city, holding aloft on long lances (what a ghastly sight!), the two severed heads dripping blood.

This estimate of the number involved can only have been very approximate, and must surely be an exaggeration. But the impression of shock at seeing the 'common people' violently take control of the streets comes over loud and clear. Korais went on to report how amid general panic, 'many government ministers, dukes, counts, duchesses, countesses and other great ladies of the queen's court, and five princes of the blood' had fled 'helter-skelter' from Paris to Versailles. Summing up his experiences for his friend shortly afterwards, with an understatement that can be forgiven in someone writing without the benefit of hindsight, he added: 'The year 1789 has been a terrible year for France, its memory will stand forever throughout history.'[1]

Korais was right. The French Revolution had begun.

A Portuguese diplomat, writing from Paris at the same time, reported, 'in all the world's annals there is no mention of a revolution like this one'. From the distance of the Prussian capital, Berlin, almost a decade later, the poet and scholar Friedrich Schlegel would sum up a commonplace that had become widespread among Germans by then: the Revolution in Paris had been 'an almost universal earthquake, an immeasurable flood in the political world'. The Swiss-born Madame de Staël, the writer and socialite who had been close to the action during the early years, in retrospect described its most violent excesses as 'an unprecedented accident that will not recur for thousands of centuries'.[2]

Across the Channel, in England, the Irish politician, essayist and member of the British parliament, Edmund Burke, was swift to condemn everything about it before most of these excesses had even taken place. In his *Reflections on the Revolution in France*, published in 1790 and an instant bestseller, Burke diagnosed a 'great crisis, not of the affairs of France alone but of all Europe . . . All circumstances taken together, the French Revolution is the most astonishing that has hitherto happened in the world.' At the opposite extreme was the English poet William Wordsworth, who spent some months in Paris at the height of the Revolution as a young man – though his often-quoted words would not be written until much later, and would not see print until 1850, after the poet's death that year:

Bliss was it in that dawn to be alive,
But to be young was very Heaven![3]

Modern judgements on the French Revolution generally agree that its effects were to transform all of Europe utterly – but not on much else about it. Was it a continuation of the Enlightenment by other means, as many observers at the time assumed? Or was it rather a violent negation of everything the *philosophes* had stood for? *How* exactly was Europe permanently changed, given that so many of the innovations introduced in France between 1789 and 1795 would sooner or later be reversed? Was this a completely unexpected bolt from the blue? Or was it part of a longer process – an 'age of revolution' – that had been launched by the American Declaration of Independence in 1776 and would take several more decades to work itself out? As recently as 1981 an influential study set out to argue that 'the French Revolution is over', implying that even after two hundred years, for many people the events of the 1790s represented unfinished business – as, for some, perhaps, they still do today.[4]

Was it, for all its horrific violence, a progressive movement, an unavoidable blip on the road towards greater human happiness? Or was it, as many contemporaries saw it, both within and outside France, a regression into barbarism that would lead only to dictatorship at home and a doomed imperialist adventure abroad?

The State System Shredded

It began as a perfect storm. The Bourbon dynasty had cemented in place an absolutist form of monarchy in which the state had increasingly been identified with the person of the king. Louis XIV, a century earlier, may not in reality have said '*L'état c'est moi*' ('The state is myself'), but he is on record as having said things that sound very like it. The French parliament had not met for almost two centuries. That meant that when things went wrong, the head of state was left exposed. And by the summer of 1789 things in France were going very badly indeed. The royal exchequer had been bankrupt for three years; Louis XVI finally bowed to pressure to recall parliament to try to sort out the crisis. Extreme weather, as so often, acted as a catalyst: the previous summer's harvest had been so poor that by July 1789 bread had become scarce and riots were breaking out all over the country.

A month after the storming of the Bastille, a newly formed National Assembly wrested control of the government from the king. Its members on 26 August signed a document, the *Déclaration des droits de l'homme et du citoyen* (*Declaration of the Rights of Man and the Citizen*); on 5 October the hapless Louis XVI gave it his signature. According to Article 3, 'The principle of all sovereignty resides in the *Nation*'. This word now rapidly took on a set of meanings that it had never possessed before. Article 6 adopted the phrase that had first been used by Rousseau, to begin: 'The law is the expression of the general will'. The traditional political state, embodied in the monarch, with everybody else ranked in hierarchical degrees as subjects, had been turned on its head. Sovereignty now lay with the people: no longer subjects but *citizens*, it was they who constituted the *nation*. The era of the nation state had arrived.[5]

Along with the new idea of citizenship went an updated concept of political liberty that went all the way back to the democratic city states of ancient Greece and the Roman Republic: all citizens were equal before the law, 'whether to protect or to punish'. The liberty of the revolutionary citizen also carried a distinctly Enlightenment flavour: 'Liberty consists in being able to do everything that does not harm others.' It would soon emerge that citizenship was going to carry a burden of obligations not spelt out in that original document; to turn subjects into citizens would prove a costly process in blood and violence. But the same rights and obligations now extended to minority Protestants and Jews – though not to women.[6]

Beginning in the summer of 1789, existing hierarchies were swept away. Along with aristocratic titles and privileges, in the first year, went the wealth and property of the Catholic Church – diverted to shoring up the national finances. Elaborate civic rituals and pageants were devised to replace religious worship with veneration for the nation. A new revolutionary calendar replaced the names of the months and bewilderingly divided them, on the decimal principle, into weeks of ten days. At a stroke the rhythms and the routines of age-old agricultural life were upended, along with the saints' days and other seasonal festivals that had punctuated them for centuries. In public documents even the name of God was replaced by the vaguer 'Supreme Being', while the secular slogan 'Liberty, Equality, Fraternity' became the new Holy Trinity. A 'Festival of Reason' was held in the cathedral of Notre-Dame in Paris in November 1793. In words attributed to Count Mirabeau, an ardent revolutionary despite the aristocratic title he had had to renounce, 'the Declaration of the Rights of Man has become a political Gospel and the French Constitution a religion for which people are prepared to die'.[7]

But it soon became apparent that not everyone was of the same mind. In November 1790 an attempt was made to nationalize even the Catholic Church: priests were obliged to swear loyalty to the secular state. Many refused; the backlash turned the Revolution into outright civil war. In parts of rural France where religious sentiment remained strong, counter-revolutionary violence provoked retaliation by the state on a scale that still has the power to shock, today. The general sent at the head of an army to quell the counter-insurgency in the Vendée, in western France, reported to the ruling National Convention, shortly after Christmas 1793:

> The Vendée is no more . . . According to your orders, I have trampled their children beneath our horses' feet; I have massacred their women, so they will no longer give birth to brigands. I do not have a single prisoner to reproach me. I have exterminated them all . . . Mercy is not a revolutionary sentiment.

Even that was not enough. State violence devised a new depravity when slave ships lying idle in the harbour at Nantes were crammed with captive counter-revolutionaries penned in their lower decks, sunk in the mouth of the River Loire, and then raised to be reused once each load of prisoners had drowned. As many as 400,000 men, women and children may have lost their lives in that campaign; it has been described as 'proportionally . . . in the front rank of the atrocities of modern European history'.[8]

Back in the capital, a 'Reign of Terror', as it has been called ever since, was well and truly under way. Right from the first days of the Revolution, the militant populace had shown a predilection for severing heads. It was a genial doctor and penal reformer by the name of Joseph-Ignace Guillotin who shortly afterwards proposed to the Assembly a method of decapitation that would be swift and supposedly painless. When the first guillotine was erected in the Place de la Révolution (today the Place de la Concorde) in October 1792, it would soon prove its worth – less, perhaps, in reducing the suffering of its victims than in enabling the state to dispose of its enemies at an industrial rate. The deposed Louis XVI, who had already been forced to abdicate to make way for a republic, became an early victim on 21 January of the next year; his queen, the unpopular Marie-Antoinette, nine months later. During the period of the Terror, between March 1793 and August 1794, the number of people publicly executed in this way reached a chillingly precise count of 2,639. The orgy of judicial killing reached its peak in the summer of 1794. It ended only after the chief architect of the Terror, Maximilien Robespierre, went to the guillotine himself at the end of July.[9]

Within France, order would slowly be restored after the frenzy of those eighteen months. But by that time, the Revolution had already begun to pass beyond the borders of the newly proclaimed nation. It wasn't so much that the monarchical powers in the rest of Europe ganged up to try to suppress or reverse what was happening in France. That would become part of it, especially after the declaration of the Republic and the execution of the king and his Austrian-born queen. But more fundamentally it was the new definition of the *nation* that brought France into inevitable conflict with its neighbours. When the German princes who had inherited rights to property and tax revenues in the German-speaking provinces of

Alsace and Lorraine objected to having their lands taken from them by the National Assembly, they were not impressed to be told that 'it is not the treaties of princes which govern the rights of *nations*'. What chance now for the 'states system' that had struggled for so long to maintain a balance of power in Europe?[10] A nation state, founded on the 'general will' of its citizens, was starting to rip up the rule book.

War began between France and a temporary coalition made up of most of its neighbours, including Britain, in 1792. For several years, fortunes tipped now one way, now the other. The nadir, for France, came in the spring of the next year. The Revolution, spearheaded by the National Convention, hit back with a whole new kind of warfare. A decree of mass conscription issued on 23 August 1793 turned every French citizen into a soldier – explicitly on the model of the Athenian citizen army that had defeated the Persians at Marathon some 2,500 years before. Perhaps a million strong, the French Revolutionary Army was to be the embodiment of the *nation* in arms – as is still celebrated in the ferocious words of the marching song that was first written for the forces defending the Rhine in that year and almost a century later would become the country's national anthem: the 'Marseillaise'. Its refrain begins 'To arms, citizens' ('Aux armes, citoyens'), and continues with a plea to 'let their foul blood soak our fields' – meaning the blood of any would-be invader.

On 17 November 1793, addressing the Convention, Robespierre himself spelt it out: 'Should all Europe declare against you, you are stronger than Europe! The French Republic is as invincible as reason; it is as immortal as truth. When liberty has made a conquest of such a country as France, no human power can drive her out.'[11] Not so long before, rulers had roused their subjects to defend the 'liberties of Europe', whatever exactly that might mean. Now liberty was both absolute and universal; but paradoxically it could only take practical, political form by being embodied in the 'will' of a nation. This was a conundrum that would perplex much of the politics of the next century. In the meantime, it was all or nothing; it was the French nation against the rest.

The stalemate lasted until 1796. It was broken very largely by the actions of one man. Napoleon Buonaparte came from an Italian-speaking family on the island of Corsica, which had become part of France as recently as 1770. In French, his name became 'Bonaparte', and before long he would become known as Emperor Napoleon I. As a very young man Napoleon had distinguished himself as an artillery officer; in 1795 he had earned his spurs as a revolutionary when he ordered cannon to be fired into a crowd of royalist counter-insurgents who tried to storm the Tuileries Palace. Now entrusted with command of the Republic's armies in Italy, Napoleon knew how to make the most of French manpower, traumatized and heavily militarized as it was by the events of the previous few years. After a string of French victories, the Austrian Empire was forced to the negotiating table in 1797. The Treaty of Campo Formio, signed that year, took the largest royalist power in Europe out of the war. Austria was obliged to give up a significant amount of territory in Italy and even more influence among the German-speaking states of the Holy Roman Empire. The map of mainland Europe was beginning to be redrawn.

Within France, the years that followed were marked by Napoleon's rapid rise through a series of roles that were closely modelled on ancient Rome: from 'First Consul' (in effect dictator, after a military coup), to 'Consul for life', and then to his coronation as emperor in 1804. For the ceremony a replica of the crown worn by Charlemagne for *his* imperial coronation, just over a thousand years before, had been specially commissioned. As well as drawing on remote history, Napoleon cemented his position through a series of popular votes. In this way he was able to claim that he still embodied the 'general will', even though he alone now issued the orders. A tactical agreement, known as the 'concordat', signed with the Catholic Church in the person of Pope Pius VII in 1801, took the heat out of religious opposition. France was a monarchical state once more – but with a difference. No longer did a royal dynasty rule through an inherited 'divine right' that had been bestowed by God; this time it was the French nation, made up of citizens and personified by its charismatic and seemingly invincible emperor, that sought to impose its will on the rest of Europe.

Opinions about Napoleon were sharply divided during his life-time: for some he was little less than a god; for others, 'Boney' became the caricature bogeyman conjured up by at least one gen-eration of British parents to terrify their children. The passage of time has added many nuances, but we are no nearer to a consensus today. A blockbuster Hollywood film, made in English and released in 2023, sparked a new round of public controversy in both English and French. Some modern historians have cast Napoleon as little more than a war criminal, responsible for the deaths of up to six million people; at the opposite end of the spectrum he has been hailed as 'the Enlightenment on horseback', a whirlwind that swept away the lingering cobwebs of medieval Europe and brought ideas of human progress, reason and religious toleration into every home and hearth throughout the European continent.[12]

At first, in many parts of Europe, Napoleon was seen as a lib-erator. Among those who benefited were the continent's Jews, who were granted full rights of citizenship and no longer obliged to live in segregated ghettos. A new law code, known as the *Code Napoléon* and modelled on the compilation of Roman law that had been drawn up on the orders of the emperor Justinian some thir-teen hundred years before, gave a uniform set of laws to the whole of continental Europe for the first time since the collapse of the Roman Empire. According to Napoleon himself, speaking once it was all over and he was far away, living as a prisoner on the British outpost of St Helena in the South Atlantic, his intention had been that 'Europe would be nothing more or less than a single people; and everyone, wherever they went, would find themselves in a common fatherland.'[13] But during his years in power, most Euro-peans on the receiving end seem to have been in little doubt: unlike the Enlightenment, which may have been French-led but had been a truly European movement, Napoleon's empire was French in name and in fact.

For the best part of a decade, from 1803 to 1812, every state in Europe, as well as the Russian and Ottoman empires on its borders, would be drawn into a shifting series of alliances either with or against Napoleon's France. Many would experience pitched battles on their soil on a scale never seen before. With the exception of the old adversaries Britain and France, most would change sides at least once before the conflict was over. While nobody knows for sure, the estimate of six million men killed in battle between 1792 and 1815 is probably not wide of the mark.

States of all sizes disappeared off the map for good. At the large end of the scale was the Holy Roman Empire. Francis II wound it up voluntarily, in 1806, partly to prevent Napoleon taking the imperial title for himself – but continued to rule as Emperor Francis I of Austria, in effect as Napoleon's vassal. A new 'Confederation of the Rhine' swept up the smaller remnants of the former empire. In the south, the Italian peninsula was consolidated into three large kingdoms to replace the dozens of independent city states, duchies and papal lands that had existed before. Europe would never be the same again.

Napoleon's rule began to unravel very quickly during the autumn and winter of 1812. The trouble with his programme of conquest was that every new gain created a need to defend frontiers that stretched ever farther away from France.[14] In order to secure the 'Grand Duchy of Warsaw' that he had created in Poland, Napoleon decided there was nothing for it but to turn against his ally of the moment, Russia. The imperial *Grande Armée* that began to cross the Niemen river from Poland into Russia at the end of June 1812 numbered more than half a million men – including roughly half that number who had been forcibly conscripted from German-speaking states. They got as far as Moscow, after narrowly defeating the tsar's army at the battle of Borodino on 7 September; but the Muscovites abandoned their city and burned it to the ground. The story of Napoleon's humiliating retreat through the snows of the Russian winter, and the decimation of his army by frostbite, enemy action and desertion, is one of the best known in all modern European history. Half a century later Leo Tolstoy would shape it into the climactic episode of one of the greatest novels ever written, *War and Peace*.

From the same story Tolstoy also derived a theory of history that has fared less well, though it still has its adherents. According to this, it is only an illusion that 'great men' such as Napoleon or his adversary Tsar Alexander I direct or 'cause' historical events. Tolstoy detected an 'incredible symmetry' between the 'movement of people from west to east' that had started out from Paris with the Revolution of 1789, reaching as far as Moscow in 1812, and the 'east-west counter-movement' that began with Napoleon's retreat, and ended up back at 'the starting point of the first movement, Paris', before fading away. The actions and behaviour of millions of men, Tolstoy concluded, were not a matter of free will or choice at all, but must be determined by forces of nature as immutable as Newton's laws.[15] A further subtlety he might have considered, but did not, would have been to contrast the self-willed actions of Napoleon with the millennia-old movement of peoples into Europe from the east. Not even a Napoleon (or, a century later, a Hitler) could buck *that* trend.

Be that as it may, there *was* something symmetrical about the counter-surge that followed Napoleon's retreat from Russia. Within three years, troops from Russia, as well as from Prussia and Austria, and even Tsar Alexander himself, would have taken up residence in Paris not once, but twice. In the immediate aftermath of the retreat, a new set of alliances lined up Russia and Britain, at opposite ends of Europe, with Austria and Prussia, former vassals of Napoleon, in the middle. In October 1813, in the 'battle of the Nations', fought outside the German city of Leipzig, the combined forces of almost all of continental Europe routed Napoleon's troops. Three months earlier, a British expeditionary force in the Iberian peninsula, along with its Spanish and Portuguese allies, had decisively defeated the

French in the Basque country. The allies now began to close in on France.

Napoleon was forced to abdicate in April 1814 and was sent into exile on the Italian island of Elba. At the beginning of May, overseen by the victors, the brother of the executed Louis XVI returned from exile; an uncrowned heir had died in the meantime, so the new king became Louis XVIII. The Bourbon monarchy was back; the wars were over (or so everybody thought). But the European 'states system', based on the balance of power, that had precariously held together for almost two centuries, lay in tatters; it could not be so easily stitched together again. The task that faced the winners on the battlefield and the architects of the future peace was to make sure that the devastation of the past twenty-two years could never be repeated. For that, a whole new system would have to be devised.

Towards a 'Concert of Europe'

Even while the wars had been at their height, statesmen at the farthest ends of the continent had begun to realize that a European emergency on this scale could only be met with a European solution. In 1804 and 1805 the foreign minister of Russia and the prime minister of Great Britain (William Pitt the Younger) had exchanged proposals for future 'reciprocal relations of the European states', based on a 'sort of code of international law' or 'a general and comprehensive system of public law in Europe'.[16] At the time, any ideas of a future peace once Napoleon had been defeated could only be wishful thinking. Nine years later, and with the four major powers of Europe converging on Paris, ready to deliver the *coup de grâce* to the Napoleonic regime, their time had come.

The movement of armies from one end of the continent to the other had brought sovereigns, commanders-in-chief and government ministers into close proximity with one another – something that had probably never happened in Europe before. Tsar Alexander went everywhere at the head of his troops; soon he would be joined by King Frederick William III of Prussia. By the end of 1813, the Austrian foreign minister, Prince Clemens von Metternich, was flitting about Europe to negotiate both with his emperor's allies and, on their behalf, with Napoleon. In a panic at the prospect of being left out, the British government took the unprecedented step of sending its own foreign minister, Robert Stewart, Viscount Castlereagh, to the continent to join the negotiations in person.

The pattern for the next eight years – if not for the whole of the next century – was set when the foreign ministers of Austria, Britain, Prussia and Russia sat down at a whist table in the small town of Chaumont, described by one of them as 'dirty and dull', on the River Marne in northern France, on 1 March 1814. 'It was agreed that never were the stakes so high at any former [whist] party,' wrote another.[17] The document they signed eight days later was called a 'Treaty of Union, Concert, and Subsidy' – already in its title heralding what would later come to be known as the 'Concert of Europe'. In it the four powers committed themselves to 'draw closer the ties which unite them for the vigorous prosecution of a War undertaken for the salutary purpose of putting an end to the miseries of Europe'. The treaty also speaks of 're-establishing a just balance of power' and maintaining 'the equilibrium of Europe' for the next twenty years.[18]

The Treaty of Chaumont has been described as 'a completely new departure in the history of international relations'. On the one hand, it set up a cartel of Great Powers as the future 'arbiters of Europe', to the exclusion of smaller states, regions, or the emerging aspirations of nations. On the other, it set the scene for a new type of diplomacy, in which senior members of their respective governments met in person to thrash out their differences around a table; and this they increasingly did 'in the name of "Europe" rather than overtly acting for themselves'.[19] At Chaumont it had been foreign ministers. Once peace had been concluded with France at the end of May, and a congress of 'All Powers engaged on either side of the present War' had been called for Vienna in the autumn, the diplomatic stakes would rise even higher. Heads of state themselves now prepared to join the highest representatives of every government in Europe to descend on the Austrian capital.[20]

The host was the emperor Francis I of Austria, though the hardest of the hard work was borne by his foreign minister Metternich, *his* long-suffering secretary, Friedrich von Gentz, and an army of police spies recruited for the occasion. The Emperor of All the Russias and the King of Prussia made their ceremonial entry into Vienna together on 25 September 1814, accompanied by Francis, who had ridden out to welcome them. Also present for varying lengths of time were the kings of Denmark, Bavaria and Württemberg, as well as dozens of minor princes, many of whom no longer had a state to call their own, and hundreds of lesser noblemen and functionaries. Even the Pope was expected at Vienna, although in the event he sent his Secretary of State instead. So many monarchs, aristocrats and high officials of so many different nationalities, representing so many different states, had never been seen all in one place before.

During the autumn of 1814, expectations ran extraordinarily high. After all these years of fighting and devastation, Europe was swept by an intense burst of euphoria. All eyes were on Vienna. The emperor Francis commissioned the greatest composer of the age, Ludwig van Beethoven, together with the now forgotten poet Alois Weissenbach, to produce a cantata to be performed at the opening concert. 'Europe stands!' begins the Chorus; the soprano, representing Vienna, exults: 'I am Europe – no more a mere city.' 'On my shattered walls,' she concludes, 'Europe is rebuilding itself.'[21] From the diaries and letters of those who were there, down to the richly researched scholarly accounts published two hundred years later, we know that everybody at the Congress was talking about 'Europe'. But what did they mean by it? The answer would have to be made up as they went along. And in the meantime, they found much to distract them.

For several months, a spirit of 'almost frenzied frivolity' seemed to trump the serious business of statecraft. Delegates, along with their wives, mistresses and retainers, were treated to a seemingly never-ending succession of fancy-dress balls, sumptuous dinners, performances of opera and theatre, firework displays, winter sleigh-rides, hunting parties where captive animals could be slaughtered in their hundreds, military parades, even on one occasion a re-enactment of a medieval tournament, followed by a Renaissance feast. The witticism that began to circulate in French – *Le Congrès danse mais il ne marche pas* – only partially survives in English trans-lation: 'The Congress dances but it doesn't work.' A member of the Austrian imperial family complained in his diary, before most of the festivities had even got under way: 'Nothing but visits and return visits; eating, fireworks, illuminations. For 8–10 days I haven't been able to get anything done. What a way to live!'[22]

By Christmas it was becoming clear that the Congress was indeed *not* working, at least not in the sense that many of the participants and most outside observers had been led to expect. No plenary session of all the delegates from all over Europe had yet been held – and indeed none ever would be. Business was being done behind closed doors, among the representatives of the major powers. And some of that was becoming increasingly acrimonious. But none of this was enough to blunt the optimism of Castlereagh when at a ball at the Hofburg Palace on New Year's Day, 1815, he leant forward and whispered in the ear of Tsar Alexander, 'Now the golden age is beginning.'[23]

The diplomatic process was grinding on by fits and starts, and party fatigue had begun to set in, when Vienna was rocked at the beginning of March 1815 by the news that Napoleon had gone missing from his island exile on Elba. Within a month the former emperor was back in Paris; his war-weary people were rallying to his renewed call to the colours. Louis XVIII, who had so recently reclaimed the French throne for the Bourbons, fled the country for a second time. Suddenly Europe was at war once again. From the British Isles to the Urals, armies were again strengthened and began ponderously moving towards the French frontiers. In the event, Napoleon attacked first; the decisive battles were fought on the soil of today's Belgium. The battle of Waterloo, fought on 18 June 1815, was won by British and Prussian armies, respectively under the command of the Duke of Wellington and General Gebhard Blücher. Napoleon's 'Hundred Days' were over.

Rather remarkably, while the fate of Europe still remained to be decided on the battlefield, the foreign ministers and diplomats gathered in Vienna had carried on with their business, regardless. The Final Act of the Congress was signed a mere nine days before the battle. Even as men were dying in their thousands on the fields of Quatre Bras, Ligny and Waterloo, in the Austrian capital the last of the weary negotiators were packing their bags and summoning up the horses and carriages that would take them home – journeys that, for some, would last several weeks. Had the battle gone the other way, as it very nearly did, their labours would have been wasted.

As it was, the provisions of the Final Act defined jurisdictions and frontiers from end to end of continental Europe. One of its most striking compromises was the creation of a sprawling 'German Confederation', which looked like nothing so much as the pale ghost of the Holy Roman Empire, presided over by Austria. Often described as a 'restoration' (at the time and since), the arrangements signed off at Vienna were more new than old, despite the efforts of rulers and their governments to cover over the traces.[24]

The Final Act also rolled up – or diplomatically shelved – a number of other matters that had been the subject of heated debate during the previous eight months. In a world before railways, in which rivers were the main arteries of long-distance trade across the continent, a series of articles for the first time set out common regulations guaranteeing freedom of navigation and the levying of tariffs – a distant precursor, perhaps, of today's European Single Market. An annex summed up inconclusive arguments about the slave trade: while they had no trouble in condemning the trade in human beings as immoral, the most exalted and powerful statesmen of Europe could not agree to outlaw it. Closer to home, the emancipation of Jewish communities, particularly in the German-speaking states, had stalled since Napoleon's defeat; the Congress did its best to reinstate rights for Jews, although it could not prevent backsliding by several states. Equal citizenship for Europe's Jews, which had begun in France with the Revolution and had been exported by Napoleon, still had some way to go.[25]

When it came to Europe's eastern borderlands, we can see with hindsight that the Congress and its immediate aftermath marked the high point of Russia's integration with the rest. This was noted at the time, too; the possibility that Russian influence might extend even further was a constant concern for the other negotiators at Vienna. But however much they might distrust him, the forced retreat of the *Grande Armée* from Moscow had left Tsar Alexander I as one of the most powerful men in Europe. At the same time, Russia itself – or rather its governing class – had never been as European, or would be again, as it was in 1815. The tsar himself, the grandson of German-born Catherine the Great, was by descent more German than Russian; his foreign ministers during the wars and afterwards were Polish, German and Greek. French had become the polite language of the Russian elite – as Tolstoy would in due course remind his readers throughout more than a thousand pages of *War and Peace*.

It was Alexander's personal influence, too, that foisted upon the new alliance an explicitly Christian dimension. Both Castlereagh and Metternich had been keen to involve the Ottoman Empire in the negotiations and the final arrangements hammered out at Vienna. The Ottomans, after all, had been drawn into more than one European alliance during the wars against France. But to bring an Islamic power to the table was too much for Alexander. One reason for this must surely have been the long-standing hostility between Europe's two powerful eastern neighbours. But Alexander raised a different objection. His own religious convictions had taken a turn towards Christian mysticism since the invasion of his country by Napoleon. A document drawn up by the tsar and unveiled in September 1815 invited the allied sovereigns 'to base the direction of [their] policy . . . on the sublime truths taught by the eternal religion of God the redeemer'. Privately ridiculed by Metternich, and reported by Castlereagh to the British cabinet as the product of an unsound mind, the Holy Alliance, as it became known, would be duly signed and published in St Petersburg on Christmas Day. But the omission of the Ottoman Empire from the treaties would turn out to have consequences.[26]

More far-reaching than the Vienna Final Act or the pieties of the Holy Alliance were the measures taken afterwards by the four allied powers to police the continent in future. Napoleon's escape from Elba and the events of the 'Hundred Days' had shown how shaky was the edifice constructed during all those months of diplomacy at Vienna.[27] All the more necessary, therefore, that there should be no going back to the failed 'system' of the previous century. After Waterloo, the diplomatic action – and many of the same actors, including Tsar Alexander, King Frederick William of Prussia, Metternich and Wellington – moved to the French capital. A second Peace of Paris, signed in November 1815, once again restored Louis XVIII to his throne, confirmed Napoleon's permanent exile to St Helena, and trimmed the eastern borders of France less generously than before.

On the same day, the formation of a Quadruple Alliance was announced. Its members were Austria, Britain, Prussia and Russia. Echoing the provisions of the wartime Treaty of Chaumont, this new treaty for the first time specified a mechanism for enforcement that would extend far into the future. The sovereigns themselves, or in their absence 'their respective Ministers', would meet at regular intervals 'for the consideration of the measures . . . for the maintenance of the peace of Europe'.[28]

Today we would call these meetings 'summits'; then, they were known as congresses. The principles of the congress system, as it would come to be called, were most fully set out at the first in the series, held three years later, in the autumn of 1818. The venue chosen was Aix-la-Chapelle, which once upon a time had been Charlemagne's capital and is today the German city of Aachen. France, after three years of good behaviour, was admitted to the club, which now became the Quintuple Alliance. In an annex to the diplomatic communiqué issued on their behalf on 15 November, the five monarchs affirmed their determination to maintain the status quo established in 1815. They also claimed the right to intervene in situations where 'other Governments shall formally claim their interference', which is a diplomatic way of saying: if anything in any way resembling the French Revolution should ever occur again.[29]

In this way was formed the 'Concert of Europe', as it would become known. Instead of relying on the fortunes of war to maintain a precarious balance of power, governments from London to St Petersburg, from the Arctic Circle to the Mediterranean, signed up to the principle that, from now on, disputes and rivalries were to be resolved by discussion and consensus among them. A new idea of Europe had been forged out of the trauma of the French Revolutionary and Napoleonic Wars. It would last (just about) until 1914.

An Age of Revolutions?

At the highest level of governments that was all very well. But lower down the scale, some of those actual or potential 'citizens' whose 'general will' had been briefly mobilized by the French Revolution had other ideas of their own.

Writing in London in defence of the revolutionaries across the Channel, the veteran of American independence, Thomas Paine, had written as far back as 1791: 'It is an age of Revolutions, in which every thing may be looked for.' Paine identified the essentials linking the revolutions in America and France as 'national sovereignty, and Government by representation'.[30] Today, with the benefit of more than two centuries of hindsight, we call these, respectively, 'nationalism' and 'liberalism'. At the time, and for the next fifty years or so, the twin concepts would remain inseparably intertwined, just as they had been in the French Revolutionary proclamation of the 'Rights of Man', from which Paine took the title for his own pamphlet. If the real source of power in a state was to be not the monarch or the government but the 'sovereign people', then indeed, as Paine seemed to be suggesting, anything was possible. (That was exactly what many others, including his adversary Edmund Burke, found so horrifying.)

These ways of thinking reached far beyond politics. In the creative arts, a set of trends was gathering momentum and in due course would come to be known as Romanticism. The movement began in northern Europe, with poetry, drama and essays published in German and English in the last decades of the eighteenth century; soon it would be taken up in music and the visual arts. By the 1820s, the Romantic movement had reached into every corner of Europe. Romanticism has been described as itself a kind of revolution.[31] It aspired to nothing less than the liberation of the creative energies of mankind; like the Enlightenment before it, Romanticism could never have arisen anywhere but in Europe, or at any other juncture in history.

A further potent ingredient in the mix was the idea that had begun with Herder in the 1780s: that nations were defined by their *differences* from one another, and that each nation possessed a distinctive 'character' of its own. Nowhere did this idea gain a greater hold than in the German states that had been subjected to several years of either direct rule or overlordship by Napoleon. While French imperial troops patrolled the streets of Berlin outside, the German professor of philosophy Johann Gottlieb Fichte had given a series of lectures that he published in 1808 with the title *Reden an die deutsche Nation* (*Addresses to the German Nation*). Pulling together the ideas of Rousseau, Herder and the growing Romantic movement, Fichte built up an image of a nation – and specifically his own – as a kind of corporate actor in the world. The future was to be forged by the newly discovered force of the human *will*, generated from below rather than dictated from above, and gathered into the collective creative impulse of the nation.[32]

After 1815, ideas variously linked to these were swirling around Europe. But little notice was taken of them at the great congresses where all the important decisions were being taken – except by the

secret police. And as most states applied some degree of prevent-
ive censorship, there were limited opportunities even to air them in
public, let alone act upon them. Ironically enough, it was the very
determination of the architects of the congress system to prevent
any repetition of the French Revolution that drove the opposition
underground and gave it an unavoidably revolutionary character.

Across northern Europe, the traditional drinking and duelling
clubs that had long been a feature of German university life rapidly
expanded and became heavily politicized. In October 1817, to mark
three hundred years since Martin Luther's act of defiance against
the Catholic Church, a mass protest was staged at the Wartburg
castle in Saxony. This was where Luther had been given refuge; the
event served as a reminder that German nationhood could trace its
origins all the way back to the Protestant Reformation. Books were
symbolically burnt – as they had been, back then, by the Inquisition. This and other signs of radical dissent crossed a line when one
of the writers whose books had been consigned to the flames, the
playwright August von Kotzebue, was assassinated by a militant student two years later. On the orders of Metternich, now Chancellor
as well as foreign minister of Austria, strict controls were placed on
universities and further restrictions imposed on the press throughout the German Confederation.

Further south, in 1820 and the spring of 1821, a wave of revolutions swept Europe from Portugal to the Italian peninsula. In Spain,
Portugal, Naples (capital of the 'Kingdom of the Two Sicilies') and
in Piedmont, senior army officers and political leaders seized power;
describing themselves as 'liberals', they tried to impose constitutions to limit the power of the restored monarchies. The national
histories of all these different parts of Europe, as they would later
be written, have tended to isolate each of these events; today, historians are more inclined to see them as connected and as part of a
Europe-wide pattern.[33] And that is certainly how they were viewed
by the likes of Metternich and Tsar Alexander, even if a hefty dose
of paranoia had crept into those high places by the 1820s.

More percipiently, the English poet Percy Bysshe Shelley, from his self-imposed exile in Tuscany, celebrated the constitutionalist *putsch* in Spain in 1820 in his 'Ode to Liberty', written shortly afterwards. The spread of liberty across the continent, Shelley wrote, is like wildfire in the heavens or the subterranean force that drives volcanic eruptions:

> A glorious people vibrated again
>   The lightning of the nations
>
>   . . .
>
>   as with its thrilling thunder
> Vesuvius wakens Etna, and the cold
>   Snow-crags by its reply are cloven in sunder . . .[34]

Despite this enthusiasm, all of these revolutionary movements were soon suppressed. By the spring of 1821, when only the Spanish constitutionalists still held out, it looked as though claims to the sovereignty of *nations* and their citizens had been nipped in the bud in the south, just as they already had in the German states. 'Citizens' were once again to be subjects everywhere; Metternich and the 'Concert of Europe' ruled.

It was in the south-eastern corner of the continent that this began to change, and in spectacular fashion. In February and March 1821 the tide of revolutionary fervour that had been sweeping eastwards reached the Balkans. The Greek Orthodox populations scattered throughout the region rose up against their Ottoman masters. This time there was no question of a bloodless take-over by well-disciplined army officers; the Greek Revolution that began in 1821 was at least as bloody as the French Revolution had been. Horrific reprisals by the Ottoman authorities meant that for all who became involved there could be no going back; it was kill or be killed.

Even if the Greek rank and file had been culturally cut off from Europe for centuries and had little idea of what had been going on in the rest of the continent, many of their leaders were highly educated men who had studied at universities in Europe and were following events and ideas closely. The first of no fewer than three provisional constitutions for an independent Greece was signed off by a National Assembly on the first day of 1822 – and sent to the British political philosopher Jeremy Bentham for comment and approval. However improbable it might have seemed to many throughout Europe at the time, during the 1820s, in the southern half of today's mainland Greece and the islands in the Aegean, out of the disparate Orthodox Greek populations would be forged a modern nation, according to the meaning which that word had first begun to acquire during the Revolution in France.[35]

Right at the start, leaders of the Greek Revolution issued appeals for 'the aid of all the civilized nations of Europe' in 'a just and sacred enterprise'; this, they said, was to be nothing less than the 'regeneration' of the people which, as every child of the Enlightenment by this time knew, had laid the foundations for European civilization itself. And the call was heeded – not by the sovereigns and governments to which it was addressed, but by individuals of all social classes. They came from almost every part of Europe, a few even from as far away as America. Between 1821 and 1826, more than a thousand volunteers arrived in Greece to take up arms.

The stories of these 'philhellenes', as they came to be known, were often tragic. Their efforts and their sacrifices were quite out of proportion to any impact most of them were able to make on the ground. Almost a third died, as often from disease as in battle – the fate of the most famous of them all, the British poet and celebrity, Lord Byron, who died of fever. As many again returned home broken and disillusioned by their experiences. But behind them, spread out from one end of Europe to the other, a much larger network of support organizations and pressure groups began to exercise a powerful effect on public opinion and in that way also on governments.[36]

Historians have often wondered, since, what it was that induced so many individuals, of so many different nationalities and backgrounds, to enlist, in one way or another, in a war in a far corner of the continent whose people and whose modern history they knew next to nothing about. Some thought they were refighting the Crusades, in a war 'of the Cross against the Crescent': Christian Europe (the Europe of the Holy Alliance) was pushing back against Islam, after centuries on the back foot. But just as important, if not even more so, was Europe's cultural debt to ancient Greece that had been invoked in that first appeal addressed to its 'civilized nations'. It was Shelley, again, who famously wrote in 1821, shortly after the revolution had begun: 'We are all Greeks. Our laws, our literature, our religion, our arts have their root in Greece. But for Greece . . . we might still have been savages and idolaters.' Either way, the philhellenes were Europeans who saw in this distant conflict something of their own at stake. Those Greek leaders had judged their target audience well.[37]

It was this pressure from below, rather than any principles of the congress system, that brought together the three powers with naval interests in the eastern Mediterranean to try to resolve the conflict. The governments of Britain, France and Russia agreed in 1826 to set up a standing conference in London on the subject of Greece. The next year, a joint naval task force was despatched to the region. Charged with the contradictory mission of imposing peace by force of arms, the expedition ended up destroying the Ottoman fleet in the battle of Navarino, fought in the coastal waters of the southwest Peloponnese in October 1827. The way was now open for Greece to be recognized as an independent state. The Greek Revolution ended, not on the battlefield, but in a room in the Foreign Office in London. There, on 3 February 1830, the representatives of the three governments put their signatures to a diplomatic protocol guaranteeing Greek independence.

By 1833, Greece had a new king, imported from Europe (from Bavaria); ten years later a constitution and a parliament would follow. Grandiose plans were drawn up – and largely fulfilled, too – to create a new capital city in Athens, complete with all the public institutions that might be expected of an ultra-modern European kingdom: a royal palace, university, parliament, national library, an Academy, an archaeological museum – even, among the first, an astronomical observatory. All of these were housed in buildings conceived in homage to the classical ruins at the city's centre, and following the latest European fashions in architecture and town planning. Ostentatiously, here was Europe reclaiming ground that had long ago been lost to the Ottomans. The long-term significance of these events is only now being fully appreciated by historians, two hundred years after they happened; a study published in 2025 sums it up: 'In 1830 the European border moved from the Adriatic to the Aegean, where it remains to this day.'[38]

But if 'modern' Greece was (and is) a *European* state, it was also, just as ostentatiously, and right from the beginning, conceived and constructed as a *national* one. At this time it was still possible to be both, without tension or contradiction. An accident of birth places Greece at the very beginning of the formation of the Europe of nation states that we know today. It had been accomplished through a combination of violent revolution, diplomacy and intervention by three of the five Great Powers of Europe at the time. A template had been set for other nations, bigger players on the European stage, to follow.

No sooner had the Great Powers signed off on independence for Greece, than the 'lightning of the nations' struck again – within a few months right across the continent, from Paris to Warsaw, from Brussels to central Italy. In France, Charles X, the last surviving brother of the executed Louis XVI, had been trying to roll back the limited powers of parliament under the constitution that had been imposed by the victors back in 1814. In response, in July 1830, a new tactic in urban warfare suddenly sprang up: Parisians began to rip up the squared stones that cobbled their streets and build them into barricades; topped with items of household furniture and any other material that might be to hand, these proved formidable obstacles to the troops sent in to restore order. The stand-off that followed would be immortalized three decades later by Victor Hugo in his panoramic novel of France after Napoleon, *Les Misérables*.

A month later, in Brussels, a performance of an opera with a local patriotic theme sparked similar scenes. The mostly French-speaking, mostly Catholic middle class of the city had never been reconciled to being rolled up by the Vienna Congress into a newly minted Kingdom of the Netherlands. Now resurrecting an ancient tribal name that went back to Julius Caesar's accounts of his conquests two thousand years before, the revolutionaries demanded national sovereignty of their own for the southern half of the Dutch kingdom, to be known as Belgium. At the same time, agitation for a united Germany and a united Italy disturbed the peace in parts of the German Confederation and the Italian peninsula. And then at the end of October, army officers seized control of the streets in Warsaw in a doomed attempt to restore the independent Polish kingdom that had been partitioned out of existence among its neighbours during the previous century.

From the point of view of the long-serving Metternich, these events added up to nothing less than 'the collapse of the dam in Europe'. As late as 1831, when the crisis in France was well on the way to a less dramatic resolution, Metternich could still write to a Russian correspondent, 'The directing committee in Paris will triumph and no government will remain standing.'[39] The reality was more varied, and more nuanced. In Poland, the revolt was totally crushed by Tsar Nicholas I, with the consequence that the Poles lost even the limited autonomy they had been granted by the Vienna settlement; the effective western frontier of Russia now extended further into Europe than at any other time before 1945. In France, a 'citizen-king', known as Louis-Philippe rather than by a regnal number, ruled in the name of 'the will of the nation' and by a tweak of wording became 'King of the French', which was thought to sound less absolutist than the traditional 'King of France'. Citizens were very far from being 'sovereign' again, but they were perhaps allowed to be a little more than mere subjects.[40]

Only the Belgians came out of it with a clear win – thanks, once again, to a conference of the Great Powers, so to that extent still within the spirit of the post-1815 system. The kingdom of Belgium was signed into existence by the representatives of all five of the Vienna powers in January 1831 – on condition of its neutrality, thereby inadvertently setting up one of the triggers for the First World War.

After 1830 the cause of nations and their emancipation continued to gather pace. And for the time being, it was still very much a *pan-European* movement. This was nowhere more evident, during the 1830s and 1840s, than in the writings and actions of the Italian journalist and serial instigator of revolts Giuseppe Mazzini. When he launched a campaigning organization called 'Young Italy' in 1831, some 60,000 Italians responded. Mazzini believed in 'a federal system of European Democracy, such that an uprising by one Nation would find the others ready to support it with deeds'.[41] Utopian, perhaps – but Mazzini's words and actions testify to a coherent *alternative* vision to the 'Concert of Europe'. A 'European Democracy' would obviously have to be driven from below, not from above by monarchs and Great Powers. This was perhaps the first time that the idea of Europe was explicitly linked to the democratic ideal.

It all came to a head in the first months of 1848. Printed slogans were pasted on walls, barricades were thrown across streets, demonstrators took over city centres, hard-pressed soldiers with conflicting loyalties either changed sides or opened fire on their fellow citizens, or both. These things happened in Palermo and Naples in January; in Paris in February; in Vienna, Berlin, Milan and Venice in March. Governments fell like ninepins. Monarchs and their courts fled their capital cities. Constitutions in great numbers were rushed into print. 'This was the only truly European revolution that there has ever been,' writes Christopher Clark in a magisterial study of these events published in 2023: 'the same words rang out everywhere: constitution, liberty, freedom of the press, association and assembly, civil (or national) guard, franchise reform'. Here was Shelley's 'lightning of the nations' in action as never before; the poet's metaphor of subterranean volcanic activity was never more apt. To the twenty-first-century historian, the revolutions of 1848 seemed more like 'the particle collision chamber at the centre of the European nineteenth century', in which, at a crucial moment, 'we enter the fission phase, in which almost simultaneous detonations create complex feedback loops'.[42]

For a few dizzying months in the spring and early summer of that year, it really did look as though, in the words of Thomas Paine back in 1791, 'every thing may be looked for', anything was possible. The mood across continental Europe at that time has been compared to the 'Arab Spring' of 2011.[43] But just as in the Muslim world in the second decade of our own century, it was not to be.

Nations in Conflict

For a few months at a time, though not the same months in different parts of the continent, it was almost as though a ghostly embryo of the future shape of Europe could be discerned through the tumult. France was once more a republic. A united Italy seemed to be rapidly emerging. North of the Alps, the thirty-nine separate jurisdictions that made up the German Confederation began to look much more like the federal state of today when an elected *National* Assembly came together in Frankfurt-am-Main to deliberate on their future. To the south and east, in the twin cities on either side of the River Danube, Buda and Pest, the Hungarian Diet (or parliament) declared first autonomy and then outright independence from Austria; elsewhere in eastern Europe, Croats, Czechs, Slovaks, Romanians, Ukrainians and Poles all launched bids for national recognition of their own. Further into the Balkans, in Bucharest a 'Provisional Government of Wallachia' ousted joint Russian and Ottoman overlordship to create a forerunner of today's Romania.

But it was not yet time for this embryo to be born. In all these places liberal reformers fell out with radicals demanding power for the entire mass of the people, in a version of Rousseau's 'general will'. It was no accident that the *Communist Manifesto*, by Karl Marx and Friedrich Engels, written in German but published in London, was slipped out at the end of February 1848, just as the continent-wide revolutions were gathering momentum. Its opening sentence has been much quoted since: 'A spectre is haunting Europe – the spectre of communism.' That claim, too, was a ghostly harbinger; it was far from being true then and would not become so until much later.[44] But it was in the white heat of that year's revolutions that the origins of the 'class war' of later times are to be found. A new fault line was opening up: between, in the classic terminology of twentieth-century Marxism, the liberal 'bourgeoisie' and the 'proletariat'.

And then there was the cause of nations, or nationalism as we now call it. It had been all very well for Mazzini to argue that democratic nation states would naturally be united by a common interest and come together. But what actually happened was the exact opposite. There was an immense swathe of central Europe, from southern Denmark in the north right through into the Ottoman Empire in the south, where communities that shared different languages, customs and traditions had been living cheek by jowl for centuries. If new nations were to be formed, based on the sovereignty of their peoples, who exactly *were* those people? How were they even to recognize one another? What did they have in common?

As the Austrian Empire seemed ready to collapse, Croats, Serbs and Romanians lined up alongside their former Austrian rulers *against* an independent Hungary, rather than be forcibly turned into Hungarians. The fate of Hungarian secession was sealed when the young, newly crowned emperor of Austria, Franz Joseph I, went on literally bended knee to Tsar Nicholas I of Russia to ask for help. By that time everyone could see that conflict between nations was likely to prove every bit as deadly as the old European fault lines had been. When the crunch came, it was the old empires that hung together, not the new nations struggling to free themselves from their grip. The result was that by the end of 1849 the revolts had been crushed everywhere. The spirit of the 'Concert of Europe' had won through after all – even if its last surviving architect, Metternich, had been forced to flee his home in Vienna and seek refuge far away in England. Everybody was back where they had started.

But not quite. Out of the 'particle collision chamber' of the revolutions had emerged new leaders, able and willing to exploit the immense popular appeal of the idea of *national* sovereignty that had briefly taken over the streets of Europe's cities. In the hands of these men, the newly unleashed force of nationalism was no longer to be the means towards a more liberal, representative type of government, but rather an alternative to it. Strongman rulers would now be able to claim legitimacy in the name of their nation, without having to transfer too much of their power to the people or their elected representatives. Enter, in France, Louis-Napoleon Bonaparte, nephew of the emperor of the same name, elected president of the French Second Republic in December 1848; enter Otto von Bismarck, confidant of King Frederick William IV of Prussia during the revolutions and later all-powerful 'Minister President' under his successor; enter Victor Emmanuel II, king of Sardinia and Piedmont from 1849.

These were the men who would transform Europe over the next twenty years. Bonaparte in 1852 followed the example of his uncle to become the emperor Napoleon III; Bismarck during the 1860s became the architect of a new German Empire, united under the leadership of Prussia but excluding the Germans of Austria; Victor Emmanuel became the beneficiary of the Italian movement known as the *Risorgimento*, or 'regeneration'. Austrian, Bourbon and papal rule in different parts of the peninsula were driven out to create a single kingdom of Italy during the same decade. Elsewhere, the principalities of Wallachia and Moldavia gained their independence as Romania in 1859. Within the Austrian Empire, the Hungarians managed to negotiate a degree of autonomy after all, with the creation of a 'Dual Monarchy' in 1867, known from then on as Austria-Hungary.

The map of Europe was changing, and in ways that could never have been foreseen, still less permitted, under the terms of the Vienna settlement in 1815. The most serious challenge to that settlement, which came close to derailing it altogether, came in the 1850s. Britain and France allowed themselves to be dragged into the latest trial of strength between Europe's two eastern neighbours, Russia and Turkey. This was the time when Turkey was becoming known as the 'sick man of Europe' – a belated and backhanded way of acknowledging a geopolitical reality that so many had tried to deny, or defy, since the time of Süleyman the Magnificent. It was fear that the 'sick man' might actually die, and in so doing pave the way for Russia to expand into the eastern Mediterranean and the Balkans, that induced Napoleon III, as he now was, and the British prime minister Lord Aberdeen, to intervene to prop him up.

The Crimean War, which lasted from 1853 to 1856, ended in defeat for Russia, with no real gain for the victors. But it did result in far-reaching changes to both of the great empires that bordered Europe to the east. On the Turkish side, the 'sick man' was granted a reprieve that in the event would last for more than half a century. In piecemeal fashion, during that time, the Ottomans would make a concerted effort to become, in various ways, more 'European'. It was a process that was controversial within the empire at the time, and in hindsight would store up trouble for later.

In Russia, too, Tsar Alexander II introduced reforms. The most drastic of these was the emancipation of his country's vast class of serfs – counted in their thousand as 'souls' that were literally owned by landlords and the main indicator of wealth among the Russian elite. But just as significant in the long run was a turn by that same elite away from Europe after the humiliation of the Crimean War. The Russian Empire was as multi-ethnic and multilingual as the Ottoman or the Austrian; but educated Russians now began to discover a Russian national identity and to champion the cause of the Slavs more broadly as a nation within and against the European powers. While the émigré Russian novelist Ivan Turgenev, who had left Russia in 1854, could write, 'I am a European, and I love Europe', and elsewhere, 'we Russians belong in language and in nature to the European family', his compatriot Fyodor Dostoyevsky in the 1870s would become a leading figure in the 'pan-Slavist' movement, arguing passionately that Russia was 'not Europe at all'.[45]

In Europe itself, the violent passions that had given the lie to Mazzini's ideal of a European national movement after 1848 were bursting out everywhere as the century moved into its second half. The first new nation states, Greece and Belgium, had been born in blood (a great deal more of it in the first case than in the second). It was bloody battles, again, beginning in 1859 and continuing until 1871, that liberated Italy and unified Germany, to create the two most powerful and influential of the new nation states on the continent.

Before Germany could be united, a brief but costly war had to be fought between the Germans of Prussia and the Germans of Austria in 1866 – essentially over which of these two German-speaking powers would take the lead. Prussia won (against the odds), and as a result Germany's national destiny was assured. Unification was almost complete in 1870, but some of the German states were still holding back. Events then showed just how devastatingly divisive the process of national unification could be. A combination of devious diplomacy by Bismarck and rashness on the part of Napoleon III sparked war between France and Prussia in July that year. The wavering German states immediately fell into line behind Prussia; French defences were quickly overwhelmed, although the war would drag on for six months.

Napoleon first surrendered, then abdicated and went into exile in England. Paris came under siege in September. Altogether about 140,000 French soldiers were killed in the war, and as many again wounded. Civilians often bore the brunt of the fighting; villages were burnt to the ground. German reprisals against irregular resistance were particularly vicious. In one incident, 'Prussian troops . . . set the buildings alight, bayoneted the inhabitants and threw them, still living, onto the flames.'[46] On 18 January 1871, with the French capital still under siege, a few miles away, at the royal complex of Versailles that had been built for Louis XIV, an assembly of German regional princes and military leaders came together to proclaim King William I of Prussia as *Kaiser* (emperor) of a newly united Germany. The German Second Empire, or *Reich*, had begun. The humiliation of defeated France was intentional, symbolic and unanswerable. And even then, the war was not quite over.

A new French republican government had capitulated; but in

Paris a workers' 'Commune' seized control in March. For two months the *Communards* defied both the victors and their own government, in a dramatic re-enactment of scenes from the Revolution of 1789. When French government troops finally broke into the city in May 1871, a week of bloodshed left between six and seven thousand Parisians dead, many of them executed in cold blood; another 40,000 faced arrest, with many later deported to a penal colony in the Pacific.[47] When the final peace treaty was signed, the same month, it detached the German-speaking regions of Alsace and Lorraine from France and assigned them to Germany. The cost of German national unification, beyond its borders, would not be easily forgotten or forgiven.

Writing some twenty years after it was all over, the French novelist Emile Zola chose to end his novel *La Bête humaine* (*The Human Beast*; the title serves as a trigger warning) in the summer of 1870. A steam train is gathering speed in the darkness of night, carrying recruits from Brittany to Paris on their way to the front. In the driver's cab, the driver and his fireman are locked in a deadly embrace, each intent on murdering the other. Still entwined, the two men fall to their deaths, mangled beneath the iron wheels. Nothing, now, can stop the driverless machine roaring down the tracks. The novel ends:

> Who cared about the victims obliterated in its path? Was it not, after all, headed for the future, careless of the blood it spilled? With no driver, surrounded by darkness, like a blind, deaf beast unleashed in the midst of death, on and on it hurtled, laden with this cannon fodder, these soldiers, already stupid with tiredness, drunk and singing.[48]

8.

'Heart of Darkness'

1871–1945

'Dr Livingstone, I presume?' The often-quoted words may never in reality have been spoken. But the meeting of two Europeans, close to the Equator at the heart of another continent, on 10 November 1871, would have consequences far beyond anything that either man could have imagined. David Livingstone was a Scottish missionary who had set out into the interior of Africa from Zanzibar on the east coast five years earlier; no news of his expedition had been heard since. The Welsh-born journalist Henry Morton Stanley had spent much of his life in the United States and was on a mission for the *New York Herald* to find the missing missionary. Stanley caught up with Livingstone at a place called Ujiji (today in western Tanzania), on the shore of Lake Tanganyika. When Stanley's story made the headlines in New York several months later, the scoop quickly found its way back to Europe. The journalist's columns and the book he published shortly afterwards turned Livingstone into a hero and helped set in motion a 'scramble for Africa' that would galvanize the nations of Europe during the next four decades.[1]

Livingstone had gone to Africa not only to convert souls; he had also been the latest of a number of British adventurers willing to risk hardship and danger in search of the answer to a mystery as old as the *Histories* of Herodotus. Where, in the centre of the African continent, was the source of the River Nile? Livingstone never found the answer; but in the course of several expeditions he did discover something else that had almost as great an impact back home. This was a thriving and brutal trade in slaves carried on by

Arab and Swahili militias and traders in the interior of the continent. To combat this, Livingstone's idealistic vision for European intervention in Africa was summed up in his motto, the 'three Cs': 'Commerce, Christianity and Civilization'.

There was always going to be a veneer of philanthropy and Christian piety about European expansion into Africa. But there was a fourth 'C', which in practice would trump all the rest: competition. And it wasn't only Africa. Suddenly, during the second half of the nineteenth century, Europeans were everywhere: toppling a dynasty in China and inspiring another to emulate them in Japan; displacing the 'Indians' from the 'wild west' of the United States and Canada; colonizing Australia and New Zealand. Before the next century was far advanced, they would even have reached the uninhabitable Poles. But in all this frenetic endeavour there was a particular allure about the vast blank area on European maps that represented the interior of the 'dark continent', as Africa was first dubbed in 1878. No one, it seemed, could control what was happening. The runaway train was gathering speed. Where it was headed now, nobody could know.

'The Horror! The Horror!'

Until this time Europeans had taken rather little interest in the overseas continent that lay nearest to their own shores. During the great expansion across the oceans that had begun with the voyages of Columbus at the end of the fifteenth century, Africa had been seen more often as a barrier to reaching the fabled east by way of the Atlantic than as a land of opportunity in its own right. Europeans had made permanent homes in only a few areas around the African coast: the Portuguese in Angola and Mozambique, Dutch and British settlers in the hinterland of the Cape of Good Hope. Otherwise, the European presence had been largely confined to trading posts dotted along the western coastline. It was from these last that some 11 million Africans from the interior had been transported to be sold as slaves in European colonies in North and South America and the Caribbean. That infamous trade had finally come to an end as recently as the first half of the nineteenth century.

The 'scramble' started out from an unlikely quarter. Even before he came to the throne in 1865, King Leopold II of the Belgians was a man possessed by a single idea. On a paperweight made out of a piece of marble taken from the Parthenon in Athens, he had inscribed the words: *'Il faut à la Belgique une colonie'* ('Belgium must have a colony').[2] Belgium was a small country, hemmed in by more powerful neighbours. After the Prussian victory over France, and the emergence of an even stronger Germany just over the border, the neutrality that had been guaranteed along with Belgian independence began to seem like a fragile thing (just how fragile, Leopold's successor would discover in 1914). Overseas possessions, Leopold was convinced, would make up for this.

Leopold was a rich man in his own right; and when he failed to persuade a succession of ministers of his own government to back him, in 1878 he recruited Stanley to colonize the basin of the Congo river for him, more or less single-handedly. For the next thirty years, the Congo Free State would be the personal fief of the Belgian king. Stanley would have preferred to work for the British government of Benjamin Disraeli, but had been turned down. At the time, no European government was enthusiastic about venturing into the interior of Africa.

But a vacuum was opening up in the heart of the 'dark continent'. Already by the start of the next decade, the very same governments that had been reluctant before were now falling over one another in the rush to fill it. France, still smarting from its humiliation by Prussia, and particularly from the loss of Alsace and Lorraine, was looking to find compensation elsewhere, and ended up ruling over huge swathes of west Africa. Britain, at the time the world's greatest naval power by some margin, was determined to keep it this way. That meant keeping control of maritime trade routes, particularly around the Cape of Good Hope at one end of the continent and through the Suez Canal (which had opened in 1869) at the other.

In southern Africa, during the last years of the nineteenth century and into the next, Britain would fight a series of wars against native Zulus and the descendants of Dutch colonists, known as Boers. At the opposite end of the continent, after bombarding the Mediterranean port city of Alexandria in 1882, the British also took effective control of Egypt for several decades and went on to fight a series of brutal campaigns in Sudan.

While this was going on, newly unified Germany and Italy could hardly afford to be left behind. Bismarck, now Imperial Chancellor, had at first held back, but during the 1880s gave the green light to German colonies in South West Africa (in today's Namibia); soon these would be followed by 'German East Africa' and smaller possessions in the west of the continent, in Togoland and Cameroon. Italy fared less well, but not for want of trying. A costly failure to conquer Ethiopia left only a stretch of coast in the Horn of Africa in Italian hands. But then, in 1911, just when it seemed that the scramble must be over, war with the Ottoman Empire gave Italy control of the two provinces facing the Mediterranean that would later be known as Libya. By that time, the only African territories *not* ruled in one way or another by a European power were Ethiopia and the tiny enclave of Liberia, created for freed slaves re-imported to their home continent from the United States.[3]

The effects of this frenzy of conquest and colonization were highly controversial at the time, as indeed they have continued to be ever since. One of the most thoughtful and evocative responses to these events, while they were still going on, was published in London in 1899. Joseph Conrad is best known for his stories of life at sea, based on his twenty years of service in the British merchant navy. A permanent exile from his native Poland, Conrad would go on to make his home in Britain and become one of the greatest novelists of his generation writing in English. His novel *Heart of Darkness* is based on his experiences in the early 1890s when he had captained a paddle steamer on the Congo river. It tells of an expedition upriver to relieve a remote outpost where a legendary trader (or plunderer) of ivory has 'gone native' in the jungle. The trader's name, Kurtz, is German; 'his mother was half-English, his father was half-French', we learn: 'All Europe contributed to the making of Kurtz.'[4]

By the time the expedition catches up with him, Kurtz is dying from fever. From the fragments of his story that emerge through his delirium, and from the dying man's papers, we learn that Kurtz had started out with the civilizing ideals of a Livingstone; since then, with no other company in these alien surroundings, he has reverted to the primitive, instinctual savagery that Conrad's story repeatedly identifies with the condition of the African natives. 'Exterminate the brutes', the sometime idealist has scrawled over his own idealistic musings. At the heart of the civilized European, the story seems to be telling us, lurks the very same darkness that civilization claims to enlighten among the 'primitive' peoples of the world. Too far gone for redemption, Kurtz dies with the words: 'The horror! The horror!'[5]

But there is more to Conrad's novel than this. The story of the expedition to find Kurtz is told as a tale within a tale. The novel itself begins and ends with a group of men aboard another boat on another great river, this time the lower reaches of the Thames at nightfall, while 'The air . . . seemed condensed into a mournful gloom, brooding motionless over the biggest, and the greatest, town on earth.'[6] It is in this setting that the worldly-wise old sailor, Marlow, begins to reminisce about his adventure in Africa.

What sets him off is the reflection that this too had once been 'one of the dark places of the earth'. Two thousand years ago, Roman conquerors must have looked upriver into the same darkness where London now lies. Marlow's conclusion about the ancient Romans reads very like Conrad's own critique of what Europeans were doing in Africa in his own day, couched in the homespun idiom of the old sailor: 'The conquest of the earth, which mostly means the taking it away from those who have a different complexion or slightly flatter noses than ourselves, is not a pretty thing when you look into it too much.' And after Marlow has finished his tale, the last words of the novel bring us back to the Thames where night has now fallen over London, and the river 'seemed to lead into the heart of an immense darkness'.[7] In Conrad's story, Europe looks into its own dark heart.

The second half of the nineteenth century brought more Europeans than ever before into close contact with peoples whose appearance and way of life seemed irredeemably alien from their own. The European 'family' might have chosen to divide itself up into self-governing nations; but the human family, if such a thing even existed, was far more diverse. Christian thinkers still believed that all human beings were descended from Adam and Eve; but if this was true, the lineage contained far more branches than were accounted for in the Bible. Several strands of scientific inquiry, carried out mainly in Britain, France and Germany, came together when Charles Darwin published *On the Origin of Species* in 1859. Quickly popularized as the 'theory of evolution', Darwin's researches proposed that biological competition, working out over millions of years, had brought into existence the entire present-day animal kingdom, including man. It was a notion that chimed perfectly with the spirit of the age. And if the whole of nature was locked in the same kind of deadly competition as the rival nations of Europe, what chance did that leave for the peoples of the rest of the world?

By the time Darwin's theory was published, a new term had already entered the language of European public discourse – or rather, an old and rather imprecise term had begun to acquire an apparently scientific meaning. The word was *race*. The peoples of different continents and regions of the world could be designated according to unalterable biological characteristics; taken together, these added up to the definition of a race. A whole pseudo-science began to be built around differences of skin pigmentation and physical variations in the shape of the human skull. In a book published in 1850 with the title *The Races of Men*, the English anatomist Robert Knox anticipated Conrad's Kurtz by half a century, when he contemplated the possibility of a 'war of extermination' against the 'dark races', which he believed were inherently 'inferior'.[8]

Three years later, in 1853, came the first volume of a 1,200-page *Essay on the Inequality of the Human Races*, written in French by the self-styled 'count' Arthur Gobineau. Almost exactly a century had passed since Rousseau had published his *Discourse on the Origin and Foundations of Inequality among Men*. Back then, the assumption of the Enlightenment had been that inequality was an evil; how was it to be explained and, if possible, mitigated? But nineteenth-century Europe positively thrived on inequality. According to Gobineau, 'History shows that all civilization derives from the white race, and that a society is great and brilliant only so far as it preserves the blood of the noble race that created it.'[9]

The race in question had by this time acquired a name: 'Aryan', derived from linguistic research into the supposed origin of the Indo-European group of languages. Learned associations devoted to the new science of anthropology (very different from the academic subject as it exists today) sprang up over the next few years in Paris, London, Moscow, Berlin and Vienna. In tandem, during the 1860s, there grew up a pseudo-science, known at first as 'racial psychology' and later as 'eugenics'. Lasting well into the next century, eugenics had as its object the maintenance and 'improvement' of the 'superior races', while contemplating with equanimity the 'gradual extinction' of those deemed inferior.[10]

Ideas like these were widespread across Europe by the turn of the twentieth century. In 1900, when Kaiser Wilhelm II of Germany sent troops to join seven other European nations, along with Japan and the United States, in putting down the 'Boxer' rebellion in China, his personal orders to them as they embarked were: 'No quarter will be given! Prisoners will not be taken! . . . [M]ay the name German be affirmed by you in such a way in China that no Chinese will ever again dare to look askance at a German.' Although Germany, in the event, played only a minor role, it has been estimated that as many as 100,000 Chinese may have been massacred, most of them by Europeans, during that campaign.[11]

Four years later, in South West Africa, the military commander sent out from Germany to crush a rebellion by the Herero people devised a plan for literal extermination, driving 'perhaps 8,000 men, with twice that number of women and children, thirsty and starving, with the remnants of their cattle and horses' into the Omaheke desert to die. As one German colonial administrator commented at the time, 'To secure the peaceful settlement of whites in the face of a native tribe that is absolutely incapable of culture and given to robbery may require nothing less than its annihilation.'[12] As a result, over several years, many thousands of Herero and Nama people of the region were in effect murdered.

Defining European identity in terms of race had consequences nearer home too, though as yet they were mild by comparison with actions overseas. For more than a millennium after the conversion of the Roman emperor Constantine, while Europeans had defined themselves by their Christian religion, the continent's Jewish communities had been ostracized, persecuted or expelled because of their different religious beliefs and practices. By the second half of the nineteenth century, Jews had finally been accepted as equal members of most European societies – except in Russia and Russian-controlled Poland, where the old religious mentality persisted. But along with legal equality fell a new shadow. Today we call it antisemitism. If Jews were descended from the ancient inhabitants of Israel and Judaea, they must belong to a different race from other Europeans.

Never mind that Jewish communities had existed all over Europe for longer than the ancestors of many European nations had done; the 'Semitic' race was different from the 'Aryan'. In the words of Houston Stewart Chamberlain, an Englishman who took German citizenship, married the daughter of the composer Richard Wagner and wrote in German, 'the Jewish people is and remains in Europe an Asiatic people alien to our part of the world'.[13] In the eyes of those who espoused the new racial theories, the supposed purity of the European, 'Aryan' race was threatened not only by its inferiors on other continents but even within its own heartland. And as a result, a European minority found itself once again a target for persecution, this time because its people were supposed to belong to a different race.

By the end of the first decade of the twentieth century, Europeans had never been so prosperous at home or so powerful abroad. Railways criss-crossed Europe and were reaching across Asia and North America; bigger and faster steamships carried more and more people and goods over seas and oceans. Industrial production, concentrated in Europe's north-west and in parts of its centre, reached new heights. Advances in medicine were bringing exponential increases in life expectancy; killer diseases were succumbing to vaccination and newly discovered cures. Scientific discoveries and technological inventions, in both Europe and North America, were transforming the world: the wireless telegraph, electric light, the motor car, the aeroplane. In the arts, the same decade gave birth to monumental symphonies by Gustav Mahler, culminating in his 'Symphony of a Thousand'; Marcel Proust embarked on the ultimate work of literary introspection in the novel *In Search of Lost Time*, which eventually would fill seven large volumes; the sculptor Auguste Rodin and the painter Claude Monet were at the height of their powers – all of them, in their way, unsurpassable.

Europeans had achieved all these things, along with their descendants on other continents. It has been estimated that by 1914, eleven 'Western' powers 'controlled nearly three-fifths of all territory and population [in the world] and more than three-quarters (a staggering 79 per cent) of global economic output'.[14] But with supremacy came the fear of losing it. The horror that Conrad's fictional character had discovered in the heart of Africa had yet to be visited upon Europeans' own 'dark continent'. And when it came, they would have nobody to blame but themselves.[15]

The End of the Old Order

While Prussian troops had been marching into France in September 1870, and before the noose had yet closed around Paris, the French writer and intellectual Ernest Renan published an open letter to a German counterpart in which he lamented the inability of the

'European family' to intervene to settle differences among its members. In place of conflict, Renan thought there ought to be 'a kind of central authority, a kind of congress of the United States of Europe'. The next year, when it was all over and the magnitude of the French defeat had still been sinking in, Renan returned to the correspondence. 'Europe is a confederation of States united by the shared idea of civilization,' he wrote.[16]

Others, caught up in the turmoil of that time, thought similarly. Also in 1871, before the final peace treaty had even been signed, the veteran poet and novelist Victor Hugo, long an advocate of some form of European unity, had raised cheers from a French audience when he spoke of a future 'United States of Europe; the continental federation' that would ensure 'the liberty of Europe, the peace of the world'. A few years later, in a newspaper article, Hugo went further: 'Europe needs a European nationality, a single government, an immense brotherly arbitration, democracy at peace with itself . . .'[17]

But *Realpolitik*, a German word that was becoming current at just this time, spoke a different language. As Bismarck expressed it with characteristic bluntness, in a handwritten note, scribbled in French, in 1876: 'Whoever speaks of Europe is wrong.' There was no arguing with the 'Iron Chancellor'.[18] When Renan returned to the subject a decade after the Franco-Prussian War had ended, in an essay from 1882 that remains a classic to this day, he still thought that eventually the nations of Europe would 'probably' give way to a 'European confederation'. But he qualified the idea immediately:

> Such, however, is not the law of the century we are living in. At the present time, the existence of nations is good, even necessary. Their existence is a guarantee of freedom, which would be lost if the world had only one law and master.

A nation, Renan concluded in that essay, is 'the expression of a great solidarity . . . a plebiscite of every day'.[19] An idea of Europe that went back to the French Revolution had been given new life and was moving forward: Rousseau's 'general will' could only be expressed by the collective 'soul' (Renan's word) of the *nation*. The 'liberties of Europe', which had been the talk of the eighteenth century, had been replaced – perhaps for good – by the liberty of each of the continent's nations. And those liberties were bound to come into conflict.

Despite the setbacks to democratic participation in the immediate aftermath of the 1848 revolutions, that 'plebiscite of every day' was spontaneously taking place all over Europe during the second half of the nineteenth century. The business of government was reaching farther than ever before through the social strata. Nationalism, it has been aptly said in hindsight, was becoming a 'mass phenomenon' at this time, the result of a gradual 'nationalization of the masses' that had begun during those failed revolutions.[20] No European state was yet a full democracy in the sense that we understand the term today. The extent of the franchise varied enormously across the continent. Bismarck in 1871 allowed the vote to all adult German men. In Britain, between 1867 and 1884 the proportion of adult males entitled to vote increased only from about one-third to about two-thirds. Women, everywhere, would have to wait until well into the next century.[21]

Still, almost every country had a parliament of some sort. An increasing number of voices began to make themselves heard, not only in parliamentary assemblies, but also through a burgeoning popular press and in the arts and entertainment. Far from finding common cause with other, similarly motivated nationalities, as Mazzini had once hoped, these voices that spoke for nations were becoming more shrill than ever.

The conflicting claims of national identities were creating tension not only across national borders but *within* states too. In the Austrian Empire, after 1849, no fewer than nine languages had been approved for use in schools and official publications: German, Hungarian, Italian, Romanian, Polish, Czech, Ukrainian, Slovene and Croatian; at least another ten were in daily use somewhere in the emperor's dominions. Still typical of everyday life at the turn of the twentieth century was the case of the Hungarian soldier who 'wrote his diary in four different languages – German for regimental matters, Slovene when thinking about his girlfriend, Serbian for songs he recalled, and Hungarian for his sexual fantasies'. But that would soon be a thing of the past. In the classic novel that charts the declining years of the Habsburg monarchy, *The Radetzky March* by Joseph Roth, written some two decades later, a scene set very shortly after this time has a character observe, presciently: 'People have stopped believing in God. Nationalism is the new religion. People don't go to church. They go to nationalist meetings.'[22]

It was against this background that the system of consensus diplomacy, which had been hastily devised in 1814 and 1815 to prevent another European war, was about to undergo its severest test yet.

Once again, events in the continent's south-eastern corner led the way. Bulgaria, Greece, Montenegro and Serbia had all won their independence from the Ottoman Empire in the course of the previous century. In October 1912 they banded together in an attempt to drive the Ottomans out of Europe altogether. By March the next year they had very nearly succeeded; the First Balkan War, as it soon became known, ended in yet another conference convened by the Great Powers of the day. The Treaty of London, signed at the end of May 1913, imposed new frontiers on the region, to replace the ones that had been negotiated at a congress held in Berlin back in 1878. The Ottomans were restricted to a small zone around Istanbul, while Bulgaria, Greece and Serbia made huge gains in the loosely defined areas that had been known since ancient times as Macedonia and Thrace. More than a million Muslims fled the Balkans for the safety of Anatolia.

But already the spirit of national rivalry was too strong for the century-old congress system to contain it. A month after the signing of the treaty, Bulgaria went to war against its former allies, determined to carve out a larger share of the spoils. The Second Balkan War lasted only six weeks, and the aggressors came off much the worst. This time the peace treaty was negotiated in the Balkans, by the Balkan powers themselves, and signed in the Romanian capital, Bucharest. European leaders were nowhere to be seen.

The first shot in what promised to be a third Balkan conflict was fired by another nationalist, a Serbian this time, on 28 June 1914. Gavrilo Princip's victims were the Archduke Franz Ferdinand, heir to the throne of Austria-Hungary, and his wife Sophie. The place was Sarajevo, capital of the former Ottoman province of Bosnia-Herzegovina, which Austria had formally annexed as recently as 1908. The 'old' emperor, Franz Joseph, had been on the throne since 1848; for several years, expectations for the future of the empire had been focused on his heir. Royal and political assassinations had become frighteningly common in Europe, and the wider world, by this time (the equivalent of terrorist atrocities today). Franz Ferdinand was the highest-profile victim yet.

As Austria and Serbia geared up to fight a local war in the Balkans, it should still have been possible for concerted diplomacy by the European powers to resolve the conflict, or at least to contain it. Instead, each government on its own account chose to activate alliances and treaty obligations that had been drawn up during the previous two decades as a kind of insurance policy against the very thing that was now happening. By the time the formal declarations of war began on 1 August 1914, the imminent third Balkan conflict had escalated to become the 'European War', soon to be known as the 'Great War' or the 'War to end Wars', and eventually as the First World War. The whole conflict would last, with intermissions, for thirty-one years. And Europe would never afterwards recover its place in the world.

The world war was a titanic clash of empires, three on each side. Austria-Hungary, together with the German Reich, made up the Central Powers, which were joined by the Ottoman Empire in October 1914. Against them stood Britain, France and Russia, collectively known as the *Entente* or the Allies. Each of the six had a European city as its capital and seat of government. But only Austria ruled over lands (and a diversity of peoples) that belonged wholly within

Europe. Britain and France on the one side, and Germany on the other, held sway over diverse populations on far-flung continents, while the Ottoman and Russian empires extended far into Asia. This was how a European civil war turned into a global conflict. Nearer home, the continent's smaller states found themselves either ground up in the mill (the fate of Belgium and Romania above all) or exempted by geography, to enjoy an impoverished neutrality on the sidelines; this was the case with the Netherlands, Scandinavia, Spain and Switzerland.

Four years later, when armistices signed in October and November 1918 brought the immediate conflict to an end, only two of the six empires were left standing. First to buckle had been Russia, where the Bolshevik Revolution of October 1917 upended the entire social order and ushered in a civil war that would cause even more deaths and suffering than the world war had done. The German and Austrian empires imploded just as the guns fell silent, to become nation states with republican governments and borders yet to be determined. The Ottoman state would eke out a nominal existence, with its capital, Istanbul, under Allied occupation for five more years until it, too, was swept away, to be replaced by a national republic. Only Britain and France held on to their imperial possessions, and gained others at the expense of the losers – but all of those lay overseas. After 1918, the age of empires in Europe was over; the time had come for nation states to sweep the board.

No one had planned any of this. Even the most ardent nationalist would have struggled to justify the human cost of four years of 'total war' – a term first coined in 1917. The killing and the devastation had been on a scale that is still hard to imagine. Close to nine million soldiers lost their lives; almost as many again returned home mutilated in body or in mind, or both, and would spend the rest of their lives as invalids or cripples. Seven million more had been captured and spent time in often brutal prisoner-of-war camps. Civilian deaths directly caused by the war amounted to almost another six million.[23]

Reflecting on these horrors in the immediate aftermath, thoughtful Europeans once again began to shine a spotlight on their own civilization and what the 'father of psychoanalysis', Sigmund Freud, would later call its 'discontents'. Freud himself, drawing on his experience with patients returning to Vienna from the front, by 1920 had come to the conclusion that among the hidden instincts of the human mind must be one that drives us towards death (later popularized as the 'death drive'). The idea that supposedly civilized Europeans might be doomed to seek their own self-destruction was not confined to psychological speculation. In a two-volume historical essay published in 1918 and 1922, the German historian Oswald Spengler predicted the downfall, or decline (the German word is ambiguous), of the 'West', which he believed was part of an inevitable historical process and would happen sometime after the year 2000.

More succinctly, the American poet Ezra Pound, who had been living in London since before the war, reflected in a poem published in 1920 that all this destruction had been 'For an old bitch gone in the teeth, / For a botched civilization'. Pound's friend and fellow American, T. S. Eliot, also living in London, in 1922 published the long poem that for several generations would sum up the desolation and devastation of the war and its aftermath, *The Waste Land*. In its closing lines we read, 'These fragments I have shored against my ruins', followed by a prayer for peace in the oldest known language of the Indo-European family, Sanskrit.[24]

Back in 1914, just as the conflict was beginning, the British Foreign Secretary, Sir Edward Grey, had famously remarked, 'The lamps are going out all over Europe, we shall not see them lit again in our life-time.' After it was over, the French general Marshal Foch is said to have predicted that all that had been won was 'an Armistice for twenty years'.[25] Both would be proved right. The darkness that Europe's national obsessions had brought upon the continent would be slow to lift; its terrible heart still lay some two decades in the future.

False Dawn

No such gloomy sentiments were on show when crowds turned out to welcome the arrival of Woodrow Wilson, President of the United States of America, at the French port of Brest on 13 December 1918. It was the first time that a serving US president had ever travelled to Europe. A massive injection of American troops and firepower, during the last eighteen months of the war, had made possible the breakthrough on the Western Front; American money was already shoring up the tottering European powers. Now Wilson was here in person to seal the peace, at the conference that would shortly come together in the French capital.

The special train that took the president and his entourage to Paris was cheered all along its route by local people who had turned out in the middle of the night – the exact reversal of the nightmare scenario that had been conjured up by Zola with his runaway steam train on the very same tracks in 1870. Wilson arrived in Paris to a hero's welcome. And in another echo of that earlier war, deliberate this time, the official opening of the peace conference took place on 18 January 1919, the anniversary of the coronation of the first German Kaiser at nearby Versailles.[26]

The spirit of the conference was captured by the British writer and socialite Harold Nicolson, who had been part of the Foreign Office delegation: 'We were journeying to Paris, not merely to liquidate the war, but to found a new order in Europe. We were preparing not Peace only, but Eternal Peace. There was about us the halo of some divine mission.'[27] This was a peace conference unlike any other before it: instead of European governments gathering around a table to carve up the continent, this time an outside arbiter had appeared; perhaps there really was something of the *deus ex machina* about the American president – or as the British prime minister, David Lloyd George, more pithily put it, afterwards: 'the idealistic President regarded himself as a missionary whose function it was to rescue the poor European heathen from their age-long

23–24. (*above*) Contrasting portraits of the Holy Roman Emperor Charles V, both by Titian and painted in 1548: as victor against German Lutheran princes at the battle of Mühlberg (1547) (*left*), and as a civilian and respected capitalist (*right*).

25. (*left*) *Europa Regina* (Map of Europe as a Queen) based on a drawing of 1537 by Johannes Putsch (Johannes Bucius Aenicola). 'This anthropomorphized continent was, it seemed, made for its emperor, Charles V, and vice versa' (p. 157).

26. (*above*) Paris, 24 July 1572. Detail from *St Bartholomew's Day Massacre*, by François Dubois (*c.* 1572–84).

27. (*right*) Charles-Irénée Castel de Saint-Pierre, *Project to Render Peace Perpetual in Europe* (1713), the second of two volumes, title page.

PROJET
POUR RENDRE
LA PAIX
PERPETUELLE
EN EUROPE.
TOME II.

A UTRECHT,
Chez ANTOINE SCHOUTEN,
Marchand Libraire.
M. DCC. XIII.

28–29. Philosophers of the Enlightenment: Baron de Montesquieu (*left*) and Jean-Jacques Rousseau (*right*).

30–31. 'Enlightened despots': Frederick II of Prussia (ruled 1740–86) (*left*) and Empress Catherine II of Russia (ruled 1762–96) (*right*).

32. The Congress of Vienna, 1814–15, coloured print, based on a watercolour of 1815 by Jean-Baptiste Isabey, depicting the arrival of the Duke of Wellington (*far left*) on 3 February.

33. The 1848 revolutions imagined: *The Universal Democratic and Social Republic* by Frédéric Sorrieu (lithograph, after 1848).

4. The Paris Peace Conference, 1919. A plenary session in the Clock Room at the Ministry of Foreign Affairs, Paris, during the preparation of the Peace Treaty.

–36. Imagining a European Union in the interwar years: Count Richard Coudenhove-alergi at the Pan-Europa Conference, Berlin, 1930 (*left*), and French prime minister Aristide riand in the 1920s (*right*).

37. The architects of the post-Second World War order: Joseph Stalin, Franklin D. Roosevelt and Winston Churchill at the Tehran Conference, November 1943.

38–39. The architects of the future European Union: Jean Monnet (*left*) and Robert Schuman (*right*).

40–41. Posters announcing Europe's good times: 1947 (*left*), 1960 (*right*).

42. The breaching of the Berlin Wall, 9–10 November 1989.

43. Refugees at Gevgelija, North Macedonia, 2016.

44. Donetsk Academic Regional Drama Theatre, Mariupol, Ukraine, destroyed 16 March 2022. The word *DETI* painted on the pavement is Russian for 'children', a warning that the building was being used as a shelter.

worship of false and fiery gods'. Either way, it was Wilson, 'with his high but narrow brow, his fine head with its elevated crown and his dreamy but untrustful eye', who would dominate the proceedings of the conference for the next six months.[28]

Wilson's blueprint for world peace was designed to keep the Europeans from one another's throats. Central to this was a new organization to be called the 'League of Nations'; its purpose would be 'to provide the collective security that, in a well-run civil society, was provided by the government, its laws, its courts and its police'. It was very much the president's personal initiative to push this project, right from the start of the conference. The British and French were much less enthusiastic. But despite backsliding and objections on the European side, the League was voted into existence on 28 April 1919. By the start of the next year, when the peace conference was formally wound up, the League of Nations could boast a membership of forty-eight states.[29]

Along with his idea for the League of Nations, Wilson brought to the conference two related, overriding principles. One was democracy; the other has come to be known as the 'self-determination of nations'. To Congress in 1917 Wilson had declared: 'The world must be made safe for democracy. Its peace must be planted on the tested foundations of political liberty.' Idealistic the president may have been, but he was no altruist. It has been pointed out that 'Wilson's aim was not so much to make the "world safe for democracy", as to make America safer in the world through the promotion of democracy.'[30] This was a tough-minded calculation that would hold good for almost exactly a century and profoundly affect the history of Europe, even if not always in terms that Wilson could have imagined.

Exactly what the American president had in mind when he spoke of the 'autonomous development' (or as we more commonly say today, the 'self-determination') of nations was not very clear at the time, and has kept historians busy speculating ever since. It seems to have been not very different from Renan's 'plebiscite of every day': the idea that the people who make up a nation should have the right to choose their form of government, and that a nation state should be made up of those who want to live in it. Within months of leaving Paris again, a 'chastened' Wilson would concede that there were aspects to this that he hadn't foreseen – which was quite some understatement.[31]

But if Wilson ever entertained second thoughts, it was already too late. By the end of 1919, and very much at his prompting, the conference had wished into existence a raft of new states. Carved out of the former Austrian and Russian empires were Finland, Estonia, Latvia, Lithuania, Czechoslovakia, the 'Kingdom of Serbs, Croats, and Slovenes' (later known as Yugoslavia), Poland, Austria and Hungary. Two more states, not foreseen or in theory even permitted by the peace conference, would quickly follow at opposite ends of Europe: the Irish Free State, which won its independence from the United Kingdom in December 1922, and the Republic of Turkey, which formally replaced the lingering remnant of the Ottoman Empire the next year. All of these were *nation* states. The Europe of nations, which had been fighting its way into existence for most of the past century, had finally arrived.

Of these new states all but one was a republic; only the Kingdom of Serbs, Croats and Slovenes was a monarchy (because the Serbs had a royal family already and it would do for the rest). All had democratic constitutions; more people than ever were given the right to vote (in some countries, including women for the first time). In these new democracies, power often tended to shift away from the executive towards parliament; many adopted proportional representation, giving more of a voice than ever before to the elected representatives of the people. As the constitution for the German Republic, proclaimed in the historic city of Weimar in 1919, expressed it: 'All political authority is derived from the people.'[32] What had been literally and dangerously revolutionary in Paris in 1789 was now political orthodoxy from one end of Europe to the other.

The influence of America (the only real winner of the world war) no doubt had something to do with this. But it has also been observed that in Europe 'the war itself had been a democratizing process'; after the mobilization of whole societies on such a scale it was inevitable that 'Mass politics was here to stay'. Whatever the reason, this first Europe-wide experiment in democracy has justly been described as a 'novelty'. Despite its origins in ancient Greece and Rome, democratic government in modern Europe still had shallow roots in 1918.[33]

New Borderlands

The almost messianic optimism of those months in Paris would soon turn out to have been premature. The heads of government, including Woodrow Wilson, went home after a victor's peace had been imposed on Germany in June 1919. But most of the business of peacemaking had barely begun. Wilson himself suffered a debilitating stroke in October and would lose the presidential election the next year. The United States never did join the League of Nations that had been his brainchild; this first American intervention in the politics of the Old World would prove short-lived. As a consequence, the League itself would become 'in practice a largely European affair'.[34] Once again, Europeans were on their own to sort out their difficulties among themselves.

Several of the new or drastically reshaped nation states that had come into existence were in the grip of civil war, or fighting against each other, or both, while the peace conference was going on, and for some time afterwards. Others, on the geographical margins of Europe, after birth pangs no less traumatic, proved to be stillborn: among them Armenia, Azerbaijan, Georgia and Ukraine. For all the claims made for the Paris Peace Conference, at the time and since, the reality was that the First World War ended not with the armistices of 1918 but five years later when the Treaty of Lausanne, signed on 24 July 1923, brought the last of these conflicts to an end, making peace between the newly created Turkish Republic and several wartime allies.[35]

With minor exceptions (such as Ireland, and an attempt by Italy to annex part of Croatia in 1922), these new or continuing wars were all about defining new borders for Europe in the east. The Russian Civil War, which began after the revolution of October 1917 and lasted until 1922, is usually seen as a purely internal conflict, driven by class and ideology; but it was also a battle to define a line of demarcation between the new Europe of capitalist nation states and newly communist Russia. No fewer than thirteen European nations sent troops to fight against the Bolsheviks. Further south, the 'Greco-Turkish War' of 1919 to 1922, also known as the 'Turkish War of Independence', was as much instigated by Britain, France and Italy as by the local claims of Greece or the Turkish nationalist movement led by Mustafa Kemal, who would later take the name Atatürk (Father of the Turks). Farther afield, Germans took part in battles for Armenia and Georgia; a British force was for a time engaged in Azerbaijan. French, German, Greek and Polish troops all fought in Ukraine.

In the summer of 1920, in an episode remembered ever afterwards as the 'miracle on the Vistula', Polish forces led by their new head of state, Józef Piłsudski, pushed back the Red Army of Vladimir Lenin from the gates of Warsaw and paved the way for a new frontier that moved the border several hundred miles further east. A treaty signed in Riga in March the next year detached from Russia large chunks of today's Belarus and Ukraine, with their populations, and handed them to Poland. In August 1921, in the heart of Anatolia, a Greek army came close to defeating Kemal and the Turkish nationalist movement outside their provisional capital of Ankara. But this time the strategic 'miracle' (or brilliant generalship) came from the other side; not only was the Greek expeditionary force expelled from Anatolia, but in the aftermath the surviving civilian population of Greek Orthodox Christians, numbering almost 1.5 million, would be permanently displaced to Greece.

Russia, now ruled by Lenin and the Bolsheviks, in December 1922 became the Union of Soviet Socialist Republics, or USSR for short. The Soviet state, from the beginning until its dissolution on the last day of 1991, was never a *European* power in the way that tsarist Russia had partially been. Nominally, at least, it had been founded on a political system, communism, that had been devised by two Germans, Karl Marx and Friedrich Engels. But for all its lip service to the internationalist vision of the *Communist Manifesto*, by the middle of the 1920s the USSR had already remodelled the old tsarist Russian nationalism so as to forge a new 'Soviet nationality', based on communism, 'as a radical *national* alternative to international capitalism', and therefore to Europe.[36]

The Republic of Turkey founded by Kemal Atatürk was a nation state based on the geographical heartland of Anatolia and the Turkish language, deliberately shorn of its Ottoman heritage and purged of the ethnic and religious minorities that had come with it. Atatürk's radical programme of internal reform was designed to make Turkey into a modern nation on the European model (including a secular agenda and replacement of the traditional Arabic script of the Ottomans with a version of the Roman alphabet). But despite these reforms before the Second World War, and the fluctuating relationship of successive Turkish governments with European institutions after it, modern Turkey has always remained politically and geographically apart from Europe.

These shifts were clearly signalled right at the beginning: in 1918 the Russian capital was moved out of Europe, from St Petersburg (or Petrograd as it was then called) back to Moscow, reversing the change made two centuries earlier by Peter the Great. Similarly, in 1923 the Turkish capital was moved from the European shore of the Bosphorus to Ankara in the Anatolian interior. Since that year, Turkey has retained a foothold in Europe only in Istanbul and its immediate hinterland, along with two islands in the Aegean close to the straits.

By the time the 'Great War' *really* ended, in the summer of 1923, Europe's political border was more clearly defined than ever before; it had also moved farther east than it had lain for many centuries. The dividing line between Europe and Asia now ran almost straight from the White Sea on the north-west coast of the USSR to the western Black Sea (just west of Odessa) in the south, then continued southwards from the straits of the Dardanelles down the eastern side of the Aegean Sea until it meets the Mediterranean.

No longer was the continent bounded on its eastern flank by great empires that were simultaneously both inside and outside the tent – and more opposed to each other than either of them was to Europe. Some of these boundaries would shift greatly during the next hundred years, indeed some of them are again bitterly contested in the 2020s. But between 1918 and 1923 a new geopolitics had been created, one that more or less still exists today. All this had come about at a human cost that was literally incalculable. As many as 12 million lives may have been lost during the Russian Civil War; between 1911 and 1923 it has been estimated that one in five of the total population of the Ottoman Empire perished.[37]

Dreams of Utopia

In the English-speaking world, the fictional portrayal in the 1942 film *Casablanca* of Victor Laszlo, the handsome, charismatic hero of resistance against Nazi occupation, is probably better known than the real-life Count Richard Coudenhove-Kalergi on whom the character was based. Born in Tokyo, the future architect of a new post-war vision for Europe was about as cosmopolitan as it was possible to be. The son of an Austrian diplomat and a Japanese geisha, whom his father had married after his birth in 1894, the young Richard had been educated in the Austrian Empire while it still existed. On his father's side the son could claim an unusual spread of European ancestry: Flemish, Polish, Greek and Norwegian as well as Austrian. Gifted in languages, and reputedly fluent in no fewer than sixteen, Coudenhove-Kalergi wrote in German. In 1922 he founded an organization called *Paneuropa-Union*, which still exists. The next year he published its manifesto, *Pan-Europa*. This would earn him the undying hatred of Adolf Hitler, who in *Mein Kampf* would shortly afterwards describe him as a 'cosmopolitan bastard' and later still add *Pan-Europa* to the list of books banned in the German Third Reich.[38]

By 1923, thoughtful Europeans were increasingly looking either east or west with diametrically opposing sentiments of hope and fear. For idealistic socialists in every country, the USSR represented a model for a future utopia; for many more, the 'red threat' of Soviet communism became a bogeyman that would haunt governments and civil authorities throughout Europe until the end of the 1980s. For others again, America had long been seen as the 'land of opportunity'; now American businesses were expanding into Europe at an unprecedented rate, American capital was beginning to dominate the world. Was the 'American dream' something that Europeans should import into their own continent? Or was that, too, a threat to be resisted?

Coudenhove-Kalergi had a stark answer. While Europeans vainly look towards either Russia or America, he wrote in *Pan-Europa*, the truth is that 'Neither the West nor the East will rescue Europe. Russia wants to conquer it, America wants to buy it.' This passage was tactfully excised from the English translation that was published in New York three years later.[39] With remarkable prescience, Coudenhove-Kalergi went on to argue that both equally represent dictatorship: military in the case of Russia, 'financial' in the case of America. The solution was to be found in what he called a 'political-economic union'. Essentially this would mean creating a customs union and disbanding national armies. Nation states were here to stay, he argued – but he strongly debunked the idea that nations have any racial basis, and therefore that national identity is fixed. A nation is, rather, a 'community of culture'; national identity can be acquired. The way to resolve the tensions that were evident at the time in many parts of Europe, where national minorities had ended up inside the 'wrong' borders, Coudenhove-Kalergi argued, would be not to change the borders, but to do away with borders altogether.[40]

This vision from 1923 has some poignant resonances in the 2020s. Its author went to some lengths to explain why his Europe left out

Britain – because its worldwide empire made it a different kind of power. Prophetically, Coudenhove-Kalergi suggested that the United Kingdom's accession 'would be possible after the end of the British Empire'. But in the meantime, he thought that English should be taught in schools throughout Pan-Europa and used as the common language of its institutions (exactly as happens, in practice, in the EU today). And at a time when it was still not quite certain whether the communist 'Reds' or the royalist 'Whites' would prevail in the Russian Civil War, Coudenhove-Kalergi thought the outcome would make little difference to Europe. No fewer than three times he makes the point: 'The common aim of all Europeans, regardless of party or nation, ought to be to prevent an invasion from Russia.' That may have sounded hysterical in 1923; just over a hundred years later, and long after the collapse of the Soviet Union in 1991, it no longer does.[41]

Coudenhove-Kalergi himself conceded that his plan might seem like just another utopia. And there was indeed something incorrigibly patrician and aloof about both the man and his plan; in an era of mass political mobilization, the titled aristocrat from a vanished empire was unlikely to have much direct appeal to the European masses. But this time – and it really *was* the first time – serious politicians with access to the levers of power were beginning to think along similar lines. In January 1925 no less a person than the current and future prime minister of France, Edouard Herriot, declared before his country's Chamber of Deputies, 'It is my greatest wish to live to see the realization of the United States of Europe.'[42] Two years later, the veteran French politician who had already held prime-ministerial office several times, Aristide Briand, became an enthusiastic supporter of the Pan-Europa movement; he became its honorary president in 1927.

This was endorsement at the highest political level. And Briand was not done yet. On 5 September 1929, on behalf of France, he presented the twenty-six other European members of the League of Nations with a plan for a 'European Federal Union'. The next year a fuller version of the plan was drawn up, on Briand's instructions, by the French diplomat Alexis Léger – who many years later would win the Nobel Prize in Literature under the pseudonym of Saint-John Perse.[43]

This outlined the basis for a new 'European Union' – reviving the name that had first been proposed by Charles-Irénée Castel de Saint-Pierre at the time of the Peace of Utrecht, a little over two centuries before. The new structure was to be at once a 'federation' and based on the 'absolute sovereignty and . . . entire political independence' of nation states. The contradiction was obvious at the time and has often been pointed out since; it is one that has not been resolved by today's EU either. Briand and Léger proposed to 'proceed from the simpler to the more complex . . . by a constant evolution and by a kind of continuous creation' – as their successors would also do after the Second World War. But unlike their later counterparts, they ruled out a customs union and placed political convergence first, before an economic one. Still, in considering these questions at all, and in such a forum, the Briand Plan marked a huge step forward.[44]

In September 1930 the League agreed to set up a committee tasked with 'the Study of a European Union'.[45] Then, as now, it was the surest way to kill a proposal. Briand himself was given the task of chairing the group. Committee and proposal died together with their architect, a year and a half later.

Between Briand's first approach to the League of Nations and the full presentation of his plan in May 1930, momentous events on the other side of the Atlantic had changed the course of European history. Economic recovery in the Old World, after the world war, had been patchy at best. Most Europeans were probably better off towards the end of the 1920s than they had been at the beginning; but the 'roaring twenties' had only truly roared in the United States. Then quite suddenly, and seemingly without warning, during the week of 22 October 1929, the bubble burst. The Wall Street Crash or Great Crash of 1929 has often been compared to the Global Economic Crisis of 2008. The effects, as the new decade of the 1930s began, were no less global, and even more dramatic. In Europe, the impact would be unevenly spread over several years, but no country would come out of it unscathed. Governments and financial institutions scrambled to protect their own. During the Great Depression, as it was called, that followed, nobody was talking about international cooperation any longer; the nations of Europe, instead of pooling their resources and working together, began to pull apart.

As the post-war system of open trade and unfettered capitalism collapsed, states tried to defend their economies by putting up tariff barriers; it was called 'protectionism'. Imports became too expensive; markets for exports disappeared. Currencies were devalued; the international gold standard was abandoned by one country after another; on both sides of the Atlantic, millions of people lost their jobs and fell into poverty. The new watchword became 'autarky', or self-sufficiency; in the words of the historian Mark Mazower, 'in the 1930s the financial facts of life forced a new economic nationalism on Europe'.

If the combination of free-market capitalism with democracy couldn't provide the security or even basic economic survival that people craved, what were the alternatives? Communist Russia was doing very well, thanks to the series of Five-Year Plans and rigorous state control under Lenin's successor, Joseph Stalin. The extent of coercion involved, and later in the decade the sheer terror imposed by the Soviet dictator on his people, would not be fully understood in Europe until after the Second World War – and have their deniers even today. But the communist system did at least show that state intervention in the economy might work. On varying scales, most European states tried something of the sort during the 1930s. And according to Mazower, experiments with 'state-led national capitalism' were remarkably successful – at least in economic terms. The cost would prove to be political.[46]

This was because economic nationalism inevitably fed into every other sort of nationalism. And plenty of those had already been simmering close to boiling point in many parts of Europe throughout the relatively good times of the 1920s. More or less every European state, new or old, was now a *nation* state. But fulfilment of a dream that had been assiduously nurtured by its dreamers for more than a century made nobody happier; the creation of national borders never seemed to bring the security that the architects of peace in 1919 had promised. In central and eastern Europe, majorities tried forcibly to assimilate minorities, and failing that, to intimidate them; minorities felt themselves under threat, and none more so than the continent's Jews, who now found themselves tarred with the brush of Bolshevism, or high finance – or sometimes, bizarrely, of both together. If nations had somehow failed to take full control of their own destiny, the only remedy seemed to be to double down. The nationalist dream of utopia was turning into a nightmare.

The systems of representative democracy that had proliferated in 1919 were quickly found wanting. The slide towards authoritarian regimes ruled by a single strongman had begun well before the Crash of 1929: in Italy the former socialist Benito Mussolini had begun the trend when he seized power in 1922; Spain took the same path the following year, Portugal and Poland in 1926. But in the 1930s the slide became an avalanche. By 1939, approximately three-fifths of all Europeans, living in sixteen states, were subject to authoritarian regimes of various types; only eleven states in the north and west, if one includes Iceland, were still parliamentary democracies.[47]

The blanket term 'fascism' has often been used to describe the European dictatorships of this period. Strictly speaking it applies only to Mussolini's Italy; the name derives from the *fasces*, bundles of rods carried by officials of the ancient Roman Republic as a symbol of order and discipline. To the extent that these regimes had a coherent ideology (and most did not), it lay in the negative one of a visceral hatred of socialism, whether in its parliamentary form or as militantly represented by the USSR. Social class, particularly the claims of the rapidly growing urban working class, was one of the great dividing lines in Europe at this time. But authoritarian regimes proved adept at neutralizing pressures from below – by nationalizing them. Mussolini had after all been a socialist once. And the party that in 1933 would take control of Germany and bring

Adolf Hitler to power had been founded more than a decade earlier as the National Socialist German Workers' Party, later to be known as Nazis. But at the core of all these regimes lay an extreme, pathological, one might even say hysterical veneration for the idea of the nation.

The Nazis coined the term *Volksgemeinschaft*, meaning 'people's community'. Far more than any other authoritarian regime in Europe, they defined the 'people' in terms that derived directly from the obsession with race that had dominated much of Europe during the previous century – and this, ironically, at a time when the science supposed to underpin it was already in headlong retreat within the international scientific community.[48]

For all these reasons, the Europe that stumbled out of the world-wide slump of the 1930s was more divided against itself than perhaps at any time in the past. When the two most powerful of the new authoritarian regimes, Hitler's Germany and Mussolini's Italy, pro-claimed a joint 'Axis' in 1936, it was neither a relationship of equals nor based on a shared project, other than the tactical advantage of both. The two governments were by that time investing heavily in an arms race against the rest of the continent, at once as a route to economic recovery and as preparation of the ground for future conquests. South of the Alps, Mussolini set the ball rolling in 1935 with the invasion of Ethiopia (successful this time) and dreamed of a new Roman Empire that would once again encompass the lands all around the Mediterranean. Further north, Hitler's 'Third Reich' claimed the mantle of the (very different) Holy Roman Empire and the second German Empire that had been created by Prussia in 1871; but Nazi territorial ambitions would soon soar far beyond the reach of either.

Meanwhile, beyond the Pyrenees, Spain became the cockpit of a mortal combat between nationalism and internationalism, between fascism and a 'popular front' made up of socialists and communists. Between 1936 and 1939 the Spanish Civil War drew in combatants from every part of Europe, and some from much farther afield. Nazi Germany and Fascist Italy backed the nationalist rebellion by General

Francisco Franco, which with their help eventually succeeded; the Soviet Union lent support to the 'popular front' government of the Spanish Republic, though not enough to save it. While other governments stood aloof, volunteers in their thousands flocked to Spain to aid the republican cause. Europeans from every nation killed one another and were killed in Spain, in a microcosm of the much larger European civil war that had begun back in 1914 and was about to be rekindled across the continent, and eventually over much of the globe.

Unconditional Surrender

Europe finally reached its own 'heart of darkness' between 1941 and 1945. This was when ideas of exterminating whole races regarded as inferior, which had first been aired and then tried out in the 'dark continent' of Africa half a century before, came to be applied with scientific precision at the heart of Europe itself. During those four years, the Nazi Reich embarked on the systematic murder of six million Jews, transported from every corner of the continent to death camps in Germany and Poland. The peculiar horror attached to the Holocaust, also known by the Hebrew term 'Shoah', perhaps lies in the efficiency with which the Nazis mobilized the most up-to-date technology and logistics (the heritage of the Enlightenment) for the purpose of killing human beings on an industrial scale, without precedent in human history. Later generations have continued to grapple with the testimony it bears to the 'banality of evil' – a capacity for ordinary individuals to accept the unspeakable into their daily lives.[49]

The targets of Nazi genocide were not exclusively Jews. The Romani people (often called 'gypsies' in many languages) were also targeted on racial grounds. Like the Jews, Romani communities had become an established part of life in many regions of Europe – in their case since at least the fourteenth century. Half a million Romani suffered the same fate as the Jews during the same years.[50]

Individuals deemed to be 'sexually deviant' or mentally deficient were routinely murdered too, regardless of their 'race'. And if combatants belonging to western European nations could usually be assured of treatment according to the established international conventions governing warfare at the time, no such restraints applied to Slavs or other 'lesser' peoples who came within the sights of trigger-happy Nazi conquerors. In eastern Europe, the Second World War became a war of extermination.

By 1942, either directly or through subservient allies, Hitler ruled most of continental Europe from the Atlantic coast to the Black Sea and the Gulf of Finland, from the Arctic Ocean to the Mediterranean. Only Portugal, Spain, Sweden and Switzerland were allowed to maintain a neutrality that posed no threat to the Reich. But apart from mass killing, the new masters of the continent seem to have had little idea what to do with their mastery. To the extent that Hitler ever possessed an idea of Europe, it was as nakedly German as Napoleon's had been French – only far darker, and more nihilistic.

The notion of German supremacy had been around since at least 1930, when it had been couched in the unmistakably racial terms of a 'Nordic Europe'. In a speech in 1936, Hitler had looked forward to a time when Germany would keep order in the 'European house'. In the aftermath of the conquest of much of northern and western Europe in the spring and early summer of 1940 a Nazi official announced that his country was taking over 'the ordering of Europe'. Six months later a 'great European New Order' (*Neuordnung Europas*) was unveiled by Hitler in a speech to a mass rally at the Berlin Sports Palace. Later, during 1941, a first 'European Congress' was held in the same city, a 'song for Europe' was broadcast on German radio, and in November a Nazi newspaper declared: 'the United States of Europe has at last become a reality'. As late as May 1943, by which time Germany was decidedly on the back foot, Hitler was still exhorting his party chiefs 'to create a unified Europe' as the means to 'seize the leadership of the world' – with the telling rider that 'Europe can only be given a coherent structure through Germany'.[51] The utopia dreamed up by Coudenhove-Kalergi in *Pan-Europa* had been turned into the most extreme dystopia imaginable.

But far from creating a 'coherent structure', the true reality, to quote Mark Mazower again, was that 'Nazi governance was never more chaotic than during the war'; in practice the 'New Order' amounted to little more than organized looting of the continent's resources (material and human) for the benefit of the Reich. This in turn, as the fortunes of war began to turn after the end of 1942, would increasingly involve desperate measures to shore up the war effort. By that time, German claims to be fighting 'a European crusade against Bolshevism', or even more bizarrely to be engaged in 'a struggle for the whole of Europe and thus for the whole of civilized humanity', had become nothing more than a grotesque appropriation of the language of the Enlightenment to defend its exact opposite.[52]

It is doubtful whether Hitler had ever intended to rule over quite as much of Europe as he ended up doing.[53] Throughout the 1920s and 1930s the thrust of Nazi ideology had always been towards expansion of Germany to the east. Until the summer of 1939 the two greatest threats to Europe, as it then existed, had been Stalin's Soviet Union from the outside and Hitler's Third Reich from within. Sooner or later the great fight to the death was going to be between the two totalitarian dictatorships at opposite ends of the ideological spectrum.

But then, in August 1939, the rest of Europe had been blindsided by the announcement of an incongruous pact: Hitler and Stalin had, in effect, agreed to carve up eastern Europe between them.[54] Faced with this hostile and seemingly united front in the east, Britain and France stumbled into a war to defend Poland – a country that, geographically and strategically, was beyond the reach of any help that either of them could have given. The consequence was that, having mopped up most of Poland, Hitler in 1940 turned westward and then, in spring, 1941, south into the Balkans.

It was only after these moves that Hitler was ready to return to the goal he had cherished all along. Without warning or even any formal declaration of war, during the early hours of Sunday, 22 June 1941, Operation Barbarossa launched a massive attack on Germany's erstwhile ally, the Soviet Union. The only European power still holding out against Nazi Germany was Britain, backed by the considerable resources of its overseas empire and economic support from an as yet uncommitted United States. The alliance between imperialist Britain and the communist USSR that followed was as incongruous as Stalin's previous deal with Hitler had been. Once America had entered the war, after the attack by Japan on Pearl Harbor in December 1941, a new dynamic quickly came into play. The future course of the war would be determined by the three-way alliance of America, Russia and Britain (the last also a rallying point for resistance to Nazism in continental Europe) against Hitler and his European satellites.

On 2 February 1943 the German Sixth Army surrendered outside the city of Stalingrad (today's Volgograd on the River Volga). The winter battle for Stalingrad had been one of the most vicious of the entire war. At horrific cost to both sides, Operation Barbarossa now turned into a slow retreat westwards. On other fronts, the Germans and Italians had been beaten in North Africa after the second battle of El Alamein the previous October and November. In July 1943 a combined British and American expedition landed in Sicily; two weeks later the Italian dictator Mussolini was overthrown and the new Italian government changed sides. Allied forces pushed northwards through Italy, despite a furious rearguard action ordered by Hitler.

Scenting victory, the three Allied leaders met together for the first time at the end of November 1943. The venue chosen was in the Iranian capital, Tehran. Neutral Iran had been invaded and occupied jointly by Britain and the Soviet Union two years before, in order to secure the supply of Iranian oil to Russia – a harbinger of the approach the prospective victors would take towards Europe, too. Franklin D. Roosevelt was in poor health but had set his sights on winning an unprecedented fourth term as American president in the election of 1944; Stalin was well known to be paranoid; Winston Churchill, for Britain, behind his trademark cigars and sonorous speaking manner, was evidently well aware of the fading influence of the British Empire. His was also the only voice for Europe in the room.

Roosevelt brought to the table only one red line, and from this he never wavered: the war could end with nothing less than the unconditional surrender of Germany. Stalin had a more complex agenda. While his pact with Hitler had lasted, the Soviet Union had annexed almost as much territory in eastern Europe as the Nazis had, stretching from Finland to the Black Sea coast of Romania. Once the Germans had been ejected, the Russian dictator expected to get it all back. Soviet war aims may not from the beginning have been quite as coherent and consistent as they have been presented in the myth-busting *Stalin's War* by Sean McMeekin, published in 2021; but from this point on they surely were. It may well have been his determination to push Soviet power westwards into Europe, rather than the hope of reducing the cost in Russian lives on the Eastern Front, that led Stalin at the Tehran conference to browbeat Churchill and Roosevelt into committing to an invasion of Europe from the west the following year. This was the 'second front' that would become known as Operation Overlord.[55]

Overlord was launched on the beaches of Normandy on 6 June 1944, known ever afterwards as D-Day. It has been called 'almost certainly the most ambitious operation in the history of warfare'. The fleet of more than 5,000 ships that transported and backed up the landing force was 'the largest . . . that had ever put to sea'. The 130,000 soldiers who went ashore in the first wave on that morning were American, British and Canadian, with support from other British overseas dominions and smaller contingents of exiles from occupied Europe.[56]

The continent had been invaded countless times, over many millennia, from the east; only once, so far as is known, from the south (in the eighth century, by Muslims from North Africa). It had never before been invaded from the west, the direction in which Columbus and his successors had set out at the end of the fifteenth century. In a sense, Overlord was the revenge of the New World upon the Old. It proved that the Atlantic was no longer the defining barrier that it had always been until then. And even so, the invasion would never have been possible had not the British Isles been available as a bridgehead where the invasion force, the ships and aircraft from across the Atlantic could muster within easy striking distance of the continent. No one may have thought of it in quite those terms at the time, but on 6 June 1944 the geopolitical position of Europe in the world changed for ever.

Two days before D-Day, American forces pushing up through Italy from the south had entered Rome; then on 22 June, the third anniversary of Hitler's attack on the Soviet Union, Stalin launched Operation Bagration, an overwhelming attack across the entire Eastern Front, all the way from Ukraine in the south to the Baltic in the north. The Third Reich was now under attack from every side. It still took almost a year, and some of the most destructive fighting of the entire war, before the Allies could advance far enough into Germany to enforce Roosevelt's long-cherished unconditional surrender – after Hitler's suicide on 30 April 1945. Ironically enough, Roosevelt himself had died of a cerebral haemorrhage just three weeks earlier.

During the final weeks, while the Americans with their British and other allies were advancing through Europe into Germany from the west and the Red Army from the east, General Dwight Eisenhower took the decision to halt the advance at the River Elbe, so as to allow the Russians to reach Berlin first. The only European leaders within reach of the driving seat were Churchill and General Charles de Gaulle, representing newly liberated France. Neither of them stood a chance of getting a hand on the wheel, though Churchill did try.[57] When peace was declared on 'Victory in Europe' day, 8 May 1945, the stage had already been set for the partition of Europe between the world's two new superpowers, the United States and the Soviet Union, that would last for almost half a century.

Since at least 1871, the nations of Europe had been set on a course that could only lead to ever greater conflict. The darkest of their instincts had been taken out on the inhabitants of another continent, Africa, until in 1914 they had turned on each other. The lamps that had been extinguished all over Europe, then, had only fitfully flickered since. The most recent bloodletting had taken the continent to new depths of darkness. Now that it was over, if you look at it from the point of view of Europe, rather than of the embattled nations, it was Europe that had lost. Unconditional surrender indeed.

9.

Europe Partitioned

1945–1989

Within days of the German surrender, Churchill despatched a telegram to the new American president, Harry S. Truman. Marked 'Top Secret' and dated 12 May 1945, it set out the British prime minister's fears of the advancing Soviets: 'An iron curtain is drawn down upon their front. We do not know what is going on behind.'[1]

In this climate of rapidly growing mutual suspicion among the victors, there was no place for a grand peace conference to round off the end of six years of war. A meeting of the leaders of the United States, the Soviet Union and Britain, held at Potsdam, the old royal residence on the outskirts of Berlin, during the second half of July 1945, was no substitute for the months-long gatherings of European leaders that had followed the Napoleonic Wars in 1814 and 1815 in Vienna or the First World War in Paris in 1919. Europe's voice at Potsdam was further weakened when the results of the British general election, held earlier that month, were announced while the conference was in full swing, and Churchill had suddenly to be replaced by his country's new prime minister, his wartime deputy and leader of the Labour Party, Clement Attlee. Much of the discussion was about the still unfinished war against Japan; back in Europe, arrangements were drawn up for Germany and Austria to be split into four zones of occupation (the fourth being assigned to France).

It's often said that, in contrast to the First World War, the outcome of the Second World War left the boundaries of states mostly unchanged. But at Potsdam the American and British sides were powerless to resist Stalin's unilateral decision to strip from Germany the greater part of the historically German-speaking lands of East Prussia, Pomerania and Silesia, and assign them instead to a newly installed communist regime in Poland – an arrangement that would have to wait until 1990 to be ratified between the two states. The Prussian city of Königsberg, which had once been a centre of the eighteenth-century Enlightenment and the lifelong home of the philosopher Immanuel Kant, became the Russian fortified port of Kaliningrad, as it remains today. No one was in a position, either, to prevent Russia from annexing part of Finland, the whole of the three Baltic states (Estonia, Latvia and Lithuania), a large chunk of eastern Poland and a slice of Romania. The borders of Russia now reached further into Europe than at any time since Tsar Alexander I had secured his share of the spoils at the Congress of Vienna in 1815.[2]

Almost a year after 'Victory in Europe' day, on 5 March 1946, at Westminster College in Fulton, Missouri, Churchill famously elaborated on his theme of an 'iron curtain . . . across the Continent' for the benefit of an audience that included President Truman himself. And he ended: 'this is certainly not the Liberated Europe we fought to build up. Nor is this one which contains the essentials of permanent peace.'[3] Indeed it was not. Britain and France had gone to war in 1939 to try to stop Hitler and Stalin from carving up Poland between them. Now Stalin had made good almost all the gains he had made from that unholy alliance and was adding others, through communist proxy regimes in Eastern Europe.

Just as had happened after the previous world war, the formal ending of this one did not bring peace everywhere. Londoners might jump for joy in the fountains of Trafalgar Square, but victory over the Nazis meant very different things in other parts of Europe. During the last days of the war, and for some time afterwards, as the Red Army moved into Germany, mass rape had once again become a weapon of conquest. In Berlin alone, according to one account, 'over 90,000 women and girls visited doctors and clinics . . . as a result of rape. No one can say how many kept silent.' The total number of raped women in eastern Germany between 1945 and 1947 may have been as many as two million.[4]

During the same period, the forced displacement of populations became a regular occurrence: somewhere between 12 and 14 million German-speakers were expelled, often violently, from cities, towns and villages in Czechoslovakia, Hungary, Poland, Romania and Yugoslavia that had been home to their ancestors for hundreds of years. Deportations in the opposite direction involved the compulsory return to the Soviet Union of prisoners of war who had been liberated from German prison camps by American and British forces. The same applied to forced labourers who had been taken from Russia to Germany by the Nazis, as well as east Europeans and Russians who had sought refuge by fleeing westward. More than five million deportees were sent to the Soviet Union, often then to be incarcerated in gulag labour camps or even executed.[5]

Meanwhile, in most of the countries that had experienced Nazi occupation, liberation brought those who had taken part in resistance face to face with their compatriots who had acquiesced or even collaborated with the occupiers. The extreme case was Greece, where open civil war had begun as early as 1943, while the Nazis had still been in charge. In Greece, as elsewhere, the most effective resistance had been organized by communists, theoretically affiliated to the Soviet Union but in practice backed by Britain and, to a lesser extent, by America. When the war ended, and first the British, and then the Americans, faced the prospect of the Communist Party taking power in Greece, the former backers of wartime resistance intervened to prevent it. Elsewhere in the Balkans, in Yugoslavia and Albania, scarcely less deadly tussles went the other way, leaving communist regimes in charge.

Very similar ingredients for conflict were present in other parts of Europe too. In Belgium, which ended the war in a condition not very different from Greece, civil war was only narrowly averted. In France, where millions had acquiesced in the Nazi-approved puppet regime of Marshal Pétain, based in the central town of Vichy, the subject would remain virtually taboo for decades afterwards. The same has been said of Czechoslovakia, Finland, Poland, the former Baltic states, and even of continental Europe as a whole.[6]

By the spring of 1947, President Truman had fully taken on board the warnings of Churchill and others. What became known as the 'Truman Doctrine' was triggered by the civil war in Greece, whose outcome still hung in the balance, and the fear that Turkey, too, might be drawn into the Soviet sphere of influence. Addressing Congress on 12 March, the president called for a massive injection of economic and military aid to those two countries; at the same time he articulated a view of his own country's new-found role in the world that would have a profound influence on the emerging shape of Europe for the best part of a century. Without mentioning Stalin, the Soviet Union, or Russia, Truman argued that 'totalitarian regimes imposed on free peoples, by direct or indirect aggression, undermine the foundations of international peace and hence the security of the United States'. And he continued: 'The free peoples of the world look to us for support in maintaining their freedoms. If we falter in our leadership, we may endanger the peace of the world – and we shall surely endanger the welfare of our own nation.'[7]

Truman's predecessor, Woodrow Wilson, had had exactly the same idea in the aftermath of the First World War. But shortly afterwards, America had retreated into isolation again – and Europeans, left to their own devices, had gone on to make a spectacularly bad fist of managing their own affairs. This time, having contributed, as Truman put it, over $300 trillion towards winning a second worldwide conflict, the United States was not going to make the same mistake again. America was now ready to confront its superpower rival. And that meant staying in Europe – not for Europe's sake, but for America's. The 'Cold War' had begun.

In the end, the drawing of the Iron Curtain down the middle of the continent would prove a piecemeal affair. The fate of Czechoslovakia remained to be determined until 1948, when a Soviet-backed coup installed a communist regime and brought the country into the eastern bloc. In the same year, the communist regime of Josip

Broz Tito in Yugoslavia broke away from Stalin; for the duration of the Cold War, Yugoslavia would remain a grey zone between east and west, an authoritarian communist state but independent of Soviet Russia. The communist insurgency in Greece would not be defeated until 1949, when superior American firepower (but not boots on the ground) prevailed to ensure that this eastern European country would remain part of the 'West', in defiance of geography. In the same year Germany was formally split into a Federal Republic (informally known as 'West Germany') and a Democratic Republic (or 'East Germany'). The final pieces of the jigsaw would not be slotted into place until the Soviets withdrew from occupied Austria in 1955, and the infamous Berlin Wall sealed off the last chink of an opening between east and west, as late as 1961.

Geopolitics dictated that the principal battleground in the new global conflict would be divided Europe. But the decisions that mattered the most were all being taken elsewhere.

Varieties of Europe

None of this was any bar to new ideas of Europe proliferating during the 1940s and 1950s. While the war lasted, it had seemed quite a reasonable proposition, among those who resisted the Nazis, that the heyday of nation states had come and gone. Nationalism had, after all, been at the root of the conflict. In a manifesto written from an Italian jail in 1941, and widely circulated among the resistance thereafter, two imprisoned opponents of Mussolini argued for 'the definitive abolition of division of Europe into national, sovereign States' and its replacement by 'a federal reorganization' which would bring about 'A FREE AND UNITED EUROPE'.[8]

In 1946 some seventy representatives of sixteen different European states came together to establish a 'Union of European Federalists'. No less a person than Winston Churchill, in a speech delivered in Zurich in September the same year, called upon France and Germany to bury their historic differences and work together with the rest of the continent to 'build a kind of United States of Europe'. But there was still to be an exception. Britain, along with America and, Churchill still hoped, Russia, 'must be the friends and sponsors of the new Europe'. The British former prime minister still thought of his own country in imperial terms: a benign godparent to the project, Britain with its many global interests was to stand aloof.[9]

Competing ideas about how Europe might reinvent itself, now that the bloodletting was over, jostled in the imagination of statesmen (more often than not, like Churchill, out of power at the time), intellectuals and creative artists. Some of these ideas had a religious tinge, harking back to the unity of the Catholic Middle Ages; others drew inspiration from the devolved administrative structure of the Holy Roman Empire in its later years, or even looked back all the way to the earliest known attempts at federation by the Greek city states of ancient times. Others reflected a socialist, or even communist, perspective. Perhaps for the first time, efforts were made to identify a 'European spirit' and champion moral and social values associated with it – a somewhat tall order, given the inhumanity that Europeans had so recently unleashed upon each other and on those in other parts of the world.[10]

All of these strands came together at a 'Congress of Europe' held in the Dutch city of The Hague, in May 1948. More than 700 delegates attended; almost a third of them were serving members of national parliaments; trades unions and intellectuals were also well represented. Churchill, still an enthusiast and recently the founder of a 'United Europe Movement', presided; his record as a wartime leader against Nazism guaranteed prestige for the occasion. Attendees included well-known names from the pre-war generation along with national leaders whose time had yet to come (among them Harold Macmillan for Britain, Konrad Adenauer for West Germany, François Mitterrand for France). It has been suggested in hindsight that the congress at The Hague 'had the potential to develop into the European equivalent to the Philadelphia Convention of 1787', in other words to lay the foundation for a 'United States of Europe' on a similar model to the USA.[11]

Needless to say, that didn't happen. Even before they arrived at The Hague, the enthusiasts for European unity were deeply divided among themselves about what form that unity might take. Some favoured a federal model, others a looser integration at the level of cooperation among national governments. A 'Political Resolution' issued at the end of the congress urged the nations of Europe to 'transfer and merge some portion of their sovereign rights so as to secure common political and economic action for the integration and proper development of their common resources'. But no mechanism existed to make that happen; beyond goodwill, no practical steps were agreed to bring it about.[12]

The congress did achieve two long-term results, which are still with us today. The Council of Europe, bringing together the representatives of ten governments (today forty-six), was established one year later, in May 1949; and in November of the next year a new Convention for the Protection of Human Rights and Fundamental Freedoms began to pave the way for the European Court of Human Rights as we know it today. Always separate from the institutions that would later pave the way for today's European Union, and lacking any direct powers of enforcement, the Council and the Court would play an important part in European affairs in years to come. Human rights, their definition and how to uphold them, would eventually take their place in emerging ideas about post-war European identity. But these were still tentative steps.[13]

Despite the high profile of some of the players at The Hague, and despite those limited but tangible results, projects for European unity remained something of a niche interest. The war had devastated towns and cities across the continent and its islands; economies had been wrecked, whole industries and livelihoods wiped out. The overriding priority for all had to be reconstruction. In pole position to lead the process were national governments (except in Germany and Austria, where responsibility still lay with the occupying forces). Those governments themselves might be anything but stable; but at least the institutions and the levers of power necessary for rebuilding existed at the national level. There were practical reasons, therefore, for those in positions of responsibility to shelve thinking about the bigger, European picture and concentrate on delivering at home. It's perhaps not entirely surprising, then, that the most effective spur towards European unity in the late 1940s came not from within Europe but from across the Atlantic. European governments might be struggling to see beyond their own backyards, but a different idea of Europe was taking hold in Washington.

By the time that Truman announced his 'doctrine' of support for states opposing communism in spring 1947, it had become glaringly obvious to the American administration that just about every government in the Old World was struggling. Currencies had been devalued; national exchequers were on the brink of bankruptcy. Enlightened self-interest prompted two motives for further intervention: if Europe were to collapse, America would lose its most potentially lucrative market; even worse would be if bankrupt or failing European states ended up as easy prey for the Soviets. In a speech delivered at Harvard University on 5 June, Secretary of State George Marshall announced a 'European Recovery Plan'; the following April it was formally recommended to Congress by President Truman and approved.

The injection of some $13 billion worth of American aid towards the reconstruction of Europe, over the next four years, was on a scale never seen before; its effects would last into the 2020s. But not even the massive sums transferred by the Marshall Plan, as it has generally become known ever since, would have been enough on their own to bring about the extraordinary economic boom that would take off in Western Europe from the late 1940s until the early 1970s. Even so, there can be no doubt that this American intervention helped kickstart it. And tucked into the small print of the Plan was a political agenda too.

Marshall in his speech outlined the aim of 'restoring the confidence of the European people in the economic future of their own countries *and of Europe as a whole*'.[14] While he expected the

Europeans themselves to step up and take the initiative in using the aid that was to be provided, they were also to be given a steer. Within days of Congress approving the plan, an 'Organization for European Economic Cooperation' (OEEC) was founded in Paris. Fourteen European nations, including Iceland (but not yet Franco's Spain) joined, along with Turkey. It was already known that President Truman 'favoured a United States of Europe'. In his opening address to the first meeting of the OEEC, the US businessman charged with leading on implementation of the Plan, Paul Hoffman, called upon his audience to move beyond 'the old separatist lines' in the interests of 'the economic strength of Europe as a whole'. At a private gathering on the fringe of the meeting, the US Under-Secretary of State for Economic Affairs, William Clayton, made it clear that his government expected the Europeans to move towards a 'European economic federation'.[15]

Built into the Marshall Plan was the expectation that customs barriers would be reduced or eliminated and national economies opened up to one another. European unity, according to this American vision, was to be driven by economic integration; but the political dimension was in there from the beginning.

For European convinced federalists, the cautious steps taken by the new organization were nothing like enough; for the participating governments, on the other hand, they were altogether too much.[16] The upshot was that the spectacular injection of Marshall aid was duly delivered, but the economic and political unity of Western Europe that its architects had dreamed up across the Atlantic was not. The nearest thing that could be achieved – again with strong input from the US administration – was the agreement of six continental Western European nations, initiated by France, to form a European Coal and Steel Community. In this new venture, West Germany was to become an equal partner.

Announced on 9 May 1950, and sealed by a treaty eleven months later, the Community was the brainchild of the French civil servant and ardent federalist Jean Monnet, together with the pragmatic foreign minister of France, the Luxembourg-born, German-speaking

Robert Schuman. In the preamble to the 'Declaration' that ever afterwards would bear his name, Schuman expressed his regret that in the 1930s, 'A united Europe was not achieved and we had war.' Although the proposed plan was limited to the resources and processes for producing coal and steel, Schuman could state confidently: 'This proposal will lead to the realization of the first concrete foundation of a European federation indispensable to the preservation of peace.' From the perspective of the 2020s, the Schuman Plan has been called 'the game-changer that Western Europe needed'.[17]

Most accounts of the origins of today's European Union begin with the Schuman Declaration. But the truth was both more modest and more mundane. At the heart of the coal and steel agreement lay the simple fact that Western European heavy industry, and especially that of France, relied on the supply of coal, and most of it lay beneath the ground in Germany. It was national self-interest, at least as much as any far-sighted appreciation of the benefits of European integration, that brought the lead players – France and the newly empowered German Federal Republic – together to spearhead the plan: the real significance of the Schuman Plan was that it brought the western half of partitioned Germany fully, and for the first time, into the European fold.[18] Albeit still very much under the guiding hand of the United States, the European Coal and Steel Community did create the first-ever supranational organization in Europe: the six participating nations agreed to pool an element of their sovereignty, since all of them accepted, at least in theory, the jurisdiction of the Community's 'High Authority'. Perhaps unsurprisingly, this was a commitment that the Labour government under Clement Attlee declined to make on behalf of Britain, which still stood apart.

Evidently, a 'United States' on the American model would not do for Europe; but Europeans could agree on no alternative, other than more of the same, and tinkering round the edges. If that was ever going to change, it would have to be, as Schuman had foreseen, 'not . . . all at once, or according to a single plan'. The Europe of the future would have to 'be built through concrete achievements which first create a de facto solidarity'.[19]

Moment of Truth

The Europe that was supposed to be coming together as the wartime decade ended was by this time understood as exclusively *Western* Europe, which the Americans also liked to call 'free Europe'. In principle, the offer of Marshall aid, when it had first been mooted, had extended to the communist states of the east, and even to the Soviet Union itself. But Stalin had rebuffed the offer, as probably he was meant to. The rival superpower could never have accepted the degree of dependence on the American-dominated capitalist system that was already baked into the Plan. As a result, whether intended or not, aid from the Marshall Plan had the effect of driving a further wedge between the two halves of divided Europe. It was a much-truncated continent that the Americans were trying to coax towards greater integration in the years after the Marshall Plan was announced.

By 1949, this new Europe was getting back on its feet economically. But Cold War hostilities were hardening. Who on the Western side was going to defend the line that divided the continent, supposing war with Russia were to turn hot? Soviet land forces in Europe vastly outnumbered anything the Western states could muster. The answer once again, inevitably, would lie with the Americans – although this time the initiative came from the European side, and principally from Britain. First steps towards a defensive pact made up of the United Kingdom, France and the 'Benelux' countries resulted in a treaty signed in Brussels in March 1948; but the real impetus came from secret talks held by the Americans with the British and Canadians in Washington four months later. The upshot was the North Atlantic Treaty Organization, which was signed into existence in Washington, DC on 4 April 1949.

Article 5 of the treaty states: 'The Parties agree that an armed attack against one or more of them in Europe or North America shall be considered an attack against them all.'[20] In this way the treaty bound the United States to the future defence of Europe, as well as Europe to the defence of America, in the rather less likely event of that being necessary. Along with the US and Canada, the founding members were Belgium, Britain, Denmark, France, Iceland, Italy, Luxembourg, the Netherlands, Norway and Portugal, to be followed by Greece and Turkey in 1952 and West Germany three years later. A military alliance in peacetime, and on such a scale, had never been seen before.

NATO, at the time of its founding, has been described as a 'fig-leaf' and a 'bluff'. Not even American firepower came close to matching the forces available to the Soviet Union in Europe; the US administration had in any case never intended to maintain a long-term military occupation. From the point of view of American policymakers, according to one later analysis, NATO was intended to work in much the same way as the Marshall Plan: 'as a device to help Europeans feel better about themselves and manage their own affairs'.[21]

If that was the aim, it didn't work out that way. The military alliance overlapped only patchily with the economic partnership of the European Coal and Steel Community. NATO did achieve a high degree of integration among the armed forces and command structures of the participating states; but inevitably the leadership was always going to come from beyond the Atlantic, which was where the lion's share of the resources lay. As the Cold War division of Europe froze into place, Europeans on both sides of the Iron Curtain had lost control of their own defence: on the one side unwillingly to Moscow, on the other unwittingly to Washington.

In June 1950 the Cold War did indeed become hot – not in Europe, but at the far end of the Asian continent, in Korea. Both superpowers now possessed nuclear weapons; no European state yet did. The defence of Western Europe became more urgent than ever. During the next four years, while far away the Korean War fought itself to the stalemate that still exists today, plans were drawn up for a European Defence Community and an overarching European Political Community. If the European Coal and Steel Community had been a cautious start, these next steps were intended to build upon it. The prime mover this time was France; once again Britain kept its distance. With strong encouragement from the US administration, the six countries that had already come together to form the first Community (crucially including West Germany) signed a new treaty in Paris in May 1952. Under its terms, the armies of each nation would all wear a common uniform and be subject to a shared budget. The European Political Community was then to determine a common foreign policy.

This treaty has been described as 'the largest single cession of sovereignty made by the countries of Western Europe until the Treaty on European Union in 1992'; the institutional structures it envisaged amounted to 'effectively a European government-in-waiting'.[22] But there was also a sting in the tail. National sovereignty was to be surrendered not just to the institutions of the Community, but also to the supreme command of NATO, which in practice meant to America. President Dwight Eisenhower, who succeeded Truman in 1953, by the next year was putting intense pressure on the European partners to ratify the treaty.

The scheme had first been thought up by one French government; it was another that brought it down. When the final terms of the treaty were debated in the National Assembly on 30 August 1954, the deputies voted by a sizeable majority to reject it, and then spontaneously burst out in a rousing rendition of the national anthem, the 'Marseillaise'. Eisenhower's Secretary of State, John Foster Dulles, was incandescent: 'It is a tragedy that in one country nationalism, abetted by communism, has asserted itself so as to endanger the whole of Europe,' he raged not long afterwards. But tweaking the nose of the Americans seems to have been part of the point. As the French philosopher Raymond Aron would later put it, 'The satisfaction of resisting American pressure was not the least reason in voting against the EDC.'[23]

Its place was soon taken by a far less contentious scheme brokered by the British Foreign Secretary, Anthony Eden. Known as the 'Western European Union', this paid lip service to the goals of 'unity' and 'the progressive integration of Europe', but without any surrender of sovereignty to a supranational organization. By this means, West Germany was finally allowed to join NATO, albeit on conditions that would limit its military capability for decades. The Soviet Union, led by Nikita Khrushchev since the death of Stalin in March 1953, responded by corralling its Eastern European satellites into a formal alliance of its own: the Warsaw Pact was inaugurated on 14 May 1955. By this time only a handful of European states lay outside one or other of these two mutually antagonistic blocs: Austria, Ireland, Finland, Sweden and Switzerland on the Western side, Yugoslavia among communist states. The defence of Europe more than ever lay in the hands of the two superpowers that continued to face one another across the Iron Curtain.

The only serious attempts by Europeans to challenge this new reality came a little over a year later. Events were triggered almost simultaneously, and in a most dramatic fashion, by governments on each side of the divide, during ten days in late October and early November 1956.

In Eastern Europe, mixed signals coming out of the new administration in Moscow had fuelled hopes in Poland and Hungary for some relaxation of tight, communist control. In Poland, Khrushchev was able to defuse tension by making minor concessions; but in Hungary a full-scale uprising broke out on Tuesday 23 October in the centre of the capital, Budapest. A week later, the short-lived government of Imre Nagy announced a 'free, democratic and independent Hungary' and two days after that, unilaterally pulled the country out of the Warsaw Pact.[24] Soviet troops surrounded the city on 3 November and entered it the next day. Six days later the insurrection was over. More than 20,000 Hungarians were killed or wounded in the uprising, and as many again imprisoned. In the aftermath, several hundred would be executed, including Nagy himself and leading members of his government two years later; some 200,000 Hungarians would flee to Western Europe before the borders were sealed once more.[25]

While these events were at their height, on Wednesday 31 October, at the climax of several months' secret planning, Britain and France, allied with the state of Israel that had been created just eight years before, launched their armed forces against Egypt, in a bid to remove the regime of Gamal Abdel Nasser. Nasser's offence (though it was not the only one) was to court the wrong side in the Cold War: he had accepted a Soviet loan to finance the building of the Aswan Dam and bought weapons from Czechoslovakia. Thus far, there was a case for intervention that might just have been enough to win the approval, if not the outright support, of America. That, at least, seems to have been the calculation of its instigators, prime ministers Anthony Eden for Britain, Guy Mollet for France and David Ben-Gurion for Israel. But in the minds of all three, and of those members of their respective governments who were in their confidence, the Cold War and its dynamics were only incidental to their real aim – which is why they took the unprecedented risk of keeping their American allies in the dark about their plans.

Britain and France still had colonial possessions overseas, chiefly in Africa. Egypt, though never formally a colony, had been in effect a British dependency from 1882 until 1952, when the compliant King Farouk had been toppled in a revolution led by Nasser. Algeria, annexed by France as long ago as 1830, had been in revolt since 1954; the Algerian insurgents looked to Nasser as the champion of a growing Arab national movement dedicated to ousting the last remnants of colonialism in the region. From the point of view of the British and French, containing Nasser would be a way to reassert European control abroad, in the only part of the world where there still remained a chance of doing so. Israel, 'a European transplant in the heart of the Middle East', but with strategic imperatives of its own, seemed like the right partner at the right time.

A convenient pretext lay to hand, since it had been British and French capital that had built the Suez Canal across Egyptian territory to link the Mediterranean with the Red Sea, almost a century before. When Nasser nationalized the controlling Suez Canal Company in July 1956, he handed the European colonial powers the excuse they were looking for. That it was no more than an excuse is evident from the fact that financial compensation was offered to shareholders, as had been done with many other nationalizations in the past, including in Britain. It was as a bid to restore their rights to the canal that the belligerents justified their actions at the end of October.[26]

But the victors in the world war had had more than enough of European empires, at home or abroad. Naturally, if also with breathtaking hypocrisy, Khrushchev's prime minister, Nikolai Bulganin, condemned the British, French and Israeli actions in the strongest possible terms, during the very hours when Soviet tanks were mowing down civilians in the streets of Budapest. But Eisenhower and his Secretary of State, John Foster Dulles, had been blindsided too. Far more was at stake than ownership of an international waterway; an American administration was not going to underwrite an imperial adventure that might have consolidated a European controlling presence in the Middle East and North Africa, perhaps even putting Western Europe on a path to reclaiming a shred of its former status as a world power.

It wasn't Bulganin's bluffing threat to bomb London and Paris (ambiguously implying that nuclear weapons might be used) that forced first Eden and then, reluctantly, Mollet and Ben-Gurion to abort their mission; it was the fury of the American administration and the economic firepower it was able to muster against its own allies, Britain in particular. On 6 November, only hours short of achieving their military objectives, but faced with the threat of imminent bankruptcy and the collapse of their currencies, first the British and then the French announced a ceasefire and agreed shortly afterwards to withdraw their troops from Egypt.

No serious historian today, probably, would argue that the Suez campaign had been soundly conceived or would have left the world a better place if it had been allowed to succeed. But there was a European dimension to the British and French joint action that has all too often been missed. Eden himself, no enthusiast for European unity, would go out of his way, as he sought to justify his actions retrospectively in his memoirs, to invoke Europe's place in the world. It had been a European imperative, he wrote, to avoid 'a master and vassal relationship' with the United States; 'Western Europe's economic security was at stake' – ironically, since it had been his own country's economic dependence on American finance, rather than anything that happened on the battlefield, that had brought the expedition to its ignominious end, along with his own premiership.[27]

This dimension of the Suez crisis was certainly not lost on other Western Europeans at the time. The Americans may have been kept in the dark, but the partners in the Western European Union were not. Representatives of Belgium, the Netherlands, Italy and Germany had given their approval in principle to intervention against Nasser more than a month before it happened; when hostilities began, West Germany's Konrad Adenauer spoke out in favour. Not only did the German Chancellor go ahead with an official visit to Paris on the very days when French and British troops were in action in Suez, but while he was there Adenauer confided to his hosts (at least as one of them would later report his words):

> France and England will never be powers comparable with the United States and the Soviet Union. Nor will Germany. There remains to them only one way of playing a decisive role in the world, which is to unite to make Europe . . . Europe will be your revenge.[28]

Pax Americana, Pax Sovietica

Defanged at last, and no longer able to make war as they had done for centuries, European governments had quietly, instead, and often in spite of themselves, to learn the arts of peace.

By the time of Suez, the process of European 'decolonization' was already in full swing. After 1956, it accelerated rapidly. With the exception of a few scattered outposts around the world that are still in place today, the remaining overseas empires of Britain and France would disappear during the next decade; only Portugal, where the fossilized dictatorship of António Salazar continued even after the death of its founder in 1970, would go on fighting to retain its possessions in Africa for a few more years. While the superpowers raced to develop ever more, and more deadly, nuclear weapons, in Europe only Britain and France ever seriously aspired to similar programmes of their own. Britain had exploded its first atomic bomb in 1952; the French programme began two years later, with a first test in 1960. But the costs were (and remain) prohibitive; as the doctrine of nuclear deterrence came to prevail during the 1960s, the possibility of a truly independent European deterrent would become increasingly elusive. Europe's future would no longer be forged on the battlefield, or even (quite) at the highest levels of Great Power diplomacy. Instead, it would depend on the growing power of its economy.

In the wake of the Suez crisis, stalled negotiations among the 'Six', the states that had created the European Coal and Steel Community, were given a new lease of life. It was these negotiations that had brought the West German Chancellor to Paris on those fateful days of November 1956. The upshot was two further supranational Communities being signed into existence in Rome on 25 March 1957. One, known as Euratom, pooled resources for the peaceful exploitation of nuclear power; more important was the European Economic Community, or EEC. The three together would soon become known officially as the 'European Communities', but less formally as either the 'European Community' (EC) or, in English, the 'Common Market'.[29]

The preamble to the EEC treaty set out the objective: 'to lay the foundations of an ever closer union among the peoples of Europe'. Recommending its acceptance, the French foreign minister announced to his country's National Assembly that only two 'Great Powers' existed in the world, 'America and Russia'. And he continued, prophetically, 'There will be a third by the end of the century: China. It depends on you whether there will also be a fourth: Europe.' This time, the treaty passed, and no singing of the 'Marseillaise' followed the vote. A vital step had been taken along the road that would lead to the future European Union – even if, for the time being, only six nations had signed up, and Britain, having 'lost an empire but not yet found a role', in the words of US Secretary of State Dean Acheson, still stood on the sidelines.[30]

The creation of the European Economic Community in 1957 was hardly the 'revenge' that Adenauer had spoken of, if he ever really did use those words. But it *was* a truly European initiative, in a way that previous moves in the same direction had not been. And although the Treaty of Rome had been at least two years in the making, it also quietly acknowledged a new reality: the nuts and bolts of the agreement made it clear that its real scope was about housekeeping (the original meaning of the Greek word 'economy'), not restoring past grandeur.

Putting Europe's house in order would soon prove to be the order of the day, and not just among the Six. Three years later, nearly all the Western states that had not joined the EEC formed an alternative grouping, the European Free Trade Association, or EFTA. This was a far looser association; it involved 'no dilution of national sovereignty and had no aim of ultimate political integration'. But between them, the EEC and EFTA organized almost the whole of Western Europe into trading blocs that cooperated internally and competed between them. This was a far cry from the beggar-my-neighbour race to the bottom for self-sufficiency of the 1930s. And just as well – because none of the European nation states that had been created or redefined between the 1830s and the 1920s was (or is) economically self-sufficient.[31]

This is not to say that cooperation in itself was enough to bring about the extraordinary economic boom that swept through almost all of Europe between the late 1940s and the early 1970s. But whatever the precise causes, those years saw nothing less than an 'economic miracle'. The phrase was first used of West Germany, which would quickly establish itself as the powerhouse of Western Europe; but to varying degrees, and at slightly different times, the same 'miracle' and its effects would become visible everywhere. 'Most of our people,' quipped the British prime minister Harold Macmillan in a much-quoted speech in July 1957, 'have never had it so good.'[32] And it was true, all over Europe – even in the communist east, although there it was governments and their well-rewarded loyal agents that stood to gain, not populations at large. In the West, standards of living rose, year on year, for more than twenty years. During the 1960s, Western Europe achieved levels of prosperity that had never been available to so many of its people at any time in history.

Three decades before, millions of lives in Europe had been blighted by unemployment, as the international economic system had collapsed after the Crash of 1929. With the return of peace after the world war, governments increasingly saw it as part of their responsibilities to care for the well-being of their people; the first post-war decades were also the heyday of the welfare state. Governments of whatever political stripe made it their business to ensure that there were paid jobs for everybody – which in those days still mostly meant adult males. Higher rates of employment brought higher tax receipts for exchequers. And it is a remarkable fact that from the late 1940s to the end of the 1970s, Europeans in every country were content to pay out a greater proportion of their hard-earned income to their government than at any time before – or indeed since.

All this meant that governments could increase many times over the amounts that they spent on public benefits such as healthcare and education. In both West and East, far more children survived infancy than ever before; life expectancy increased. Millions more teenagers stayed on at school rather than going directly into the workforce; beyond school, universities and technical colleges opened their doors to an ever-increasing proportion of young people. In the communist system it was taken for granted that welfare, like every-thing else, was the responsibility of the all-controlling state; but even in capitalist countries, the state played a far greater role, and directly managed a larger share of the economy, than at any other time, before or since. As a result, the 1960s have been described as 'the apogee of the European state'.[33]

In most, though not yet all, of Western Europe, there was also a surprising degree of political consensus during the 1950s and 1960s. Spain and Portugal remained in their pre-war time warp, as dictatorships on the fascist model. They would be joined for seven years from 1967 by Greece, in one of the period's most bizarre aberrations. But otherwise every European state in the west was a democracy. Franchises had been extended to include almost the entire adult population. The hard-fought right of women to vote had been conceded in much of Europe after the First World War; it was now near universal, except in Switzerland, where women would have to wait until 1971 to exercise their democratic rights at the federal level. Underlying the surface divisions of political parties was a broadly social-democratic mainstream. Social democracy embedded in the rule of law, as it developed in Western Europe, demonstrated that it was possible for the state to look after the well-being of its citizens without coercively controlling every aspect of their lives. Crucially, too, it proved that the economic benefits claimed for capitalism could reach farther across the social spectrum than had ever been possible before.[34]

Sudden cracks in the peaceful status quo emerged, again almost simultaneously, in both East and West, in 1968. This time the challenge came from a section of society that had grown exponentially in the conditions of the previous twenty years, but had yet to find its place within it: namely, university students. Practical problems of accommodating the thousands more young people who now flocked to capital cities to study at ancient institutions provided flashpoints in communist Prague in October 1967 and three months later in the Paris inner suburb of Nanterre.[35] Unrest followed in several cities of France, Germany and Italy, as well as in communist Poland and Czechoslovakia. This unrest would culminate, in the West, in the mass uprising of students and industrial workers across France that paralysed the government of President de Gaulle's Fifth Republic for several weeks during May 1968, and in the East, in the failed Prague Spring, whose political leaders attempted to create a democratic version of communism 'with a human face'.

The 'May Events' in Paris fizzled out when de Gaulle announced a general election, which the government easily won. In Czechoslovakia, it took a full-scale Soviet invasion, during the night of 20–21 August, to suppress the reforms that had been introduced by the government of Alexander Dubček. By comparison with 1956, the upheavals of 1968 were little more than a footnote. In the West, nobody went to war; in the East, the invasion was accompanied by much less violence than before: unlike the ill-fated Nagy, the deposed Czech leaders were allowed to live out their days in obscurity. But once again the symmetry between events on either side of the Iron Curtain is striking. And the same can be said of their causes.

In the West, many of the slogans seen on protest marches were about 'American imperialism'. The US had been waging a war in Southeast Asia since 1965 to contain the spread of communism in the former French possessions of Vietnam, Laos and Cambodia. For many young Europeans, that war had exposed something about the Western superpower that their elders had preferred to ignore. The more it looked as though America was behaving like just another imperial power around the world, the more determined were these young Europeans to reject its dominance in their own countries. Neither the events of May 1968, nor their offshoots in far-left terrorist cells whose deadly work would continue sporadically throughout the next decade, were ever likely to change that. Like it or not, Western Europe still owed its security and its prosperity to the protective aegis provided by the United States. But the protests in Western Europe were an uncomfortable reminder of a reality that was built into the dynamics of the Cold War and would long outlast it.

In Eastern Europe, just as in 1956, the stakes were more clear-cut and the outcome starker. In Czechoslovakia – and also in Poland, where tensions stopped short of boiling over – behind the immediate spark of student discontent lay simmering resentment at Soviet dominance. But the lesson of the outcome was the same as before: the Soviets were there to stay. This was spelt out in a speech by the Soviet leader, Leonid Brezhnev, on 3 August 1968, shortly before he ordered Russian and Warsaw Pact troops into Czechoslovakia.

The 'Brezhnev Doctrine', as it would soon become known, affirmed the right of 'all the socialist countries' (meaning, in practice, the USSR) to intervene if any one of them were to deviate from 'the principles of Marxism-Leninism and socialism'.[36] In the East, just as in the West, once the dust had settled, all that had happened was that a new generation of Europeans had bumped up against the same limits as their elders had done.

A Community of Rights and Values

By 1971, peace had held throughout Western Europe for almost three decades. Since the EEC had come into operation in 1958, trade among its six members had increased by more than 300 per cent; it had become 'the world's second largest market'.[37] And four new members were queueing up to join, including Britain, which in the meantime had opted for a post-imperial role alongside its European neighbours.

But if Europe was at peace and prospering, America was not. The Vietnam War still dragged on, though it was clear by 1971 that it could not be won. Six years of a foreign war had taken their toll on the richest economy in the world; the huge trade surpluses that had made possible the enlightened self-interest of the Marshall Plan, by 1971 had turned into a deficit for the first time in almost a century.[38] In the changed circumstances, ideas about Europe were bound to change, on both sides of the Atlantic.

It was the cost of the war in Vietnam that forced President Richard Nixon, on 15 August 1971, to start calling in America's debts. At a press conference on that day he announced the end of the system of fixed exchange rates for national currencies that had been worked out at a conference of the embryonic United Nations Organization held at Bretton Woods, in New Hampshire, back in July 1944. By pegging the value of the US dollar to the price of gold, that system had provided an umbrella of economic security to the governments of the non-communist, or 'free', world ever since. At a stroke, that security had gone. Each national currency would once again have to find its own level against its competitors, bringing back spectres from the 1930s. It was the turn of European governments to be blindsided. And if the *economic* umbrella of the United States could be withdrawn so easily, and so suddenly, what guarantee was there that the *military* umbrella could be relied on in future, either?

The certainties of the 1960s (including the grim one of 'Mutually Assured Destruction', or MAD, which underpinned the theory of nuclear deterrence) were suddenly looking a lot less certain. Nixon and his National Security Advisor, Henry Kissinger, now ratcheted up pressure on European governments to pay their share of the costs for their own defence. The complaint was not new, but in the changed economic climate it began to sound more like a threat. Both sides were in an insoluble bind. European governments, with the exception of only Greece and Portugal, had stood down their military capabilities to such an extent that it would be politically close to impossible to reinstate them. They would not easily forgo the prosperity they had so recently won as the upside of outsourcing their defence to the superpower. They could rely on the fact that America had at least as high a stake in the Cold War as they did; and without full control over their own weapons and armed forces (as Suez had demonstrated), what exactly would they be paying for?

In the meantime, by 1971 the cause of political integration in Europe had stalled during the 1960s and had only recently restarted. This was almost entirely due to the dominant position of the French president, de Gaulle, who in his later years had increasingly tried to turn the European Community into a national, French project. De Gaulle resigned in April 1969, and at the end of that year a summit meeting of the heads of the six governments, in The Hague, opened up renewed prospects for cooperation. Even before Nixon's bombshell a year and a half later, but with the economic horizon already darkening, the first tentative plans for monetary union and a single currency were laid. A year later, an initiative called European Political Cooperation (EPC) was launched; negotiations began in earnest that would see Britain, Denmark and Ireland join the Community on the first day of 1973. (Norway, also included, decided after a referendum to stick with EFTA instead.)

These initiatives were taken in a very different climate, and in a different spirit, from either the abortive federalist debates of the 1940s or the negotiations of the 1950s that had brought the EC into existence. By the time the representatives of the 'Nine' came together for their first summit in Paris in October 1972, three months before the new members were officially due to join, and more than a year after the collapse of the Bretton Woods financial system, Western Europe was at last ready to 'make its voice heard in world affairs, and to make an original contribution commensurate with its human, intellectual and material resources', in the words of the communiqué issued afterwards. This time, when the member states declared 'their intention to transform . . . the whole complex of their relations into a European Union', if the language was still inelegant, the aspiration was all their own. They were no longer being nudged by the United States; quite the reverse, in fact – as we now know thanks to the publication of a private memo by Nixon, from March 1973, in which he warned against 'European unity' as a threat to America and a 'Frankenstein monster'.[39]

The fullest expression of this new-found sense of purpose came a year later. In the Middle East, by the end of October 1973, the three-week Yom Kippur War had been won by Israel, strongly backed by the United States. The oil-producing states of the Middle East, in solidarity with defeated Egypt and Syria, then imposed embargoes and hiked the price of oil to America and Europe fourfold. That was the beginning of an economic downturn for the whole of the Western world that some would say has never ended. But it also signalled a moment when the European Nine made a concerted pitch for their own, collective self-determination.

On 6 November, under the aegis of 'European Political Cooperation', a joint declaration issued in Brussels attempted to be even-handed between the two sides in the Middle East: for the first time an official document referred to the 'legitimate rights' of the Palestinian people who had been displaced since the establishment of the Israeli state. The motive for this declaration may have been dictated less by high principles than by the self-interest of the moment – since an extended embargo on Middle Eastern oil would have a much more dire effect on the economies of Europe than that of the United States. But even taking the most cynical view (which was certainly Kissinger's), this was the first time that a European institution had arrived at a unified, and distinctively European, position on a matter of foreign policy and had the confidence to declare it before the world.[40]

Just over a month later, the heads of government of the Nine met again in Copenhagen. On 14 December, at this moment of high tension, and perhaps euphoria, they issued the first-ever 'Declaration on European Identity'. This reaffirmed the goal of 'European unification' and the creation of a future 'European Union', from the Paris summit. Article 6 acknowledged that in a world dominated by a small number of superpowers, individual European states on their own could no longer exercise the kind of influence they once had done. Many other articles spelt out ways in which the European Community as a whole intended to interact with the rest of the world, including the United States. But what is most significant in this document is Article 1, which was quoted in the Introduction and highlights 'the needs of the individual . . . the principles of representative democracy, of the rule of law, of social justice . . . and of respect for human rights' as the 'fundamental elements of the European Identity'. Familiar though all these terms are today, they only really came together to define a coherent idea of Europe in the very particular geopolitical circumstances of the early 1970s.[41]

After 1973, the European Nine continued to push an agenda based on human rights at the series of Conferences on Security and Co-Operation in Europe that brought together the two superpowers and their European clients on the neutral ground of Helsinki and Geneva between 1973 and 1975. For the United States and the Soviet Union the focus was on defusing the nuclear stand-off between them, in the process reducing both the cost of the arms race and the real danger of mutual annihilation. But for the recently expanded

European Community, which had no real stake in the Great Power game and was thereby the freer to make a pitch for the moral high ground, there was an opportunity to be taken; their representatives grasped it with both hands. America was represented by Henry Kissinger, now Secretary of State as well as National Security Advisor in the administration of President Gerald Ford, who had succeeded Nixon after the latter's resignation in 1974. Kissinger's single-minded pursuit of Bismarckian *Realpolitik* left the Europeans free to take ownership of a policy that would later be credited with helping to end the Cold War and later still be adopted by the American-led 'West' for more than three decades after it was over.

On European insistence, a whole section of the Final Accords signed at Helsinki on 1 August 1975 was headed, 'Respect for human rights and fundamental freedoms'. Included among these were 'freedom of thought, conscience, religion or belief, for all without distinction as to race, sex, language or religion'. These rights and freedoms, according to the Accords, have 'universal significance' and are essential for the 'peace, justice and wellbeing . . . of all States'.[42]

Along with human rights, democracy itself was becoming consolidated throughout Western Europe during the second half of the 1970s. The three southern dictatorships, in Portugal, Greece and Spain, collapsed suddenly and in that order in 1974 and 1975; the road to full democracy and acceptance by their European peers would not be entirely smooth for any of them. But at the end of it, Greece was welcomed into the European Community in 1981; the other two, five years later. The EC, as it grew larger, was cautiously moving towards further integration, despite new economic challenges and an intensification of the Cold War in the early 1980s. Direct elections to the European Parliament were held for the first time in 1979; the long-delayed first stage towards a common currency, the European Monetary System, came into effect at the beginning of the same year.

But the most far-reaching development came in 1986, when the members of the EC, now increased to twelve, signed the Single European Act. Its most practical and immediate effect was to create, by a deadline of the end of 1992, an 'internal market . . . without internal frontiers in which the free movement of goods, persons, services and capital is ensured'. It was at this practical level that an enthusiastic proponent of the Act was the British Conservative prime minister, Margaret Thatcher. 'In retrospect', it has been suggested, 'it is clear that . . . Thatcher thought she was turning the Community into a market economy administered by national governments'. But the preamble to the Act makes clear that there was much more to the common endeavour than this. The signatories committed themselves to establishing a 'European Union' by the same deadline (as indeed would happen). This was to be founded on 'the European idea', which was not explicitly defined but was linked to the principles of democracy, 'human rights and fundamental freedoms', and a 'Social Charter' consisting of 'freedom, equality and social justice'. Just so far had the once-revolutionary slogan of 'liberty, equality, fraternity' come since it had been launched during the French Revolution.[43]

When the provisions of the Act came into force on 1 January 1987, for better or for worse the foundations of today's EU had been well and truly laid.

Russia Comes in from the Cold

In the meantime, a new and rather different idea of Europe was emerging from a most unexpected quarter. The two developments were not entirely unrelated; in a speech delivered in the summer of 1988, the General Secretary of the Communist Party of the Soviet Union warned the leaders of the satellite states of Eastern Europe: 'To the West of our borders there is a new giant developing, one with a population of 350 million people, which surpasses us in its level of economic, scientific and technological growth.'[44]

The General Secretary, in effect the head of government and head of state in the Soviet Union, was Mikhail Sergeyevich Gorbachev. He had been elected by the ruling Politburo to lead them in 1985, after the deaths of a string of geriatric leaders. Longevity in office was still a characteristic of the East European heads of government whom Gorbachev harangued on that day; the leaders of Bulgaria, Czechoslovakia, the German Democratic Republic and Hungary were all well into their seventies; Romania's Nicolae Ceaușescu and Poland's General Wojciech Jaruzelski were relative youngsters at seventy and sixty-five respectively. And it wasn't just the *leaders* of the Soviet bloc who were moribund. The Soviet-inspired command economy had signally failed to adapt to the worldwide economic turbulence of the 1970s and 1980s. The Soviet Union could no longer afford to keep up with the United States in the arms race while also feeding its people. The East European 'socialist republics' were in even worse shape: tied to an outmoded Soviet economy that was in no position to bail them out, they had been living since the late 1970s on credit obligingly provided by Western European and American banks.

This was part of the insoluble conundrum that confronted the fifty-four-year-old Gorbachev in 1985. He at once set himself to try to negotiate his way out of the death-spiral of the nuclear arms race and to overhaul the Soviet economy. So far-reaching were his attempts at reform that the Russian words *perestroika* (restructuring) and *glasnost* (openness) would quickly enter the daily vocabulary of news media all around the world.

Nuclear tensions had reached new heights by the middle of the decade, not least thanks to the 'Star Wars' programme announced by President Ronald Reagan in 1984. Properly known as the 'Strategic Defense Initiative' (SDI), its aim was to create a defensive shield in space that would protect the United States from attack by intercontinental nuclear missiles. At the same time, both superpowers were piling a new generation of shorter-range nuclear weapons into Europe. Many Western European governments were decidedly lukewarm about a military programme that assumed the total annihilation of their countries as the price of protecting America; on both sides of the Iron Curtain, large sections of the public were horrified and did what they could to protest against the deadly weapons placed in their midst, most conspicuously in Britain and West Germany, where most of the new missiles were based.

As the 1980s drew towards a close, each of the two superpowers still maintained more than a quarter of a million troops in East and West Germany respectively – and this was more than forty years after the end of the world war that had first brought them there.[45] Beyond Germany, American forces manned naval and airforce bases throughout the NATO countries of Western Europe; the Soviets stationed troops and weapons across the Warsaw Pact. No wonder, then, if Europeans on both sides of the divide sat up and took notice when Gorbachev began to outline a future for the continent that promised an end both to the Cold War and to the partition of Europe.

It began as little more than a catchphrase. 'Europe is our common home,' declared Gorbachev, on visits to London and Paris in 1984 and 1985, the first before he had even become General Secretary. This was perhaps no more than a polite way of reaching out to his hosts. And Gorbachev was not only famously polite; in all his engagements with foreign leaders and public appearances abroad, in the words of his biographer, 'Gorbachev came across as natural, informal, charming, and with a real sense of humour'. Personality had as much to do with it as politics; both together were the source of the 'Gorbymania' that swept through both halves of Europe during the later 1980s. But soon it would turn out that Gorbachev's idea of Europe went well beyond good public relations.[46]

Common ground between East and West, to underpin the idea, was provided by the agreements on human rights and freedoms that had been reached at Helsinki back in 1975. No fewer than thirty-three states had signed up to these; but many, including the USSR, had then chosen to ignore them. It was along the lines of these agreements that the Soviet Union was now being reformed, even if the motivation was economic rather than ethical. All that Gorbachev had to do – and it was a great deal – was to persuade everyone else that this time his country really meant what it said.

This was to be the consistent theme of the charm offensive that the Soviet leader directed towards Western Europe, in tandem with tough negotiations with President Reagan (and from January 1989, Reagan's successor George H. W. Bush) on reducing their respective nuclear arsenals.[47]

The essence of Gorbachev's idea of a 'common European home' was most fully set out in a speech he made to the Council of Europe, in Strasbourg, on 6 July 1989. There, he called for 'a restructuring of the international order existing in Europe that would put the European common values in the forefront'. Not since Tsar Alexander I had come up with the idea of a Holy Alliance in 1815 had a Russian leader so boldly claimed a place for his country at the heart of European identity; the Soviet Union, from its birth in the aftermath of the October Revolution of 1917, had more often than not defined itself by its *opposition* to capitalist Europe. As the decade of the 1980s drew to a close, Gorbachev was following closely in the footsteps of more distant Russian leaders yet, Peter the Great and Catherine the Great in the eighteenth century, in bringing his country back towards Europe. From being a threat, as so many of his predecessors had chosen to see it, Europe for Gorbachev had suddenly become an opportunity.

It followed, therefore, as Gorbachev put it in his 1989 speech, that:

> The philosophy of the concept of a common European home rules out the probability of an armed clash and the very possibility of the use or threat of force, above all military force, by an alliance against another alliance, inside alliances or wherever it may be.[48]

And Gorbachev was as good as his word. In the same year, he drastically reduced the number of Soviet troops in Eastern Europe; at the end of 1988 he had already spelt out the end of the 'Brezhnev Doctrine': there would be no more armed Soviet interventions in the satellite states. Huge reductions in nuclear weapons were agreed with the United States; and the disastrous Soviet occupation of Afghanistan, which had started in 1979, ended. By the summer of 1989, Western leaders and commentators were beginning to talk publicly of the Cold War being over.[49]

But Alexander I had addressed Europe from a position of strength, after his country's leading role in defeating Napoleon. Gorbachev, although he played his diplomatic cards with consummate skill, came as a supplicant. And his interlocutors knew it. Alexander had spoken at Vienna as the divinely anointed Emperor of All the Russias. Soviet leaders, from Lenin onwards, ruled effectively as dictators; but they could be deposed, as Khrushchev had been in 1964. How secure was Gorbachev? And how many Russians, anyway, shared his vision of a 'vast economic space from the Atlantic to the Urals where Eastern and Western parts would be strongly interlocked', or of a 'peaceful and democratic' Europe in which 'we [Russians] visualize our own future'? Was Gorbachev even sincere?[50]

At the time, no one knew the answers to those questions. Subsequent events would prove that the Soviet leader's position at home was very far from being assured. Public opinion is hard to gauge in an authoritarian system, but such evidence as exists suggests that Gorbachev did enjoy a large measure of popular support in 1989, even though this eloquent advocate of democracy never risked submitting himself to the democratic choice of his people.[51] He surely did mean what he said, and so did a small circle of his closest associates at the top of government; but if Russia was to open up towards Europe and become once again a player on the European stage, the cultural shift would take time to achieve. And time, as things turned out, was not on Gorbachev's side.

It was in Eastern Europe that the new thinking handed down from Moscow had the deepest and the most lasting impact – but not in the way it was meant to. Long before Gorbachev had given the signal that the Soviet Union was loosening its grip on the reins, all the European states in the Warsaw Pact were being pulled in two contradictory directions – at once by their *political* dependence on the USSR and their *economic* dependence on Western finance.

In Poland, discontent and economic crisis found a focus in the Catholic Church, in a revived trades-union movement that tried to fight free of communist control, and in historical memories of Russian oppression that went back almost two hundred years. In Hungary, a communist government came closest to following Gorbachev's own path of economic reform, while in Romania Ceauşescu reverted to the repressive methods of Stalin in order to pay down his foreign debts at the cost of reducing his people to penury. From the Baltic in the north to the Danube in the south, intellectuals began to revive memories of a lost 'Central Europe' that could trace its identity back to Catholic Christendom and the Holy Roman Empire, but had been brutally brushed out of history by the partition of the 1940s. The Czech novelist Milan Kundera, speaking from exile in France at the end of the 1970s, had protested:

> The post-war annexation of Central Europe . . . by Russian civilization . . . is the most significant event in the history of the West in our century, and we cannot dismiss the possibility that the end of Central Europe marked the beginning of the end for Europe as a whole.[52]

And so, by the time of Gorbachev's speech in Strasbourg to the Council of Europe, the current of events was already flowing faster, and in a different direction, which would catch everyone, including the Soviet leader, completely off guard. Between June and December 1989 one by one the communist regimes of the Warsaw Pact fell like the proverbial row of ninepins. The collapse has been described as a single 'democratic revolution'; it has been compared to the chain-reaction revolutions of 1848, many of which had happened in the very same towns and cities, and even to the epoch-changing French Revolution of 1789, whose 200th anniversary was being commemorated that year.[53]

On 4 June candidates put up by the trades union Solidarity trounced the Polish Communist Party in a free general election. Two weeks later, a reformist government in Hungary symbolically exhumed the remains of Imre Nagy, who had been executed after the rebellion of 1956, and buried them with full honours, attended by a crowd estimated at 200,000; shortly afterwards work began on dismantling the electrified fence that for three decades had barred Hungarians from migrating westwards into Austria. That summer, thousands of East Germans took advantage of travel permits that allowed them to spend their holidays in Hungary – and then crossed through the newly opened frontier into the West.

The government of the German Democratic Republic, in a desperate attempt to keep itself in existence, deposed its veteran leader, Erich Honecker, on 18 October; his successor, Egon Krenz, would last barely six weeks in the job. It was on Krenz's watch, on 9 November, that pressure from crowds gathering in the streets of East Berlin reached breaking point. The government conceded that travel into the western sector of the city would be permitted for the first time in almost thirty years. But the announcement that evening was bungled; suddenly realizing that they would not be shot dead if they tried, thousands of East Berliners poured through the check-points, climbed on top of the wall, and in some places even began to hack at the concrete that was the physical manifestation of divided Germany and divided Europe.

The very next day, far to the south, Bulgaria's ageing leader was deposed (though a change of regime would have to wait a few months longer). Next came Czechoslovakia, where the communist leadership surrendered power in the 'Velvet Revolution' later the same month. Thus far, the collapse had been remarkably free of violence. Romania, in December, would prove to be the outlier, as the megalomaniacal rule of Nicolae Ceaușescu was already in so many other ways. Demonstrations in the town of Timișoara were met by live fire from the Romanian army that left almost a hundred dead. At the end of a tumultuous week, after a palace coup, the dictator and his wife were summarily executed on Christmas Day.

The immediate causes and the course of events were different in each case; but one thing unified them. This was the end of Russian rule. The fearsome apparatus of state control and subservience to Moscow that had been put in place by Stalin in the late 1940s, and been propped up ever since by his successors and the puppet regimes of the client states, had turned out in the end to be no more than a house of cards. Whether it was reformists taking over governments, or people in their thousands taking to the streets of towns and cities, or both together, it was Europeans themselves who surged spontaneously to fill a vacuum of power. They did it without coordination among themselves, with no coherent programme, with no overarching vision, inspired by no single ideology or shared dream of utopia. Above all, they did it because they *could*.

Europe's partition had begun with the partition of Germany in 1945. Forty-four years later it ended with the breaching of the Berlin Wall, which symbolically divided a city, a nation and a continent, on the evening of 9 November 1989. Nothing better captures the essence of those largely bloodless revolutions than the photographs taken in Berlin during the first heady days, when jubilant Berliners sat on top of the hated Wall, and complete strangers from the eastern and western sectors of the city embraced one another in the streets.

Just when no one had been expecting it, Europeans had taken their destiny once more into their own hands. Now it was up to them to decide what to do with it.

10

The 'End of History' and the European Union

1989–2022

If Gorbachev had followed the example of Stalin, Khrushchev and Brezhnev before him, and sent Soviet tanks into Eastern Europe in the autumn of 1989, the Cold War would have ended very differently – almost certainly by turning 'hot' and quite possibly involving the use of nuclear weapons by the superpowers. In the event, the Soviet leader slept undisturbed through the night of 9–10 November; according to one of his aides, afterwards, it had been Gorbachev's 'secret dream . . . to wake up one morning and learn that the [Berlin] wall had fallen of its own accord' – which seems to have been pretty much what happened. The Cold War ended as it did, in the words of one authoritative historian, 'because Mikhail Gorbachev chose not to act, but rather to be acted upon'.[1] The consequence of that choice was that Gorbachev won the Nobel Peace Prize in 1990 – and a year later lost an empire.

But several months before the defining events of 1989 had even happened, a different narrative was already taking hold on both sides of the Atlantic. In the summer of that year, readers of a journal published by an American think tank were invited to consider whether the 'unabashed victory of economic and political liberalism', and the 'triumph of the West, of the Western *idea*', amounted to 'the total exhaustion of viable systematic alternatives to Western liberalism'. These words appear on the first page of an academic article by the political scientist Francis Fukuyama, provocatively entitled 'The end of history?' During the years that followed, the article's title, and the note of triumphalism of its opening paragraphs, would become talking points all over the world. First published in 1992, the book by the same author, *The End of History and the Last Man* (now without the question mark), has since become an international bestseller and several times been updated in later editions.[2]

Amid all the fierce controversy that Fukuyama has generated, it has been endlessly pointed out (not least by the author himself) that there was never any suggestion that history had come to a literal end with the end of the Cold War; the course of events would go on as before, as indeed it has. Rather, in the impending collapse of communism in the Soviet Union and Eastern Europe, Fukuyama saw the confirmation of a theory about History (in the book with a capital letter) that had been around for almost two centuries.

The theory itself went back to the German philosopher Hegel, and more particularly to an interpretation of Hegel's ideas by another thinker in the twentieth century, the Russian-born French philosopher Alexandre Kojève. It may not be entirely coincidental that during the 1950s and 1960s Kojève had been employed at the French Ministry of Economic Affairs; his work there has since been credited with a formative role in the creation of the European Community.[3] According to the theory, 'History' had always been a process moving in a single direction. Now, as Fukuyama dusted it off in the summer of 1989, that process was reaching its final, appointed 'end', or goal, as societies all over the world converged to embrace the model of 'Western' liberal democracy.

Less noticed in all the furore was that Europe, and particularly the European Community, soon to become the European Union, had a particular part to play in Fukuyama's scheme of things. And it was not a very positive one. For Fukuyama, as for Kojève before him, the 'end of history' would bring the whole world to the present condition of 'countries of post-war Western Europe – precisely those flabby, prosperous, self-satisfied, inward-looking, weak-willed states whose grandest project was nothing more heroic than the creation of the Common Market'. In the book, the life of the 'last man', a notion borrowed from another German philosopher, Nietzsche this time, that is supposed to follow the end of history, is described as 'one of physical security and material plenty, precisely what Western politicians are fond of promising their electorates'. Returning to the subject some years later, to defend himself against the charge of a specifically *American* triumphalism, Fukuyama would reiterate that 'the European Union is a much fuller real-world embodiment of the concept [of the 'end of history'] than is the contemporary United States'.[4]

None of this would have mattered very much had not these propositions gained such enormous traction in the aftermath of the ending of the Cold War. Delusional as this may seem from the perspective of 2026, for at least two decades many people in Europe, as well as in America, were willing to buy into the narrative that the normal processes of history had been left behind – and that in 1989 a US-led 'West' had triumphed over all opposition. What then, aside from the blandness of endless shopping, was to be the role of Europe in the post-historical world of the 'last man'?

The Troubled Road to Maastricht

During the tumultuous two years that followed the upheavals of 1989, it was far from obvious which direction Europe was going to take, or what kind of continent was about to emerge from the ending of partition. The European Community was still in the throes of transforming itself into the European Union. Leading the negotiations was Jacques Delors, the French president of the Commission (in effect, its executive). Already a rift had opened up between Delors and the British Conservative prime minister Margaret Thatcher. On one side was a vision rooted in the social-democratic consensus politics of Europe in the 1960s, pushed by Delors with the broad backing of eleven out of the twelve governments negotiating. On the other, Mrs Thatcher had taken her country down a very different path since her election in 1979. Her vision was much closer to the 'neoliberal', unfettered capitalism espoused by the United States, particularly under President Reagan (the so-called 'Reaganomics').

Famously, Thatcher had thrown down the gauntlet in a speech delivered in the Belgian city of Bruges on 20 September 1988. 'We have not successfully rolled back the frontiers of the state in Britain,' she declared, 'only to see them re-imposed at a European level with a European super-state exercising a new dominance from Brussels.' Two years later, at a summit of European leaders held in Rome, Thatcher spoke out with her trademark forthrightness against proposals for monetary union and what she feared would become a 'federal Europe'. In Parliament shortly afterwards, she expressed her opposition more resonantly still: 'No, no, no!'[5]

The tension was defused when Mrs Thatcher was ousted by her own party at the end of November 1990 – largely on the grounds of her intransigence on the European issue. But the clash of personalities and ideologies would cast a long shadow. And in any case – as Thatcher had quite rightly observed in her Bruges speech, before anyone had even imagined that the Berlin Wall could fall – the twelve were arguing about the future of only *Western* Europe: 'We must never forget that east of the Iron Curtain, people who once enjoyed a full share of European culture, freedom and identity have been cut off from their roots,' she had said then. By the end of 1989, they were cut off no longer. But where did Central and Eastern Europe fit into the picture that was being painted in Brussels?

Less noticed at the time, and scarcely remembered today, was an alternative vision for Europe after the end of the Cold War. This one, too, was broadly social-democratic. Its architects were Gorbachev and François Mitterrand, the French president. Mitterrand had begun his tenure as a socialist, but had then been forced by economic pressures to make a U-turn towards neoliberalism during the 1980s. Gorbachev was a recent convert to social-democratic principles, despite still being the leader of the world's most powerful Communist Party. For different reasons, which were deeply grounded in the twentieth-century history of their respective countries, both leaders wanted to see the whole of Europe come together as a freestanding bloc that would be independent of the United States. If the

Cold War was finally over, after all, and the Soviet Union no longer presented a threat, what reason could there be for American troops and American finance still to dominate the old continent?[6]

It's hard to believe that during the very same months when a French president of the European Commission, Jacques Delors, was battling Mrs Thatcher for the political soul of Western Europe, the president of France and the head of the Soviet government were seriously trying to promote a version of Europe that would have cut the ground from under both, with an even more grandiose vision of their own. Variously described as 'Greater Europe' or a 'European confederation', this was the Europe that had been conjured up in Gorbachev's Strasbourg speech, stretching all the way 'from the Atlantic to the Urals'. In such a Europe there would be no need for any defensive military alliances, either US-led NATO or the Soviet-led Warsaw Pact. And crucially, there would be a place, too, for a reformed, post-communist Russia, which in this way would continue to have a say in European affairs.[7]

Of course, it was never going to happen. Mitterrand's vision was steeped in nostalgia – at once for the socialist ideals of his youth and for a Gaullist dream in which France was destined to take the place of America in Europe. Gorbachev, although he seems to have been slow to realize it, had been left high and dry by the collapse of the communist governments of Eastern Europe; both at home and abroad he had lost the initiative and would never regain it.

The idea remained on the table until it was killed off at a summit meeting in Prague in the summer of 1991. In fact, it was already dead. Social democracy was all very well, but what mattered most for the newly liberated nations of the East was that they had thrown off Russian rule; they were not going to be enthusiastic about any arrangement that might bring it back in some diluted form.[8] Almost from the beginning, the new governments that emerged in Eastern Europe looked to Brussels for their future – and several were already in their imagination beginning to leapfrog all the way to Washington. Whatever the more complex reality, the perception was gaining ground that America had 'won' the Cold War. The newly liberated

Europeans were inclined to hug America close, rather than allow a foothold to the old oppressor.

In the meantime, at its inexorable pace, the bandwagon was rolling that would come to rest in the Dutch town of Maastricht, where on 9 and 10 December 1991 the heads of government would agree the terms of the treaty that would ever afterwards bear its name. But as the bandwagon rolled, it would repeatedly be overtaken by the rush of events, which at times would threaten to overturn it altogether.

The first of these was the reunification of Germany.

Of all the world leaders who stood helplessly on the sidelines in the autumn of 1989, the first to seize the initiative was the West German Chancellor, Helmut Kohl. Unveiling a Ten-Point Plan before the Bundestag, the parliament in Bonn, on 28 November, Kohl set out a bold programme to bring the two halves of divided Germany together into a single, democratic, sovereign state. Right from the outset, the prospects that had suddenly opened up for Europe as a whole had been trumped by the immediate aspirations of a single nation; the knee-jerk responses this prompted from other European leaders were equally grounded in pre-war national rivalries – notably from Britain's Margaret Thatcher and François Mitterrand of France. The old chestnut of the balance of power in Europe was back. Ironically enough, it was the two superpowers that between them had done the most to divide Germany and Europe in the first place that came into line first, and effectively sealed the deal, to allow reunification to happen.

George H. W. Bush, the American president, was persuaded early in 1990. He had seen the results of German opinion polls. These showed that most Germans cared a great deal more about bringing their country back together than they did about the rival military alliances of the Cold War: neutrality would be just fine for them. But from the American point of view, a neutral Germany would seriously weaken the hold of the superpower over its European allies. Better to throw his weight behind reunification, Bush calculated, if by doing so he could keep a united Germany within the NATO fold, than to soothe atavistic fears in Europe. So the American admin-istration came out in favour, with the condition that the *whole* of reunified Germany must be a member of NATO. Gorbachev held out for as long as he could against the expansion of the US-led alli-ance into territory that still was part of the Warsaw Pact; but he, too, had recognized the momentum sweeping the two Germanies. Eventually, Gorbachev gave way, after an oral promise from US Secretary of State James Baker that in future 'there would be no extension of NATO's jurisdiction one inch to the east'.[9]

Why the Soviet leader failed to extract a written guarantee for that pledge is a question that has been repeatedly asked ever since. But one reason must surely be that the economy of the USSR in 1990 was in free fall. Gorbachev's plea for a financial bailout from the United States went largely unanswered; but West Germany was booming, and Kohl could afford to be generous – to the tune of some 60 billion Deutschmarks (about £20 billion at the time). Some of this was even earmarked to pay the cost of food and barracks back in Russia for more than 300,000 Soviet troops who between 1991 and 1994 would be withdrawn from the former East Germany.[10]

Once Gorbachev had given his consent to the two Germanies being reunited, at a meeting with Kohl in July 1990, there was noth-ing left for the other European leaders but to embrace the new reality, despite their earlier misgivings. It would now become their task to bind the newly empowered Germany more closely than ever into the Union that was still under construction. And to be fair, no one was more enthusiastic about that process than Chancellor Kohl: further integration into Europe would be the best way to ensure that his country could never again return to its Nazi past. And so, amid scenes of general rejoicing on the streets of Berlin on 3 Octo-ber 1990, the German Democratic Republic ceased to exist; its five *Länder*, or provinces, became formally incorporated into the Fed-eral Republic of Germany.

The speed of German reunification had taken everyone totally by surprise. Almost as rapidly, on Europe's eastern borders, the oppos-ite process was gathering momentum. Once again, the motor for change was national sentiment; but this time it was geared towards separation. All around the perimeter of the Soviet Union, the 'socialist republics' that had been inherited from the old empire of the tsars were rediscovering national identities of their own. Some of those had a European past to tap into. The Baltic republics of Estonia, Latvia and Lithuania had enjoyed independence as recently as between the world wars; long before that, they had been part of Catholic Europe during the later Middle Ages. Moldavia and parts of Belarus and Ukraine also had European heritages from various times in the past. Further afield, if to a lesser degree, the same could be said for Georgia, Armenia and Azerbaijan. All three had bid unsuccessfully to become European-style nation states in the aftermath of the First World War, before being absorbed into the Soviet Union.

Even before the communist collapse in Eastern Europe, several of these republics had begun to challenge the authority of Moscow. Gorbachev's principled renunciation of the use of force in Europe didn't extend within the borders of the Soviet Union itself. Nationalist protesters had been shot and killed by the Red Army in Tbilisi, the capital of Georgia, in April 1989 and in Baku, capital of Azerbaijan, in January the following year. But it was in the three Baltic republics that the most serious stand-off occurred, because this one threatened to derail the whole idea of a peaceful end to the Cold War. On 23 August 1989, the fiftieth anniversary of the pact between Hitler and Stalin that had handed their countries over to the Soviets, almost two million people came together to form a human chain that linked the three capital cities of Lithuania, Latvia and Estonia – namely, Vilnius, Riga and Tallinn.[11] In its way, this was as spontaneous and profound a demonstration of popular will as the breaching of the Berlin Wall would be a few months later.

In March the following year, the elected regional government in Lithuania, under the unlikely leadership of the bespectacled pianist and professor of music at the Vilnius Conservatory, Vytautas Landsbergis, declared its independence from Moscow. Gorbachev responded by imposing an economic boycott. For more than a year after that, all three republics teetered on the brink of full independence – and Western governments held back from forcing the issue, for fear of the wider consequences. Bloodshed came to the streets of Vilnius and Riga in January 1991. So soon after the frontiers and status of reunited Germany had been settled, no one could say for certain where the boundary of the new Europe would end up.

At the same time as the clashes in the Baltic capitals, a much bigger conflict was being fought far away in the desert of Kuwait on the Persian Gulf. The Gulf War of January and February 1991 brought together a coalition of some forty-two nations, under the auspices of the United Nations and led by the United States, to eject the forces of the Iraqi dictator, Saddam Hussein, from the neighbouring oil-producing state of Kuwait, which they had occupied the previous August. While the Cold War had lasted, decisive international action on this scale would have been unthinkable; now, even the Soviet Union had grudgingly to acquiesce. By the time the war ended, with the capitulation of the Iraqi generals on the last day of February, it was clear for all to see that the world was no longer symmetrically divided between two superpowers; now there was only one, and that was the United States. Leadership of the successful coalition against Saddam had served as a stand-in for any actual victory in the Cold War. Europeans, like everybody else, would have to get used to living in a unipolar world.

Back in Europe, the retreat of the Soviet Union and the accompanying collapse of communism had been remarkably bloodless – except in Romania. A new challenge now emerged in precisely that grey area which had managed to straddle the Cold War divide: Yugoslavia. The federal state of Yugoslavia had been ruled as a communist dictatorship by Josip Broz Tito from 1944 until his death in 1980. A decade later it was still holding together – but only just. Yugoslavia had never been occupied (or 'liberated') by the Red Army; it had never been a member of the Warsaw Pact or directly subservient to Moscow. Tito's rule had been modelled in many ways on Stalin's; but unlike any other communist ruler he had allowed his people to join the tide of southern European 'guest workers' who helped to sustain the West German 'economic miracle' – and in doing so, to send back much-needed hard currency to their home country.

It's often said that the wars which accompanied the break-up of Yugoslavia during the 1990s were nationalist struggles; and that is certainly how they were portrayed at the time and have been remembered, since, in each of the successor states. But the truth is that Yugoslavia *was* a nation state; it had been one of those created out of the collapse of empires at the end of the First World War. Until the late 1980s, at the earliest, there was no good reason to suppose that it would prove to be a failed one (as another, Czechoslovakia, would also become in 1993 – though without the violence). The South Slavs, or Yugo-Slavs in their own language, shared at least as much to bind them into a nation as the Germans or Italians; the regional dialects of what used to be known as Serbo-Croat were never as different from one another as, say, Piedmontese is from Sicilian. But the six republics and two 'autonomous provinces' that made up the federal Yugoslavia did not share the same history.[12]

A three-way fault line ran through Yugoslavia; and this could be traced back through anything between five hundred and a thousand years. Slovenia and Croatia, including the Adriatic coastline all the way down to Dubrovnik, had always been part of Catholic Europe; Serbia, Montenegro and the rest of the south had once been part of the Orthodox Christian empire of Byzantium, and later of its Muslim successor, the Ottoman Empire. The 'ethnic' hatreds that broke out in 1991 and generated such horrific violence on all sides were not truly ethnic at all, but religious and cultural. Communities broke apart along the lines of religion and the popular cultures that each had separately inherited from the past: Catholic, Orthodox and Muslim. Along with these, to add to the toxic mix, were the choices that individuals and groups had made during the testing time of four years of Nazi occupation during the Second World War, and which had never been forgotten. As the Yugoslav nation state shattered during the 1990s, Europe was confronted with the ghosts of a history that stretched all the way back, beginning with living memory, far beyond the origins of nations or nationalism.

On 25 June 1991 state parliaments in Slovenia and Croatia declared their independence. The federal president, Slobodan Milošević, sent in the Yugoslav National Army; Slovenian forces fought against them for control of border posts and the main airport outside the capital, Ljubljana. Within days a high-level deputation of three foreign ministers from the European Community had arrived in Belgrade, the capital of federal Yugoslavia. According to the lead delegate, Luxembourg's Jacques Poos, in response to a question from an American journalist, 'European governments had a special responsibility to act in a crisis that threatened European stability. "This is the hour of Europe," he said. "It is not the hour of the Americans." '[13] History has not been kind to that oft-repeated soundbite. The violent break-up of Yugoslavia was indeed a European problem, and the time was indeed ripe for the European Community to come up with a European solution. But if this was the 'hour of Europe', then Europe blew it.

Fighting in Slovenia lasted only ten days; but in Croatia a vicious intercommunal conflict raged for the next six months. At the same time, the Yugoslav army, in effect now Serbian-controlled, shelled and largely destroyed the historic Croatian town of Dubrovnik on the Adriatic coast. The member states of the European Community signally failed to pull together, let alone to influence the course of events on the ground. Attempts to mediate were further thrown into disarray when the German foreign minister, Hans-Dietrich Genscher, unilaterally jumped the gun by recognizing the breakaway republics in December, just two months after Germany's own reunification. Croatia, the logic went, could present itself 'as an integral part of a civilized Catholic, central European culture while denigrating its Serbian neighbour as a representative of the barbaric, despotic Orient'. The fault lines that were tearing Yugoslavia apart were Europe's own.[14]

And finally, there was the collapse of the Soviet Union. Ever since Mikhail Gorbachev had embarked on his charm offensive towards the West, there had always been a lurking suspicion in Western capitals that sooner or later he might be toppled in a coup d'état – and then everything might have to begin again from scratch. On Sunday, 18 August 1991 it happened. While the Soviet president (as he had now become) was on holiday in Crimea, tanks moved into central Moscow. The Kremlin was once again in the hands of communist hardliners. Except that it wasn't. The hero of the hour was a former associate and by this time a fierce rival of Gorbachev, Boris Yeltsin. Yeltsin had gone one better than his boss by standing for election – and winning – as president of the Russian Soviet Republic (by far the largest of the republics that made up the Soviet Union). He it was who now faced down the hardliners and the tanks. Within days the coup had crumbled. But so had what was left of Gorbachev's authority.

On 8 December, the day before the heads of European governments were finally due to meet at Maastricht to seal the birth of the European Union, at a hunting lodge in a forest in western Belarus the leaders of Russia, Belarus and a newly independent Ukraine secretly signed an agreement: 'as founding states of the USSR . . . that the USSR as a subject of international law and a geopolitical reality ceases its existence'.[15] As one Union came into existence in the West, another disintegrated in the East. On Christmas Day 1991, Gorbachev recognized the fait accompli and announced his resignation. The Soviet Union was formally dissolved on the last day of the year; its place was taken by the Russian Federation (more or less equivalent to the 'old' Russia of the tsars) and the Commonwealth of Independent States, consisting of most of the former 'socialist republics' – but not the three Baltic states, which now were free to reclaim their place in Europe.

With all this going on around it, it's something of a wonder that the European Union ever got to be born at all.

Peak Europe?

The chief architects of the agreement that was thrashed out during thirty-one hours of intense negotiations at Maastricht on 9 and 10

December 1991 were Helmut Kohl for Germany and François Mitterrand for France. The purpose of the meeting was more than to follow up on the Single European Act of five years before. German reunification and the imminent dissolution of the Soviet Union had given a whole new momentum to ideas of a united Europe. This was to be Europe's chance for a concerted response. The results of opinion polls in the member states were, for once, encouraging.[16] But, as always, national priorities and lingering anxieties about the 'balance of power in Europe' drove the debate – even now, when there was so much less power to balance.

Chancellor Kohl and his foreign minister would have liked to push for greater political integration; but that would have been too much for Mitterrand, and out of the question for Britain's John Major, who had replaced Margaret Thatcher as Conservative prime minister and would have a difficult enough hand to play, between his European partners on the one hand and a 'eurosceptic' press and governing party back home. And so it was decided that the European Union would be founded on monetary union instead.

Since the early 1970s, the 'mighty' Deutschmark, as it used regularly to be described, had become the dominant currency in Europe and an international reserve currency to rival the American dollar. All European governments, whether they liked it or not, were to some extent tied by the strict fiscal policies of the German central bank, the Bundesbank. From the point of view of the French, and many of the others, a new common currency and a new central bank to oversee it would break that dominance. But Kohl would only agree to this on condition that the European currency and the European bank were run according to German principles – a decision that would store up serious problems for later. Significant concessions were granted to Britain, which was allowed to opt out of the single currency, as well as from a 'social chapter' designed to regulate aspects of working practices across the member states.

The treaty that established the European Union and set out this agenda was formally signed by representatives of the twelve governments when they returned to Maastricht on 7 February 1992. It is not an exciting document. It wasn't meant to be. Much the largest part of it is framed as a series of revisions to the earlier treaties that had created the European Community. What the heads of government had agreed to, back in December, was still a work in progress. The spirit of the Schuman Declaration of 1950 was very much alive, four decades later; the new Europe was being built incrementally, in halting stages.

But among these stages, Maastricht stands out as a step-change. First of all, there was the European Union itself, which at a stroke replaced the separate 'Communities' that made up the EC. Citizens of member states were automatically enrolled as citizens of the Union, with 'the right to move and reside freely within the territory of the Member States' and to vote in elections to the European Parliament. More powers were given to the Parliament. The European Council, made up of heads of government (and not to be confused with the Council of the European Union, also known as the 'Council of Ministers'), would set the policy agenda. The Commission retained its role as the executive of the new Union, its members nominated by national governments.[17]

The 'democratic deficit' that is often claimed against these arrangements – and has been only slightly mitigated by subsequent treaties – is equally often exaggerated, by comparison with other democratic systems. The method of election to the European Parliament, based on proportional representation, is more directly representative of the choices of the electorate than, for example, the British or American 'first past the post' system, in which changes of government often hinge on a handful of votes cast in 'marginal constituencies' or 'swing states'. The members of the European Council and the Council of Ministers *are*, by definition, elected (by national electorates); and a Commission whose members have been nominated by national governments is scarcely less democratically accountable than an American administration, appointed by the president and approved by Congress.

The real objections to the Maastricht Treaty that were raised at the time, and have not gone away, always came from national governments and mass media. Limited though the innovations were, the passage of the treaty through national parliaments was often stormy, and nowhere more so than in the United Kingdom; there, the Conservative government of John Major was almost brought down by 'eurosceptic' colleagues whom in an unguarded moment the prime minister was heard to describe as 'bastards'.[18] In three states, Denmark, France and Ireland, the issue was put to a referendum. The Danes at first voted 'no', until they, too, were given the same conces-sion as Britain to opt out of the single currency; this was enough to change the minds of a sufficient number of Danish voters to swing the result the other way in a rerun. The French referendum passed by the narrowest of margins, causing serious embarrassment to Mit-terrand's government. Only the Irish gave the treaty a convincing thumbs-up, with almost 70 per cent of votes cast in favour. It wasn't until all these hurdles had been passed that the Maastricht Treaty finally came into force on 1 November 1993.

For the newly defined citizens of the Union, the effects were less than dramatic. The most consequential change was the abolition of border controls and customs checks at frontiers within the Schen-gen Area (so called after the town in Luxembourg where an initial agreement had been reached in 1985). This happened only gradually throughout the 1990s, before being enshrined in European Union law as late as 1999 – once again with an opt-out for the United King-dom, along with Ireland. Governments now began to issue national passports in a standard design with a burgundy cover and the words 'European Union' in the relevant language printed above the name of the issuing country. The European flag began to appear more frequently alongside national flags on public buildings in most member states (but again, conspicuously, not the United Kingdom).

On the geographical periphery of the European Union, lifestyles began to look and feel more 'European'. In Greece, 'the traditional men-only *kapheneion*, where elderly denizens played backgammon, drank coffee and disputed the contents of the daily newspapers, began to be displaced by smart bars where young people of both sexes would congregate'. In Britain, warm beer and instant coffee began to give way, respectively, to chilled lager and machine-made coffees such as americano and cappuccino, usually served with dexterity by a new type of young person called a *barista* (often originating, like the names, from Italy). Soggy, thick-cut chips served in greasy newsprint and consumed on the street had to compete with a new craze for 'French fries'; the traditional 'spit and sawdust' pub began to offer upmarket food menus, and eventually even to allow children inside. But what one historian of the EU terms the 'EUphoria' of this decade was in practice largely restricted to Brussels insiders, academics and a smattering of more or less idealistic enthusiasts, usually affiliated to centrist political parties.[19]

In the meantime, not far away, war had again flared up in the Balkans in spring 1992. This time the focus was on Bosnia and Herzegovina. A five-way split pitted Christian Orthodox Bosnian Serbs, backed by Serbia, against Catholic Christian Bosnian Croats, backed by Croatia, and all the rest against Bosnia's Muslims (mostly the descendants of local people who had converted to Islam under Ottoman rule). The failure of European peacemaking was even more abject this time. It was during this conflict, which dragged on for three years, that the ugly term 'ethnic cleansing' came to be coined. The massacre of some eight thousand Muslims, carried out by Bosnian Serb forces outside the town of Srebrenica in July 1995, has been called 'the worst single war crime committed in Europe since 1945'. Men and boys were shot in cold blood 'under the very noses of Dutch, French and other European soldiers who were there to protect them in the name of the United Nations'. In Sarajevo, the ruined capital of Bosnia, by 1995, 'Europe had become a dirty word'.[20]

From the beginning of the Yugoslav wars, the American administration, first under George H. W. Bush, then under Bill Clinton, had hung back from involvement in what was quite reasonably seen as a purely European issue. But after the massacre at Srebrenica, and spurred on by his personal commitment to 'humanitarian intervention', Clinton mobilized NATO to bomb the Bosnian Serb army into retreat. The talks that finally brokered peace in Bosnia and Herzegovina were held far from Europe, at an airbase outside the city of Dayton, Ohio; from the end of 1995 a force of some 60,000 NATO troops was stationed in the region to ensure that its terms were kept. In the final round of war, fought over the independence of Kosovo from Serbia in 1998 and 1999, the decisive role was once again played by NATO, which controversially began bombing Belgrade in March 1999. In all these operations, the armed forces of several European states were heavily involved. But it was American leadership of the transatlantic alliance that belatedly enforced peace in the Balkans. When push came to shove, the hard power of NATO had trumped EU soft power many times over.

Despite these failures, it was beyond its own borders that the European Union generated the strongest enthusiasm during the 1990s – at the level both of governments and of public opinion. Throughout Eastern Europe, states new and old queued up to join the EU. With an irony whose significance has yet to be fully explored, this included every one of the successor states that took the place of the federal Yugoslavia. No sooner had these new nations finished fighting their 'ethnic' battles for self-determination than they were eager to hand back part of it to the supranational EU. Less surprisingly, perhaps, the same was true of the former Soviet satellites, and of most of the handful of European states that had remained officially neutral during the Cold War (with the notable exception of Switzerland).

All this highlighted a problem that EU leaders had recognized right from the start of the Maastricht process. As early as June 1993, the European Council had 'agreed that the associated countries in Central and Eastern Europe that so desire shall become members of the European Union' – but only 'as soon as an associated country is able to assume the obligations of membership by satisfying the economic and political conditions required'. The way these obligations were defined in turn laid down the essential principles underlying the European Union as it still exists today. As well as economic criteria, which were daunting enough for states just emerging from decades of a communist command economy, candidates had to have 'achieved stability of institutions guaranteeing democracy, the rule of law, human rights and respect for and protection of minorities'.[21]

The door was open; but the entrance was quite a narrow one. And how far did the invitation extend? Already on the candidate list were two Mediterranean islands that had won their independence from British colonial rule in the 1960s: Cyprus and Malta. So was Turkey. If you went back far enough, Anatolia had been solidly part of the Roman Empire, and then of its Byzantine successor, for more than a thousand years. Muslim Turkey had first registered its application to join the European Community back in 1987; with fluctuating degrees of enthusiasm on both sides, negotiations with the European Union would continue until as recently as 2019, when they were effectively frozen.

Even Russia, as it moved towards democracy under the leadership of Boris Yeltsin in the early 1990s, seems at one stage to have contemplated applying.[22] And what about the successor states to the Soviet Union that lay between the borders of Russia and the Eastern European candidates for membership: states that included Belarus, Moldova, Ukraine, even the Caucasian republics? If a new 'dividing line in Eastern Europe' was emerging, it would prove before long to be highly unstable, and eventually the cause of a new war.[23]

All this excitement abroad undoubtedly contributed to 'EUphoria' in Brussels during the 1990s. After all, 'When people are beating at your door, asking to be allowed in, you conclude that you are doing things right.'[24] Within the European Union, too, in traditionally 'eurosceptic' Britain, the Labour government led by Tony Blair, which came to power after a landslide electoral victory over the Conservatives in 1997, was markedly more pro-EU than its predecessors had been. On taking office, the Blair government immediately waived one of the two opt-outs that had been granted for Britain by the Maastricht Treaty, in adopting the 'social chapter' and enshrining its provisions in UK law. Blair's instinct to reverse the other opt-out, too, and join the project for monetary union after all, would only narrowly be overruled by his Chancellor of the Exchequer and future successor, Gordon Brown.

By the time the common currency, now named the euro, went into circulation on 1 January 2002, the European Union had increased in size from twelve to fifteen members (with the accession of Austria, Finland and Sweden in 1995); a further ten would soon be cleared to join in 2004. The EU was now 'the largest trading bloc in the world, ahead of the United States and China in volume of exports and imports'. Soft power was paying off. The Europe that was emerging at this time has been called (by a historian not overly sympathetic to the project) 'a paragon of the international virtues: a community of values and a system of inter-state relations held up by Europeans and non-Europeans alike as an exemplar for all to emulate.'[25]

As the new millennium began, the British prime minister had earned respect abroad for his robust support of humanitarian intervention in former Yugoslavia and elsewhere. It has been said that 'If popular elections for a European president had been held then, Blair would surely have come out well ahead of any alternative candidate . . . Blair seemed poised for destiny in Europe.'[26]

But events took a different course. The terrorist attacks on the United States on 11 September 2001, known ever afterwards as '9/11', were of a scale and audacity never matched by any act of terrorism before or (so far, thankfully) since. Whatever may have been the ultimate aims of the instigators of the plot, its effect was to lay a trail that led the mighty American military machine deep into the traditional 'graveyard of empires' – Afghanistan. Heading a military alliance that included NATO but would eventually involve other countries as well, America would remain bogged down in Afghanistan for the next twenty years. To cap it all, and surely beyond the wildest dreams of the 9/11 plotters, the administration headed by George W. Bush (son of H. W.) further committed American arms to toppling the dictatorial regime of Saddam Hussein in Iraq in March 2003.

The Iraq War divided Europe down the middle. In a fateful decision, Britain's Tony Blair abandoned any ambitions he may have harboured for himself or his country in Europe and hung his fortunes on the success (and, as he seems genuinely to have believed, the justice) of the American cause. The strongest opposition to the Iraq War came from the governments of France and Germany, which challenged the premise on which the invasion of Iraq had been launched (that Saddam possessed 'weapons of mass destruction' capable of reaching Europe) and correctly predicted the longer-term consequences for the Middle East and Europe. In the run-up to the invasion, American media and some members of the administration deliberately tried to drive a wedge between a moribund 'old Europe' and a brave 'new Europe' in the east that had recently been liberated from communist rule and was now much more willing to applaud the 'shock and awe' administered by US firepower.

The actual split in Europe was more complex than that, but none the less serious. Ranged against France and Germany, and alongside the United Kingdom in support of the American action, were four EU governments (Denmark, Italy, Portugal and Spain) along with three candidate members (the Czech Republic, Hungary and Poland). Only weeks after a European Council meeting had agreed that the EU would follow a common line on Iraq, at the end of January the leaders of these eight countries published an open letter with the title, 'Europe and America Must Stand United'. No wonder that some German commentators, at the time, began to describe the Iraq War 'as being waged over the meaning of Europe'.[27] Once again, the gravitational pull of the superpower was exerting a distorting effect on the politics of the Old World; the institutions of the EU could do nothing to prevent it.

A year after the invasion of Iraq, the European Union celebrated its greatest single expansion ever. On 1 May 2004 the fifteen Western members were joined by ten new ones: Cyprus, the Czech Republic, Estonia, Hungary, Latvia, Lithuania, Malta, Poland, Slovakia and Slovenia – all of them, bar Malta, extending the reach of the Union eastwards. Two more (Bulgaria and Romania) were slated to follow three years later. The original twelve signatories of the Maastricht Treaty had more than doubled; if a Union of twenty-five states was to be effectively organized, it would be urgently necessary to

overhaul the 'work in progress' that had been devised in the different world of the early 1990s.

In preparation for enlargement, modest updates to the treaty had
already been made, in the treaties of Amsterdam signed in 1997,
and of Nice in 2001. Now that it had happened, the next step took
the form of a 'Convention on the Future of Europe'. Chaired by
the former president of France, Valéry Giscard d'Estaing, the Convention brought together more than a hundred representatives of
participating governments as well as from the institutions of the
European Union. The outcome was a 'draft Treaty establishing
a Constitution for Europe'. It was presented to a meeting of the
European Council in the Greek city of Thessaloniki in June 2003.
Although much of the text was carried over from earlier treaties,
the Convention seems sincerely to have been driven by the desire
to present, in a single document, an accessible and even appealing
statement of what the EU was all about.[28]

The draft begins with an epigraph that goes all the way back to
the aftermath of the Persian Wars, when democracy and Europe
had both been invented: 'Our Constitution . . . is called a democracy because power is in the hands not of a minority but of the
greatest number.' These words are supposed to have been spoken
by the Athenian statesman Pericles in the year 431 BCE, in praise of
his city's political system; they had been recorded not long afterwards by the historian Thucydides. An upbeat preamble follows:
'Europe is a continent that has brought forth civilisation . . . its
inhabitants, arriving in successive waves from earliest times, have
gradually developed the values underlying humanism: equality
of persons, freedom, respect for reason.' The preamble continues
by celebrating the 'cultural, religious and humanist inheritance
of Europe', together with values that include human rights and
'respect for law'. It affirms the belief 'that reunited Europe intends
to continue along the path of civilisation, progress and prosperity,
for the good of all its inhabitants'.[29]

For a whole year, the draft was picked over in meetings of government bodies and officials all over Europe. By the time a revised text

was approved by the European Council in June 2004, the preamble had been toned down and the quote from Thucydides had gone. The Constitution had then to be ratified by twenty-five national governments. Over the next few months, eleven did so (including two, Luxembourg and Spain, by popular referendum). But in other countries, predictable and powerful forces were ranged against it, and none more vociferous than the right-wing press in Britain. 'A thousand years of sovereignty are about to be buried by undertaker Blair,' ranted the populist daily, *The Sun* (whose owner had never lived in Britain); a more sober weekly magazine, *The Economist*, had already published a cartoon of the original draft in a wastepaper basket, with the caption, 'Where to file it'.[30] The *coup de grâce* for the Constitution came from national referenda in France and the Netherlands during the first half of 2005. Of French voters, 55 per cent rejected it; of Dutch voters, 62 per cent.

Shorn of the most interesting – and approachable – bits of the rejected Constitution, a revised Treaty of Lisbon was eventually approved by the heads of government at the end of 2007. The word 'Constitution' was dropped. Perhaps ominously, for the first time an article was added that made provision for a state to *leave* the European Union. Several of the tweaks to governance that had been proposed in the Constitution were carried over into the treaty, the most significant being a slight strengthening of the executive. The President of the Council was now to be elected from the heads of government who made up its numbers; previously this role had rotated around the member states, changing every six months. The 'High Representative' for foreign affairs, a role that went back to the Amsterdam Treaty of 1997, was given a new title and greater authority to speak for the EU as a whole. If it's true that Henry Kissinger had once complained, 'Who do I call if I want to talk to Europe?', now there was an answer.[31]

This treaty, too, would have a difficult passage towards ratification; it finally made it into law in all EU states (twenty-seven of them, now that Bulgaria and Romania had joined) two years later, on 1 December 2009. No less than its predecessors, the Lisbon

Treaty represented unfinished business; it was still conceived as part of a work in progress. And it remains unfinished to this day, because there has never yet been another. By 2009, had 'peak Europe' already passed?

The Bankruptcy of Nations

The Lisbon Treaty was in the final stages of ratification when a meeting of European finance ministers took place in Luxembourg. In the words of the finance minister of Greece, George Papaconstantinou, whose government had been elected to office a mere two weeks earlier, 'Juncker presided . . . speaking in English, French and German, chairing in a haze of smoke . . . Nobody dared remind him he was in a non-smoking building.' Jean-Claude Juncker was prime minister of Luxembourg and a future president of the European Commission. When the representative of the Greek government had finished his report on the state of his country's finances, a stunned silence fell on the room. Once it had been broken, the president of the European Central Bank cautiously expressed his disbelief: how could the true state of the Greek economy have been so seriously misrepresented until that moment? Outside, facing waiting journalists, Juncker put it more bluntly: 'The game is over.'[32]

So began a crisis that would soon be described by Germany's Chancellor Angela Merkel as 'the worst . . . in Europe since the Second World War', with the future at stake, not only of the single European currency, the euro, but even of the European Union itself.[33] For the best part of a decade, its effects would blight the lives of citizens in four countries on the geographical periphery of the EU: Portugal, Ireland, Greece and Spain – collectively shamed in English by the acronym 'PIGS'. In Greece, the worst affected, the economy shrank by a quarter, personal incomes fell by a third, unemployment rose to 27 per cent and double that among young people. Businesses failed, public services were reduced; the number of suicides soared.[34]

What could have gone so badly wrong in such a short time?

The single European currency had been launched into relatively calm economic seas; during its first years, a fair wind had filled its sails. By the time of that Luxembourg meeting in 2009, sixteen member states had joined what had become known as the Eurozone. Except for Britain and Denmark (exempted by the Maastricht Treaty), it was expected that the rest would follow once they met the necessary conditions. The world's economic system had become more integrated than ever, trade was flourishing. A new era of globalization was bringing boom times to much of the world, including Europe. There was heady talk of an end to the 'boom and bust' cycles of the past.

But when a new financial storm swept across the world in 2008, it turned out that the good ship Eurozone had been fitted with too much sail, and not enough draught below the waterline to keep it from capsizing in rough water. Much has been written in hindsight about the design flaws that had been built into the single currency from the beginning; some had warned about them at the time. The financial crash of autumn 2008 was not caused by Europe or the Eurozone; as is so often the case with real storms too, this one came from across the Atlantic. A collapse of confidence in American banks had sent tsunami waves through the entire world's closely interlocked banking system. Just as had happened back in 1929, a crisis created in the United States caused a worldwide recession. Europe was not immune. But as the rest of the world began to climb out of recession after only a year, by the time that the Lisbon Treaty was finally ratified at the end of 2009, Europe – or rather the Eurozone – was plunging towards a separate crisis that was all its own.

The European sovereign-debt crisis, as it is technically called, reached its height between 2010 and 2012, but would not be finally over in all parts of the Eurozone until the second half of the decade. The key word here is 'sovereign'. A sovereign debt is the money owed by a sovereign state; traditionally, a state unable to pay the interest due on its debts is in default; devaluation of the currency follows, and 'restructuring' of the debt. There was never any question that the Eurozone as a whole might be in this position; but what so shocked that meeting in Luxembourg in October 2009 was the discovery that at least one of the states that made up the zone, Greece, was. And soon enough it turned out that Greece was not alone. In addition to the so-called 'PIGS', question marks even arose over Italy, one of the largest economies in Europe.

In this crisis, national governments that were in credit, ever mindful of their voters, jibbed at coming to the rescue of their debtor peers on the southern and western periphery. Instead of pooling the resources available to 'the largest trading bloc in the world', EU decision-making descended into a tug of war between richer (supposedly more prudent) and poorer (or more profligate) European states. At the heart of the problem were the notions of fiscal prudence that had been baked into the euro project from the start – at the insistence of German politicians haunted by memories of the hyperinflation that had wrecked their country in the aftermath of the First World War.

A 'troika' of institutions was mobilized in 2010 to impose discipline on the nations at risk of default: the European Central Bank (still run on lines laid down by its predecessor, the Bundesbank), the European Commission, and – at the insistence of the German government, apparently not able fully to trust the other two – the US-based International Monetary Fund (IMF). In the words of one EU insider, writing a decade afterwards, 'Germany defined the terms and drew the red lines for national bailouts that had never been supposed to happen . . . It was not a glorious chapter in the history of European institutions.'[35]

A speech by the president of the European Central Bank (ECB), Mario Draghi, in London in July 2012, is credited with having turned the tide: 'Within our mandate, the ECB is ready to do *whatever it takes* to preserve the euro.' Following through on this promise, a European Stability Mechanism was created in October of that year by the heads of government of the Eurozone states. This enables the bank to borrow on international markets in order to provide loans (conditional on good behaviour) to member states in financial difficulty.

As a solution, the Stability Mechanism was a long way short of the mutualization of debt that applies within a state. The sovereign-debt crisis had shown more starkly than ever the difference between a voluntary union of sovereign states and a single state with full control over its currency and financial system. It would take two further crises in the next decade, the Covid pandemic and war in Ukraine, to loosen the constraints that had been imposed on the ECB from the beginning and give the European institutions real power to borrow and invest on behalf of the Union as a whole.[36]

Even after Draghi's intervention, there still remained a very real possibility that Greece, or conceivably another of the debtor states, might default and be forced to leave the Eurozone, perhaps even the Union. Nobody knew what might happen then, because nothing like this had been imaginable at the time when the rules had been written. The crunch came in July 2015. A populist far-left government in Greece had been refusing for six months to accept new terms laid down by the 'Troika'. With all banks closed in Greece and a chaotic exit from the single currency only days away, the country's latest finance minister, the charismatic Yanis Varoufakis, had to concede that his bluff had been called and resigned. Greece finally accepted the punitive conditions attached to a third bailout from the European Central Bank. Slowly the crisis began to recede across Europe.

It had been a close-run thing. But at the end of the day the Eurozone and the institutions of the European Union, as well as the nation states that were most affected, had learnt from their mistakes. The members of the European family really were stronger together, even if the bonds of mutual trust had been stretched close to breaking point and the strongest had been seen to bully the weakest without compunction. At the end of the day, the national interests of all were still better served by holding together.

By 2015 a new crisis was bursting across the southern shores of Europe. America's wars in Afghanistan in 2002 and Iraq in 2003 had destabilized whole regions stretching far to the south and east. Then in 2011 the failed 'Arab Spring' had led to the collapse of regimes and civil wars from Libya in the west to Syria in the east; in Syria and Iraq the brutal fundamentalist movement known variously as Daesh, Islamic State, or ISIS was terrorizing Shia Muslims and Christian minorities. For the millions of people in those regions whose livelihoods had been destroyed and who daily faced the threat of extreme violence or death, the best hope they could imagine for safety and the chance to rebuild their lives lay in Europe – if only they could get there.

From the Middle East and North Africa one route lay through Turkey and into Bulgaria or Greece across a narrow land border, another across the Aegean from Turkey to the nearest Greek islands. A third, so far as we know without precedent in the whole history and prehistory of the continent, lay across the open sea from Tunisia or Libya to the nearest points of Italy, the large island of Sicily and the tiny one of Lampedusa. In 2013 the number of 'irregular' migrants arriving in the European Union by these routes stood at just over 100,000. Two years later it had jumped to 1.8 million.[37] Tragic scenes were filmed on the beaches of Greek islands, where tourists had not long before gone to soak up the sun and a carefree Mediterranean lifestyle; now, drowned children were being fished out of the shallows. The world's press began to report harrowing stories of whole shiploads of migrants drowning while trying to cross from Africa to Italy in overcrowded and unsafe boats. Once they reached shore, thousands of helpless, desperate people had to be housed and looked after. In the front-line states, Italy and Greece, local institutions were overwhelmed.

The places where the migrants came ashore were not usually their intended destinations; most were hoping to make new lives for themselves and their dependants in the more prosperous, and perhaps more welcoming, states of northern Europe, particularly Germany and Sweden.[38] A much smaller number, perhaps because they already spoke English or had relatives there, were determined to risk a further dangerous sea crossing to reach Britain; that number, too, was rising dramatically in 2015 and 2016.

Faced with the appearance of a new and completely unprecedented crisis on its borders, Europe collectively panicked. Efforts at EU level to restrict the movement of migrants through agreements with Turkey and Tunisia, at the time and since, have been condemned by some as cynical and by others as insufficiently effective. But the most immediate, and potentially far-reaching, symptom of panic in 2015 was on the part of *national* governments. For the first time since 1989, barriers and fences once again began to be erected in Europe – almost all of them on the continent's *internal* borders. This was the beginning of a reversal of the principle of 'free movement' enshrined in the Maastricht Treaty and embodied in the Schengen zone, where frontier formalities had been abolished since the 1990s.

Before the end of 2015, in sheer frustration at the attitude of other European governments, Germany's long-serving Chancellor Merkel announced that those refugees already in Europe would be made welcome in Germany: *Wir schaffen das* ('We'll fix that'), she famously declared at a press conference in August that year. But the problem was not so easily fixed – because the buck stopped not with the EU institutions but with national governments; and these in their turn were susceptible to the fervour being whipped up among their electorates by politicians who played on nationalist fears. This is why a plan put forward by the European Commission in 2015 to redistribute migrants according to a quota system throughout the EU has never been fully implemented.

The national, and more particularly the *nationalist*, backlash was not only against the new arrivals but against the European Union itself. In this way the Union became the victim of its own success. The more desperately outsiders pressed to come inside, the more discontented became some of those already there. Opinion polls in 2015 showed that immigration had become 'the number one issue of concern for people across Europe'.[39] Populist political parties of the far right thrived on whipping up nativist fears of Muslims arriving from other continents, often with a different skin colour, and potentially linked to the terrorism that was rife in the countries they had fled. It made matters worse that terrorist atrocities in

Europe had continued sporadically, ever since coordinated suicide bombings had killed several hundred people in Madrid in 2004 and London in 2005. The EU's open borders, among its most significant achievements and chief selling points, were being blamed. Euro-scepticism was on the rise.

Despite these internal strains, reaching back to the sovereign-debt crisis that had not yet been fully resolved, only one member state chose to take the nuclear option of leaving the European Union. Against expectations, this was not Greece, the country that had suffered the worst from the efforts of the European institutions to save the Eurozone, but the United Kingdom, which had been among the least affected either by the debt crisis or by mass migration across the Mediterranean. The word 'Grexit' had been conjured up for a departure that never happened; instead it morphed into 'Brexit', which did. In a referendum held on 23 June 2016, voters in the UK voted by a narrow margin (51.9 to 48.1 per cent) to leave the EU; the formal break finally took place on 31 January 2020. To adapt the words of US Secretary of State Dean Acheson, spoken almost sixty years before, Great Britain had now lost both an empire *and* a role.

For the rest of Europe, the most tangible effect of Brexit was to douse the enthusiasm of all those throughout the continent who had been beating the same drum as the 'Brexiteers'. No other country or mainstream political party has so far chosen to follow the same path; the protracted negotiations for withdrawal, and the fractured politics that would tear apart the United Kingdom's governing Conservative Party for more than three years, were generally seen as being in no one's interest to emulate. Otherwise, the institutions of the European Union and the remaining twenty-seven member states have been little affected. Brexit was simply a local symptom of the deeper problems that confronted the whole of Europe during the decade of the 2010s.

Those problems have not gone away since. But all of them would soon be dwarfed by a different challenge that, almost unnoticed, had been building on Europe's eastern borders ever since the ending of the Cold War.

Countdown to War

Just as the bombs had begun to drop on Belgrade, back in March 1999, the North Atlantic Treaty Organization, NATO, had welcomed into its ranks the first former communist members to join the alliance. The pledge made to Gorbachev on behalf of George H. W. Bush, never to do so, back in 1990, had been conveniently brushed aside in the meantime. The new members were the Czech Republic, Hungary and Poland. Five years later, the process had gathered pace, with seven more Central and Eastern European states joining in 2004, at the same time as several of them also joined the European Union.

Precisely what purpose NATO would continue to serve, now that the Cold War was over and its adversary, the Warsaw Pact, had been dissolved back in 1991, had been a hot topic for conversation throughout the 1990s. At one point there had even been talk of Russia joining the alliance.[40] At the turn of the millennium, NATO's successful interventions in the former Yugoslavia had given at least short-term justification for keeping it in existence. No one had quite intended this, but the upshot was that American forces were as deeply entrenched in Europe as they had ever been. And the Europeans had once again unwittingly outsourced their defence, this time to the only superpower left standing. By 2009, NATO had twenty-eight members, one more than the EU at the time. But quite what this massive military alliance was for nobody seemed to know for sure.

If the purpose of the transatlantic alliance was left unclear, so was the always elusive dividing line marking out Europe on the map. In 1945, Stalin had driven that line all the way westwards as far as the River Elbe in Germany; since the end of the Cold War in 1989, it had been quietly drifting back in the opposite direction. Between them, by 2009, the EU and NATO reached all the way eastwards to the borders of Finland and the Baltic states with Russia, of Poland with Belarus and Ukraine, of Hungary and Romania with Ukraine, and of Romania with Moldova and Transnistria. But with separate leaderships and different agendas in Washington and Brussels, that had been the result of no concerted policy either. The two fudges – over the purpose of NATO and the boundaries of Europe – were about to be compounded, with explosive results.

The first warning signal came in February 2007. Addressing an international gathering in Munich, the Russian president, Vladimir Putin, complained that 'NATO expansion does not bear any relation to the modernization of the Alliance itself or to ensuring security in Europe'. Instead, he argued, 'it represents a serious provocation', by which he meant, to Russia.[41] The next year, the alliance received formal applications to join from two former Soviet republics, Georgia and Ukraine. The United States and some Eastern European members were ready to defy the anticipated Russian objections and say yes; but vetoes by France and Germany (not coincidentally the twin motors of the Eurozone, if not quite of the EU as a whole) meant that no definitive answer was given, then or later. The door to Ukraine and Georgia becoming NATO members at some unspecified time in the future was left open. In this way an unresolved issue was allowed to fester for more than a decade.

In the meantime, the Russian foreign ministry warned of 'new dividing lines in Europe' and threatened 'appropriate measures'. What those might be was made abundantly clear in August 2008, when Russian troops entered Georgia, ostensibly to back local separatists in two regions of the country. Those parts of Georgia have remained under effective Russian control ever since. To what extent the *people* of either Georgia or Ukraine at that time actually wanted to join an alliance whose name and rationale refer to an ocean many thousands of miles from their borders remains disputed. But Europe, and specifically the European Union, was a different matter.[42]

A summit held in Prague on 7 May 2009 brought together the highest officials of the European Union, leaders and foreign ministers from all twenty-seven EU member states and their opposite numbers from Armenia, Azerbaijan, Belarus, Georgia, Moldova and Ukraine. It ended with a joint declaration of an 'Eastern Partnership' between the EU and these former Soviet republics. Even in the straitened circumstances of that year, the EU was offering unspecified 'financial support' to each of these countries in return for 'commitments to the principles of international law and to fundamental values, including democracy, the rule of law and the respect for human rights', along with economic reforms that would align them with EU standards. The partners could expect accelerated 'political association' with the EU and 'the foundation for Association Agreements' at some unspecified time in the future. Not on the table was future *membership* of the Union, though you had to read the text of the declaration quite carefully to be sure.[43]

Not so long before, a partnership like this might well have had a place in it for Russia. That was already out of the question by 2009. Russia, under Putin's presidency from 2000 to 2008, had rowed back from the reforms that had been initiated by Gorbachev and been taken further under Yeltsin. By 2009, Putin had stepped down to become prime minister – temporarily, as it would turn out – but was still very much in charge of an increasingly authoritarian system. The commitment that the EU was asking of its Eastern partners was the exact opposite of everything that twenty-first-century Russia stood for.

It may be that the leaders of the European Union thought their own soft power would be a safer bet than the hard power of NATO as a way of extending Europe's influence still further eastwards. It was not. Even if nobody in those days thought it remotely likely that conventional warfare would return to Europe or its near neighbourhood, the EU leaders ought to have known that they were playing with fire.

The hazard built into the Eastern Partnership wasn't just about provoking the proverbial Russian bear. Each of the six partner states was now on the front line in what some were already beginning to call a 'new cold war'.[44] Their own societies were divided right down the middle. None had experienced independent statehood for more than a few turbulent years, if that; none possessed embedded democratic institutions or a tradition of the rule of law. On the other hand, all had lived for decades under the authoritarian rule of the tsars and then of the Soviet Union. While some among their populations looked westwards with hope for a different future, others still hankered after the familiar certainties of the past – or were attracted by the 'kleptocratic' capitalism that had emerged in Russia and in these states themselves since 1989, offering irresistible temptation for a powerful few.

In encouraging these states to become more European, and in seeming to dangle the possibility of future membership of an even larger EU, the Eastern Partnership risked stoking those divisions further. The Russian foreign ministry was not wrong in identifying 'new dividing lines'; only, they were not new at all. They were (and are) the age-old dividing lines between Europe and Asia. All that was happening was that they were shifting once again.

The flashpoint would prove to be Ukraine.

The independence of Ukraine had been formally guaranteed in 1994 by a binding memorandum signed in Budapest by the United States, Russia and the United Kingdom, with China and France as later signatories. In return, the Ukrainian government had, with some reluctance, agreed to give up the nuclear weapons that had been stationed on its territory by the now defunct Soviet Union.[45] At the time, the very existence of the Ukrainian state had seemed precarious. Riven by fault lines created by the shifting geopolitical tectonic plates of Europe and Asia, going back centuries, Ukraine in the 1990s could so easily have gone the same way as Yugoslavia. One authority on international relations, writing in the middle of that decade, had even predicted that it was much more likely that Ukraine would split in two, along the religious divide between its Catholic west and Orthodox east, than that Ukrainians would ever fight against Russians.[46]

The moment of decision for Ukraine came in November 2013.

The country's president, Viktor Yanukovych, was invited to the third summit of the Eastern Partnership, held in Vilnius. There he was expected to follow the example of his Georgian and Moldovan counterparts and sign an Association Agreement with the European Union. Yanukovych had close business ties with Moscow and a distinctly authoritarian streak of his own – he had locked up the leader of the opposition and other political opponents. Thus far, EU officials had been prepared to hold their noses; in return for signing the agreement, Ukraine's political prisoners would be set free. But at the last minute, under intense pressure from Russia, Yanukovych refused to sign. The price Ukraine was obliged to pay for Russian oil had already been hiked to a level that would soon bankrupt the country. Worse, Vladimir Putin, once again president of the Russian Federation, 'threatened to occupy the Crimea and a good part of southeastern Ukraine, including the Donbas'.[47]

From December 2013 until February the next year, the centre of Kyiv, the Ukrainian capital, was convulsed by a series of popular demonstrations in favour of the European Union. Whether deliberately or not, an ill-considered statement issued on behalf of the EU foreign ministers can only have fanned the flames: if the contested agreement 'did not constitute the final goal of EU-Ukraine cooperation', in the words of the statement, then presumably the door was left open for full accession after all?[48] A few days later, on 18 February, violence broke out in Kyiv's Maidan Square; the mayhem lasted for several days. Yanukovych fled to Russia, and a newly elected government pledged to sign the Association Agreement after all.

On 27 February 2014, Putin made good on his threat; Russian troops seized control of Crimea and shortly afterwards embarked on a war of attrition in the Donbas region of eastern Ukraine. During the next eight years, this undeclared war would cause the deaths of some 14,000 people – including the passengers and crew of a Malaysian airliner flying from Amsterdam to Kuala Lumpur, shot down in July 2014 as what the language of war callously terms 'collateral damage'. The effect of all this was dramatically to unite Ukraine 'across ethnic, linguistic, religious, and cultural lines', particularly under the leadership of its strongly pro-EU president, Volodymyr Zelensky, who was elected in 2019. Aggression from outside was melding together a nation out of disparate elements that in other circumstances might well have pulled apart.[49]

Then came the worldwide pandemic of Covid-19 that broke out in the first months of 2020. While it lasted, the conflict in eastern Ukraine, like so much else, was frozen in place. The longer-term effects of the pandemic are still being weighed – on the health of individuals, on societies and on the world economy. But its effects on one individual would lead directly to consequences that could yet prove more dire than the pandemic itself.

Vladimir Putin, isolated for many months from all but a very limited inner circle, and absent from public view, seems to have spent his time brooding over Ukraine. In a long essay published in July 2021, Putin argued that Russians and Ukrainians are a single people who share a single history. There had never been a distinct Ukrainian nation until the idea had been conjured up by Europeans in the nineteenth century, he wrote; then and now, the purpose of those Europeans had been nothing less than to create 'a barrier between Europe and Russia, a springboard against Russia'. Ukraine's president wasn't mentioned by name. But the warning to Zelensky and his people was loud and clear: 'we will never allow our historical territories and people close to us living there to be used against Russia'.[50]

It soon turned out that Putin had been plotting more than just a historical essay during his months of isolation. As the pandemic finally began to ease during the last months of 2021, Russian troops massed along the borders of Ukraine, both in Russia itself and in its pliant neighbour Belarus. The international community watched with mounting alarm. The world's television channels showed pictures of meetings between the Russian president and a succession of visiting heads of government, separated by the length of a table five metres long – an ostentatious parody of the 'social distance' introduced by governments as a protection against the Covid virus. To one foreign leader after another Putin gave assurances that the military build-up was purely an exercise; there was no intention to invade Ukraine. American intelligence warned otherwise, though many European leaders, including Zelensky, were sceptical.

In the meantime, on 17 December 2021, bypassing the Europeans entirely, the Russian foreign ministry issued the text of a proposed treaty with the United States. Included in its preamble was a reminder 'that a nuclear war cannot be won and must never be fought' – the first of a number of implied threats to come. Among the terms of the draft was that 'The United States of America shall undertake to prevent further eastward expansion of the North Atlantic Treaty Organization and deny accession to the Alliance to the States of the former Union of Soviet Socialist Republics.' All nuclear and other heavy weapons were to be withdrawn from within reach of the territory of either side – meaning in effect that NATO would have to remove its military arsenal from Eastern Europe.[51]

Here, several decades too late, would have been the written guarantee that Gorbachev had failed to elicit, back in 1990. In the minds of Putin and his inner circle at the Kremlin, fogged by overly long Covid isolation, the shape of Europe was still something that could be settled between the superpowers of the last century. Instead, this time it would have to be decided on the battlefield.

And so the world awoke on that morning of 24 February 2022 to images on television and social media of Russian tanks passing through deserted border posts, unopposed on their way to seize control of Ukraine's major cities: the capital Kyiv and Kharkiv. No one seems to have expected the Ukrainians to resist. But they did. In response to an offer of sanctuary in the United States, President Zelensky is reported to have said, 'The fight is here; I need ammunition, not a ride.' Addressing his people in a video address on the third day of the invasion, he put it more emotionally: 'I am here. We are not putting down our arms. We will be defending our country, because our weapon is truth, and our truth is that this is our land, our country, our children, and we will defend all this.'[52] The president may not have realized how closely his words channelled those put into the mouths of the Greek defenders of *their* land, two and a half millennia before, by the first historian, Herodotus.

Epilogue
Mariupol and After

The port city of Mariupol, in eastern Ukraine on the Sea of Azov, had been close to the front line since 2014. Ukrainian defence forces were well dug in, to the east of the city, facing the parts of the Donbas that were already under Russian control. On the morning of 24 February 2022, everybody thought that the attack would come from there. From that first morning, the sounds of gunfire could be heard in the centre of Mariupol; the first reports of casualties were coming in. Those who could rushed to the railway station; but too few left while it was still possible. Soon there would be no more trains. It was the advance of Russian troops from the rear, crossing the isthmus from Russian-controlled Crimea, that sealed the fate of Mariupol. By the end of February, the city had been encircled. Indiscriminate shelling and bombing took out electricity, gas and water services; mobile-phone networks were cut off; people were reduced to melting snow to boil water for cooking.[1]

The siege of Mariupol in the spring of 2022 lasted for almost three months. The Russian commanders used the tactics they had perfected during the civil war in Syria, in the service of the dictator Bashar al-Assad. They pulverized the city with artillery from the ground and bombs from the air until there was almost nothing left. The particular horror of twenty-first-century warfare was captured when a heavily pregnant woman, covered in blood, was photographed in the ruins of a bombed maternity ward.

By mid-March, more than a thousand civilians, mostly women and children, had taken shelter in the neoclassical building of the Donetsk Academic Regional Drama Theatre; the Russian word *deti* (children) had even been chalked in huge letters on the open space in front of it as a warning. On 16 March the theatre was targeted by artillery shells, fire ripping through the ruins. It is still not known for certain how many were killed outright or trapped under the rubble and later died. Eventually, the defenders were confined to the giant Azov steel works, known as Azovstal. A complex of underground bunkers beneath it had been built to withstand a nuclear strike during the Cold War. But concrete-busting bombs broke through. Two months, to the day, after the destruction of the theatre, more than two thousand survivors of the Azov Regiment surrendered and were taken into Russian captivity. The siege of Mariupol was over. And a long and deadly war of attrition was just beginning.

Images of these events were captured by the courageous Ukrainian journalist Mstyslav Chernov and his team in the 2023 documentary, *20 Days in Mariupol*. In a jarring juxtaposition with the Hollywood entertainment industry, the film won an Oscar for best documentary in 2024. But this, perhaps, is the nearest equivalent in the twenty-first century to Herodotus writing up on scrolls of papyrus the results of his inquiry into the events of the Persian Wars and their causes. Now, as then, it's the *telling* that turns events into history.

As recently as the 1990s, the worldwide triumph of a 'Western idea' based on liberal democracy was supposed to have marked the 'end of history'. Ukrainians, back in 2014, had overwhelmingly voted to make that idea their own. And that is why, when Zelensky appealed to the EU and to NATO in the spring of 2022 to help his people fight for that 'Western idea', his appeal was heeded – and not only by these institutions and by national governments, but also by millions of ordinary citizens who opened their homes to welcome Ukrainian women and children fleeing the conflict, and who donated money to charities organizing relief in the war zone.

Over the next three years, huge shipments of armaments, training for military personnel, and economic support were provided to Ukraine. A very large part of that contribution came from America, followed at some distance by Germany, the United Kingdom and almost every member of the European Union. Two previously neutral

European states and EU members, Finland and Sweden, joined the NATO alliance, which was therefore strengthened, rather than weakened, by Putin's gamble. Massive economic sanctions imposed by the United States, the EU and individual European states aimed to isolate Russia from worldwide trade and financial systems. Despite backsliding by some EU governments, and discordant voices raised on both sides of the Atlantic, it was an impressive show of solidarity.

But it was not enough. By the end of 2024, Ukrainian forces were on the back foot on the battlefield. Russia, far from being isolated economically or diplomatically, had deepened its alliances with other parts of the world, in particular China, Iran and nuclear-armed North Korea. A summit held in the Russian city of Kazan in November 2024 brought together representatives of more than thirty countries, including twenty-two heads of state or government and the secretary-general of the United Nations.[2] Then in January 2025 an incoming administration in the US threatened an approach very different from that of its predecessor – not only towards Ukraine but towards Europe in general, and crucially also towards Russia.

The shift was very publicly demonstrated during the following months, when official statements from the White House and choreographed scenes beamed to the world's television channels attempted to characterize President Zelensky as a 'dictator' and himself to blame for the aggression against his country. Then on 15 August came a highly staged summit meeting between the presidents of Russia and the United States in the US state of Alaska – a territory which, just like Ukraine, had once been Russian. That event seemed to mark the end of Russia's isolation by a 'West' that perhaps no longer existed; but, far from being the diplomatic breakthrough proclaimed by some at the time, it brought no immediate prospect of a let-up in the fighting on Europe's eastern borders. In the meantime, the European Union and European governments, despite being excluded from negotiations, were scrambling to devise ways to provide continued support for Ukraine for as long as the conflict might last, or credible guarantees to oversee any possible ceasefire negotiated over their heads.

As this book went to press, it still seemed all too likely that any promised end to the war in Ukraine could only be an imposed, temporary truce, one which would leave the 'gates of Europe' wide open to the east – and once again carve up the continent without any regard for its people, as last happened in 1945.[3] In that case, the fate of Mariupol could well become the fate of more European cities in the months and years to come.

In the second half of the 2020s it is no longer the rule of law or liberal democracy that is in the ascendant around the world, but Russian-style authoritarianism. Despite valiant efforts by European political leaders to preserve as much as they can of the post-Second World War order, the task facing them in the years to come will be to adapt to a multipolar world in which Europe stands alone, one in which long established rules for international engagement are being torn up daily. That task, logically, ought to bring with it an opportunity: for Europeans and their governments to slay the demons of the past and rise above the jealous rivalries among nation states that a century ago brought the continent to its 'heart of darkness' and the unconditional surrender that followed.[4]

But the very opposite of that seemed to be envisaged by a new 'idea of Europe' which emerged from across the Atlantic at the end of 2025. According to a 33-page *National Security Strategy of the United States of America* issued by the White House on 4 December, 'American diplomacy should continue to stand up for genuine democracy, freedom of expression, and unapologetic celebrations of European nations' individual character and history.' The same document welcomes 'the growing influence of patriotic European parties' – evidently a reference to political parties of the far right, such as Alternative für Deutschland, which had been explicitly endorsed earlier in the year by the US vice-president.[5] The far from enlightened self-interest of those in charge of American policy implied a blueprint for Europe that would see current democratic systems replaced by the kind of 'democracy' practised in Russia and Hungary; long-established norms of free speech by the unregulated spread of harmful content and misinformation on (US-run) digital platforms; and the EU itself by the kind of atavistic nationalism that was last seen in the 1930s. Less noticed in the frenzy of commentary that followed the publication of this document was the total absence of any reference to the rule of law.

At the start of 2026, it is impossible to predict how European governments and electorates might respond to these multiple challenges. In foreign policy, there have been encouraging signs of greater cooperation, if some way short of unity, among European states. Concerted efforts are well under way to invest in the continent's defence. But it remains to be seen how far national electorates will continue to back those efforts, at a time when public attention seems more preoccupied with issues such as the cost of living and the impact of mass immigration on communities than with geopolitical threats which could actually have a greater effect on everybody's lives. In parts of eastern Europe where the populist-nationalist parties now favoured by American policy have come to power, far-right governments are already drawing their countries back towards the orbit of Russia, which they had only recently escaped.

And yet, if governments of even middle-sized nation states seem increasingly incapable of satisfying the demands of their electorates, that may be all the more reason to invest, instead, in *European* solutions. While dissatisfied voters across Europe are being drawn towards nationalist solutions that would only make their problems worse, the one solution that has never yet been seriously attempted is *more* Europe, rather than less. In a world dominated by states the size of China, Russia and the USA, an effective European administration would be able to pull on levers unavailable to any national government – and to stand up for the interests of its citizens in the face of those giants. Could not those citizens themselves, irrespective of background or national allegiance, come together to consolidate a collective identity for Europe as a whole? Inspired by the lessons of geography and history, could not Europeans of every nationality discover the same inspiration in their *European* identity as their forebears drew from the national identities of the nineteenth and twentieth centuries? The result would be not the 'superstate' that some dread but more like a 'super-nation'. And who knows, it may already be happening among the generations born after 1989.

Otherwise, the nation states of Europe risk ending up like the city states of the ancient Greeks – so obsessed with preserving their autonomy from each other and so fixated on their 'individual character and history' that they fall, one by one, into the grip of a more ruthless neighbour. If that were to happen, an authoritarian, Russian-dominated empire could end up stretching, undifferentiated, all the way from the Atlantic to the Pacific; even the term 'Europe' would no longer have any meaning, and indeed the story told in this book would become redundant, perhaps even erased from memory – not an end of *History*, but a literal end to the history of *Europe*.

On the other hand, if the study of history tells us anything, it is that things never turn out in the way you might expect. Who could have foretold that a tiny collection of Greek city states would repel the invading Persians in the fifth century BCE, and a century and a half later an expedition from Europe would overcome the largest empire in the world at the time? Who could have foretold that the teaching of an obscure preacher in Galilee would become the foundation for a world religion – and also for a way of organizing politics and society that would define a whole continent for almost two millennia? The same could be said of the extraordinary voyages of Europeans around the world, which began at the end of the fifteenth century and culminated in colonization all over the globe four centuries later. And so it goes on. Like every good story, history is made up of surprises.

Notes

Where quotations have been translated from another language and no translator is credited, translations are my own.

Introduction

1 Raphael Behr, 'This war will shake politics into a new sobriety', *The Guardian* (2 March 2022), Journal section, 1–2.

2 See, for example, Norman Davies, *Europe: A History* (London: Bodley Head, 2014 [1996]), xvii, 47.

3 Ian Morris, *Geography is Destiny: Britain and the World, a 10,000-Year History* (London: Profile, 2022), 7, 9 and *passim*.

4 Davies, *Europe*, 8, 10–12; Anthony Pagden, 'Europe: Conceptualizing a continent', in Anthony Pagden (ed.), *The Idea of Europe: From Antiquity to the European Union* (Washington, DC: Woodrow Wilson Center and New York: Cambridge University Press, 2002), 33–54 (see 46–7); Tim Marshall, *Prisoners of Geography*, rev. edn (London: Elliott & Thompson, 2025 [2015]), 11 (cross). And see pp. 180–81 and 303 below.

5 Johannes Krause and Thomas Trappe, *A Short History of Humanity: How Migration Made Us Who We Are*, trans. Caroline Waight (London: W. H. Allen, 2021 [2019, in German]), 198 (North America); Richard Broome, *Aboriginal Australians: A History since 1788* (London: Allen and Unwin, 2019), 78–9 (Australia).

6 The positive case is made by Niall Ferguson, *Civilization: The West and the Rest* (London: Penguin, 2011), xxvi and *passim*; Julio Crespo MacLennan, *Europa: How Europe Shaped the Modern World* (New York: Pegasus, 2018), xii and *passim*. For the opposite trend among some recent historians see, for example, Caroline Elkins, *Legacy of Violence: A History of the British Empire* (London: Bodley Head, 2022).

7 For a thoughtful critique of these widely accepted generalizations see Jean-Paul Demoule, *The Indo-Europeans: Archaeology, Language, Race, and the Search for the Origins of the West* (Oxford: Oxford University Press, 2023 [2014, in French]).

8 Ian Morris, *Why the West Rules – For Now: The Patterns of History and What They Reveal about the Future* (London: Profile, 2010), 110–12; Krause and Trappe, *Short History*, 20–22, 72–3, 100–102, 214.

9 Yuval Noah Harari, *Sapiens: A Brief History of Humankind* (London: Vintage, 2014), 41–4, 161; Morris, *Why the West Rules*, 60–73, 558; David Reich, *Who We Are and How We Got Here: Ancient DNA and the New Science of the Human Past* (Oxford: Oxford University Press, 2018).

10 Ferguson, *Civilization*, 12–13, 19–49, 305; Walter Scheidel, *Escape from Rome: The Failure of Empire and the Road to Prosperity* (Princeton, NJ: Princeton University Press, 2019).

11 Stella Ghervas, *Conquering Peace: From the Enlightenment to the European Union* (Cambridge, MA: Harvard University Press, 2021), 5 and *passim*.

12 'Document on The European Identity published by the Nine Foreign Ministers on 14 December 1973, in Copenhagen', articles 2 and 4: <https://www.cvce.eu/content/publication/1999/1/1/02798dc9-9c69-4b7d-b2c9-f03a8db7da32/publishable_en.pdf>.

13 See in particular Anthony D. Smith, *Nationalism: Theory, Ideology, History* (Cambridge: Polity, 2001); Paul Lawrence, *Nationalism: History and Theory* (London: Pearson, 2005); Joep Leerssen, *National Thought in Europe: A Cultural History* (Amsterdam: Amsterdam University Press, 2006).

14 'Document on The European Identity', article 1.

1. The Beginning of History and the Invention of Europe

1 Herodotus, *Histories*, book 6, chs 48–9 and 101–18. Several translations of this work are available and include the standard book/chapter divisions referenced here. See further: trans. Aubrey de Sélincourt, rev. edn, with notes by John Marincola (London: Penguin, 2003 [1954]); Constantinos Lagos and Fotis Karyanos, *Who Really Won the Battle of*

Marathon? A Bold Re-Appraisal of One of History's Most Famous Battles, trans. John Carr (Barnsley, Yorkshire and Philadelphia, PA: Pen and Sword, 2020 [2015, in Greek, with illustrations and maps]).

2 Pausanias, *Guide to Greece* [2nd century CE], trans. Peter Levi, 2 vols (London: Penguin, 1979), 1.45–6 (monumental painting); Sonya Nevin, *The Idea of Marathon: Battle and Culture* (London: Bloomsbury Academic, 2022), 88, 118–20, 167–8 (runner and sources); 156–8 (Romans).

3 Athena Leoussi, 'The battle of Marathon and European identity', in Beatrice Heuser and Athena Leoussi (eds), *Famous Battles and How They Shaped the Modern World, c. 1200 BCE–1302 CE* (Barnsley, Yorkshire, and Philadelphia, PA: Pen and Sword, 2018), 46 (French Revolution), 50 (John Stuart Mill, review of George Grote, *History of Greece* [1846], quoted); 45 (German historians).

4 Timothy Rood, 'From Marathon to Waterloo: Byron, battle monuments, and the Persian Wars', in Emma Bridges, Edith Hall and P. J. Rhodes (eds), *Cultural Responses to the Persian Wars: Antiquity to the Third Millennium* (Oxford: Oxford University Press, 2007), 292–3 (W. S. Gilbert); Michael Llewellyn Smith, *Olympics in Athens: 1896–2004* (London: Profile, 2004), 180, 183–4 (Marathon race).

5 Paul Cartledge, *Democracy: A Life*, 2nd edn (Oxford: Oxford University Press, 2018), 32, 55, 75.

6 Herodotus, *Histories*, book 1, Preface.

7 Herodotus, *Histories*, book 7, ch. 135.

8 Kurt Raaflaub, *The Discovery of Freedom in Ancient Greece* (Chicago, IL: University of Chicago Press, 2004 [1985, in German]), 60, 79, 86, 256.

9 Herodotus, *Histories*, book 7, ch. 104.

10 Edith Hall, *Inventing the Barbarian: Greek Self-Definition through Tragedy* (Oxford: Clarendon Press, 1989).

11 Naoíse Mac Sweeney, *The West: A New History of an Old Idea* (London: W. H. Allen, 2023), 13–22, 35–7; Josephine Quinn, *How the World Made the West: A 4,000-Year History* (London: Bloomsbury, 2024), 210–13.

12 Herodotus, *Histories*, book 4, ch. 45; for 'Europe' and 'Asia' before Herodotus see John Marincola, 'Introduction', in *Histories*, trans. de Sélincourt, xviii–xix.

13 Herodotus, *Histories*, book 1, Preface–ch. 4 (ch. 4 quoted).

14 Herodotus, *Histories*, book 7, chs 5, 8a, 8c.

15 Herodotus, *Histories*, book 7, chs 50, 54.

16 Herodotus, *Histories*, book 8, ch. 109; book 9, ch. 116. See also Rosalind Thomas, *Herodotus in Context: Ethnography, Science and the Art of Persuasion* (Cambridge: Cambridge University Press, 2000), 98–100; Simon Price and Peter Thonemann, *The Birth of Classical Europe: A History from Troy to Augustine* (London: Allen Lane/Penguin, 2010), 115–17.

17 Herodotus, *Histories*, book 4, ch. 45.

18 Demosthenes, *Philippics*, book 3, chs 30–31; see also Ian Worthington, *Demosthenes of Athens and the Fall of Classical Greece* (Oxford: Oxford University Press, 2013), 220–23.

19 Raaflaub, *Discovery*, 157–65.

20 Ian Worthington, *Philip II of Macedonia* (New Haven, CT: Yale University Press, 2008), 4.

21 Respectively: Simon Hornblower, *The Greek World, 479–323 BC*, 4th edn (Abingdon: Routledge, 2011), 268, citing in translation Isocrates, *Philip*, 137 (written in 346 BCE); Arnaldo Momigliano, 'Terra marique', *Journal of Roman Studies*, 32 (1942), 53–64 (see 56), citing Theopompus of Chios, fragments 27, 256.

22 Worthington, *Philip II*, 160.

23 Price and Thonemann, *Birth*, 143.

24 A. B. Bosworth, *Conquest and Empire: The Reign of Alexander the Great* (Cambridge: Cambridge University Press, 1993), 35, 259; for the fullest ancient account, see Diodorus of Sicily, *The Library, Books 16–20: Philip II, Alexander the Great and the Successors*, trans. Robin Waterfield (Oxford: Oxford University Press, 2019), 94–5.

25 Respectively: Diodorus of Sicily, *Library*, book 17, ch. 17, paragraphs 1–2; Arrian, *The Campaigns of Alexander*, trans. Aubrey de Sélincourt (London: Penguin, 1971), 66.

26 Diodorus of Sicily, *Library*, book 18, ch. 4, paragraph 4. Compare Arrian, *Campaigns*, 213, 348–9.

27 *Anthologia Graeca*, book 16, poem 6 (addressed to Philip V, c. 200 BCE), cited in Momigliano, 'Terra marique', 56–7 (my translation); see also Price and Thonemann, *Birth*, 175. I am grateful to Professor Thonemann for directing me to this source.

28 Emily Mackil, *Creating a Common Polity: Religion, Economy, and Politics in the Making of the Greek Koinon* (Berkeley, CA: University of California Press, 2013), 1 and n. 3.

29 Polybius, *Histories*, book 2, chs 37, 38, 42. For a translation of parts of this work see Polybius, *The Rise of the Roman Empire*, trans. Ian Scott-Kilvert, selected with an introduction by F. W. Walbank (London: Penguin, 1979).

30 Graham Shipley, *The Greek World after Alexander, 323–30 BC* (London: Routledge, 2000), 136–7; Paul Cartledge, *The Spartans: An Epic History* (London: Pan, 2013), 236–7.

31 Walbank, 'Introduction', in Polybius, *Rise*, 9–40 (see 37 on Montesquieu); Peter Thonemann, *The Hellenistic Age: A Very Short Introduction* (Oxford: Oxford University Press, 2018), 27 (US and state constitutions); Shipley, *Greek World*, 133–40; Gustav Adolf Lehmann, 'Greek federalism, the rediscovery of Polybius, and the framing of the American constitution', in Hans Beck and Peter Funke (eds), *Federalism in Greek Antiquity* (Cambridge: Cambridge University Press, 2015), 512–23.

32 Greg Woolf, *Rome: An Empire's Story* (Oxford: Oxford University Press, 2012), 18–19, 38–9, 44.

33 Plutarch, 'Pyrrhus', in *Hellenistic Lives*, trans. Robin Waterfield (Oxford: Oxford University Press, 2016), 231 and (for commentary) 351, 452.

34 F. W. Walbank, *The Hellenistic World* (London: Fontana, 1992), 228, citing Heracleides Ponticus [fourth century BCE] (Rome a Greek city); Hellanicus of Lesbos [fifth century BCE] (Trojan story).

35 Polybius, *Histories*, book 2, ch. 2; Walbank, *Hellenistic World*, 229–30.

36 Walbank, 'Introduction', 12–15; Polybius, *Histories*, book 1, ch. 1 (quoted).

37 Walbank, *Hellenistic World*, 158.

38 Polybius, *Histories*, respectively: book 2, ch. 40 and book 1, ch. 2 (for the latter compare book 15, ch. 9).

39 Only a few paragraphs survive of Polybius's account of these events. The fullest ancient account is Pausanias, *Guide to Greece* [second century CE], trans. Peter Levi, 2 vols (London: Penguin, 1979), 1.256–68.

2. 'Power without End'

1 Livy, *History of Rome from the Founding of the City*, book 22, chs 54–5. Several translations of the surviving portions of this work are available and include the standard book/chapter divisions referenced here. See further: Livy, *The Early History of Rome*, trans. Aubrey de Sélincourt (London: Penguin, 1960), and Livy, *The War with Hannibal*, trans. Aubrey de Sélincourt (London: Penguin, 1965).

2 Livy, *History*, book 22, ch. 57.

3 Simon Price and Peter Thonemann, *The Birth of Classical Europe: A History from Troy to Augustine* (London: Allen Lane/Penguin, 2010), 214.

4 Polybius, *Histories*, book 38, ch. 21, trans. W. R. Paton, 6 vols (Loeb Classical Library, Cambridge, MA: Harvard University Press, 1922–7), 6.437.

5 Livy, *History*, book 1, chs 4–7; Cicero, *Republic*, book 2, ch. 4, trans. Niall Rudd in Cicero, *The Republic and The Laws* (Oxford: Oxford University Press, 1998), 36 (without the murder of Remus).

6 Livy, *History*, book 2, ch. 1; Mary Beard, *SPQR: A History of Ancient Rome* (London: Profile, 2015), 128–9.

7 Price and Thonemann, *Birth*, 189; Greg Woolf, *Rome: An Empire's Story* (Oxford: Oxford University Press, 2012), 71; Beard, *SPQR*, 184–92.

8 Valentina Arena, *Libertas and the Practice of Politics in the Late Roman Republic* (Cambridge: Cambridge University Press, 2012), 28, 66.

9 Peter Stein, *Roman Law in European History* (Cambridge: Cambridge University Press, 1999 [1996, in German]), 1–2.

10 Woolf, *Rome*, 70, 71, 104, 278, but see map on p. 127 ('Mediterranean empire'); Dexter Hoyos, *Rome Victorious: The Irresistible Rise of the Roman Empire* (London: I.B. Tauris, 2019), 47, 49 (lack of plan).

11 Plutarch, 'Tiberius and Gaius Gracchus', in *Roman Lives*, trans. Robin Waterfield (Oxford: Oxford University Press, 1999), 19–20, 38, 98–9, 113–14. On the politics see Beard, *SPQR*, 216, 221–34; Edward J. Watts, *The Romans: A 2,000-Year History* (London and New York: Basic Books, 2025), 138 ('political tool').

12 Beard, *SPQR*, 248–50; Joel Allen, *The Roman Republic and the Hellenistic Mediterranean: From Alexander to Caesar* (Medford, MA: Wiley Blackwell, 2020), 202–4.

13 Plutarch, 'Sulla', in *Roman Lives*, trans. Waterfield, 212.

14 Pliny the Elder, *Natural History* [*c.* 75 CE], book 7, ch. 25; Beard, *SPQR*, 284 ('up to a million').

15 Watts, *The Romans*, 154, 649 (n. 68).

16 Plutarch, 'Antony', in *Roman Lives*, trans. Waterfield, 425–6.

17 Beard, *SPQR*, 340, 354; Woolf, *Rome*, 19, 20, 151, 163 (*imperium*).

18 Respectively: Neville Morley, *The Roman Empire: Roots of Imperialism* (London and New York: Pluto Press, 2010), 69 ('kleptocracy'); Peter Wells, *The Battle That Stopped Rome* (New York: Norton, 2004), 278 ('institutionalized terror'), and see also Hoyos, *Rome Victorious*, 2, 193–5; Edward Gibbon, *The History of the Decline and Fall of the Roman Empire*, abridged edn, ed. David Womersley (London: Penguin, 2005), 83; Mary Beard, *Emperor of Rome: Ruling the Ancient World* (London: Profile, 2023), 407 and *passim*.

19 Virgil, *Aeneid*, book 1, lines 277–8; book 6, lines 851–3.

20 Horace, *Odes*, book 4, poem 15 ('To Augustus'), lines 12–16.

21 Price and Thonemann, *Birth*, 262.

22 Woolf, *Rome*, 182 ('*civilitas*'); Charlton Lewis and Charles Short, *A Latin Dictionary* (Oxford: Oxford University Press, 1879), entry: *humanitas* (quoted).

23 Anne Kolb, '*Via ducta* – Roman road building: An introduction to its significance, the sources and the state of research', in Anne Kolb (ed.), *Roman Roads: New Evidence – New Perspectives* (Boston, MA: De Gruyter, 2019), 3–21 (see 9); Victor von Hagen, *The Roads That Led to Rome* (London: Weidenfeld and Nicolson, 1967), 8, 24.

24 Von Hagen, *Roads*, 65 (courier service); 51 (Golden Mile).

25 Beard, *SPQR*, 509–10; Josephine Quinn, *How the World Made the West: A 4,000-Year History* (London: Bloomsbury, 2024), 277–8.

26 Pliny the Elder, *Natural History* [*c.* 75 CE], book 3, ch. 1; Strabo, *Geography* [early first century CE, in Greek], book 2, ch. 5, paragraph 26.

27 Tacitus, *Annals*, book 1, respectively: ch. 11 and ch. 9.

28 Anthony Birley, *Hadrian: The Restless Emperor* (Abingdon: Routledge, 1997), 111–19, 128–38, 151–3, 209–10.

29 Tacitus, *Annals*, book 1, chs 4, 81.

30 Tacitus, *Agricola and Germania*, trans. Harold Mattingly, rev. edn (London: Penguin, 2009), 3–4; J. B. Rives, 'Introduction' in the same

volume, xxxiii and 'Notes', 71, n. 3; Tacitus, *The Annals of Imperial Rome*, trans. Michael Grant, rev. edn (London: Penguin, 1996), 173 (quoted).

31 Marcus Aurelius, *To Himself* [*Meditations*], respectively: book 6, ch. 16; book 4, ch. 3; book 8, ch. 51.

32 Galatians, 1.1; 1.4; 5.22–3; 5.1; Romans, 8.2 (New English Bible). On date and context see Charles Freeman, *A New History of Early Christianity* (New Haven, CT, and London: Yale University Press, 2011), 47–65.

33 Larry Siedentop, *Inventing the Individual: The Origins of Western Liberalism* (London: Allen Lane / Penguin, 2014), 60–62.

34 Matthew, 22.21; Galatians, 4.7; Tertullian cited in Peter Brown, *The Body and Society: Men, Women, and Sexual Renunciation in Early Christianity* (New York: Columbia University Press, 1988), 83.

35 Myles Lavan, 'The spread of Roman citizenship, 14–212 CE', *Past and Present*, 230 (2016), 3–46; Beard, *SPQR*, 527–9; Watts, *The Romans*, 275–6.

36 Stein, *Roman Law*, 20–21; Michael Kulikowski, *Imperial Triumph: The Roman World from Hadrian to Constantine, AD 138–363* (London: Profile, 2016), 100–101.

37 Woolf, *Rome*, 191, 213; Kulikowski, *Triumph*, 175 (new walls for Rome).

38 Peter Heather, *The Fall of the Roman Empire: A New History* (London: Pan Macmillan, 2006), 58–62.

39 Heather, *Fall*, 28, 117–18; Kulikowski, *Triumph*, respectively: 258, 200 (quoted).

40 Lactantius, *De Mortibus Persecutorum* [*On the Deaths of the Persecutors*], ch. 5, ed. and trans. J. L. Creed (Oxford: Clarendon Press, 1984), 10–11.

41 Robin Lane Fox, *Pagans and Christians in the Mediterranean World from the Second Century AD to the Conversion of Constantine* (London: Penguin, 1988), 425 (on motives), 450–59, 550–54; Peter Heather, *Christendom: The Triumph of a Religion* (London: Allen Lane, 2022), 20–25 (estimate of numbers).

42 A. H. M. Jones, J. R. Martindale and J. Morris, *The Prosopography of the Later Roman Empire*, 3 vols (Cambridge: Cambridge University Press, 1971–92), 1.223.

43 Peter Weiss, 'The vision of Constantine', *Journal of Roman Archaeology*, 16 (2003), 237–59; Timothy Barnes, *Constantine: Dynasty, Religion and*

Power in the Later Roman Empire (Oxford: Blackwell, 2011), 74–80. See, most recently, Heather, *Christendom*, 4–19.

44 Eusebius, *Oration in Praise of the Emperor Constantine*, ch. 1, paragraph 6, delivered in the year 332; Greek text in I. A. Heikel, *Eusebius Werke*, vol. 1 (*Die griechischen christlichen Schriftsteller* 7 (Leipzig: Hinrichs, 1902), 195–259.

3. *'Waiting for the Barbarians'*

1 Ammianus Marcellinus, *The Later Roman Empire (AD 354–378)*, trans. Walter Hamilton (London: Penguin, 1986), 417.

2 See, for example, Walter Goffart, *Barbarian Tides: The Migration Age and the Later Roman Empire* (Philadelphia, PA: University of Pennsylvania Press, 2006); Guy Halsall, *Barbarian Migrations and the Roman West, 376–568* (Cambridge: Cambridge University Press, 2007); C.P. Cavafy, *The Collected Poems*, ed. Anthony Hirst, trans. Evangelos Sachperoglou (Oxford: Oxford University Press, 2007), 14–17 (quoted, my translation).

3 Peter Heather, *The Fall of the Roman Empire: A New History* (London: Pan Macmillan, 2006), 145.

4 Heather, *Fall*, 181–2 (numbers); Ammianus Marcellinus, trans. Hamilton, 435–7 (battle, 435 quoted).

5 Ammianus Marcellinus, trans. Hamilton, 423, 425, 433, 440.

6 Bryan Ward-Perkins, *The Fall of Rome and the End of Civilization* (Oxford: Oxford University Press, 2005), 24–7 (negative opinions); Heather, *Fall*, 67–70 (superiority); Yves Dauge, *Le Barbare: Recherches sur la conception romaine du barbarie et de la civilisation* (Brussels: Latomus, 1981), 19–20, and Edward James, *Europe's Barbarians: AD 200–600* (London: Pearson Longman, 2009), 11 (not racist).

7 Julius Caesar, *Seven Commentaries on the Gallic War*, trans. Carolyn Hammond (Oxford: Oxford University Press, 1996), 129–30.

8 Tacitus, *Germania*, ch. 46 [98 CE], in Tacitus, *Agricola and Germania*, trans. Harold Mattingly, rev. edn (London: Penguin, 2009), 57 (translation slightly adapted); James, *Europe's Barbarians*, 26–30.

9 Peter Heather, *Empires and Barbarians: The Fall of Rome and the Birth of Europe* (Oxford: Oxford University Press, 2009), 3–9, 598 and Map 1.

10 Heather, *Fall*, 159–61 (160 quoted); Heather, *Empires*, 74–7.

11 Ward-Perkins, *Fall*, 32–3, 40–41.

12 Ammianus Marcellinus, trans. Hamilton, 411–12. For modern assessments see Michael Kulikowski, *Imperial Tragedy: From Constantine's Empire to the Destruction of Roman Italy, AD 363–568* (London: Profile, 2019), 75–80, 83–5; Heather, *Empires*, 158–64, 209–14; James, *Europe's Barbarians*, 45–7.

13 Peter Heather, *Christendom: The Triumph of a Religion* (London: Allen Lane, 2022), 172–6.

14 Ammianus Marcellinus, trans. Hamilton, 416.

15 Heather, *Fall*, 184–7.

16 Heather, *Fall*, 194–9, 205–11.

17 Heather, *Empires*, 191–3; Kulikowski, *Tragedy*, 123–42 ('cold war': 122).

18 Heather, *Fall*, 211–16; Heather, *Empires*, 193–201 (Alaric's objectives); Ward-Perkins, *Fall*, 53 (map of Gothic migration route).

19 Heather, *Fall*, 211–27 (see 221 for debt in gold, 224 for size of army).

20 Heather, *Fall*, 227–9 (227 quoted); Kulikowski, *Tragedy*, 144, 148–9; Ward-Perkins, *Fall*, 21–2; Ammianus Marcellinus, trans. Hamilton, 45, 178 (quoted).

21 St Jerome, cited in Ward-Perkins, *Fall*, 28.

22 St Augustine, *Concerning the City of God against the Pagans*, trans. Henry Bettenson, rev. edn (London: Penguin, 2003), 87.

23 Orientius, *Commonitorium* [*c.* 430], quoted in translation in Heather, *Fall*, 207.

24 Sidonius Apollonaris [fifth century], quoted in translation in Heather, *Fall*, 196–7.

25 *The Gothic History of Jordanes* [*c.* 550], trans. Charles Mierow (Princeton, NJ: Princeton University Press, 1915), 102; Marcellinus Comes [early sixth century], *Chronicle*, ed. J. P. Migne (*Patrologia Graeca*, vol. 51), see respectively: years 454; 447.

26 Heather, *Empires*, 207–8, 223, 234–9.

27 Arnoldo Momigliano, cited in Ward-Perkins, *Fall*, 31 ('noiseless fall'); Judith Herrin, *Ravenna: Capital of Empire, Crucible of Europe* (London: Allen Lane, 2020), 77–85.

28 Herrin, *Ravenna*, 89–136.

29 Gregory of Tours, *The History of the Franks* [late sixth century], trans. Lewis Thorpe (London: Penguin, 1974), 144; Heather, *Empires*, 305–32.

30 Chris Wickham, *The Inheritance of Rome: A History of Europe from 400 to 1000* (London: Allen Lane/Penguin, 2009), 76–108.

31 Heather, *Empires*, 347–8; see also Wickham, *Inheritance*, 101–2, 134, 147, 157, 200.

32 Ward-Perkins, *Fall*, 138–68 (see 139, 142: population); Joseph Tainter, *The Collapse of Complex Societies* (Cambridge: Cambridge University Press, 1988), 128–52.

33 Averil Cameron, *The Mediterranean World in Late Antiquity, AD 395–700*, rev. edn (London: Routledge, 2012 [1993]), 23 (population); Paul Stephenson, *New Rome: The Roman Empire in the East, AD 395–700* (London: Profile, 2021), 53.

34 *Codex Justinianus*, cited in translation in Stephen Mitchell, *A History of the Later Roman Empire, AD 284–641* (Oxford: Blackwell, 2007), 270; see also Peter Sarris, *Justinian: Emperor, Soldier, Saint* (London and New York: Basic Books, 2024), 119–20.

35 Peter Heather, *Rome Resurgent: War and Empire in the Age of Justinian* (Oxford: Oxford University Press, 2018), 120–23, 139–42, 164–79; Herrin, *Ravenna*, 151–9.

36 Peter Sarris, *Empires of Faith: The Fall of Rome to the Rise of Islam, 500–700* (Oxford: Oxford University Press, 2011), 158–9; Kulikowski, *Tragedy*, 309–10.

37 Heather, *Empires*, 386–406; Wickham, *Inheritance*, 480–84; James, *Europe's Barbarians*, 95–101.

38 John of Ephesus [sixth century], cited in Sarris, *Empires*, 181 ('Slavonians'); Mark Whittow, *The Making of Orthodox Byzantium, 600–1025* (Basingstoke: Macmillan, 1996), 49–50, 74–7.

39 John Haldon, *The Empire That Would Not Die: The Paradox of Eastern Roman Survival, 640–740* (Cambridge, MA: Harvard University Press, 2016), 31–55.

40 *The Chronicle of Theophanes* [ninth century], trans. Harry Turtledove (Princeton, NJ: Princeton University Press, 1982), 88–91; Haldon, *Empire*, 52–4.

41 Anthony Kaldellis, *Romanland: Ethnicity and Empire in Byzantium* (Cambridge, MA: Harvard University Press, 2019), ix–xv.

42 Edward Gibbon, *The History of the Decline and Fall of the Roman Empire*, ed. David Womersley, vol. 3 (London: Penguin, 1996), 336; Heather, *Christendom*, 372, for a more modest modern assessment of the significance of the battle.

43 Chronicle of Isidore Pacensis, written in 754, quoted by Denys Hay, *Europe: The Emergence of an Idea*, rev. edn (Edinburgh: Edinburgh University Press, 1968 [1957]), 25.

44 Janet Nelson, *King and Emperor: A New Life of Charlemagne* (London: Allen Lane/Penguin, 2019), 69–76; Rosamond McKitterick, *Charlemagne: The Formation of a European Identity* (Cambridge: Cambridge University Press, 2008), 71–4.

45 The Donation of Constantine (*Constitutum Constantini*) [late eighth century], cited in translation in Nelson, *King*, 355, see further 353–6; Heather, *Christendom*, 375–6.

46 Wickham, *Inheritance*, 144, 146–8, 377; Heather, *Christendom*, 367–72.

47 Norman Davies, *Europe: A History* (London: Bodley Head, 2014 [1996]), 298 (summary of campaigns); Einhard, 'The life of Charlemagne', in *Einhard and Notker the Stammerer: Two Lives of Charlemagne*, trans. David Ganz (London: Penguin, 2008), 23–4 (Saxons).

48 Peter Frankopan, *The Silk Roads: A New History of the World* (London: Bloomsbury, 2015), 27–62.

4. A Tale of Two Empires

1 Janet Nelson, *King and Emperor: A New Life of Charlemagne* (London: Allen Lane/Penguin, 2019), 491 ('skin'); 382, citing in translation the *Annals of the Kings of the Franks*, see further 380–85; Einhard and Notker the Stammerer, *Two Lives of Charlemagne*, trans. David Ganz (London: Penguin, 2008), 121, n. 66 (Charlemagne's height).

2 Laury Sarti, *Orbis Romanus: Byzantium and the Legacy of Rome in the Carolingian World* (Oxford: Oxford University Press, 2024), 19–20.

3 '[Karolus Magnus et Leo Papa]', in Ernst Dümmler (ed.), *Poetae latini aevi Carolini* (Berlin: Weidmann, 1881), 368, lines 92–4 (also known as the 'Paderborn epic').

4 Einhard, 'The Life of Charlemagne', trans. Ganz, 36 (building of Aachen); Nelson, *King*, 356–9; Rosamond McKitterick, *Charlemagne: The Formation of a European Identity* (Cambridge: Cambridge University Press, 2008), 157–71; Judith Herrin, *Ravenna: Capital of Empire, Crucible of Europe* (London: Allen Lane, 2020), 362, 393, 399, 481, 489 (for the role of that city).

5 Einhard, 'Life', trans. Ganz, 16, 18 ('barbarian'), 121 (classical allusions). On Einhard see McKitterick, *Charlemagne*, 7–20.

6 Nelson, *King*, 466 ('heir of Rome'); Einhard, 'Life', trans. Ganz, 36 (literacy), 40 (tombstone, quoted, emphasis added); 38 (law codes). On the last see also McKitterick, *Charlemagne*, 275–8.

7 Judith Herrin, *Women in Purple: Rulers of Medieval Byzantium* (London: Weidenfeld and Nicolson, 2001), 78, 91.

8 For the latest survey of the available evidence, see Sarti, *Orbis*, 27–33.

9 Einhard, 'Life', trans. Ganz, 38 ('angry'); Nelson, *King*, 458 (recognition by Michael I); 494 (citing Charlemagne's letter to Michael, my translation).

10 Mark Whittow, *The Making of Orthodox Byzantium, 600–1025* (Basingstoke: Macmillan, 1996), 104.

11 Averil Cameron and Judith Herrin (eds and trans.), *Constantinople in the Early Eighth Century: The Parastaseis Syntomoi Chronikai (Introduction, Translation, and Commentary)* (Leiden: Brill, 1984).

12 Chris Wickham, *The Inheritance of Rome: A History of Europe from 400 to 1000* (London: Allen Lane / Penguin, 2009), 394–5, 401–4; Nelson, *King*, 429–35 (proposed division of empire).

13 Peter Heather, *Christendom: The Triumph of a Religion* (London: Allen Lane / Penguin, 2022), 381–3; William Chester Jordan, *Europe in the High Middle Ages* (London: Allen Lane / Penguin, 2001), 13–16; Dan Jones, *Powers and Thrones: A New History of the Middle Ages* (London: Head of Zeus, 2021), 259–61.

14 Peter Sawyer, 'The age of the Vikings and before', in Peter Sawyer (ed.), *The Oxford Illustrated History of the Vikings* (Oxford: Oxford University Press, 1997), 1–18 (see 3–8).

15 Janet Nelson, 'The Frankish empire', in Sawyer (ed.), *Vikings*, 19–47 (see 29–30); Peter Heather, *Empires and Barbarians: The Fall of Rome and the Birth of Europe* (Oxford: Oxford University Press, 2009), 453–6, 458.

16 Thomas Noonan, 'Scandinavians in European Russia', in Sawyer (ed.), *Vikings*, 134–55; Heather, *Empires*, 475–6.

17 Peter Wilson, *The Holy Roman Empire: A Thousand Years of Europe's History* (London: Allen Lane / Penguin, 2016), 34 (quoted), 49–50.

18 Constantine Porphyrogenitus [909–959], *De administrando imperio*, Greek text ed. G. Moravcsik; English trans. R. J. H. Jenkins, rev. edn, 2 vols (Washington, DC: Dumbarton Oaks Center for Byzantine Studies, 1967), 1.7–9 (citing Theophanes Continuatus, translation adapted); 2.10 (on title).

19 Constantine Porphyrogenitus, *De Caerimoniis* (Preface, my translation); Averil Cameron, *The Byzantines* (Oxford: Blackwell, 2006), 35–6, 72–3.

20 *De administrando*, 1.66–7 (ch. 13).

21 *De administrando*, 1.13 ('secret'); 1.44–65 (chs 1–12); 1.180–81 (ch. 41).

22 Paul Stephenson, *Byzantium's Balkan Frontier: A Political Study of the Northern Balkans, 900–1204* (Cambridge: Cambridge University Press, 2000), 71–4; Anthony Kaldellis, *Streams of Gold, Rivers of Blood: The Rise and Fall of Byzantium, 955 A.D. to the First Crusade* (Oxford: Oxford University Press, 2017), 120–27.

23 Anthony Kaldellis, *Romanland: Ethnicity and Empire in Byzantium* (Cambridge, MA: Harvard University Press, 2019), 267 and ch. 7 *passim*; 271–2.

24 *Eisagoge*, attributed to Patriarch Photius, cited in translation in Anthony Kaldellis, *The Byzantine Republic: People and Power in New Rome* (Cambridge, MA: Harvard University Press, 2015), 17–18; see also 75–82 on laws.

25 Wilson, *Holy Roman Empire*, 29–33 (29 quoted).

26 Quoted in translation in Martin Rady, *The Middle Kingdoms: A New History of Central Europe* (London: Allen Lane / Penguin, 2023), 58 (emphasis added).

27 *Dictatus Papae*, cited in translation in Ernest Henderson (ed. and trans.), *Select Historical Documents of the Middle Ages* (London: George Bell, 1910), 366–7 (articles 1–2, 9, 12, 19, 6, 27).

28 Berthold of Reichenau, 'Chronicle' [*c.* 1080], in I. S. Robinson (ed. and trans.), *Eleventh-Century Germany: The Swabian Chronicles* (Manchester: Manchester University Press, 2008), 142–63 (160 quoted).

29 See, for example, Heather, *Christendom*, 470–71; Wilson, *Holy Roman Empire*, 58; Jordan, *Europe*, 92.

30 Jordan, *Europe*, 5, 8–10; Jones, *Powers*, 228, 393.

31 Heather, *Empires*, 515–76; Ian Morris, *Geography is Destiny: Britain and the World, a 10,000-Year History* (London: Profile, 2022), 148–85.

32 Peter Frankopan, *The First Crusade: The Call from the East* (London: Vintage, 2013), 97–100; Kaldellis, *Streams*, 285–7.

33 Frankopan, *First Crusade*, 33, 57–70.

34 Frankopan, *First Crusade*, 17–25; Michael Angold, *Church and Society in Byzantium under the Comneni, 1081–1261* (Cambridge: Cambridge University Press, 1995), 22–7.

35 *Chronicles of the First Crusade, 1096–1099*, ed. Christopher Tyerman (London: Penguin, 2011), 2, 9–10 (translated extracts, respectively, from Robert of Rheims and Fulcher of Chartres).

36 Robert of Rheims in *Chronicles*, 3–4 (quoted); see also Fulcher in *Chronicles*, 6, 9.

37 Jonathan Phillips, *Holy Warriors: A Modern History of the Crusades* (London: Vintage, 2010), 5; George Demacopoulos, *Colonizing Christianity: Greek and Latin Religious Identity in the Era of the Fourth Crusade* (New York: Fordham University Press, 2019), 5–9 and *passim*.

38 *Chronicles*, 4 (Robert), 10 (Fulcher).

39 Christopher Tyerman, *The World of the Crusades* (New Haven, CT, and London: Yale University Press, 2019), 74–5.

40 Phillips, *Holy Warriors*, 11 (kings); Tyerman, *World*, 227 (quoted).

41 Frankopan, *First Crusade*, 202–6; Kaldellis, *Streams*, 295–301.

42 Raymond of Aguilers, in *Chronicles*, 328–9.

43 Tyerman, *World*, 105–7, 111–14 and Map 5.

44 Cited in Jonathan Phillips, *The Second Crusade: Extending the Frontiers of Christendom* (New Haven, CT: Yale University Press, 2007), 269.

45 Tyerman, *World*, 195 (citing the *Itinerary of King Richard*, quoted); 222 (casualties).

46 For the fullest modern accounts see Michael Angold, *The Fourth Crusade: Event and Context* (London: Pearson Longman, 2003) and Jonathan Phillips, *The Fourth Crusade and the Sack of Constantinople* (London: Pimlico, 2005); on causes and historical significance see Roderick Beaton, *The Greeks: A Global History* (London: Faber and New York: Basic Books, 2021), 323–33, and Edward J. Watts, *The Romans: A 2,000-Year History* (London and New York: Basic Books, 2025), 600–622.

5. Breaking Out – Breaking Up

1 Pope Innocent III, 'On the misery of Man', in Bernard Murchland (ed. and trans.), *Two Views of Man* (New York: Frederick Ungar, 1966), 3–4 (quoted).

2 *Crusade and Christendom: Annotated Documents in Translation from Innocent III to the Fall of Acre, 1187–1291*, ed. Jessalynn Bird, Edward Peters and James Powell (Philadelphia, PA: University of Pennsylvania Press, 2013), 106–7; Peter Heather, *Christendom: The Triumph of a Religion* (London: Allen Lane / Penguin, 2022), 507–10.

3 Jacques Le Goff, *The Birth of Purgatory*, trans. Arthur Goldhammer (London: Scolar Press, 1984 [1981, in French]).

4 Heather, *Christendom*, 560–67, 583.

5 Heather, *Christendom*, 574–5.

6 William Chester Jordan, *Europe in the High Middle Ages* (London: Allen Lane / Penguin, 2001), 208, 209, 234–5 (Magna Carta); Norman Davies, *Europe: A History* (London: Bodley Head, 2014 [1996]), 360 (vassal kings).

7 Larry Siedentop, *Inventing the Individual: The Origins of Western Liberalism* (London: Allen Lane / Penguin, 2014), 209, 221.

8 Dante Alighieri, *De Monarchia*, book 2, chs 3–8 (book 1, ch. 2 and book 2, ch. 3 quoted).

9 Dante, *De Monarchia*, book 3, chs 12–15.

10 Dante Alighieri, *La Divina Commedia: Paradiso*, canto 33, line 145 (emphasis added).

11 Patrick Boyde, *Dante Philomythes and Philosopher: Man in the Cosmos* (Cambridge: Cambridge University Press, 1981), 96–111.

12 Dante Alighieri, *La Divina Commedia: Inferno*, canto 26, lines 112–20, 141.

13 Nicholas Morton, *The Mongol Storm: Making and Breaking Empires in the Medieval Near East* (New York and London: Basic Books, 2022), 89–91; Martin Rady, *The Middle Kingdoms: A New History of Central Europe* (London: Allen Lane/Penguin, 2023), 2–3 ('dogmen'); Ian Morris, *Why the West Rules – For Now: The Patterns of History and What They Reveal about the Future* (London: Profile, 2010), 391 (quoting the English chronicler Matthew Paris [1200–1259]).

14 Morton, *Mongol Storm*, 91, 136–7.

15 Peter Frankopan, *The Silk Roads: A New History of the World* (London: Bloomsbury, 2015), 177–80 (Mongols and Russian Empire).

16 Dante, *Inferno*, canto 17, lines 14–17.

17 Morton, *Mongol Storm*, 235–6.

18 Quoted by Frankopan, *Silk Roads*, 184.

19 Morris, *Why the West Rules*, 395–6.

20 Morton, *Mongol Storm*, 317–19.

21 Peter Frankopan, *The Earth Transformed: An Untold Story* (London: Bloomsbury, 2023), 295, 304–6.

22 Giovanni Boccaccio, *Decameron*, ed. and trans. G. H. McWilliam (London: Penguin Classics, 1995), 5–6, 12.

23 Jordan, *Europe*, 297 (numerical estimates, end of Middle Ages); Dan Jones, *Powers and Thrones: A New History of the Middle Ages* (London: Head of Zeus, 2021), 501 ('too many'); see also Frankopan, *Earth Transformed*, 305.

24 Donald Nicol, *The Last Centuries of Byzantium 1261–1453*, 2nd edn (Cambridge: Cambridge University Press, 1993 [1972]), 241–2 (242 quoted, paraphrasing Cantacouzenus [John VI Cantacuzene], *Historiae*, book 3, pp. 276–9).

25 Nicol, *Last Centuries*, 275, 284–5, 290–91, 300.

26 David Abulafia, *The Discovery of Mankind: Atlantic Encounters in the Age of Columbus* (New Haven, CT, and London: Yale University Press, 2008), 33 (Dante), 36–7, 83–4 (Portuguese expeditions).

27 Enea Silvio Piccolomini (1454), quoted in translation in Alex Drace-Francis, *European Identity: A Historical Reader* (London: Macmillan International/Red Globe Press, 2013), 15.

28 Felipe Fernández-Armesto, *1492: The Year Our World Began* (London: Bloomsbury, 2010), 36–8, 97–9; Abulafia, *Discovery*, 13 (Columbus described).

29 'Digest of Columbus's log-book on the first voyage made by Bartolomé de las Casas', in *The Four Voyages of Christopher Columbus*, ed. and trans. J. M. Cohen (London: Penguin, 1969), 37–8.

30 Fernando Cervantes, *Conquistadores: A New History* (London: Allen Lane/Penguin, 2020), 20–21; *Four Voyages*, 300 ('Fourth voyage: Columbus's letter to the sovereigns of Spain').

31 Fernández-Armesto, *1492*, 1–11, 185; Cervantes, *Conquistadores*, 12–13.

32 *Four Voyages*, respectively: 220–22, 226 ('earthly Paradise'); 122 (slaves); 120, 265, 274 (conquests); 38 (letters to princes), on which see also Abulafia, *Discovery*, 27–30; 300–301 (gold).

33 Abulafia, *Discovery*, 183–6, 213.

34 Quoted in Cervantes, *Conquistadores*, 191.

35 William Shakespeare, *A Midsummer Night's Dream* [*c.* 1598], Act 2, Scene 1, line 175; Andrew Wheatcroft, *The Habsburgs: Embodying Empire* (London: Viking/Penguin, 1995), xv (map: The Habsburg world empire in 1580).

36 Morris, *Why the West Rules*, 407–17; Fernández-Armesto, *1492*, 223–7, 247–50.

37 Diarmaid MacCulloch, *Reformation: Europe's House Divided, 1490–1700* (London: Allen Lane/Penguin, 2003), 76–9, 106; Peter Mack, 'Humanism and the classical tradition', in Gordon Campbell (ed.), *The Oxford Illustrated History of the Renaissance* (Oxford: Oxford University Press, 2019), 11–44.

38 Jonathan Jones, *Earthly Delights: A History of the Renaissance* (London: Thames and Hudson, 2023), 15–16.

39 Mark Greengrass, *Christendom Destroyed: Europe 1517–1648* (London: Allen Lane/Penguin, 2014), 101–19.

40 Greengrass, *Christendom*, 246–7.

41 Greengrass, *Christendom*, 259 ('kaleidoscope'), 262 (number of 'independent entities'); Brendan Simms, *Europe: The Struggle for Supremacy, 1453 to the Present* (London: Allen Lane/Penguin, 2013), 1 ('representative

assemblies'); David Parrott, 'War and the state, *c.*1400–*c.*1650', in Campbell (ed.), *The Oxford Illustrated History*, 45–81 (mercenary armies).

42 Peter Wilson, *The Holy Roman Empire: A Thousand Years of Europe's History* (London: Allen Lane/Penguin, 2016), 165.

43 Geoffrey Parker, *Emperor: A New Life of Charles V* (New Haven, CT, and
London: Yale University Press, 2019), 376–8.

44 Parker, *Emperor*, 99–100, 184, 523–4, Plates 25, 27; Wheatcroft, *Habsburgs*, 103–4, 119.

45 Greengrass, *Christendom*, 30–31.

46 Parker, *Emperor*, 171–3 (171 cited, quoting a letter of 18 May 1527).

47 Parker, *Emperor*, 529, citing the Polish historian Władysław Pociecha,
writing in 1947.

48 Greengrass, *Christendom*, 14–17.

49 Barbara Stollberg-Rilinger, *The Holy Roman Empire: A Short History* (Princeton, NJ: Princeton University Press, 2018 [2013, in German]), 12–16.

50 Caspar Hirschi, *The Origins of Nationalism: An Alternative History from
Ancient Rome to Early Modern Germany* (Cambridge: Cambridge Uni-
versity Press, 2012), 184 (quoted), 192 (Election Capitulation); see also
Parker, *Emperor*, 103–4.

51 MacCulloch, *Reformation*, 123.

52 Parker, *Emperor*, 123 (Charles); MacCulloch, *Reformation*, 131 (Luther).

53 MacCulloch, *Reformation*, 116–17.

54 MacCulloch, *Reformation*, 159 (quoted); Wilson, *Holy Roman Empire*,
592–3 (numbers).

55 Parker, *Emperor*, 464–9 (abdication), 512 ('impossible empire').

56 MacCulloch, *Reformation*, 277.

6. Becoming European – Inventing Civilization

1 *Die Reisen des Samuel Kiechel*, ed. K. D. Hassler (Stuttgart, 1866), 102,
cited in translation in Martin Rady, *The Middle Kingdoms: A New History
of Central Europe* (London: Allen Lane/Penguin, 2023), 224.

2 Diarmaid MacCulloch, *Reformation: Europe's House Divided, 1490–1700*
(London: Allen Lane/Penguin, 2003), 172–89, 194–7.

3 MacCulloch, *Reformation*, 304.

4 Mark Greengrass, *Christendom Destroyed: Europe 1517–1648* (London: Allen Lane/Penguin, 2014), 490; MacCulloch, *Reformation*, 322–3.

5 MacCulloch, *Reformation*, 275.

6 MacCulloch, *Reformation*, 295.

7 Felipe Fernández-Armesto, *The Spanish Armada: The Experience of War in 1588* (Oxford: Oxford University Press, 1988).

8 Greengrass, *Christendom*, 407 (numbers).

9 James Cameron Lees, *St Giles', Edinburgh* (Edinburgh: Chambers, 1889), 209.

10 Johann Grimmelshausen, *The Adventures of Simplicius Simplicissimus*, trans. Mike Mitchell (Sawtry, UK: Dedalus, 1999); Geoffrey Parker, *Global Crisis: War, Climate Change and Catastrophe in the Seventeenth Century* (New Haven, CT, and London: Yale University Press, 2013), 249 (numbers).

11 Greengrass, *Christendom*, 641.

12 Quoted in Brendan Simms, *Europe: The Struggle for Supremacy, 1453 to the Present* (London: Allen Lane/Penguin, 2013), 38–9.

13 MacCulloch, *Reformation*, 499 (Richelieu), 500 (quoted).

14 Simms, *Europe*; Tim Blanning, *The Pursuit of Glory: Europe 1648–1815* (London: Allen Lane/Penguin, 2007).

15 Quoted in Simms, *Europe*, respectively: 53, 42.

16 Norman Davies, *Europe: A History* (London: Bodley Head, 2014 [1996]), 7.

17 Blanning, *Pursuit*, 101.

18 See for example Niall Ferguson, *Civilization: The West and the Rest* (London: Penguin, 2011), 36–49, 259–94.

19 Latin text and Italian translation in Luca D'Ascia, *Il Corano e la tiara: L'Epistola a Maometto II di Enea Silvio Piccolomini (papa Pio II)* (Bologna: Pendragon, 2001), 237–8 (quoted), 242. On the significance of this text see Denys Hay, *Europe: The Emergence of an Idea*, rev. edn (Edinburgh: Edinburgh University Press, 1968 [1957]), 83–4.

20 Marc David Baer, *The Ottomans: Khans, Caesars and Caliphs* (London and New York: Basic Books, 2021), 92–3, 96–9 ('Renaissance prince'), 143; Philip Mansel, *Constantinople: City of the World's Desire, 1453–1924* (London: Penguin, 1997), 22–3.

21 Caroline Finkel, *Osman's Dream: The Story of the Ottoman Empire, 1300–1923* (London: John Murray, 2005), 115–16.

22 Rady, *Middle Kingdoms*, 212, 214.

23 Andrew Wheatcroft, *The Enemy at the Gate: Habsburgs, Ottomans and the Battle for Europe* (London: Bodley Head, 2008), 150–51.

24 Baer, *Ottomans*, 109–10; Finkel, *Osman's Dream*, 291–2, 336–8.

25 Blanning, *Pursuit*, 237 (Louis XIV); Mark Galeotti, *A Short History of Russia* (London: Ebury Press/Penguin, 2021), 84, citing Johann Georg Korb (quoted).

26 Galeotti, *Short History*, 88.

27 Blanning, *Pursuit*, 237–9; Geoffrey Hosking, *Russia and the Russians: From the Earliest Times to the Present*, 2nd edn (London: Allen Lane/Penguin, 2012 [2001]), 205–6.

28 Andrew Rothstein, *Peter the Great and Marlborough: Politics and Diplomacy in Converging Wars* (Basingstoke: Macmillan, 1986), 124 (Leibniz, quoted); Blanning, *Pursuit*, 238 ('Imperator').

29 Paul Stock, *Europe and the British Geographical Imagination, 1760–1830* (Oxford: Oxford University Press, 2019), 157–9 (see also 178–82); P. J. von Strahlenberg (1730), cited in translation in Alex Drace-Francis, *European Identity: A Historical Reader* (London: Macmillan International/Red Globe Press, 2013), 46–50.

30 Catherine II, *The Grand Instructions to the Commissioners Appointed to Frame a New Code of Laws for the Russian Empire*, trans. M. Tatischeff, ch. 1, art. 6; ch. 2, art. 9 (London, 1768), 70–71, cited in Drace-Francis, *European Identity*, 77–8; on European influence see Ritchie Robertson, *The Enlightenment: The Pursuit of Happiness, 1680–1790* (Allen Lane/Penguin, 2020), 666–8.

31 Lucien Frary, *Russia and the Making of Modern Greek Identity, 1821–1844* (Oxford: Oxford University Press, 2015), 24.

32 Edward Gibbon, *The History of the Decline and Fall of the Roman Empire*, abridged edition, ed. David Womersley (London: Penguin, 2005), 441.

33 Derek Heater, *The Idea of European Unity* (Leicester and London: Leicester University Press, 1992), 26 (quoted); 24–6 (publication history and attribution to Henry IV).

34 Heater, *Idea*, 32 ('tidy mind'; ancient Greek city states); 33 (senate); 27, 33 ('equilibrium').

35 Heater, *Idea*, 31 (Sully on Muscovy, Turkey); 53–5 (Penn); William Penn, *The Peace of Europe: The Fruits of Solitude and Other Writings* (London: Dent, n.d.), 11 (quoted).

36 Heater, *Idea*, 66–72; Shane Weller, *The Idea of Europe: A Critical History* (Cambridge: Cambridge University Press, 2021), 33, 38 ('European Union'); Abbé de Saint-Pierre, *Projet pour rendre la paix perpétuelle en Europe* [1713], ed. Simone Goyard-Fabre (Paris: Garnier, 1981); for a summary see 71–84.

37 Ritchie Robertson, *Enlightenment*, 1, citing John Locke, *Essay Concerning Human Understanding* (1690), book 2, ch. 21.

38 John Robertson, *The Enlightenment: A Very Short Introduction* (Oxford: Oxford University Press, 2015), 80.

39 Anthony Pagden, *The Enlightenment and Why it Still Matters* (Oxford: Oxford University Press, 2013), 83.

40 Jonathan Israel, *Radical Enlightenment: Philosophy and the Making of Modernity, 1650–1750* (Oxford: Oxford University Press, 2001), vi; Paschalis Kitromilides, *Enlightenment and Revolution: The Making of Modern Greece* (Cambridge, MA: Harvard University Press, 2013), 43–51, 126–33 (Evgenios Voulgaris).

41 Ritchie Robertson, *Enlightenment*, 416; Diderot in *Encyclopédie, ou Dictionnaire raisonné des sciences, des arts et des métiers* (Paris, 1751–72), 5.635, 5.642 (quoted), available online at <http://enccre.academie-sciences.fr/encyclopedie>; John Robertson, *Enlightenment*, 95–6, and Ritchie Robertson, *Enlightenment*, 419 (reception).

42 Romilly *fils* in *Encyclopédie*, 16.390–95, online (quoted); Jonathan Israel, *Enlightenment Contested: Philosophy, Modernity, and the Emancipation of Man, 1670–1752* (Oxford: Oxford University Press, 2006), 615–30 (Islam).

43 Stock, *Europe*, 139.

44 Frederick II of Prussia, *On the Forms of Government and the Duties of Sovereigns* [1777], cited in translation in Blanning, *Pursuit*, 292–3.

45 Jean Starobinski, 'Le mot civilisation', in his *Le Remède dans le Mal. Critique et légitimation de l'artifice à l'âge des Lumières* (Paris: Gallimard, 1989), 11–59 (see 14), citing Mirabeau, *L'Ami des hommes* [1756], 136.

46 Jaucourt in *Encyclopédie*, 17.741, online.

47 John Robertson, *Enlightenment*, 63–4.

48 Pagden, *Enlightenment*, 230–46.

49 Montesquieu, *Persian Letters*, trans. Margaret Mauldon (Oxford: Oxford University Press, 2008), 30 (quoted); Ritchie Robertson, *Enlightenment*, 605–6.

50 Voltaire, *Candide* [1759], 2nd edn, trans. and ed. Robert M. Adams (New York and London: Norton, 1996), 74–5.

51 *Du Contrat social*, in Jean-Jacques Rousseau, *Collection complète des oeuvres*, vol. 1 (Geneva, 1782), 204; online at <www.rousseauonline.ch>; Joep Leerssen, *National Thought in Europe: A Cultural History* (Amsterdam: Amsterdam University Press, 2006), 83.

52 Respectively: Montesquieu, *Pensées*, no. 318, cited in Anthony Pagden, *The Pursuit of Europe: A History* (Oxford: Oxford University Press, 2022), 3; Voltaire, *Essai sur l'histoire du siècle de Louis XIV* [1751], trans. M. P. Pollock (London, 1926), cited in Drace-Francis, *European Identity*, 64.

53 Rousseau, *Considérations sur le gouvernement de Pologne* [1771–2], ch. 3, in *Collection*, vol. 1, 427, online.

54 Gibbon, *History* (abridged edn), 441–2.

7. 'The Lightning of the Nations'

1 Letter to Demetrios Lotos (Paris, 8 September 1789), in Adamantios Korais, *Complete Original Works, Vol B1: Letters (1774–1814)* (in Greek), ed. G. Valetas (Athens: Dorikos, 1964), 122–8 (125, 127 quoted).

2 Respectively: Gavin Murray-Miller, *Revolutionary Europe: Politics, Community and Culture in Transnational Context, 1775–1922* (London: Bloomsbury Academic, 2020), 31; Rosa Mucignat and Sanja Perovic, 'Introduction: Radical transnationalism: The French Revolution in Europe's political imagination', in R. Mucignat and S. Perovic (eds), *The French Revolution Effect (Comparative Critical Studies*, vol. 15, no. 2) (Edinburgh: Edinburgh University Press, 2018), 139–50 (see 139); Martin Thom, *Republics, Nations and Tribes* (London: Verso, 1995), 15.

3 Edmund Burke, cited in Brendan Simms, *Europe: The Struggle for Supremacy, 1453 to the Present* (London: Allen Lane/Penguin, 2013), 144; William Wordsworth, *The Prelude* (London: Moxon, 1850), 299 (Book 11).

4 Enlightenment: Contrast Jonathan Israel, *A Revolution of the Mind: Radical Enlightenment and the Intellectual Origins of Modern Democracy* (Princeton, NJ: Princeton University Press, 2010), 224, with John Robertson, *The Enlightenment: A Very Short Introduction* (Oxford: Oxford University Press, 2015), 116; for discussion see Ritchie Robertson, *The Enlightenment: The Pursuit of Happiness, 1680–1790* (Allen Lane / Penguin, 2020), 725–31. Age of revolution: Marisa Linton, 'The intellectual origins of the French Revolution', in Peter Campbell (ed.), *The Origins of the French Revolution* (Basingstoke: Palgrave, 2006), 139–59; Eric Hobsbawm, *The Age of Revolution* (London: Weidenfeld and Nicolson, 1962). Modern perspectives: François Furet, *Interpreting the French Revolution* (Cambridge: Cambridge University Press, 1981), 1 (quoted); Mucignat and Perovic, 'Introduction', 141.

5 Website of the French Presidency (emphasis added): <https://www.elysee.fr/la-presidence/la-declaration-des-droits-de-l-homme-et-du-citoyen>; see also Joep Leerssen, *National Thought in Europe: A Cultural History* (Amsterdam: Amsterdam University Press, 2006), 89, 92; Murray-Miller, *Revolutionary Europe*, 28, 40–41.

6 Website of the French Presidency, respectively: articles 6, 4.

7 Michael Burleigh, *Earthly Powers: Religion and Politics in Europe from the Enlightenment to the Great War* (London: Harper Perennial, 2006), 81 (Mirabeau), 83, 86 (calendar); Ritchie Robertson, *Enlightenment*, 728 ('Festival of Reason').

8 Norman Davies, *Europe: A History* (London: Bodley Head, 2014 [1996]), 705 (quoting General François Westermann), 706 ('*noyades*'); Tim Blanning, *The Pursuit of Glory: Europe 1648–1815* (London: Allen Lane / Penguin, 2007), 345 (number, quoted).

9 Davies, *Europe*, 700 (guillotine); Ritchie Robertson, *Enlightenment*, 724 (numbers).

10 Blanning, *Pursuit*, 617–18, citing Merlin de Douai on behalf of the National Assembly (emphasis added); on the states system see also Simms, *Europe*, 148.

11 Leerssen, *National Thought*, 137 (citing 'La Marseillaise' in translation); Mark Jarrett, *The Congress of Vienna and its Legacy* (London: I.B. Tauris, 2014), 23, citing Robespierre's address to the National Convention, 17 November 1793.

12 Contrast, for example, Claude Ribbe, *Napoleon's Crimes: A Blueprint for Hitler* (London: Oneworld, 2007 [2005, in French]); Andrew Roberts, *Napoleon: A Life* (London: Penguin, 2015); on the Ridley Scott film, see Andrew Roberts, 'Non! Napoleon was a greater man than this movie myth', *The Sunday Times* (19 November 2023), main section, p. 15 (quoted).

13 Emmanuel de Las Cases, *Mémorial de Saint-Hélène*, 2 vols (Paris, 1842), 2.143–5, cited in translation in Alex Drace-Francis, *European Identity: A Historical Reader* (London: Macmillan International/Red Globe Press, 2013), 101, reporting Napoleon's words from August 1816.

14 Simms, *Europe*, 170.

15 Leo Tolstoy, *War and Peace*, trans. Anthony Briggs (London: Penguin, 2005), respectively: 1321 (Epilogue, Part II, ch. 2); 1318 (ch. 1, quoted).

16 Jarrett, *Congress*, 39, 41, citing instructions from Adam Jerzy Czartory-ski (Russian foreign minister) to his ambassador to London (1804) and William Pitt to Count Vorontsov, 19 January 1805.

17 Glenda Sluga, *The Invention of the International Order: Remaking Europe after Napoleon* (Princeton, NJ: Princeton University Press, 2021), 87–92 (87 quoted, citing Metternich to Wilhelmine von Sagan, 8 March 1814); Adam Zamoyski, *Rites of Peace: The Fall of Napoleon and the Congress of Vienna* (London: Harper Perennial, 2008), 167 (citing Castlereagh to Foreign Office, 9 March 1814).

18 Treaty of Chaumont: <https://en.wikisource.org/wiki/Treaty_of_Chaumont>.

19 Zamoyski, *Rites*, 168 (quoted), on exclusion and nationalism see further 562–4; contrast Jarrett, *Congress*, 70 (quoted), 150–51.

20 Jarrett, *Congress*, 65, citing Treaty of Paris, 30 May 1814, in translation.

21 Quoted in translation in Mats Andrén, *Thinking Europe: A History of the European Idea since 1800* (New York and Oxford: Berghahn, 2023), 24–5; Zamoyski, *Rites*, 356–7, 376.

22 Desmond Seward, *Metternich: The First European* (London: Viking Penguin, 1991; reprint: Lume Books, 2021), 108 ('frivolity'; quotation from Prince de Ligne); Zamoyski, *Rites*, 278 (citing the diary of Archduke John of Austria, 29 September 1814).

23 Jarrett, *Congress*, 90, 94, 149 (no plenary session); 377 (quoted).

24 Matthijs Lok, *Europe against Revolution: Conservatism, Enlightenment, and the Making of the Past* (Oxford: Oxford University Press, 2023), 237–8.

25 Jarrett, *Congress*, 125–49; *The General Treaty of the Final Act of the Congress of Vienna, 9 June 1815*: <https://en.wikisource.org/wiki/Final_Act_of_the_Congress_of_Vienna>.

26 Jarrett, *Congress*, 148 (Ottomans); 173–8 (177: Castlereagh to Cabinet); Zamoyski, *Rites*, 414–15 (Ottomans); 520 (text of the treaty cited).

27 Jarrett, *Congress*, 164–5.

28 Jarrett, *Congress*, 168, citing Article 6 of the Quadruple Alliance, 20 November 1815.

29 *Congress of Aix-la-Chapelle (1818)/Maintenance of the Peace of Europe*, Annex C: <https://en.wikisource.org/wiki/Congress_of_Aix-la-Chapelle_(1818)/Maintenance_of_the_Peace_of_Europe#Annex_C:_Peace_of_Europe,_Union_of_the_Five_Powers>.

30 Thomas Paine, 'Rights of man: Being an answer to Mr. Burke's attack on the French Revolution' [1791], in *Common Sense, Rights of Man, and Other Essential Writings of Thomas Paine* (New York: Signet, 2003), 256.

31 See, for example, Isaiah Berlin, *The Roots of Romanticism* (Princeton, NJ: Princeton University Press, 1999), xiii, 1 and *passim*; Tim Blanning, *The Romantic Revolution* (London: Weidenfeld & Nicolson, 2010).

32 Leerssen, *National Thought*, 112–14; Berlin, *Roots*, 91–2.

33 Maurizio Isabella, *Southern Europe in the Age of Revolutions* (Princeton, NJ: Princeton University Press, 2023), 17, 28 and *passim*.

34 'Ode to Liberty', lines 1–2, 182–4, in Percy Bysshe Shelley, *The Major Works*, ed. Zachary Leader and Michael O'Neill (Oxford: Oxford University Press, 2003), 466–74.

35 Isabella, *Southern Europe*, 192; see also Roderick Beaton, *Greece: Biography of a Modern Nation* (Allen Lane/Penguin, 2019), 74–111.

36 Roderick Beaton, 'Philhellenism', in Paschalis Kitromilides and Constantinos Tsoukalas (eds), *The Greek Revolution: A Critical Dictionary* (Cambridge, MA: Harvard University Press, 2021), 593–613 (594 for 'Manifesto addressed to Europe', quoted).

37 William St Clair, *That Greece Might Still Be Free: The Philhellenes in the War of Independence* (Cambridge: Open Book, 2008 [1972]), 128–31; Yanni

Kotsonis, *The Greek Revolution and the Violent Birth of Nationalism* (Princeton, NJ: Princeton University Press, 2025), 247, 279, citing the Swiss financier and philhellene Jean-Gabriel Eynard in 1826; Percy Bysshe Shelley, 'Preface', *Hellas*, in Shelley, *The Major Works*, 549 (quoted).

38 Kotsonis, *Greek Revolution*, 315–16.

39 Quoted, respectively, in Richard Evans, *The Pursuit of Power: Europe 1815–1914* (London: Allen Lane/Penguin, 2016), 70; Simms, *Europe*, 194.

40 Evans, *Pursuit*, 66.

41 Giuseppe Mazzini, 'Note autobiografiche', in *Scritti di Giuseppe Mazzini: Politica ed Economia*, vol. 1 (Milan: Sonzogno, n.d.), 118.

42 Christopher Clark, *Revolutionary Spring: Fighting for a New World, 1848–1849* (London: Allen Lane/Penguin, 2023), 398–9 (constitutions); 1, 342 (quoted); 4, 295 (quoted).

43 Clark, *Revolutionary Spring*, 7, 344–5, 352.

44 Simms, *Europe*, 215.

45 Shane Weller, *The Idea of Europe: A Critical History* (Cambridge: Cambridge University Press, 2021), 104 (Turgenev), 108–9 (Dostoyevsky); see also Geoffrey Hosking, *Russia and the Russians: From the Earliest Times to the Present*, 2nd edn (London: Allen Lane/Penguin, 2012 [2001]), 313–14.

46 Evans, *Pursuit*, 265 (numbers), 264 (quoted).

47 Evans, *Pursuit*, 272 (numbers).

48 Emile Zola, *La Bête humaine* (Paris: Bibliothèque-Charpentier, 1893 [1890]), 415.

8. 'Heart of Darkness'

1 Thomas Pakenham, *The Scramble for Africa, 1876–1912* (London: Weidenfeld and Nicolson, 1991), 1–3, 25–6.

2 Pakenham, *Scramble*, 13, 656.

3 Pakenham, *Scramble*, 667, 670 (map); Richard Evans, *The Pursuit of Power: Europe 1815–1914* (London: Allen Lane/Penguin, 2016), 643.

4 Joseph Conrad, *Heart of Darkness* [1899] *and Other Tales* (Oxford: Oxford University Press, 1990), 207.

5 Respectively: Conrad, *Heart of Darkness*, 208, 239; see also Shane Weller, *The Idea of Europe: A Critical History* (Cambridge: Cambridge University Press, 2021), 134–5.

6 Conrad, *Heart of Darkness*, 135.

7 Conrad, *Heart of Darkness*, respectively: 138, 140–41, 252.

8 Weller, *Idea*, 129.

9 Cited in Norman Davies, *Europe: A History* (London: Bodley Head, 2014 [1996]), 735.

10 Jean-Paul Demoule, *The Indo-Europeans: Archaeology, Language, Race, and the Search for the Origins of the West* (Oxford University Press, 2023 [2014, in French]), 33–4, 328–31 (Aryans); 71–2 (anthropological societies); 94 (quoting Francis Galton in 1883).

11 Cited in Evans, *Pursuit*, 651; Ian Kershaw, *To Hell and Back: Europe 1914–1949* (London: Allen Lane / Penguin, 2015), 22 (numbers).

12 Respectively: Pakenham, *Scramble*, 611; cited in translation in Martin Rady, *The Middle Kingdoms: A New History of Central Europe* (London: Allen Lane / Penguin, 2023), 408.

13 Cited in Weller, *Idea*, 133; see also Rady, *Middle Kingdoms*, 409–13.

14 Niall Ferguson, *Civilization: The West and the Rest* (London: Penguin, 2011), 5, 144, citing figures derived from Angus Maddison, *The World Economy: Historical Statistics* (Paris: OECD, 2004).

15 This is broadly the argument of Mark Mazower, *Dark Continent: Europe's Twentieth Century* (London: Allen Lane / Penguin, 1998), though without reference to Conrad's novel.

16 Ernest Renan, *La Réforme intellectuelle et morale*, 3rd edn (Paris: Michel Lévy, 1872), 182, 197; see also Shane Weller, *The Idea of Europe: A Critical History* (Cambridge: Cambridge University Press, 2021), 131–2.

17 Cited in translation in, respectively, Anthony Pagden, *The Pursuit of Europe: A History* (Oxford: Oxford University Press, 2022), 118; Weller, *Idea*, 118. For similar commentary at the time see Mats Andrén, *Thinking Europe: A History of the European Idea since 1800* (New York and Oxford: Berghahn, 2023), 34.

18 Cited in Kiran Klaus Patel, *Project Europe: A History* (Cambridge: Cambridge University Press, 2020 [2018, in German]), 5.

19 Ernest Renan, 'What is a nation?' (edited translation of 'Qu'est-ce qu'une nation?' [1882]), in Stuart Woolf (ed.), *Nationalism in Europe, 1815 to the Present: A Reader* (London: Routledge, 1995), 48–60 (see 53, 58, 59).

20 Rady, *Middle Kingdoms*, 374; Evans, *Pursuit*, 588, 621.

21 Evans, *Pursuit*, 568; Brendan Simms, *Europe: The Struggle for Supremacy, 1453 to the Present* (London: Allen Lane / Penguin, 2013), 239.

22 Rady, *Middle Kingdoms*, 379–80 (379 quoted); Joseph Roth, *The Radetzky March* [1932], trans. Michael Hofmann (London: Granta, 2002), 177.

23 Kershaw, *To Hell*, 45 ('total war'), 91, 98 (numbers).

24 Respectively: Sigmund Freud, *Civilization and its Discontents* (London: Penguin, 2002 [1930, in German]); 'Beyond the pleasure principle' [1920, in German], in *On Metapsychology*, vol. II, in the Penguin Freud Library (London: Penguin, 1991), 269–338 (see esp. 311–12, 322, 330–31); Oswald Spengler, *The Decline of the West*, trans. Charles Atkinson (Oxford: Oxford University Press, 1991 [1918, 1922, in German]); Ezra Pound, *Hugh Selwyn Mauberley* [1920], in *Selected Poems* (London: Faber, 1948), 176; T. S. Eliot, *The Waste Land* [1922], lines 430, 433, in *Collected Poems, 1909–1962* (London: Faber, 1963), 79.

25 Viscount Grey of Fallodon: *Twenty-Five Years 1892–1916*, 2 vols (New York: Stokes, 1925), 2.20; Winston Churchill, *The Gathering Storm* (New York: Houghton Mifflin, 1948), 7.

26 Margaret MacMillan, *Paris 1919: Six Months That Changed the World* (London: John Murray, 2019 [first published as *Peacemakers*, 2001]), 23–4, 71.

27 Harold Nicolson, *Peacemaking 1919*, quoted in MacMillan, *Paris*, 95.

28 David Lloyd George, *The Truth about the Peace Treaties*, 2 vols (London: Gollancz, 1938), 1.223.

29 Respectively: MacMillan, *Paris*, 21 (quoted), 106; Kershaw, *To Hell*, 115.

30 Simms, *Europe*, 310–11.

31 MacMillan, *Paris*, 18–21 (20 quoted).

32 Mazower, *Dark Continent*, ix, 1–8 (5 quoted).

33 Kershaw, *To Hell*, 122 (quoted); Mazower, *Dark Continent*, 2–3 (novelty).

34 Kershaw, *To Hell*, 115.

35 Jay Winter, *The Day the Great War Ended, 24 July 1923: The Civilianization of War* (Oxford: Oxford University Press, 2022).

36 Mazower, *Dark Continent*, 38, 118 (original emphasis).

37 Mark Galeotti, *A Short History of Russia* (London: Ebury Press/Penguin, 2021), 148; Sean McMeekin, *The Ottoman Endgame: War, Revolution and the Making of the Modern Middle East, 1908–1923* (London: Allen Lane/ Penguin, 2015), 483.

38 Martyn Bond, *Hitler's Cosmopolitan Bastard: Count Richard Coudenhove-Kalergi and his Vision of Europe* (Montreal: McGill-Queen's University Press, 2021), 3–16.

39 Richard Coudenhove-Kalergi, *Pan-Europa* [in German] (Vienna: Pan-Europa Verlag, 1982 [1923]), xi, passage omitted from *Pan-Europe*, trans. Nicholas Murray Butler (New York: Knopf, 1926).

40 Coudenhove-Kalergi, *Pan-Europa*, 70 (customs union), 138 ('community of culture'), 148–9 (borders).

41 Coudenhove-Kalergi, *Pan-Europa*, 43 (British accession), 154 (English language); 51, 54, 58 (Russia, the last quoted).

42 Coudenhove-Kalergi, *Pan-Europa*, xi–xii (utopia); Weller, *Idea*, 163 (Herriot).

43 Pagden, *Pursuit*, 181–3.

44 'Memorandum on the organization of a régime of European federal union addressed to twenty-six governments of Europe, by M. Briand, Foreign Minister of France, May 17, 1930', *International Conciliation, Special Bulletin* (Worcester, MA: Carnegie Endowment for International Peace, 1930), 325–53 (French text and translation); 335, 351 quoted; see also 333 (customs union), 343 (political before economic convergence).

45 Pagden, *Pursuit*, 186.

46 Mazower, *Dark Continent*, 117, 128–9 (129 quoted).

47 Kershaw, *To Hell*, 245.

48 Demoule, *Indo-Europeans*, 93; Mazower, *Dark Continent*, 103–4.

49 Hannah Arendt, *Eichmann in Jerusalem: A Report on the Banality of Evil* (London: Penguin, 2022 [1963]).

50 María Sierra, *The Roma and the Holocaust: The Romani Genocide under Nazism* (London: Bloomsbury Academic, 2024).

51 Weller, *Idea*, 184–5 (Alfred Rosenberg in 1930, Hitler's 1936 speech); Pagden, *Pursuit*, 205 ('ordering'); 'Text of speech by Chancellor Adolf Hitler, at Berlin Sports Palace, January 30, 1941': <https://

www.ibiblio.org/pha/policy/1941/410130a.html>; Clifton Child, 'The concept of the New Order', in Arnold Toynbee and Veronica Toynbee (eds), *Hitler's Europe: Survey of International Affairs 1939–1946* (London: Oxford University Press, 1954), 47–51 ('celebrations', see also Pagden, *Pursuit*, 205–6); Simms, *Europe*, 378–9 (citing speech by Hitler, early May 1943).

52 Mazower, *Dark Continent*, 143 (quoted), 153–7; Mark Mazower, *Hitler's Empire: How the Nazis Ruled Europe* (London: Penguin, 2008); Simms, *Pursuit* ('crusade'), 379; Weller, *Idea*, 185–6, citing and commenting on speech by Hitler, 30 January 1942.

53 Mazower, *Dark Continent*, 147.

54 Sean McMeekin, *Stalin's War* (London: Allen Lane/Penguin, 2021), 71–177.

55 McMeekin, *Stalin's War*, 495–511.

56 Antony Beevor, *D-Day: The Battle for Normandy: 75th Anniversary Edition* (London: Penguin, 2019), xvii, xxii–xxiii, 74–5.

57 John Lewis Gaddis, *The United States and the Origins of the Cold War: 1941–1947* (New York: Columbia University Press, 2000 [1972]), 206–8.

9. Europe Partitioned

1 'Telegram from Prime Minister Winston Churchill to US President Truman, May 12th 1945', National Archives, Kew: <https://www.nationalarchives.gov.uk/education/resources/cold-war-on-file/churchill-post-yalta>.

2 Brendan Simms, *Europe: The Struggle for Supremacy, 1453 to the Present* (London: Allen Lane/Penguin, 2013), 387–8.

3 Winston Churchill, 'Sinews of peace', speech delivered at Westminster College, Fulton, Missouri, Tuesday, 5 March 1946, National Archives, Kew: <https://www.nationalarchives.gov.uk/education/resources/cold-war-on-file/iron-curtain-speech>.

4 Anthony Read and David Fisher, *The Fall of Berlin* (London: Pimlico, 1993), 438–40 (440 quoted); John Lewis Gaddis, *The Cold War* (London: Allen Lane/Penguin, 2005), 24.

5 Respectively: R. M. Douglas, *Orderly and Humane: The Expulsion of the Germans after the Second World War* (New Haven, CT, and London: Yale University Press, 2012); Tony Judt, *Postwar: A History of Europe since 1945* (London: Viking, 2010 [2005]), 30–31.

6 See, respectively, Martin Conway, 'The Greek Civil War: Greek exceptionalism or mirror of a European civil war?', in Philip Carabott and Thanasis Sfikas (eds), *The Greek Civil War: Essays on a Conflict of Exceptionalism and Silences* (Aldershot: Ashgate / Abingdon: Routledge, 2004), 17–39 (Belgium and see especially 31); Judt, *Postwar*, 115–16 (France); Sean McMeekin, *Stalin's War* (London: Allen Lane / Penguin, 2021), 651 (eastern Europe); Mark Mazower, *Dark Continent: Europe's Twentieth Century* (London: Allen Lane / Penguin, 1998), 215 ('class war' throughout Europe).

7 'Truman doctrine' (text of address to Congress, 12 March 1947), US National Archives: <https://www.archives.gov/milestone-documents/truman-doctrine>.

8 'The Ventotene Manifesto by Altiero Spinelli and Ernesto Rossi. For a Free and United Europe. A draft Manifesto' [1941], trans. E. Urgesi: <http://www.altierospinelli.org/manifesto/manifesto_en.html>.

9 Mark Gilbert, *European Integration: A Political History*, 2nd edn (Lanham, MD: Rowan and Littlefield, 2021 [2012]), 18 (quoted); Anthony Pagden, *The Pursuit of Europe: A History* (Oxford: Oxford University Press, 2022), 228–9 (Union of European Federalists); Winston Churchill, 'Speech delivered at the University of Zurich, 19 September 1946': <https://rm.coe.int/16806981f3> (quoted).

10 Shane Weller, *The Idea of Europe: A Critical History* (Cambridge: Cambridge University Press, 2021), 204–10.

11 Simms, *Europe*, 398.

12 Quoted in Mathieu Segers, *The Origins of European Integration: The Pre-History of Today's European Union, 1937–1951* (Cambridge: Cambridge University Press, 2024), 160.

13 Gilbert, *European Integration*, 31.

14 US National Archives: <https://www.archives.gov/milestone-documents/marshall-plan> (emphasis added).

15 Respectively: Simms, *Europe*, 398 (Truman); Gilbert, *European Integration*, 24; Segers, *Origins*, 137.

16 Respectively: Gilbert, *European Integration*, 24; Ian Kershaw, *To Hell and Back: Europe 1914–1949* (London: Allen Lane/Penguin, 2015), 515.

17 'Schuman Declaration', English translation at <https://european-union.europa.eu/principles-countries-history/history-eu/1945-59/schuman-declaration-may-1950_en>; Segers, *Origins*, 190, 191.

18 See, for example, Tony Judt, *A Grand Illusion? An Essay on Europe* (New York and London: New York University Press, 2011), 10–17; Ian Kershaw, *Roller-Coaster: Europe 1950–2017* (London: Allen Lane/Penguin, 2018), 164.

19 'Schuman Declaration' (see note 17).

20 North Atlantic Treaty, 4 April 1949, Article 5: <https://www.nato.int/cps/en/natohq/official_texts_17120.htm>.

21 Kershaw, *To Hell*, 518 ('fig-leaf'); Judt, *Postwar*, 150 ('bluff'; quoted).

22 Respectively: Gilbert, *European Integration*, 50–51; Simms, *Europe*, 412.

23 Gilbert, *European Integration*, 54 (Dulles); Klaus Larres, *Uncertain Allies: Nixon, Kissinger, and the Threat of a United Europe* (New Haven, CT, and London: Yale University Press, 2022), 19 (Aron).

24 Alex von Tunzelmann, *Blood and Sand: Suez, Hungary and the Crisis That Shook the World* (London and New York: Simon and Schuster, 2016), 69, 83–9, 92, 210, 253.

25 Kershaw, *Roller-Coaster*, 127; von Tunzelmann, *Blood and Sand*, 371.

26 Simms, *Europe*, 400 (on Israel, quoted); von Tunzelmann, *Blood and Sand*, 28–30 (nationalization and compensation); see further Ralph Dietl, 'Suez 1956: A European intervention?', *Journal of Contemporary History*, 43/2 (2008), 259–78 (see 260).

27 Dietl, 'Suez 1956', 260–61; Simms, *Europe*, 424–5.

28 Dietl, 'Suez 1956', 261, 268–9, 273, 277; Christian Pineau [foreign minister of France at the time], *1956/Suez* (Paris: Robert Laffont, 1976), 191, cited in translation in von Tunzelmann, *Blood and Sand*, 346–7.

29 Kiran Klaus Patel, *Project Europe: A History* (Cambridge: Cambridge University Press, 2020 [2018, in German]), 7–8.

30 Gilbert, *European Integration*, 67 (Treaty of Rome, quoted); Pagden, *Pursuit*, 248 (quoting Maurice Faure); Judt, *Postwar*, 278 (quoting Dean Acheson on Britain, 1962).

31 Kershaw, *Roller-Coaster*, 162 (EFTA, quoted); Judt, *Postwar*, 304 (self-sufficiency).

32 Quoted in Judt, *Postwar*, 324.

33 Judt, *Postwar*, 360.

34 Judt, *Postwar*, 360–86; Mazower, *Dark Continent*, 332, 340.

35 Kershaw, *Roller-Coaster*, 241, 243 (Prague); Judt, *Postwar*, 409 (Nanterre).

36 Cited in Kershaw, *Roller-Coaster*, 443.

37 Gilbert, *European Integration*, 107–8, 119 (the latter quoted).

38 Larres, *Uncertain Allies*, 121, 125.

39 Gilbert, *European Integration*, 117–18 (Paris summit, quoted); Larres, *Uncertain Allies*, 38, 192; Patel, *Project Europe*, 239 ('Frankenstein monster').

40 Larres, *Uncertain Allies*, 240; Gilbert, *European Integration*, 125.

41 Article quoted in full and discussed in the Introduction; see pp. 12, 14 above. See further Patel, *Project Europe*, 11–12, 47, 52, 70–72, 147–9, 165–71.

42 'Conference on Security and Co-Operation in Europe Final Act', 1 August 1975, Helsinki: Declaration, Article 7: <https://www.osce.org/files/f/documents/5/c/39501.pdf>.

43 Single European Act (February 1986), *Official Journal of the European Communities*, 169/1 (29 June 1987), respectively: Article 13; preamble; Gilbert, *European Integration*, 169 (Thatcher); Patel, *Project Europe*, 168 (French Revolution).

44 'Speech by Gorbachev at the Political Consultative Committee Meeting in Warsaw, July 15, 1988', in Vojtech Mastny and Malcolm Byrne (eds), *A Cardboard Castle? An Inside History of the Warsaw Pact 1955–1991* (Budapest: Central European University Press, 2005), 607–16, cited and discussed in Michael Cox, 'Who Won the Cold War in Europe? A Historiographical Overview', in Frédéric Bozo, Marie-Pierre Rey, N. Piers Ludlow and Leopoldo Nuti (eds), *Europe and the End of the Cold War: A Reappraisal* (Abingdon: Routledge, 2008), 9–19 (see 14).

45 Gaddis, *Cold War*, 250.

46 Marie-Pierre Rey, 'Gorbachev's new thinking and Europe, 1985–1989', in Bozo *et al.* (eds), *Europe*, 23–35 (see 25); William Taubman, *Gorbachev: His Life and Times* (London and New York: Simon and Schuster, 2017), 287 (quoted), see also 689.

47 Svetlana Savranskaya, 'In the name of Europe: Soviet withdrawal from Eastern Europe', in Bozo *et al.* (eds), *Europe*, 36–48 (see 45–6).

48 Mikhail Gorbachev, 'Address to the Council of Europe' [6 July 1989], cited in Alex Drace-Francis, *European Identity: A Historical Reader* (London: Macmillan International/Red Globe Press, 2013), 233–7 (236, 237 quoted).

49 Robert Service, *The End of the Cold War 1985–1991* (London: Macmillan, 2015), 403.

50 Gorbachev, 'Address': <https://www.cvce.eu/content/publication /2002/9/20/4c021687-98f9-4727-9e8b-836e0bc1f6fb/publishable_en.pdf> (passage omitted in Drace-Francis).

51 Taubman, *Gorbachev*, 427, 509; Judt, *Postwar*, 600.

52 'Afterword: A talk with the author by Philip Roth', in Milan Kundera, *The Book of Laughter and Forgetting*, trans. M. H. Heim (London: Penguin, 1980), 229–37 (230 quoted); see also Milan Kundera, 'The tragedy of Central Europe', trans. Edmund White, *New York Review of Books* (26 April 1984), 33–8; and Weller, *Idea*, 221–6.

53 Simms, *Europe*, 485 ('democratic'); Gaddis, *Cold War*, 237–8 (1789).

10. The 'End of History' and the European Union

1 William Taubman, *Gorbachev: His Life and Times* (London and New York: Simon and Schuster, 2017), 464, citing the testimony of Gorbachev's adviser at the time, Andrei Grachev; John Lewis Gaddis, *The Cold War* (London: Allen Lane/Penguin, 2005), 239 (quoted), see also 257.

2 Francis Fukuyama, 'The end of history?', *The National Interest* (summer 1989), 173–89 (173 quoted, original emphasis); Francis Fukuyama, *The End of History and the Last Man* [new edition with additional material] (London: Penguin, 2020 [1992]).

3 On Kojève see Fukuyama, *End*, 65–7; Boris Groys, *Alexandre Kojève: An Intellectual Biography* (London: Verso, 2025).

4 Respectively: Fukuyama, 'End', 175; Fukuyama, *End*, 311; 'Afterword to the second paperback edition, 2006', in *End*, 341–55 (346 quoted).

5 Margaret Thatcher, 'Speech to the College of Europe ("the Bruges speech")': <https://www.margaretthatcher.org/document/107332>;

Mark Gilbert, *European Integration: A Political History*, 2nd edn (Lanham, MD: Rowan and Littlefield, 2021 [2012]), 189–90.

6 Marie-Pierre Rey, 'Gorbachev's new thinking and Europe, 1985–1989', in Frédéric Bozo, Marie-Pierre Rey, N. Piers Ludlow and Leopoldo Nuti (eds), *Europe and the End of the Cold War: A Reappraisal* (Abingdon: Routledge, 2008), 23–35 (see 31–3); Andrei Grachev, 'From the common European home to European confederation: François Mitterrand and Mikhail Gorbachev in search of the road to a greater Europe', 207–19 in the same volume.

7 Grachev, 'From the common', 207–8.

8 Rey, 'Gorbachev's new thinking', 32.

9 George Bush and Brent Scowcroft, *A World Transformed* (New York: Knopf, 1998), 239; Gaddis, *The Cold War*, 251.

10 Tony Judt, *Postwar: A History of Europe since 1945* (London: Viking, 2010 [2005]), 641–2; Taubman, *Gorbachev*, 544, 546–50, 564 (NATO); 569 (German financial aid; other sources give different figures).

11 Judt, *Postwar*, 645.

12 See also Judt, *Postwar*, 668–9.

13 Alan Riding, 'Conflict in Yugoslavia: Europeans send high-level team', *The New York Times* (29 June 1991), section 1, p. 4.

14 Marie-Janine Calic, *Der Krieg in Bosnien-Hercegovina* (Frankfurt-am-Main: Suhrkamp, 1995), 17, cited in translation in Misha Glenny, *The Balkans 1804–1999: Nationalism, War and the Great Powers* (London: Granta, 1999), 637.

15 Serhii Plokhy, *The Last Empire: The Final Days of the Soviet Union* (New York: Basic Books; London: Oneworld, 2014), 301–16 (309 quoted).

16 'Maastricht Treaty hailed as great leap forward despite Major concessions', *The Guardian* (12 December 1991) ('31 hours'); Ian Kershaw, *Roller-Coaster: Europe 1950–2017* (London: Allen Lane/Penguin, 2018), 425 (opinion polls); Gilbert, *European Integration*, 204–5.

17 'Treaty on European Union', *Official Journal of the European Communities*, C 191 (July 1992), 1–112.

18 *The Guardian* (25 July 1993).

19 Roderick Beaton, *Greece: Biography of a Modern Nation* (London: Allen Lane / Penguin, 2019), 350 (quoted); Gilbert, *European Integration*, 207–35 ('EUphoria').

20 Timothy Garton Ash, *Homelands: A Personal History of Europe* (London: Bodley Head, 2023), 179–80.

21 Copenhagen European Council, 21–22 June 1993: Presidency Conclusions, article 7: <https://www.europarl.europa.eu/enlargement/ec/cop_en.htm>.

22 Brendan Simms, *Europe: The Struggle for Supremacy, 1453 to the Present* (London: Allen Lane / Penguin, 2013), 496.

23 Kershaw, *Roller-Coaster*, 418 ('dividing line'); Richard Sakwa, *The Lost Peace: How the West Failed to Prevent a Second Cold War* (New Haven, CT, and London: Yale University Press, 2023); Serhii Plokhy, *The Russo-Ukrainian War* (London: Allen Lane / Penguin, 2023), 92–3.

24 Gilbert, *European Integration*, 215.

25 Respectively: Kershaw, *Roller-Coaster*, 459; Judt, *Postwar*, 799.

26 Brendan Simms, *Britain's Europe: A Thousand Years of Conflict and Cooperation* (London: Allen Lane / Penguin, 2016), 202–3.

27 Eckart Woertz, Manon-Nour Tannous and Achim Rohde, 'The Iraq war as a war over the meaning of Europe', *Middle East Journal*, 77/3–4 (2024), 439–60 (see, respectively, 452, 439–40).

28 Magdalena Frennhoff Larsén, 'Enlargement, treaty reform and crises, 1993–2021', in Brigitte Leucht, Katja Seidel and Laurent Warlouzet (eds), *Reinventing Europe: The History of the European Union, 1945 to the Present* (London: Bloomsbury Academic, 2023), 65–83 (see 71–3).

29 'Draft treaty establishing a Constitution for Europe', *Official Journal of the European Union*, C 169 (18 July 2003), 1–105 (Preamble, quoted); Patel, *Project Europe*, 146–7, 171 (Thucydides).

30 Gilbert, *European Integration*, respectively: 228–9, 226.

31 For the disputed authenticity of Kissinger's remark see Klaus Larres, *Uncertain Allies: Nixon, Kissinger, and the Threat of a United Europe* (New Haven, CT, and London: Yale University Press, 2022), 77.

32 George Papaconstantinou, *Game Over: The Inside Story of the Greek Crisis* (privately published, 2016), 34, 37.

33 Charles Dallara, *Euroshock: How the Largest Debt Restructuring in History Helped Save Greece and Preserve the Eurozone* (New York: Rodin, 2024), 17 and n.

34 Beaton, *Greece*, 381.

35 Loukas Tsoukalis, *Europe's Coming of Age* (Cambridge: Polity, 2023), 30–34 (31, 34 cited).

36 Gilbert, *European Integration*, 252 quoted, emphasis added; 'European Stability Mechanism – Main Features, Instruments and Accountability', European Parliament briefing document, 11 October 2019: <https://www.europarl.europa.eu/RegData/etudes/BRIE/2014/497755/IPOL-ECON_NT(2014)497755_EN.pdf>; Tsoukalis, *Europe's Coming of Age*, 87.

37 European Commission: 'Statistics on migration to Europe' (11 April 2024): <https://commission.europa.eu/strategy-and-policy/priorities-2019-2024/promoting-our-european-way-life/statistics-migration-europe_en>.

38 Kershaw, *Roller-Coaster*, 514.

39 Tsoukalis, *Europe's Coming of Age*, 38.

40 See for example Sakwa, *Lost Peace*, 69–71; Garton Ash, *Homelands*, 162–3.

41 Quoted in Plokhy, *War*, 86–7; for an account more sympathetic to the Russian point of view see Sakwa, *Lost Peace*, 86–8.

42 Contrast Sakwa, *Lost Peace*, 86 ('No more than 20 per cent of Ukrainians at the time'), with Plokhy, *War*, 85–90.

43 Council of the European Union: 'Joint Declaration of the Prague Eastern Partnership Summit, Prague, 7 May 2009', Article 16 (financial support), Article 1 (commitments), Articles 2, 5 (association): <https://ec.europa.eu/commission/presscorner/detail/en/pres_09_78>.

44 Sakwa, *Lost Peace*, 199–217.

45 Plokhy, *War*, 72–4.

46 Samuel Huntington, *The Clash of Civilizations and the Remaking of World Order* (London and New York: Simon and Schuster, 2002), 37, 166–7.

47 Plokhy, *War*, 94–5, citing a television interview with a Ukrainian official in 2018.

48 Gilbert, *European Integration*, 255, quoting Council of the European Union, 3921st meeting, Foreign Affairs, 10 February 2014.
49 Plokhy, *War*, 132–3 (132 quoted).
50 Cited in Plokhy, *War*, 137.
51 Foreign Ministry of the Russian Federation: 'Treaty between The United States of America and the Russian Federation on security guarantees', 17 December 2021, articles 4 (quoted), 6, 7: <https://mid.ru/ru/foreign_policy/rso/nato/1790818/?lang=en>.
52 Cited in Plokhy, *War*, 164–5.

Epilogue

1 This paragraph and the two following draw on press coverage at the time, and particularly on the Special Report, 'Mariupol – the ruin of a city', by Shaun Walker, Isobel Koshiw, Pjotr Sauer, Morten Risberg, Liz Cookman and Luke Harding, *The Guardian* (24 February 2023), 4–7.
2 'Outcome of the 16th BRICS Summit in Kazan, Russia', European Think Tank (8 November 2024): <https://www.europarl.europa.eu/think-tank/en/document/EPRS_ATA(2024)766243#:~:text=Under%20Russia's%20presidency%2C%20BRICS%20(acronym,October%20in%20Kazan%20(Russia>.
3 For the expression: Serhii Plokhy, *The Gates of Europe: A History of Ukraine*, rev. edn (New York: Basic Books, 2021 [2015]).
4 See, for example, Marc de Vos, *Superpower Europe: The European Union's Silent Revolution* (Cambridge: Polity, 2024).
5 *National Security Strategy of the United States of America, November 2025* (released 4 December 2025), p. 30 quoted: <https://www.whitehouse.gov/wp-content/uploads/2025/12/2025-National-Security-Strategy.pdf>.

Index